Housing Desegregation and Federal Policy

Urban and Regional Policy and
Development Studies
Michael A. Stegman, Series Editor

Housing Desegregation and Federal Policy

Edited by John M. Goering

MAR 2 5 1987

The University of North Carolina Press

Chapel Hill and London

© 1986 The University of North Carolina Press

All rights reserved

Manufactured in the United States of America

Library of Congress Cataloging-in-Publication Data

Housing desegregation and federal policy

   (Urban and regional policy and development studies)
Includes bibliographies and index.

   1. Discrimination in housing—United States—
Addresses, essays, lectures. 2. Housing policy—
United States—Addresses, essays, lectures.
3. United States—Race relations—Addresses, essays,
lectures. 4. Discrimination in housing—Law and
legislation—United States—Addresses, essays, lectures.
I. Goering, John M. II. Series.
HD7293.H584   1986   363.5'1   86-1404
ISBN 0-8078-1707-4
ISBN 0-8078-4156-0 (pbk.)

"Changing Racial Attitudes toward Residential Integration"
(Chapter 7 of this work) draws upon tables reprinted from *Racial
Attitudes in America: Trends and Interpretations*, by Howard
Schuman, Charlotte Steeh, and Lawrence Bobo (Cambridge:
Harvard University Press, 1985). The tables are reprinted with
permission of the publishers. Copyright 1985 by the President and
Fellows of Harvard College.

The opinions expressed in the essays by John M. Goering are
those of the author and do not necessarily reflect the views of the
U.S. Department of Housing and Urban Development or the U.S
government.

To Mother,

      With Love!

         Jack

Contents

Preface

The impetus for this reader arose out of my experience with civil rights policy and legislative events over a six-year period as program manager for fair housing research and evaluation issues for the Office of Policy Development and Research at the U.S. Department for Housing and Urban Development (HUD). At close range, I have observed most of the debates, decisions, and indecision as HUD has sought to implement both Title VI of the Civil Rights Act of 1964, which banned discrimination in federally assisted housing, and Title VIII of the Civil Rights Act of 1968, which outlawed discrimination in most of the private housing market. The strengths and limitations of these two legislative mandates have much to do with the current state of the movement for housing desegregation in America. Virtually all legislation is, however, flawed if only in the inability to anticipate future problems and the ingenuity of men and women in circumventing the law. Walter Mondale's promise on the floor of Congress in 1968 that the soon-to-be-passed Fair Housing Law would replace segregated ghettos by "truly integrated housing patterns" has proved to be just such an unfulfilled prediction. A variety of local and national— social, political, and programmatic—issues have contributed to this still in-complete civil rights promise. This book provides an accounting of much that has happened between the passage of those civil rights mandates and the present.

From within the walls of HUD, hundreds of civil servants and political appointees have sought over the past two decades the means to enforce the country's civil rights requirements, knowing all too well the obstacles in their path. Commitment has worked beside disaffection and confusion in an effort to enforce ambiguous, somewhat unpopular laws. Programs and regulations have frequently become the subject of litigation and legislative revision. HUD's civil rights mandate has thus unevenly evolved as a result of a variety of federal and state court decisions, executive branch programmatic initiatives, congressional revanche, and sporadic regulatory initiatives.

Having witnessed many of these external and internal pressures regarding the issue of housing desegregation, I felt pushed to provide a wider audience with a broad-ranging, "multi-disciplinary" assessment of the diverse voices, interests, and evidence heard from my vantage point at HUD. At one time I believed that holding a conference, bringing together a range of viewpoints and evidence, could facilitate a clearer mandate for action either within HUD or without. I now realize that no single event, sharing viewpoints and data, will overcome the substantial political and institutional obstacles in the path of achieving housing desegregation.

This book is itself only one step out of many needed to clarify, extend, and promote increased understanding and perhaps greater tolerance for housing integration. My hope is that a similar anthology, prepared a decade from now, will record that decisions were made, action was taken, and the evils of segregation and discrimination were noticeably lessened.

This volume does not include contributions from the broad range of interest groups concerned with these issues. The American Enterprise Institute, the Heritage Foundation, the Potomac Institute, the Leadership Conference on Civil Rights, the National Committee Against Discrimination in Housing, the NAACP, and National Neighbors are all likely contributors to the dialogue on civil rights and desegregation. The views of current or past political figures also are not directly included, although some reference is made to their opinions. The reader may also miss statements and assessments of actions taken by state or local governments or by private community organizations. This collection is deliberately—although by no means exclusively—focused on federal policies and programs.

In addition to my experiences at HUD, there have been a number of colleagues and friends who have played a role in developing my thinking on the topic of desegregation. Before joining HUD, I learned a great deal about the complexities of racial housing policies working with the Office of Neighborhood Stabilization within the New York City Commission on Human Rights. Eleanor Holmes Norton, then chairperson of the Commission, encouraged my research interests and tolerated my naiveté. While at HUD, I benefited greatly from working with George Schermer, a man whose rectitude puts weaker men to shame. I also have a deep professional debt to the staff and leadership of many of the private fair housing centers throughout the country. Working with them over several years taught me about many of the obstacles to civil rights enforcement. A number of attorneys have also helped knock some of the rough edges off my understanding of legal and regulatory issues in fair housing; among them are John Knapp, Harry Carey, Steve Sachs, Larry Pearl, David Deutsch, Rich Stearns, John Herold, and Pat Hampton. I would also like to thank George Galster and Jane Karadbil who provided valuable comments on earlier drafts of my introductory material.

Personally my deepest debts are owed to Danilo and Felicidad. They have given me the encouragement, support, and care I needed to complete this book.

John M. Goering

Housing Desegregation and Federal Policy

Introduction

JOHN M. GOERING

"Atlanta is Open to You!" the billboard poster reads, apparently offering black families the prospect of living in a home of their choice, anywhere in the city. For some, there will indeed be opportunities to live in racially mixed neighborhoods. Others, however, will see this poster as another reminder of the failed promises of the civil rights struggles of the 1960s. The Atlanta they see is, like most American cities, still largely segregated. Over 85 percent of Atlanta's black population, roughly 200,000 people, would have to move in order to achieve an even distribution of blacks and whites. The fact that Atlanta is statistically slightly less segregated today than it was a decade ago means a great deal to the few families who have found their way out of segregated neighborhoods, but little to the bulk of blacks still living in ghettos.

There are many reasons why America has achieved so little progress in desegregating housing opportunities. At the heart of these reasons is a pervasive uncertainty felt by most whites and many blacks about whether they really want to build and sustain racially integrated communities. What is the point of residential integration? Is it worth all of the social, fiscal, and political costs associated with it? And if it is a worthy national goal, whose job is it to promote desegregation? If the federal government is the choice, what tools does it have to eradicate or even weaken the walls of racial segregation?

Answers to these questions do not come from any single discipline or from comprehensive research aimed at the causes of and impediments to housing desegregation. Lawyers, social scientists, courts, and federal policy analysts have separately, and for years, sought answers and provided arguments concerning housing integration. This book brings together most of these diverse, but intercrossed, threads of policy analysis and debate to provide a portrait of the state of housing desegregation efforts in America in the 1980s.

Understanding how well or poorly the process of housing desegregation is working is facilitated by understanding where the process is pointed as well as where it started. The first section in this collection focuses on the legal and political issues surrounding the goal of housing integration. Housing integration in this instance refers only to the stable sharing of a residential area by whites and minorities and not to any personal interaction or social mixing.[1] How important is the goal of housing integration to whites and blacks, and what are the constitutional and legal problems associated with achieving this objective? These questions are addressed with the legal analyses related primarily to federal law, leaving for others the task of examining the relevance of any state or local laws to the problems of housing desegregation.

The second section provides evidence documenting the extent of segregation as it is experienced by black and Hispanic citizens. The slight declines in housing segregation experienced by blacks, in cities like Atlanta, have not been shared by all Hispanics, leaving room for questions about how different minority groups experience opportunities for housing integration in cities and suburbs throughout the United States. This section also includes statistical analyses of a variety of social and demographic factors as they help explain levels of segregation. Among the major contributors to the level of segregation is the practice of racial discrimination by real estate agents and rental property managers. Such evidence provides clear proof of the extent to which deliberate or inadvertent discrimination acts to sustain segregation. The malleability of racial discrimination, by means of law enforcement, appears as one of the major themes interwoven throughout many of the papers in this collection.

Racial discrimination, as well as demographic and economic factors, is insufficient, however, to explain either the support for or antagonism to housing desegregation and integration. Assessing the attitudinal and sociological pressures associated with racial residential mixing is crucial to understanding the prospects for stable racial integration. The third section of this book provides a brief look at both attitudinal and social issues as they relate to private sector housing. Cumulatively, the first three sections of this collection provide the reader with a sense of the constraints, opportunities, and reasons for promoting the goal of housing integration.

One big piece missing from the puzzle of whether and how it is possible to achieve housing integration is the role of federal legislation, policies, and programs. Although federally subsidized housing constitutes only a small share of the nation's total housing stock, it is often argued that only federal intervention can overcome the major obstacles in the path of achieving a more integrated society. Housing desegregation refers to any of the procedures used to move from a racially separate society to one in which housing integration, or racial residential mixing, is a realistic option for blacks and whites. To what extent have federal housing programs fostered either segregation or desegregation? How have changing congressional civil rights requirements influenced the patterns of dispersal of assisted households? Must the federal government, especially the U.S. Department of Housing and Urban Development (HUD), use only color-blind criteria in implementing its programs, or may race be used in selecting and placing households in publicly assisted housing?

Providing a balanced and current assessment of federal policies is complicated by recent disagreement over the nature of the federal government's responsibility for housing integration. According to the assistant attorney general for civil rights at the U.S. Department of Justice, there is no federal requirement to promote housing integration and a probable prohibition on the use of race-conscious methods (Mariano 1984:1). A former general counsel at HUD, however, rejects this interpretation of federal law, finding clear legislative justification for the goal of housing integration (McGrew 1984:5). Such basic disagreements will not be quickly nor easily resolved, because they go to the heart of the federal government's responsibility and liability for ending housing segregation. Amendments to the Fair Housing Act of 1968 may be submitted to Congress in 1986 with the prospect that hearings and debate may clarify this federal responsibility.

The disagreements between present and former federal officials are partly a symptom of disagreements that are widely held by black and white Americans. Whites seem to have grown tired of civil rights issues, becoming more disinterested in or resistant to the housing rights of minorities. Black organizations and households also question the benefits and stigma associated with programs for desegregating schools and housing. Many question the costs and wonder about the benefits that appear to be experienced by relatively few. Housing industry groups, such as the National Association of Realtors, sensing this legal and popular discontent, are also pressing to eliminate certain practices promoting housing integration (North 1983a, 1983b; DeMuth 1984:E1).

Popular discontent and legal uncertainty may seem like a strange context for conducting careful policy analysis. It is, indeed, because of the raw feelings and political jousting that a balanced assessment is most needed. At a time when partisan ideology tries to establish public policy, it is most useful to attempt a dissection of legal and empirical issues. This reader was designed, therefore, to offer the best legal and empirical discussion of issues to those concerned about housing desegregation. It attempts to provide clearer definitions where issues have not been neatly defined; it offers legal precision and doubts in place of simple policy declarations; and it provides evidence concerning the operation of a variety of federal programs at a time when such evidence is currently available to only a handful of people in Washington or is the subject of protracted litigation in federal courts.

This reader has been constructed in the simple belief that it is impossible to make any progress on behalf of housing integration unless there is a willingness to expose doubts, evidence, uncertainties, and, most importantly, legal and practical options. Perhaps after a process of assessment and debate, it will appear useful to uphold the policy of housing integration but to do nothing further to achieve its implementation. Perhaps there will be strong enough political pressure to abandon the goal as legally unsound and overly costly. Still other voices may prevail and a clearer legislative and programmatic agenda for housing desegregation may be established.

Whatever the likely course of events, it seems clear that nothing will change suddenly or without considerable debate and litigation. Americans will not move suddenly to totally disavow the goal of integration. The question remains as to how much importance will be given to implementing the goal, what legal tools and programs will be available for use, and how long it will take for public officials and neighbors—white and black—to lose their fear of integrated housing.

The focus of this collection is, it should be noted, largely on the issues of *racial* integration in housing. Little attempt is made to address all of the complex and distinctive issues related to the segregation or integration of religious or national origin groups, such as Hispanics or Asians. This choice was made both because more is known about racial factors and because of the inadequacy of research on other groups (Feagin and Feagin 1978). Many of the characteristics and findings regarding race may, of course, be applicable to the problems experienced by other groups. It is clear, however, that there are substantial difficulties involved in extending analyses and remedies based on race to other groups in society (Wasserstrom 1977; Schuck 1980; Ford Foundation 1984). Research and policy analysis on black Americans will, it is hoped, extend benefits to others in search of housing integration.

NOTE

1. To early advocates of the goal of housing integration, the realization of this objective would be "a situation in which white and nonwhite families not only live in a spatially mixed community but also accept one another, associate without self-consciousness, and do not look forward to release from each other as neighbors" (Weaver 1956:94). Such social integration would vary from place to place, and would be preceded by some form of spatial integration (Hunt 1959:208; Hamilton and Bishop 1976). At a minimum, a spatially integrated area can be defined as having one or more minority residents. Thus, the remaining white, elderly households left behind in an otherwise minority enclave could be said to create spatial integration; the black families living within a gentrifying white community also represent statistical integration.

More realistically, residential integration implies both the mixing of more than just token or minimal numbers of the opposite race as well as a measure of stability in their occupancy. Stable spatial residential integration thus means the racial mixing of households over a reasonable period of time, with the assurance of reasonably stable replacement of black and/or white outmovers. Operationally, such areas have been identified as places in which people believed the area will "still have both Negroes and whites moving in during the next five years" (Bradburn, Sudman, and Gockel 1970:7) or in which time series data recorded no net change in the proportion of white and nonwhite residents between decennial censuses (Taeuber and Taeuber 1965: 106).

REFERENCES

Bradburn, Norman, Seymour Sudman, and Galen Gockel. 1970. *Racial Integration in American Neighborhoods.* Chicago: National Opinion Research Center.
DeMuth, Jerry. 1984. "Integration Maintenance Opposed by Realtor Group." *Washington Post*, 21 July.
Feagin, Joe, and Clairece Feagin. 1978. *Discrimination American Style: Institutional Racism and Sexism.* Englewood Cliffs, N.J.: Prentice-Hall.
Ford Foundation. 1984. *Hispanics: Challenges and Opportunities.* New York: Ford Foundation.

Hamilton, David, and George Bishop. 1976. "Attitudinal and Behavioral Effects of Initial Integration of White Suburban Neighborhoods." *Journal of Social Issues* 32: 46–47.

Hunt, Chester. 1959. "Private Integrated Housing in a Medium Size Northern City." *Social Problems* 7: 195–209.

McGrew, Jane. 1984. "Integration Is Goal of Housing Policy." *Los Angeles Times*, 15 July.

Mariano, Ann. 1984. "Fair Housing Law Questioned." *Washington Post*, 11 July.

North, William. 1983a. "Today's Real Estate Industry Challenges." *Texas Realtor* (May): 6–9.

———. 1983b. "Realtors Seek Resolution of Fair Housing Dilemma." News release, National Association of Realtors, Washington, D.C., 12 September.

Schuck, Peter. 1980. "The Graying of Civil Rights Law." *The Public Interest* 60 (Summer): 69–93.

Taeuber, Karl, and Alma Taeuber. 1965. *Negroes in Cities*. Chicago: Aldine.

Wasserstrom, Richard. 1977. "Racism, Sexism, and Preferential Treatment: An Approach to the Topics." *UCLA Law Review* 24 (February): 581–622.

Weaver, Robert. 1956. "Integration in Public and Private Housing." *The Annals* 304 (March): 86–97.

Section I
Perspectives on Housing Integration

Introduction

JOHN M. GOERING

When construction of 120 townhouses for low-income families began in Spring 1980 in the Whitman Park area of Philadelphia, the neighbors draped their doors in black crepe in protest (McGrew 1981). In suburban areas of Washington, D.C., newly arrived black families are often greeted by a cross-burning by local Ku Kluxers (Valente 1983). In 1984, there were over thirty attacks by whites on the homes of blacks living in integrated areas in Chicago, including firebombings and stonings (Blackistone 1985). Resistance to the arrival of minority families, as well as to public housing that might be used by them, is a longstanding, continuing part of life in most American cities. It occurs throughout most parts of the country—in New York, Boston, Chicago, Memphis, St. Louis, Cleveland, and San Antonio.

The desegregation of housing for minorities still appears as one of America's most unsettled civil rights frontiers, despite the passage of civil rights laws in the 1960s. Americans now fairly willingly use the same bathrooms, water fountains, and restaurants regardless of race. Minority access to voting rights and to equal employment is reasonably well-entrenched in American legal and social values. Even school desegregation, with all of its contentiousness, generally is recognized by citizens and courts as a valid objective. There remain, however, high levels of resistance and uncertainty about housing integration, with confusion, ambivalence, and disinterest seemingly as apparent now as they were thirty years ago (Abrams 1955; Weaver 1956). The apparent intractability of racial segregation has paralyzed decision makers and led some to conclude that it is time to abandon the goal of housing integration (Piven and Cloward 1980; Downs 1982; Stuart 1982:A1).

Despite these doubts, racial desegregation remains an objective vigorously pursued in dozens of courts throughout the country. The city of Parma, Ohio, for example, was found guilty in 1980 by a federal court of purposefully and illegally excluding blacks from its community (*U.S.A. v. City of Parma* 1980). In Texarkana, Arkansas, a federal appeals court ruled in 1983 that the city and the U.S. Department of Housing and Urban Development had deliberately acted to support a policy segregating blacks in public housing and ordered them to remedy the situation by desegregating their projects with all deliberate speed (*Clients' Council v. Pierce* 1983). In Toledo, Ohio, a federal judge ruled in 1983 that the Toledo Housing Authority had to increase housing opportunities in surrounding suburbs to end a pattern of purposeful discrimination and segregation (*Jaimes v. Lucas* 1983). More recently, the federal government has sued the city of Cicero, Illinois, for policies that deliberately excluded minorities from housing and employment opportunities in the city, creating an illegally all-white enclave (Maitland 1983). Similar cases and charges are being pursued in Yonkers, New York; Cincinnati, Ohio; Memphis, Tennessee; St. Louis, Missouri; Kansas City, Missouri; Glastonbury, Connecticut; Charlottesville, Virginia; and New York City (Kurtz 1983:A2).

Citizens and civil rights organizations continue to charge that their constitutional or legal rights have been violated either by excluding them from the benefits of interracial residential living or by trapping them in black or minority ghettos. Nothing has been done, the charge is made, by federal, state, or local officials to disrupt the segregative status quo. Public policymakers have succumbed to local racist practices and sustained segregated living, decades after it was declared illegal (*Jaimes v. Lucas* 1983; *Clients' Council v. Pierce* 1983; Schnapper 1983).

The responses to such charges vary from case to case and frequently raise questions about the limits of judicial oversight. Federal agencies may reject requests for certain forms of relief or remedy, claiming that no intentional discrimination or violation occurred, that Congress has empowered federal agencies and not courts to determine corrective action in cases where civil rights have been violated, and that, even if the U.S. government were found guilty of fostering segregation, there currently are virtually no housing resources available to promote effective desegregation. In one case in Boston, for example, the plaintiffs requested 3,000 units of integrated housing, a request that was labeled by the Justice Department as a "massive judicial intrusion." Courts might be able to order the elimination of barriers to the development of housing for minorities, but cannot, the federal government replied, order the actual development of that housing as a remedy because Congress has not appropriated funds for either public housing production or assisted housing construction.[1] The claim of fiscal restraint will increasingly confront courts and policymakers with substantial difficulties as decisions are made to allocate dwindling housing resources to meet the nation's diverse housing needs. The options available to federal courts are, therefore, to a degree circumscribed by legislative, fiscal, and administrative decisions.

These limitations suggest the imperative need for a national policy on housing desegregation. Framing a national policy on housing integration is, as Orfield points out in this section, a necessity to ensure that federal housing programs do not intensify the problems of ghettoization. He reminds us of the now unfashionable truth that ghettos not only persist but are expanding. Fair housing laws are insufficient, he argues, to overcome the combination of class and racial impediments to desegregation. Federal and local officials, who often violate the Constitution and civil rights laws, must develop new policies and plans for desegregation that go beyond the mere enforcement of antidiscrimination statutes. Desegregation plans, he stresses, should link efforts at school and housing desegregation, reducing resistance to unpopular techniques such as busing and thereby increase the marketability of housing desegregation programs. A national program for integration, he concludes, "is the only decision compatible with the core values of our society."

The fact that there is not unanimity on either the priority or the means to achieve desegregation is highlighted in the next analysis by Leigh and Mc-Ghee. Unlike Orfield, they see other priorities and choices for the minority community. Integration may be too "utopian" a goal, with only dim prospects for its realization.[2] Better and more affordable housing, rather than integration, would come first in their priorities. They list reasons for supporting a national integration policy, but also find reasons why the National Urban League might be opposed to one. Central to their opposition, as well as to that of many other fair housing advocates, is the prospect that race-conscious practices will be adopted to restrict the housing choices of minorities in the name of promoting integration. The National Urban League would oppose, they state, "any action that would maintain housing integration by denying free access to minority group members."

Being at the lower end of the pecking order of civil rights priorities is not, then, the only limitation facing the movement for housing integration. It suffers from the more fundamental limitation that in the promotion of stable interracial communities some minorities may be denied their equal housing rights. Polikoff, in this section, thoughtfully addresses many of the key and controversial legal issues that are associated with linking fair housing laws to the promotion of residential integration. Responding to large-scale housing institutions whose practices may directly or indirectly foster segregation is identified, rightly, as a major legal frontier. Several contributors to this section worry about the design of desegregation programs where race is an explicit consideration. The National Urban League, for example, sides with fair housing policies that emphasize choice, regardless of whether the outcome is segregation or some form of integration.

The final contribution to this section is written by one of the major fair housing attorneys in the United States. Polikoff has been plaintiffs' attorney in the *Gautreaux* case (see Vernarelli, Chapter 9 below, for a discussion of the case). He is also currently engaged in litigation regarding integration maintenance or racial diversity programs in Chicago. After reviewing current legal and political issues, he focuses on the specific constitutional and legal standards that would have to be met to implement counseling efforts. He argues that they offer an alternative to approaches that emphasize only freedom of choice and those that use coercion through racial quotas. The compelling interests, the necessity of the means, and the burden and fairness of the specific program must be assessed in order to determine its legality. Polikoff's conclusion leaves a substantial legal challenge as well as critical research recommendations appropriate for both local and national audiences.

Although the contributors to this section oppose, or are reluctant to recommend the use of, race-conscious integration quotas, their use is a live, although extremely controversial, part of current legal and policy debate regarding housing integration. One fair housing activist, engaged in a court suit over racial quotas used to maintain integration, argued:

> Integration is a laudable goal, but must minorities who have suffered and still suffer the burdens of racism and the resulting segregation in society, now bear the brunt of society's meager efforts to integrate? A black who is denied an apartment in an attempt to maintain a racially segregated community and a black who is denied an apartment in order to maintain an integrated community are in the same position. They have been denied an apartment because they are black. (Hoeber 1980)

The outright denial of housing to minorities in order to maintain an existing balance or ratio of majority to minority households is a prominent, contentious aspect of the fair housing movement in the United States.[3]

Over a decade ago, prominent policy analysts argued that one of the essential factors determining the racial stability of an area is "a workable mechanism ensuring that whites will remain in a majority—such as some type of quota system—that is both legal and credible" (Downs 1973:99). The use of such racial housing quotas has been noted for years (Deutsch and Collins 1951: 15–16; Grier and Grier 1960:71–74; Bradburn, Sudman, and Gockel 1970: 76–86; Molotch 1972:111; Ackerman 1974; Milgrim 1977). One developer when asked was quite frank in his justification for using quotas: "We're getting some flack from the human relations people and the feds too. They say we are manipulating. I'll tell you something. We are manipulating and I'll tell you something else—we're building more houses, selling more houses, selling to more Negroes, and getting more integration our way than we would if we did it their way" (Schermer and Leven 1968:26).

Such a reaction has been common among developers as well as some citizen groups (McEntire 1960:212–15; Goodwin 1979:159–63). In Oak Park, Illinois, for example, certain areas were exempted from fair housing law enforcement to enable racial proportions to be maintained, although the implementation of a 30 percent minority quota was rejected (Berry 1979:300–301). Quotas, establishing a numerical threshold for the proportion of blacks residing in a building or community, continue to be attractive for two reasons: they are relatively simple and straightforward to administer, and they act to immediately reduce or eliminate the fears of whites that they will become a numerical minority. That is, virtually all quotas establish whites as the dominant percentage. The use of quotas requires none of the complex assessments spelled out by Polikoff; indeed, they are being used in a number of housing developments across the United States.[4]

The use of "benign" quotas to establish or maintain racial integration does indeed appear to many to conflict with the rights of individuals protected by Title VIII of the Civil Rights Act of 1968. The problem of developing legally acceptable standards for race-conscious integration management confronts the issue that such affirmative criteria frequently act as a ceiling. "Integration management activities that effectively limit black representation in a municipality to no more than the metropolitan wide ratio ascribe the force of law to the proposition that blacks must everywhere constitute a minority" (Lake and Winslow 1981:322).

Federal courts have produced modest but by no means definitive clarification of some aspects of the legality of quotas. In a case involving the Housing Authority of Beaver County, Pennsylvania, a federal court ruled that the authority's use of quotas to "balance" the racial distribution of its tenants was illegal. The authority's use of a ceiling quota, limiting minority participation, violated the Constitution and fair housing laws by denying blacks access to housing solely because of their race and because of the burden or stigma imposed on them. The court decided that individual blacks may not be made to suffer exclusion in an effort to protect the broader societal interest in preventing resegregation. Only a temporary and "precisely tailored" racial goal might be acceptable, one in which the quota "includes as many black residents as is compatible with the need to avoid resegregation" or tipping (*Burney v. Housing Authority of Beaver County* 1982:15,998:590).

Another pending case involving the use of racial quotas in a federally assisted housing project in New York City dramatically illustrates the complexity and controversy surrounding the use of quotas. In 1979, a class action suit was brought by black families who stated that they were denied apartments in the Starrett City complex in Brooklyn because of their race and the existence of a fixed racial quota (*Mario v. Starrett City* 1979). Starrett City, which includes 46 buildings housing over 5,800 families, admitted to the use and necessity of a 70 percent white–30 percent minority quota in order to maintain an interracial community. As a result of this restriction, and the tight rental housing market in New York, the waiting period for blacks soon lengthened to twenty months whereas for whites it was two months.

For some supporters of Starrett City's policy, there was convincing evidence that but for its racial quota the development would have surely tipped, destroying the racial integration in the community. No other way was known to preserve the integrated character of Starrett City that would have less of a discriminatory effect. White fears over tipping could only be allayed through a restriction on the proportion of minorities to approximately one-third the total population. The defendant's expert witness, Oscar Newman, carried forward the logic of this position:

> The fear of taking a morally disturbing position [the use of occupancy controls] has served to perpetuate a far greater immorality: the polarization of American society and the segregation of blacks to intolerable living conditions for generations to come. . . . The public institutionalization of a set limit for minority participation, therefore, works to attract majority residents just as it prevents minority residents from overwhelm-

ing it. It serves, not only as a mechanism for stabilizing an integrated community, but as a device to allow the tipping point to increase a few points without bringing about white flight. (Newman 1983:203, 205)

More recently, Newman (1985) has gone further in predicting that the use of racial quotas throughout the United States could almost assuredly double the number of minorities currently in residence without leading to resegregation.

An apparent settlement of the Starrett City litigation was reached in May 1984, allowing Starrett to continue its use of quotas with the provision that its ceiling be raised slightly and that other projects throughout the city be made available to minorities. One month later, however, the U.S. Department of Justice filed suit in federal court charging that the policy of using racial quotas violated federal fair housing law by denying blacks access to apartments based on race. The federal government's intervention at the "last moment" (Fried 1984:33) brought it into close alignment with the original accusations by the plaintiffs. That is, the use of the quota denied housing opportunities to minorities in violation of federal fair housing law. "Such a denial of rights to minorities cannot be justified by a purported need to give effect to the racial prejudices of others." (*U.S.A. v. Starrett City* 1984:11). Starrett City's success in achieving integration was at the expense of discriminating against large numbers of blacks and Hispanics.

Currently, no decision has been reached by the court on the suit filed by the Department of Justice. The suit has, however, brought to the surface many previously unspoken disagreements within the civil rights and minority communities (Morley 1984). The NAACP, despite its long support for school integration, is likely to oppose the settlement in Starrett, agreeing with the Department of Justice. The attorney for the NAACP reacted bitterly to Starrett's quota, because it preys on white flight and supports the view that whites feel safe and comfortable only when they are in the majority. Private fair housing centers, which saw in the settlement a means to open up housing opportunities outside of Starrett City, may now feel pressed to defend an agreement that appears to violate the rights of minorities.

The constitutionality and legality of quotas will most likely be resolved only by the Supreme Court. The Court may also need to rule on the legality of a broad range of race-conscious integration maintenance tools currently under litigation in New York, Chicago, and elsewhere (*Greater South Suburban v. South Suburban* 1984), clearing away some of the most pernicious obstacles to establishing national policy for housing integration. It seems unlikely, however, that the precise tailoring required in the *Burney* decision will succumb to the broad-scale social engineering suggested by Starrett's defendants. Courts will probably reluctantly, if at all, attempt to establish national or administrative programmatic requirements. They will more likely leave to others the onerous task of deciding how to systematically address the multiple needs for freedom of choice in housing and desegregation procedures to sustain stable residential integration, as well as for adequate housing for the country's minority poor.

NOTES

1. This discussion is based on documents submitted to the U.S. District Court for the District of Massachusetts in the case of *NAACP v. Pierce (Harris)* C.A. No. 78-850-S. The documents are the "Plaintiffs Proposed Form of Judgement" submitted on 26 May 1983 and "Defendants Opposition to Plaintiff's Proposed Form of Judgement" submitted on 27 June 1983.

2. "If whites have arrived at a new place, blacks have also arrived at a new place. It is a recognition that they must have economic power. There is less hysteria about integration, but equal hysteria about opportunity and justice. There is more comfort with black identity, and more talk about forming coalitions with whites who are beginning to find that Reaganomics is color-blind" (Gilliam 1982:17).

3. The following is an excerpt from a letter written to the NAACP relating the writers' concerns about racial diversity programs (the letter does not indicate what specific programs are being objected to):

> We think that the attempts of local governments all across the country to control the numbers of Black families in communities, neighborhoods, and buildings, are a far greater danger to our People (indeed to the Country) than the admitted racist activities of some real estate sales-persons. We Blacks should have enough, in the last 10 or 15 years, of the absolutely botched up job others have done in managing our utilization of our Constitutionally endowed prerogatives. But further, in our estimation, none of this preoccupation with that Realtor/Housing Center case should deter the NAACP from coming to grips with the growing pace toward the management of where we Blacks live. Outside of stepping on our freedom of speech, we know of hardly a more suppressive move that governments can take in this society, than to control where we can live. Would any other people in this Country even be thought of as fit subjects for such policies? And, would any other People not raise holy hell at the very thought that they should be shunted around from area to area, in the interests of satisfying white fear that whites will flee an area (or decline to move in)? (Communication from Michael H. Sussman, Assistant General Counsel, NAACP Special Contribution Fund, 25 January 1985)

4. A nonrandom survey of thirty housing developers found that "the creation of integrated projects required setting realistic goals on white, minority, and black participation in the project—never to exceed 40% minority" (Newman 1983:76). There is also limited evidence concerning the use of racial quotas in public housing projects. Ackerman (1974:249–51), for example, provides evidence from San Francisco indicating that federally subsidized housing projects using racial occupancy controls were more likely to be "substantially integrated." Substantially integrated projects were those with at least 20 percent minority (black, Spanish, or white) occupancy. These data do not, however, give any indication of the length of time during which projects retained

balanced, stable proportions of different racial or nationality groups. Nor do the data indicate the racial composition of the census tract or neighborhood for each of the projects. That is, substantial integration may be easier to achieve in only certain kinds of neighborhoods and may last for shorter or longer periods of time depending on other factors.

REFERENCES

Abrams, Charles. 1955. *Forbidden Neighbors.* New York: Harper and Row.

Ackerman, Bruce. 1974. "Integration for Subsidized Housing and the Question of Racial Occupancy Controls." *Stanford Law Review* 26 (January): 245–81.

Berry, Brian. 1979. *The Open Housing Question: Race and Housing in Chicago, 1966–1976.* Cambridge, Mass.: Ballinger.

Blackistone, Kevin. 1985. "Racial Violence and Harassment Escalate in Chicago Area." *The Chicago Reporter* 14 (January): 1, 6–7.

Bradburn, Norman, Seymor Sudman, and Galen Gockel. 1970. *Racial Integration in American Neighborhoods.* Chicago: National Opinion Research Center.

Burney v. Housing Authority of Beaver County. 1982. 551 F.Supp. 746 (W.D. Pa.).

Clients' Council v. Pierce. 1983. No. 82–1383 (CA–8, 6–28–83).

Deutsch, Morton, and Mary Collins. 1951. *Interracial Housing: A Psychological Evaluation of a Social Experiment.* Minneapolis: University of Minnesota Press.

Downs, Anthony. 1973. *Opening Up the Suburbs.* New Haven: Yale University Press.

————. 1982. Quoted in John McCarron, "Integration Isn't Best Path for Minorities, Forum Told," *Chicago Tribune,* 21 June, p. 4.

Fried, Joseph. 1984. "U.S. Challenges Accord in Starrett City Bias Suit." *New York Times,* 29 June, p. B3.

Gilliam, Dorothy. 1982. "The New Segregation: Two Decades of Civil Rights and Wrongs in Washington." *Washington Post Magazine,* 17 October, pp. 16–17.

Goodwin, Carole. 1979. *The Oak Park Strategy: Community Control of Racial Change.* Chicago: University of Chicago Press.

Greater South Suburban Board of Realtors and National Association of Realtors v. South Suburban Housing Center. 1984. No. 83 C 8149. Northern District of Illinois, U.S. District Court.

Grier, George, and Eunice Grier. 1960. *Privately Developed Interracial Housing: An Analysis of Experience.* Berkeley: University of California Press.

Hoeber, Betty. 1980. "Letter to the Editor." *City Limits* (June/July): 18–19.

Jaimes v. Lucas Metropolitan Housing Authority, HUD et al. 1983 C.A. 20. C. 74–86 (N.D. Ohio), 12 May.

Kurtz, Howard. 1983. "Lawsuit in Yonkers Challenges a Suburban Tradition of Bias." *Washington Post,* 2 May, p. A2.

Lake, Robert, and Jessica Winslow. 1981. "Integration Management: Municipal Constraints on Residential Mobility." *Urban Geography* 12: 311–26.

McEntire, Davis. 1960. *Residence and Race.* Berkeley: University of California Press.

McGrew, Jane. 1981. "Resistance to Change Continues to Restrict Public Housing Choices." *Journal of Housing* 38 (July): 375–80.

Maitland, Leslie. 1983. "U.S. Sues Cicero, Ill., Saying Town Policy Is to Exclude Blacks." *New York Times*, 21 January, p. 1.

Mario, Arthur, et al. v. Starrett City Associates. 1979. 79 Civ. 3096 (E.R.N.). Eastern District of New York, U.S. District Court.

Milgrim, Morris. 1977. *Good Neighborhood: The Challenge of Open Housing.* New York: W. W. Norton.

Molotch, Harvey. 1972. *Managed Integration.* Berkeley: University of California Press.

Morley, Jefferson. 1984. "Double Reverse Discrimination." *The New Republic*, 9 July, pp. 14–18.

Newman, Oscar. 1983. *Integration = Intervention: The Use of Occupancy Controls at Starrett City.* Great Neck, N.Y.: Institute for Community Design Analysis.
————. 1985. Remarks at Potomac Institute/NCDH Legal Fair Housing Conference, Washington, D.C., 10 January.

Piven, Frances Fox, and Richard A. Cloward. 1980. "The Case against Urban Desegregation." In *Housing Urban America*, edited by Jon Pynoos, Robert Schafer, and Chester Hartman, pp. 100–110. New York: Aldine.

Saltman, Juliet. 1983. "Neighborhood Change: Theories, Realities, Prospects." Unpublished report, National Neighbors, Washington, D.C.

Schermer, George, and Arthur Levin. 1968. *Housing Guide to Equal Opportunity: Affirmative Practices for Integrated Housing.* Washington, D.C.: The Potomac Institute.

Schnapper, Eric. 1983. "Perpetuation of Past Discrimation." *Harvard Law Review* 96 (February): 828–64.

Stuart, Reginald. 1982. "Schools Try to Attract Whites by Easing Integration Efforts." *New York Times*, 21 June, p. A1.

U.S.A. v. City of Parma, Ohio. 1980. 494 F.Supp. 1049.

U.S.A. v. Starrett City Associates. 1984. "Complaint for Discrimination in Housing." CV-84-2793. Eastern District of New York, U.S. District Court.

Valente, Judith. 1983. "Cross Burning, Vandalism Reported in Maryland Suburbs." *Washington Post*, 30 August, p. C2.

Weaver, Robert. 1956. "Integration in Public and Private Housing." *The Annals* 304 (March): 86–97.

Chapter One
The Movement for Housing Integration
Rationale and the Nature of the Challenge

GARY ORFIELD

The cause of fair housing hardly occupies a leading place on the nation's political agenda. Many Americans believe that the problem of discrimination has already been solved.[1] Others think that the government has already done too much. Just after the election of President Reagan, conservatives in the Senate killed a very modest fair housing enforcement bill with little reaction around the United States.[2] There have been no major demonstrations against housing segregation for more than a decade. The issue has been virtually ignored for the past two years and Justice Department enforcement of the weak federal law on the books has been drastically reduced.[3] There has in fact been very little effort for any kind of integration in recent years and yet few issues will so profoundly affect the future of our society.

Housing segregation and the possibility of integrated housing are so important to our future because race is the central structural problem of American urban society and because a family's spatial location determines so much in our sprawling, highly segregated metropolitan areas. It not only determines whether or not one's children will grow up in a multiracial setting with friends of different groups but it also determines the quality of schools, the level of municipal services, increases in housing value, relative tax burdens, ease of access to work, safety, and much else.[4]

The differences among communities within any large metropolitan area are vast. In terms of economics, educational level, community wealth, ethnic background, and other ways, they are greater, often much greater, than the difference between the United States and some separate countries. Moving from a declining part of a ghetto or barrio to a prosperous white suburb is in some ways like moving to another country. Whether this kind of move can become commonplace and stable integration can be achieved on a substantial and growing scale will do much to define whether or not we can keep alive the dream of equality in a single society. The alternative is to fulfill the prophecy of separate and unequal societies with minority families largely confined to a situation of undesired segregation and permanent inequality.

No one seriously discusses housing integration policy as a way to rapidly reverse racial inequality in urban areas. Segregation is so widespread, so deeply rooted in customs, expectations, and practices, and so strongly reinforced by differences of income and wealth at a time when many cannot afford to participate in the home ownership market, that it would be foolish to expect a rapid transformation.

The speed and comprehensiveness of the integration is not nearly so crucial as the fact that policies do create a real possibility of a different racial future. They can create channels out of the ghetto and the barrio that really work rather than find the out-migrant rapidly swamped in an even larger pattern of expanding minority segregation. One consequence can be the creation of a safety valve permitting access to the social and economic mainstream for highly motivated, highly successful minority families who are always the most frustrated with arbitrary racial distinctions. Finally, a successful policy can begin to change white attitudes by showing that integration can be stable rather than a mere prelude to a destructive racial transition.

Since the mid-sixties there has been a wide diversity of attempts to deal with the problems of the cities, from the liberal interventionist strategies of the Great Society to the antigovernment, free market philosophy of the Reagan administration. The Great Society effort embraced many approaches simultaneously. These included the War on Poverty with its community action and Headstart programs, massive compensatory education efforts under the 1965 Elementary and Secondary Education Act, expanded job training, comprehensive community-based planning in the Model Cities program, a turn toward subsidizing private housing construction and low-income home ownership, and unprecedented civil rights policies that increased black voting power, desegregated southern schools, made job discrimination illegal, and produced a federal law against housing discrimination.[5]

The programs were reduced and consolidated to some extent under presidents Nixon and Ford. Civil rights enforcement was sharply curtailed, and there was a concerted effort to increase the autonomy of the state and local governments in urban policy.[6] The Carter administration brought a partial return to programs more targeted on the poor and minorities but no major new programs.[7] The Reagan administration adopted the view that urban aid programs had actually harmed both the cities and the economy and proceeded to cut and dismantle a number while giving local officials free reign in others.[8]

The relatively brief period since the mid-sixties has seen experiments touching virtually the full range of ideas seriously discussed by urban experts. If one adds to this list the experience with policies initiated by individual state and local governments, and by federal courts in response to findings of constitutional violations, it is possible to assess the outcomes of many approaches to urban improvements.

The experience shows several important things. First, no policy directed at improving the conditions of the poor in urban areas is likely to be pursued consistently for any length of time. Policies have been extremely erratic and have changed dramatically over the past fifteen to twenty years.[9] Second, no policy is likely to receive sufficient funds, even in the most liberal times, to permit any approach to equality for the residents of the poverty areas of the great cities.[10] Third, there has been a strong tendency to abandon federal controls and strong national regulation in favor of local and state autonomy. This means that programs tend to lose what focus they had on the poor and minorities.[11] Fourth, the implementation of change in desperately poor areas is a very complex process with high risks of waste and corruption in some areas. The difficulty and the existence of these legitimate points of criticism make maintenance of the programs all the more difficult. Fifth, there is very little private interest in investment in such areas, even under the most far-reaching incentives and subsidies. Large and small experiments, from urban renewal to Model Cities, from black capitalism to community development corporations, from tax exemptions to free job training and subsidized employment programs, have failed to achieve significant ghetto economic growth or even to offset continuing declines.[12]

Not only is there a good deal of evidence that ghetto enrichment policies have been too small to make much difference and have become less rather than more targeted over time, but there is also strong evidence that even these small efforts are extraordinarily vulnerable to political attack. Both the Reagan administration and conservative governments in a number of state capitals have shown that cutting off programs channeling money into depressed minority communities can be a very popular political program. Such cutbacks appeal to the widespread white belief that urban and racial problems are not the result of institutionalized discrimination operating over time but of the personal failings of the people in the ghetto or barrio.[13] The Reagan cuts, for example, eliminated programs such as public service jobs and the poverty program and cut particularly sharply at housing subsidy programs serving very low income families in very poor areas. Although social and educational programs aimed at the middle class were largely spared in the budget fights of 1981–82, there was little politically effective defense of many of the programs intended to make separate more equal in American cities.[14] The sharp reduction in the political strength of inner cities caused by the 1982 reapportionment of Congress and state legislatures only compounded these difficulties.[15]

The ghetto enhancement strategy is based on a belief in white goodwill and willingness to continually commit large resources to dealing with ghetto problems caused ultimately by discrimination. There is no evidence, however, that whites believe that they are responsible or that they are willing to commit such resources.[16] Indeed, as middle-class minority families increasingly separate themselves from poor inner-city communities, it is not clear that there will ever be politically effective demands for such commitments.

In the decades of argument about competing strategies of "ghetto enhancement" or integration, integrationists have argued consistently that, in a white-dominated society, separate is inevitably unequal both in terms of the resources that go into a community and in terms of the way in which society values that community, its institutions, and its people. This is not true because there is something inferior about blacks and Latinos or something "magic" about white neighborhoods or schools; the basic problem that integration addresses is the problem of white prejudice and the fact of institutional and individual discrimination in favor of whites and white communities.

Whereas most integrationists believe that racial integration is a very important end in itself in a multiracial society, most minority families who prefer integrated schools and neighborhoods do so on a more pragmatic basis—the conviction that white decision makers will channel more real resources, rewards, and recognition to institutions and communities serving significant numbers of influential whites as well as blacks or Latinos. They are right.

Integration as the Only Real Alternative to Ghettoization

Segregation is not a fixed phenomenon—it is dynamic, constantly spreading, and usually associated with a wide range of negative developments for affected minority communities over time. These changes are associated with white responses to racial change and the general white inability to distinguish middle-class minority families and neighborhoods from the minority poor. Thus, although the first minority families moving into white areas near ghettos or barrios often have higher incomes and status than the whites they buy from, often epitomizing the very values that the local whites claim to defend most vigorously, the white majority commonly views them as harbingers of the neighborhood's rapid racial transformation and decline and not as assets for the neighborhood culture. Whites then proceed to act in ways that make this self-fulfilling prophecy come true. Special circumstances exist, of course, when the changes connected with movement toward racial segregation do not occur, but this cycle is still the dominant reality in most communities and the prevailing expectation of most whites.

The belief in the inevitablity of ghetto expansion is not merely a product of public fears or of prejudices in the real estate market but has also been the dominant perspective of researchers who have shaped scholarly understanding of racial change. Most of the major statistical studies of residential segregation through analysis of the 1970 census found few exceptions to the pattern of virtually complete racial transition in communities that began racial integration. A new analysis of metropolitan Chicago reports that, even though there had been a great deal of black movement out from earlier ghetto areas during the 1970s, blacks were even more likely to be concentrated in virtually all-black communities than they were a decade earlier and that all-black communities ranked far below white or integrated communities in income, employment, education, and other measures studied.[17]

The only way to avoid the by-products of this process in specific neighborhoods adjoining ghettos and to diminish the white expectations that underlie segregation is by achieving stable integration. The key process in racial transition is the virtual exclusion of many integrated or transitional communities from the white housing market. Neighborhoods usually change racially, not because of a sudden flight of existing white residents, but because of the unwillingness of enough white families to buy or rent housing.[18] The shrinkage or disappearance of white demand and a very active minority market, including buyers and renters steered by realtors believing that the community is in transition, can rapidly change the racial composition of a neighborhood. The only way to avoid this process is by maintaining an active white market for local housing and mobilizing community support for an integrated neighborhood. In a community adjoining an existing ghetto or barrio, unless there is a very high price barrier or some other special circumstances, this usually requires a concerted community effort to monitor real estate practices, deal with any telltale signs of decay, maintain well-integrated public schools, and recruit families into the neighborhood.[19]

The entire situation sometimes changes if the community can deal with the fear of resegregation. Communities that preserve stable integration and offer assurance of relative stability are no longer seen as places to flee because of predictable decline but as places in which investment is far more secure than other white areas in the path of expanding minority populations. These communities have mastered a major threat to their future and have mobilized resources and community organization that are extremely valuable for their future. Whereas housing in an area threatened by racial change is often seen by whites as a speculative investment, homes in stable integrated areas are viewed differently. Small businesses, which often leave racially changing areas, find integrated communities much more attractive.

Analysis of patterns of racial change in all metropolitan Chicago census tracts from 1970 to 1980 identified 61 stably integrated black-white tracts and 135 stable Hispanic-white tracts. In both categories these tracts ranked far above the all-minority areas and also other comparable tracts that went through racial transition during this period. The stable tracts had higher incomes, less poverty, less unemployment, and considerably higher educational levels.[20]

The situation of the neighborhood that has faced and resolved the threat of racial change is much more like that of a community undergoing "gentrification" than that of a community threatening to become a low-income ghetto. The class status of such a community is likely to be stable or rising and its attractiveness can eventually produce beneficial financial returns for those who held or made investments when the future was insecure.[21] Investment in maintenance or major rehabilitation is much more likely, and in some cases there may be a special need for special programs to prevent displacement of minority families.[22]

Fair Housing: Accomplishments and Limitations

Considerable progress has occurred since the fair housing movement first emerged in the aftermath of World War II. Like all major reforms, the solution of one set of major problems has both revealed more complex and related issues and suggested some of the ways to address them.

The campaign for fair housing began with the simple problem of apartheid, often fully supported by government and sustained by overt discrimination, intimidation, and frequent violence. Segregation of blacks in northern cities was almost total and a virtual white consensus fostered the practice. The courts upheld, and the federal government strongly encouraged, a system of racial covenants that made integrated housing illegal in many areas. Blacks were living in neighborhoods of extremely high density and deplorable housing quality, paying higher rents for worse housing.[23]

The first reform was outlawing overt discrimination. The law had to require that minority and white Americans get equal opportunity to obtain housing in the private and public sectors. More than a generation of work was necessary to win the victories stretching from the Supreme Court's decision against restrictive covenants in 1948 to the federal fair housing law in 1968. Finally, a quarter century after housing segregation had been a virtually unchallenged norm, the Congress, the president, and the Supreme Court had taken the position that overt discrimination was wrong and illegal.[24] Although there was no significant enforcement machinery, the change in goals was very significant.

These reforms have transformed the lives of significant numbers of middle- and upper-income nonwhite families and led to improved housing quality and choice for millions of black and Hispanic households. In many solid middle-class and wealthy areas that had always been all-white, a small number of blacks and other minorities has moved in without incident and now shares routinely in the lives of many well-served and privileged communities, largely insulated from the problems of the inner city.

The total confinement of minority families in dense inner-city neighborhoods is now largely a thing of the past.[25] Although some areas near ghettos have remained all white through more than a quarter century of fair housing because of their intense racial hostility, ghettos and barrios have been able to expand, often with great speed and over large distances.

Comparing the location of the black population in the mid–1940s with the 1980s in any large American city is an astonishing experience. The physical area included in segregated minority communities has expanded *exponentially*. Population increases alone do not drive this expansion. Indeed, the ghettos became much larger in a number of central cities losing black population in the 1970s. In some large metropolitan areas minority communities have expanded across city boundary lines to include dozens of square miles of suburbia.[26]

The existing housing system does not produce a stable and "efficient" boundary between the minority and white markets. The basic mechanisms of change—the desire of young minority families for better housing and neighborhoods and the specialization of certain sectors of the housing market in racial conversion—produce a powerful impulse toward continuing expansion of the boundaries of the minority areas. This now appears to occur whether or not there is any increase in the number of households. When the demand created by migration stops, this can produce a more rapid cycle of decay and collapse of neighborhoods in the heart of the minority community. Without new migrants, those moving out are not replaced by newcomers at the core of the ghetto. Because there is no white demand inside ghetto boundaries apart from the small number of areas affected by gentrification, the economic value of housing there plummets and decline and abandonment become commonplace.

Although the rapid expansion of the ghetto has not produced integration for most blacks, it has permitted the filtering process to work to eliminate much of the completely unacceptable housing stock and to upgrade the quality of housing for minority families by greatly increasing the supply of housing units in the minority housing market. Under certain circumstances, the rapid expansion of segregation, combined with the virtual absence of any white demand for housing units within minority areas, may mean that there are excess housing units and therefore a less rapid increase in prices and rentals than in the white or integrated housing markets. There is evidence that the housing situation of blacks has improved dramatically in the past generation with the lessening of the housing *overcharges* so obvious in the 1940s.[27] Fair housing deserves a good share of the credit for such changes.

The Problem Redefined

Part of the reason for the original fair housing movement was the obvious inequality in housing opportunities between whites and blacks. To a significant extent, housing is better now and fair housing has helped. The change came for a small number of black families in the way foreseen by fair housing advocates. Many others, however, live in better housing but in the midst of much larger ghettos, ghettos larger than anyone imagined a generation ago. The previous focus on black segregation is also now widening to encompass increased awareness of the existence of large barrios housing segregated low-income and working-class Hispanics. Such barrios are experiencing many problems paralleling but often different from those seen in the black ghettos.[28]

Obviously, fair housing laws and court decisions alone did not and do not produce integrated cities. As research accumulates on racial change in cities since the passage of fair housing laws, it is apparent that, although new laws ended the absolute confinement of the ghetto, they left untouched many of the basic forces that spread segregation. The most important problem is not one of prosecuting individual violators in a basically fair housing market, although this is what the new law addresses. Rather, the basic problems are very widespread institutional discrimination, the inertia of segregation, the fear of resegregation, and the behavior of both minority and white families based on a long history of residential segregation and neighborhood transition.[29] All of these factors produce a tendency to continue the spread of segregation. Special efforts, *beyond fair housing laws*, were necessary in virtually all of the substantially integrated areas adjoining existing segregated minority communities to achieve stable residential integration.[30] The nature of the special efforts and the possibility of applying them on a much broader scale provide an agenda for the next generation of efforts to achieve racially integrated urban neighborhoods.

Communities that have remained integrated have identified a number of forces that produce racial transition and devised strategies to deal with each. These forces include discrimination and steering of housing customers by brokers and rental agents; the "self-steering" of blacks and whites based on the limited knowledge by most minority homeseekers of areas any distance away from the minority communities (and thus their tendency to focus very heavy demands on nearby integrated areas); and the fear of white businesses, organizations, churches, and residents that integrated neighborhoods will soon become black or Hispanic.[31] The tendency for public schools to become minority institutions while their neighborhoods are still residentially integrated furthers the process of resegregation. Whites fear that the first signs of commercial disinvestment, declines in municipal services, declines in housing upkeep, or a rise in crime indicate that the community is in a downward spiral.[32] If subsidized housing or FHA home financing suddenly become apparent in the neighborhood on a large scale, people often perceive these actions as judgments about the area's declining future and racial change.[33]

Successfully integrated communities have found it necessary to mobilize to deal directly with these problems early in the process of racial change. Some have learned how to do so despite the lack of support or even hostile actions from city, state, and federal agencies. The lessons show that the achievement of the gains of stable integration on a large scale requires an explicit goal of integration, rather than nondiscrimination alone. More importantly, it requires at least a temporary mobilization of resources to respond to the ghettoization process and generate a steady white, as well as black, demand for housing in the area.[34]

The most important impact of success is that it permits both the old-time white residents and the minority newcomers to remain in the kind of neighborhood they want to live in—a stable community that does not face the spiral of decline that often comes after ghettoization. It permits "natural" integration in the neighborhood schools and creates the best conditions for improved race relations—conditions of equal status and shared community experience.[35] Such neighborhoods help the city both by maintaining their economic and educational vitality and by attracting and holding groups of concerned citizens who often exert considerable influence on a citywide basis.[36] Perhaps their most important function is to show other communities that the ghettoization process is not inevitable and to open the possibility of broader achievement of integration.

The Policy Agenda

Integration, like other social policy reforms, is often dismissed in the current political mood as either irrelevant or impossible. It is, in fact, an extremely powerful reform when properly implemented, because it deals with the problem of racial and class separation, school segregation, and neighborhood decline all at the same time, while creating conditions that foster better race relations. It has a positive impact on these problems in a way that is more acceptable to the public than such alternative policies as busing for school integration. There is evidence, for example, that children growing up in integrated neighborhoods have the most positive experiences in integrated schools.[37]

We have learned how to increase urban integration, not because of national policies or major civil rights campaigns, but because of practical experience in a number of individual neighborhoods and suburbs. Whites who did not want to flee, and blacks who did not want to live through the ghettoization process again, learned how to maintain integration because it was their only alternative. Studies of migration patterns and of the impact of widely divergent types of school desegregation plans that have been implemented in different cities and metropolitan areas also have increased our understanding. The courts have experimented with an extraordinary range of approaches that can now be analyzed.

These experiences indicate that successful housing integration requires concerted intervention in the housing market. They also indicate that school desegregation plans should include as much as possible of the housing market in order to encourage neighborhood integration by reducing concerns with fleeing or avoiding a neighborhood with a racially changing school.[38] Research on the impact of federally assisted housing and rent subsidies on residential and school integration shows that, in the absence of federal housing policies explicitly committed to integration and operated with an accurate understanding of the nature of urban racial change, virtually any form of housing subsidy is likely to intensify, rather than diminish, the problems of ghettoization.

Conclusion

The need now is for policies and actions that support integration on the part of local governments and school districts that have a great deal to gain from stable integration. The federal government also needs to express a position on this issue, while fostering research, supportive policies, or experiments. At a time when much of the previous urban policy has been dismantled and the next round of urban reform is being considered, an urgent need arises to recognize both what has been accomplished and what could be achieved through an aggressive attack on one of the core problems of urban America—massive and spreading residential segregation. Only a tiny investment has occurred in understanding, modifying, or eliminating the ghettoization process in contrast to the large investment in research and programs that accepts segregation as a given while trying to improve conditions within segregated minority communities. Future policy and research priorities should correct this failure.

The need for federal and local policies supporting integration addresses not only pragmatic realities of urban change but also the legal and moral imperatives of our constitutional system and national ideology. Since 1964, there has been a clear legal requirement for action to end segregation created by governmental action. The judiciary has found a history of local official action designed to segregate the public schools in virtually every city examined by federal courts.[39] Although the courts have examined the history of housing segregation by public officials far less often than school segregation, an impressive body of findings now exists that shows a history of local and federal actions designed to segregate housing. These actions have violated the constitutional guarantee of "equal protection of the laws," and they have created a constitutional requirement that government officials develop and implement plans to overcome the continuing effects of this government-imposed segregation. These must be plans for integration.

Equal protection of the laws and equal opportunity more broadly defined are not only legal goals but also a basic part of American public ideology. Most Americans believe that black and Hispanic people should have equal access to housing and neighborhoods they can afford and whites say that they are ready to accept nonwhite neighbors. In fact, most whites believe that this equal opportunity already exists.[40]

The job of researchers and responsible officials is to portray the consequences of segregation: the continuing failure of promises to make separate communities equal and the availability of workable policies. We must explain as clearly as possible the severity of contemporary segregation so that policies designed to aid integration can draw upon profound legal, empirical, and ideological roots.

There is a choice to be made. I believe that it is a choice between a clearly unworkable policy of equalizing segregation in a society where separate has always been unequal and a difficult, but possible, policy of building an integrated society. A decision to pursue integration is the only decision compatible with the core values of our society.

NOTES AND REFERENCES

1. A 1981 *Washington Post*/ABC News survey found, for example, that only 16 percent of whites believed that blacks still faced discrimination in the housing market. *Washington Post*, 24 March 1981, p. A2.

2. The bill died despite a favorable majority in the Senate because of a conservative GOP filibuster, with 78 percent of Republicans and the Republican leader unwilling to

end debate and bring the measure to a vote. *Congressional Record*, S15852, 9 December 1980; *Congressional Quarterly Almanac 1980*, 72–S, roll call 496.

3. Citizens Commission on Civil Rights, *A Decent Home: A Report on the Continued Failure of the Federal Government to Provide Equal Housing Opportunity* (Washington, D.C., March 1983).

4. John F. Kain and John M. Quigley, *Housing Markets and Racial Discrimination: A Microeconomic Analysis* (New York: National Bureau of Economic Research, 1975); Louis Harris and Associates, Inc., *A Survey of Citizen Views and Concerns about Urban Life* (Report to the U.S. Department of Housing and Urban Development [HUD], February 1978); Deborah Haines, *Black Homeowners in Transition Areas* (Chicago: Chicago Urban League, 1981).

5. Sar A. Levitan and Robert Taggart, *The Promise of Greatness* (Cambridge: Harvard University Press, 1976).

6. Michael N. Danielson, *The Politics of Exclusion* (New York: Columbia University Press, 1976); Bernard J. Frieden and Marshall Kaplan, *The Politics of Neglect: Urban Aid from Model Cities to Revenue Sharing* (Cambridge: MIT Press, 1975); White House Domestic Council, *1976 Report on National Growth and Development* (Washington, D.C., 1976).

7. *The President's National Urban Policy Report, 1980* (Washington, D.C., 1980).

8. *The President's National Urban Policy Report, 1982* (Washington, D.C., 1982); John L. Palmer and Isabel V. Sawhill, eds., *The Reagan Record* (Washington, D.C.: The Urban Institute, 1984), chap. 7.

9. The massive housing subsidy programs created in 1968, for example, were substantially abandoned in 1973 and those initiated for housing construction in 1974 were substantially abandoned in 1981.

10. This is clearly apparent in reports prepared in the late 1960s, after a historic expansion of federal assistance. *Report of the National Advisory Commission on Civil Disorders* (1968); National Commission on Urban Problems, *Building the American City* (1968).

11. All presidents elected since Lyndon Johnson have urged a larger state and local role in urban programs, and Nixon, Ford, and Reagan have campaigned for weaker civil rights enforcement.

12. Samuel I. Doctors, ed., *Whatever Happened to Minority Economic Development* (Hinsdale, Ill.: Dryden Press, 1974).

13. Robert Kuttner, *Revolt of the Haves: Tax Rebellions and Hard Times* (New York: Simon and Schuster, 1980); Gerald Pomper and Colleagues, *The Election of 1980* (Chatham, N.J.: Chatham House, 1981); Seymour Martin Lipset, ed., *Party Coalitions in the 1980s* (San Francisco: Institute for Contemporary Studies, 1981).

14. Rowland Evans and Robert Novak, *The Reagan Revolution* (New York: E. P. Dutton, 1981).

15. *Congressional Quarterly Almanac* (1981).

16. Only 28 percent of whites believed that the federal social programs of the sixties had made things better. *New York Times*/CBS Poll, *Chicago Tribune*, 16 November 1980.

17. Gary Orfield, Albert Woolbright, and Helene Kim, *Neighborhood Change and Integration in Metropolitan Chicago* (Report of the Leadership Council for Metropolitan Open Communities, July 1984).

18. Avery M. Guest and J. J. Zuiches, "Another Look at Residential Turnover in Urban Neighborhoods," *American Journal of Sociology* 77 (1971): 457–67; Henry J. Becker, "Racially Integrated Neighborhoods: Do White Families Move In? Which Ones?" (Paper presented at the annual meeting of the American Sociological Association, 1979).

19. Carole Goodwin, *The Oak Park Strategy: Community Control of Racial Change* (Chicago: University of Chicago Press, 1979); Gary Orfield, *Toward a Strategy for Urban Integration: Lessons in School and Housing Policy from Twelve Cities* (New York: Ford Foundation, 1981).

20. Orfield, Woolbright, and Kim, *Neighborhood Change.*

21. Michigan Advisory Committee to the U.S. Civil Rights Commission, *Reinvestment and Housing Equality in Michigan* (1980).

22. District of Columbia Advisory Committee to the U.S. Civil Rights Commission, *Neighborhood Renewal—Reinvestment and Displacement in D.C.* (1981); Daphne Spain, "Black-to-White Successions in Central City Housing: Limited Evidence for Urban Revitalization" (Paper presented at the annual meeting of the American Sociological Association, 1979).

23. U.S. Housing and Home Finance Agency, *Our Nonwhite Population and Its Housing* (Washington, D.C.: 1963), pp. 9–14.

24. Civil Rights Act of 1968, Public Law No. 90–284; *Jones v. Mayer*, 392 U.S. 409.

25. Citizens Commission on Civil Rights, Appendix by Karl Taeuber on "Racial Residential Segregation, 1980" (1983).

26. William P. O'Hare, Roy Chatterjee, and Margaret Shukur, *Blacks, Demographic Change, and Public Policy* (Report to HUD by the Joint Center for Political Studies, May 1982).

27. Anthony Yezer, *How Well Are We Housed? Blacks* (Washington, D.C.: HUD, 1979); John C. Weicher, *Housing: Federal Policies and Programs* (Washington, D.C.: American Enterprise Institute, 1980), chap. 2.

28. Gary Orfield and Ricardo M. Tostado, eds., *Latinos in Metropolitan Chicago: A Study of Housing and Employment* (Chicago: Latino Institute, 1983), chap. 5.

29. Becker, "Racially Integrated Neighborhoods"; Harvey L. Molotch, *Managed Integration* (Berkeley: University of California Press, 1972); Yona Ginsberg, *Jews in a Changing Neighborhood* (New York: The Free Press, 1975); Kathleen McCourt, *Working Class Women and Grass-Roots Politics* (Bloomington: University of Indiana Press, 1977).

30. Orfield, *Toward a Strategy for Urban Integration*; Goodwin, *Oak Park Strategy.*

31. Reynolds Farley, Suzanne Bianchi, and Diane Colasanto, "Barriers to the Racial Integration of Neighborhoods: The Detroit Case," *Annals of the American Academy of Political and Social Science* 441 (January 1979): 97–113; Ginsberg, *Jews in a Changing Neighborhood.*

32. McCourt, *Working Class Women*; Richard P. Taub, D. Garth Taylor, and Jan D. Dunham, *Paths of Neighborhood Change* (Chicago: University of Chicago Press, 1984).

33. Susan M. Wachter, "The 1968 FHA Amendments to the National Housing Act: Their Impact on Urban Areas," in *The Urban Impacts of Federal Policies*, ed. Norman J. Glickman (Baltimore: Johns Hopkins University Press, 1980), pp. 426–50.

34. Goodwin, *Oak Park Strategy.*

35. Gordon Allport, *The Nature of Prejudice* (Reading, Mass.: Addison-Wesley, 1954); J. Berger, B. Cohen, and M. Zelditch, Jr., "Status Conceptions and Social Interactions," *American Sociological Review* 37 (1972): 241–55.

36. In 1980 the white population in Washington, D.C., which included substantial numbers living in areas affected by gentrification, showed a higher percentage with college education than the whites in any of the suburban counties. As black suburbanization increased very rapidly, the economic differences between the blacks still residing in the central city and the whites living there became very wide. Alison Jennings, "Class and Race in Washington, D.C.: 1970–1980" (B.A. paper, University of Chicago, 1983).

37. This was an important finding of Robert Green's evaluation of desegregation experiences in metropolitan Wilmington. Experience with voluntary transfer programs has also found that white residents of integrated neighborhoods are far more willing to send their children to integrated magnet schools in other parts of the city than residents of all-white areas.

38. Christine H. Rossell, "Desegregation Plans, Racial Isolation, White Flight, and Community Response," in *The Consequences of School Desegregation*, ed. Christine H. Rossell and Willis D. Hawley (Philadelphia: Temple University Press, 1983), pp. 13–57.

39. Center for National Policy Review, "Why Must Northern School Systems Desegregate?: A Summary of Federal Court Findings in Recent Cases" (Washington, D.C., 1977).

40. *Washington Post*/ABC News Survey, *Washington Post*, 24 March 1981.

Chapter Two
A Minority Perspective on Residential Racial Integration

WILHELMINA A. LEIGH

JAMES D. MCGHEE

The purpose of this chapter is to provide an answer to the question, how does the minority community feel about the goal of residential racial integration? The first section contains a discussion of the historical search for ways to achieve residential racial integration. The next section discusses the extent of residential racial integration in the United States to date. The third section analyzes the attitudes of blacks toward residential integration, and the fourth integrates the analyses of the preceding sections.

History

"The mission of the National Urban League is to enable blacks and other minority group members to cultivate and exercise their full human potential on par with all other Americans."[1] Part of being able to exercise one's full human potential on a par with other Americans is the ability to choose the type and the location of one's residence. Home ownership has long been the means by which most Americans acquire wealth.[2] Black Americans, likewise, value the ownership of suitable housing and its associated housing bundle — including the neighborhood, schools, municipal services, and other factors to enhance their general well-being.[3]

The freedom to choose to live unharassed in any neighborhood where a person can afford the housing also is part of exercising one's full human potential. To the extent that different ethnic or racial groups of neighbors occupy housing in given locations, blacks seeking to acquire housing there also are seeking residential racial integration.

Historically, many barriers have thwarted blacks seeking the type and location of housing they want. Discriminatory hiring practices and differential wage scales have reduced the income levels of many black households and prevented them from purchasing homes.[4] Even when their incomes were not a problem, other obstacles existed. Redlining by mortgage lenders and insurance companies has meant either refusals to provide loans and mortgage insurance or their availability at higher rates or for shorter periods of time. Lenders and insurance companies have often used such practices with those seeking to buy in certain neighborhoods. Common characteristics of redlined neighborhoods often include the ethnic or racial makeup of the residents, the age of the housing stock, and the income level of the residents. Such neighborhoods are either predominantly ethnic or black, shifting toward a nonwhite majority, or located near predominantly ethnic or black areas.[5] The housing stock is generally more than fifteen years old, and the residents are primarily in the low- and moderate-income brackets.

Other barriers to the free choice of blacks and to the establishment and maintenance of racially integrated neighborhoods have been the practices by real estate agents of blockbusting and steering. Steering means directing white households to all-white neighborhoods and referring black households either to all-black neighborhoods or to integrated neighborhoods. Real estate agents thus accelerate the pace of racial change by influencing the white households in integrated neighborhoods to sell their houses, often at a loss, but certainly at less than the loss that they have been led to anticipate with the influx of more black neighbors. Real estate agents or developers buy these artificially devalued properties for resale at a markup to black households. Although it occurs most often in the home purchase market, steering also exists in the rental market. In this instance, agents often refer blacks to the units of lowest quality in the neighborhoods that brokers believe to be in transition.[6]

What have blockbusting and steering meant in terms of the ability of blacks to acquire the type of housing they want in the locations they desire? Although empirical evidence is inconsistent on the results of blockbusting, it was one of the major vehicles that enabled blacks and other minorities to acquire ownership of homes (albeit at inflated prices) in neighborhoods they might otherwise have found barred to them.[7] It is the pursuit of their desired housing bundle that has caused blacks to bump up against whites residentially. Thus, the fear among whites of residential racial integration, and the assistance of loan insurance from the Federal Housing Administration (FHA),[8] often unintentionally combined to provide "decent, safe, and sanitary dwellings" for many black families.

Extent of Residential Racial Integration

The dominant pattern of racial dispersion throughout contemporary metropolitan areas has concentrated blacks and other minorities in the inner city and whites in the outer suburbs. Residential moves by blacks to achieve racial integration have flowed largely from cities—perceived as the areas with the most crime, the worst housing, the worst schools, and the worst conditions in which to raise children—to suburbs.[9] To what extent has residential racial integration occurred in recent years? To what degree have black (and white) households functioned as if this were a desirable by-product or a worthwhile end product?

Interviews with blacks and whites in the *1978 HUD Survey on the Quality of Community Life* revealed that little actual residential integration exists. Eighty-nine percent of the whites interviewed said that they lived in all-white or mostly white neighborhoods; 52 percent of these white households lived in all-white neighborhoods. Among the blacks interviewed, 55 percent said that they lived in predominantly minority neighborhoods. Only 8 percent of the white households and 32 percent of the black households surveyed indicated that they lived in neighborhoods where half the residents were white and half were minorities.[10] Moreover, in responding to questions about the importance of the ethnic and racial background of the residents when they were deciding whether to move into a neighborhood, among residents of mostly white neighborhoods, 18 percent felt it was either important or very important, and 28 percent of those in mostly minority neighborhoods held the same view.[11] A similar finding emerges when the responses of black and white residents are analyzed separately. Twenty-eight percent of the black households and 20 percent of the white households viewed the ethnic or racial background of neighborhood residents as either important or very important.[12]

Thus, although about half of all the whites and blacks surveyed said they lived in neighborhoods with some degree of integration—from mostly black to mostly white—fewer than 10 percent of the whites and only 32 percent of the blacks live in neighborhoods that are approximately evenly integrated by race. When moving, a higher percentage of blacks than whites view the ethnic and racial composition of their new neighborhoods as important.

Statistics from the 1980 census for thirteen large American cities (New York City, Chicago, Detroit, Philadelphia, Los Angeles, Washington, D.C., Houston, Baltimore, New Orleans, Atlanta, Dallas, Cleveland, and St. Louis) confirm a trend toward increasing black suburbanization.[13] In the United States as a whole, one out of every five black Americans now lives in the suburbs, and the black population is growing faster in the suburbs than in the central cities. In only one place—New York City—did the flow of blacks to the suburbs diminish between 1960–70 and 1970–80. Although the black suburban population increase around New York City was 77,494 for 1960–70 and 68,127 for 1970–80, the percentage of suburbanites who are black increased between 1970 and 1980 from 6 to 8. In Houston, though the suburban black population increased from 3,819 for 1960–70 to 14,100 for 1970–80, because of overall population growth in this primary metropolitan statistical area (PMSA), the percentage of suburbanites who are black decreased from 9 to 6. The largest increases in the percentage of the total black suburban population occurred in Washington, D.C.—an increase from 8 percent in 1970 to 17 percent in 1980—and in Atlanta, Georgia—an increase from 6 percent in 1970 to 14 percent in 1980.

The statistics now available do not say anything about the socioeconomic levels of the new black suburbanites or whether their moves are advancing racial integration. Examination of these questions certainly is one of the areas that research on residential racial integration in the 1980s should emphasize.

However, it is possible to conclude already that both increasing numbers and percentages of blacks are voting with their feet for the suburbs, whatever that may mean for racial integration and the overall quality of their lives.

Attitudes of Blacks toward Residential Racial Integration

How do black Americans feel about the goal of achieving residential racial integration? For what reasons might they prefer residential racial integration of neighborhoods? Residential racial integration per se is not now and may never have been the desideratum among blacks. The more fundamental concern among black Americans has been freedom from impediments to the fulfillment of their human potential. If blacks get the housing units that they want, and the characteristics include a racially integrated neighborhood, they are willing to accept integration as a useful although not essential outcome.

According to opinions interviewees expressed in the *1978 HUD Survey on the Quality of Community Life*, 57 percent of all blacks and 15 percent of all whites would prefer the racial composition of their neighborhoods to be half white and half minority.[14] However, one has to temper this finding with other findings from this and other surveys about the perceived and actual accompaniments to residence in neighborhoods that are racially integrated.

Pro

As the preceding section noted, residential racial integration has become an important by-product in the search for both suitable housing and a decent residential environment.[15] As part of this decent residential environment, we assume that blacks prefer a high level of amenities—that is, quality public schools, low crime rates, responsive police and fire departments, regular garbage collection, good road maintenance, and other qualities. If living in integrated neighborhoods is the only way to acquire suitable housing, then it is certain that blacks who have that goal would not oppose racial integration. Likewise, if living in racially integrated neighborhoods provides access to quality local schools and if the acquisition of quality education is a high priority among black households, then they would not be averse to racial integration.

If living in a decent environment is defined as living in an environment with lower crime rates, particularly lower rates of crime against persons, and if the suburbs have lower crime rates, then black Americans seeking decent environments will seek residences in the suburbs. If municipal services—street cleaning, snow removal, fire and police protection, garbage collection—are part of a decent environment and if neighborhoods that are residentially racially integrated are the ones that provide high levels of municipal services, then black

Table 1. Attitudes of Residents Toward Local Amenities, by Neighborhood Composition (Percentage of Total)

	Residents of Mostly Minority Neighborhoods	Residents of Mostly White Neighborhoods
Felt Schools Excellent or Pretty Good	45	61
Felt Crime a Serious Problem	71	34
Felt Police Excellent or Pretty Good	52	69
Felt Garbage Collection Excellent or Pretty Good	70	75
Felt Fire Protection Excellent or Pretty Good	77	84
Felt Road Maintenance Excellent or Pretty Good	38	47

SOURCE: Prepared by the National Urban League Research Department from the 1978 Survey on the Quality of Community Life: A Data Book (Washington, D.C.: U.S. Department of Housing and Urban Development, 1978), pp. 226-227, 416, 424-425, and 432.

Americans will seek the localities that satisfy their desire for such services. They will then accept the racial integration that may come along with it.

Evidence from the *1978 HUD Survey on the Quality of Community Life* confirms the above reasoning to some extent (see Tables 1 and 2). Opinions expressed both by residents of minority and white neighborhoods and by blacks and whites separately indicate some of the factors that could motivate moves that may yield residential racial integration. In all instances, more residents living in mostly white neighborhoods feel that their municipal services are excellent or pretty good than do those living in mostly minority neighborhoods (Table 1). Thus, strong incentives exist to move from mostly minority neighborhoods to mostly white ones if greater satisfaction with municipal services is an objective. The uniformly smaller percentages of black than of white households feeling such high levels of satisfaction also suggest that it would be blacks (as one minority group) who would relocate from the mostly minority to the mostly white neighborhoods for these reasons (Table 2).

If blacks are working for firms that are decentralizing because land costs in the suburbs are lower than in cities and if they want to keep their jobs and decrease commuting time between home and job, then blacks who currently live in the cities may want to move to the suburbs. To the extent that the suburbs have largely white populations, black households, by pursuing easier

Table 2. Attitudes of Residents Toward Local Amenities, by Race (Percentage of Total)

	Blacks	Whites
Felt Schools Excellent or Pretty Good	59	63
Felt Crime a Serious Problem	69	29
Felt Police Excellent or Pretty Good	56	69
Felt Garbage Collection Excellent or Pretty Good	69	75
Felt Fire Protection Excellent or Pretty Good	70	72
Felt Road Maintenance Excellent or Pretty Good	31	47

SOURCE: Prepared by the National Urban League Research Department from the 1978 Survey on the Quality of Community Life: A Data Book (Washington, D.C.: U.S. Department of Housing and Urban Development, 1978), pp. 224-225, 414-415, 422-423, and 430-431.

work access, may also be racially integrating neighborhoods. Once again, residential racial integration is achieved not in its own right but as the by-product of pursuing other goals.

Con

Although there are many possible reasons to look with disfavor on residential racial integration, most of them center on the location of the process,[16] that is, in existing white neighborhoods or in existing minority neighborhoods. One objection to the residential racial integration of minorities into existing white suburban neighborhoods relates to its impact on minority voting block strength. To the extent that the movement of blacks from cities to suburban areas reduces their numbers in inner-city voting jurisdictions, they are reducing their power as the plurality or majority of voters in certain wards. This loss of concentrated voting power often means the difference between the election of a black official and a white official. Insofar as representation in elected office by a member of one's same ethnic or racial group bestows advantages upon constituents, one could argue that the suburbanization that leads to residential racial integration is not desirable for black communities as a whole.

Another objection to residential racial integration has been the dissolution of community and kinship networks. If residential racial integration requires minorities to move to a predominantly white suburb, the minority group social network—churches, civic groups, and the like—will lose members and may lose its effectiveness. The social isolation of being greatly outnumbered as a minority resident in a predominantly white suburb could only aggravate the hurt of any racially motivated harassment experienced there and would certainly lessen the willingness of minority groups to move to integrate. The personal and social costs of integration may be too high for minorities to bear willingly.

A final and slightly different type of objection to residential racial integration relates to the integration of existing minority neighborhoods by whites. Since the early 1970s, neighborhoods once predominantly black and redlined by lenders and insurers have attracted some whites as places in which to buy and renovate homes. The process whereby higher income whites replace lower income blacks, usually in declining inner-city neighborhoods, is known as gentrification and has been decried by many since first observed. Positive aspects of the process can include both spatial deconcentration of racial minorities and strengthening of the city tax base. Negative aspects are its resemblance to the "Negro removal," with which urban renewal became synonymous,[17] and the reduction of the already limited supply of housing available to low- and moderate-income people.

Insofar as the "gentry" are moving into vacant buildings without displacing existing tenants (who cannot afford to buy their units), such a process fosters the goals of neighborhood renewal and residential racial integration. However, insofar as the process displaces either tenants unable to buy their units (often converted to cooperatives or condominiums) or owners no longer able to pay the real estate taxes associated with the inflated assessed values such new investment in the neighborhood brings, then it clearly has negative effects. For example, in the major renovation areas of Washington, D.C., between 1970 and 1980, the black population decreased by 36 percent and the white population increased by 7 percent.[18] No one knows where the people who are displaced go. Because they were vulnerable to displacement from their original neighborhoods, financial constraints are likely to limit their ability to move to the suburbs and integrate neighborhoods there. Due to changes in prices or conditions brought about by neighborhood reinvestment, they no longer had the freedom to choose whether to move or to remain.

In this instance, freedom of choice for minorities over the types and locations of residences has been constrained by economics, although the changes that result include the racial integration—at least in the short run—of many neighborhoods that formerly were all black. In this case, some see the displaced as seriously "dispossessed":

> While displacement has always produced severe hardship to the lower-income, when it was caused by urban renewal or other earlier programs the "trickle down" theory provided comfort to some that lower-income

people whose homes were demolished could find housing which was being abandoned by higher-income persons. Displacement due to reinvestment turns the trickle down theory on its head; it is the higher-income who are now usurping the homes of the lower-income, leaving nothing left to trickle down.[19]

Long-term residential racial integration seems to be an elusive goal in the United States. Few neighborhoods integrated by the in-migration of blacks have remained integrated over time. The phenomenon of integration by whites through the gentrification process is still new enough that it is unclear how stable this integration may be. Although gentrification may bring about integration within some city neighborhoods in the short run, it probably will do little to further integration in the longer run and may generate increased crowding or pocket ghettos in other parts of the metropolitan areas.

The case of gentrification and the other issues discussed in this chapter demonstrate how large a part home ownership plays in creating freedom of mobility. If those who were displaced—blacks or others—had been able to buy their apartments after developers converted them to cooperatives and condominiums, they might have moved from their neighborhoods only temporarily, during renovation, rather than permanently. However, encouraging more home ownership cannot remedy, by itself, the inability of many owners to meet the property tax payments required to enable them to stay in their neighborhoods. In any case, the movement of blacks from inner-city areas either voluntarily (in pursuit of an enhanced housing bundle or racial integration in the suburbs) or involuntarily (by gentrification or reinvestment displacement) has the same net effects—of diluting black voting strength within cities and of weakening the social and cultural fabric of black communities.

Summary and Conclusion

In viewing questions from a minority perspective, it is important to remember that no single "minority community" position exists on housing or almost any other issue. The competing motives of individuals and the diversity of opinion within minority groups prevent anything resembling consensus on most issues. However, an identifiable similarity of motives and reasonably clear agreement on goals does provide a glue that binds together the fragile coalition of groups often called the "minority community." One common motive is the desire to improve the living conditions of minority group members, and a common goal is to ensure equal access to "decent, safe and sanitary dwellings."

In order to understand the minority perspective on residential racial integration, we must distinguish between the minority community as a collection of individuals with one set of motives and priorities and the organizations that represent individuals who may hold a quite different set of motives and priorities. This is not to say that the organizations are not representative of their constituencies but only that individuals may behave very differently from organizations. For example, a minority organization may have a philosophical concern that focuses on the long-range attitudinal changes that might occur as a result of a closer association between members of different races and ethnic groups. This concern might center on the idea that if people of different ethnic backgrounds lived in the same neighborhoods, their children would attend the same schools, socialize together, and thereby come to know each other as individuals rather than merely as members of another racial group. Theoretically, this would result in reduced prejudice and bigotry that might carry over into adulthood.

Similarly, parents living in integrated neighborhoods would interact in a context of mutual problems and concerns that would transcend racial and ethnic identification and, again, become individuals to one another rather than out-group members. Thus, residential racial integration may be seen as a long-term method of fostering mutual respect among various racial or ethnic groups. Nevertheless, this motive probably is not uppermost in the minds of individuals as they seek housing and other goods and services for their families. It *is* a consideration when civil rights, service, or advocacy groups form national policies or take positions on the issue of housing. Part of the difficulty in understanding the minority community's positions on residential integration stems, perhaps, from the reluctance of its organizations to express clearly and repeatedly such seemingly utopian goals. Often they are reluctant because the attainment of these goals is uncertain at best and, even if attained, no one could attribute such successes conclusively to a specific set of actions, policies, or conditions.

Historically, the National Urban League has opposed any activity that would limit for any reason the access of minority group members to any housing that they could afford. At the same time, the organization has concerned itself with limiting the diffusion of black political power, acquiring jobs, limiting urban displacement, and a myriad of other, separate issues related to housing. Although the National Urban League opposes any policy of so-called "spatial deconcentration," for example, it does not object to the movement of blacks to suburbs by personal choice. Even if this movement eventually results in neighborhoods that are no longer racially integrated, the League would oppose any action that would maintain housing integration by denying free access to housing to minority group members. The overriding issue here is better, more affordable housing for minorities, not housing integration.

Similarly, while the National Urban League condemns urban renewal projects that are merely euphemisms for "Negro removal," it recognizes that open housing means that whites also must be free to move into previously black areas, a trend occurring now in many urban centers. However, this process becomes problematic when realtors, bankers, thrift institutions, and insurers conspire to influence the process to the detriment of minority group members.

In view of the impediments that blacks face when they seek to exercise their full freedom of choice in terms of residence type and location, the National Urban League has served as an advocate for the elimination of discriminatory barriers to free choice. One such advocacy action was a court suit that the League filed against the Office of the Comptroller of the Currency and other financial regulatory agencies.[20] Although the court ruled that the organization did not have standing as a plaintiff against certain of these agencies, as a result of the suit the League obtained agreements to ameliorate the racially and sexually discriminatory aspects of the home mortgage lending process involving several institutions.

This chapter began with a statement of the mission of the National Urban League; it is appropriate to close on that same point. The National Urban League seeks to enable blacks and other minority group members to exercise their full human potential. Although the organization pursues broad policy concerns and objectives regarding residential racial integration, whatever personal choices enable minority group members to realize their life potential, the League, by its very definition, supports. Residential racial integration has been enhanced over the years by the cumulative fulfillment of the mission of the organization and by the personal choices the members of its constituency have made. We are confident that it will continue to evolve in this fashion.

NOTES

1. National Urban League, *Manual*, p. 2.
2. The use of home ownership as the primary form of wealth accumulation has been noted since the 1930s. See Gries and Ford, *Home Ownership, Income, and Types of Dwelling*, p. 1.
3. The concept of the housing bundle is explained at length in Kain and Quigley, *Housing Markets and Racial Discrimination*, pp. 256–63.
4. As far back as 1932, President Hoover's Committee on Home Building and Home Ownership noted that blacks, who are predominantly renters, are required to spend larger proportions of their incomes on rent than are other groups. It was also found that home ownership among blacks was increasing at that time despite difficulties with financing and the high interest rates paid for second mortgages, which were common for home purchases then. See Gries and Ford, *Negro Housing*, p. 71.
5. Naparstek and Cincotta, *Urban Disinvestment*, p. 10.
6. A useful discussion of both blockbusting and steering can be found in Lake, *The New Suburbanites*.
7. See Taeuber and Taeuber, *Negroes in Cities*, p. 22, for a discussion of the factors that lead to increased prices of houses after the in-migration of blacks to a neighborhood.
8. "Housing Discrimination Must Be Dealt with by HUD," p. 317.
9. *1978 HUD Survey*, p. 2.
10. Ibid., pp. 298–99.
11. Ibid., p. 610.

12. Ibid., pp. 608–9.

13. Carlson, "Blacks Increasingly Head to Suburbs," p. 29.

14. *1978 HUD Survey*, pp. 298–99.

15. In the *1978 HUD Survey*, 40 percent of all residents of a large city but only 13 percent of all residents of a medium suburban city considered the condition of the housing in their community to be a severe problem (pp. 220–21). Additionally, 51 percent of all blacks in the survey but only 16 percent of all whites considered the condition of housing in their community to be a severe problem (pp. 224–25). In mostly white neighborhoods, 19 percent of the residents felt housing conditions to be a severe problem, whereas, in mostly minority neighborhoods, 44 percent of the residents shared that sentiment (pp. 226–27).

16. An extended discussion of possible disadvantages to the residential integration of suburbs by minorities is found in Calmore, "Fair Housing vs. Fair Housing."

17. The legacy of urban renewal programs in the United States is explored in Anderson, *The Federal Bulldozer*; Wilson, *Urban Renewal*.

18. Feinberg, "D.C. Leads Country in Renovation."

19. Werner, "Displacement," p. 11.

20. *National Urban League v. Office of the Comptroller et al.*, U.S. District Court of the District of Columbia, Civil Action No. 76–718, April 1976. (The final order was filed 3 May 1978.)

REFERENCES

Anderson, Martin. *The Federal Bulldozer*. Cambridge, Mass.: The MIT Press, 1964.
"Blockbusting." *Georgetown Law Journal* 59 (October 1970): 170–89.
Calmore, John O. "Fair Housing vs. Fair Housing: The Conflict Between Providing Low-Income Housing in Impacted Areas and Providing Increased Housing Opportunities through Spatial Deconcentration." *Housing Law Bulletin* 9 (November/December 1979): 1–12.
Carlson, Eugene. "Blacks Increasingly Head to Suburbs." *Wall Street Journal*, 20 October 1981, p. 29.
Feinberg, Lawrence. "D.C. Leads Country in Renovation of Inner-City Housing." *Washington Post*, 11 December 1981, pp. B1, B5.
Gries, J. M., and J. Ford, eds. *Home Ownership, Income, and Types of Dwelling*. Vol. 4 of the *Report on the President's Conference on Home Building and Home Ownership*. Washington, D.C.: National Capital Press, 1932.
———. *Negro Housing*. Vol. 6 of the *Report on the President's Conference on Home Building and Home Ownership*. Washington, D.C.: National Capital Press, 1932.
"Housing Discrimination Must Be Dealt with by HUD." *Journal of Housing* 37 (June 1980): 315–22.
1978 HUD Survey on the Quality of Community Life: A Data Book. Washington, D.C.: U.S. Department of Housing and Urban Development, 1978.
Kain, John F., and John M. Quigley. *Housing Markets and Racial Discrimination*. New York: Columbia University Press, 1975.
Lake, Robert W. *The New Suburbanites: Race and Housing in the Suburbs*. New Brunswick, N.J.: Center for Urban Policy Research, Rutgers University, 1981.

Leigh, Wilhelmina A. "Urban Renewal, Blockbusting, and Reinvestment Displacement: A Conceptual Analysis in the Context of the Neighborhood Life Cycle." Unpublished manuscript, National Urban League, Washington, D.C., 1981.

Naparstek, Arthur J., and Gale Cincotta. *Urban Disinvestment: New Implications for Community Organization, Research and Public Policy*. Washington, D.C., and Chicago: National Center for Urban Ethnic Affairs and National Training and Information Center, n.d.

National Urban League. *Manual for Affiliates of the National Urban League*. New York, 1972.

Taeuber, Karl E., and Alma F. Taeuber. *Negroes in Cities*. New York: Atheneum, 1972.

Werner, Frances E. "Displacement: HUD's Role in Saving the Cities at the Expense of Their Resident Lower-Income Populations." Paper submitted for consideration at HUD's Consumer Forum on Displacement, Washington, D.C., 28 September 1978.

Wilson, John Q., ed. *Urban Renewal: The Record and the Controversy*. Cambridge, Mass.: The MIT Press, 1968.

Chapter Three
Sustainable Integration or Inevitable Resegregation
The Troubling Questions
ALEXANDER POLIKOFF*

A trend toward black suburbanization, beginning in the 1970s, has been documented in a number of studies.[1] Will this demographic development merely extend to the suburbs the residential segregation patterns so familiar in most of our central cities? Or does it present an opportunity for fostering racially diverse communities?

Growing numbers of suburban municipalities are grappling with the complexities of attempting to maintain themselves as racially diverse.[2] This chapter addresses some of the legal, especially constitutional, and policy questions posed by those efforts. Particular attention will be paid to race-conscious housing counseling. We will use this term to refer to an important but controversial activity: a counseling and referral service carried on by a municipal or municipally supported housing agency that collects information about racial residential patterns and encourages homeseekers to consider housing options that persons of their race are unlikely to consider (i.e., white homeseekers are encouraged to consider moving to integrated areas and black homeseekers are encouraged to consider predominantly white neighborhoods).[3] The significance of regional efforts not confined to a single municipality will also be discussed.

Background

The experience of one Chicago suburb illustrates the difficulties of attempting to maintain racial diversity. In 1967 the Commission on Human Relations of Markham, Illinois, issued a report that spoke glowingly of Markham's "stable racial integration":

> Markham enjoys substantial and stable racial integration. In the strife ridden 60's, here Negroes and whites have learned to live together as co-laborers, learn together as students, govern together as equals and worship together as brothers. We recognize the presence of problems but, we have learned that life in a community such as ours is an exciting and rewarding experience. We pledge ourselves to strive for the full attain-

*This chapter is based on a paper prepared by Business and Professional People for the Public Interest (BPI) for the Joyce Foundation of Chicago. The author gratefully acknowledges the considerable assistance of BPI attorneys Elizabeth Lassar, Howard Learner, and John Hammell.

ment of the integration goal. We welcome all people of good will to share
in this rich inter-racial life. We are pledged to demonstrate the success of
racial integration to our metropolitan area.[4]

However, the same report cast doubt on Markham's ability to make good on
its pledge to demonstrate the success of racial integration:

This Commission worked actively to implement peaceful integration and
cooperated with the Veterans's Administration, the Illinois Commission
on Human Relations and the real estate brokers handling non-white sales.
Now that we are working just as hard to maintain that integration we find
not only a lack of cooperation from these sources but actual opposition.
. . . In the past, all-Negro subdivisions have developed in the Chicago
suburbs and some suburban areas have gradually changed into non-white
sections, but we believe our situation marks the first significant extension
of the Chicago pattern of block-by-block transition to the suburbs.[5]

Markham's black population, which was about 2.5 percent in 1950, rose to 21
percent in 1960, 50 percent in 1970, and 70 percent in 1980; it was estimated
to be about 75 percent in 1984. Most neighborhoods are either entirely black
or are steadily losing their white residents. The Human Relations Commission
is defunct.[6]

The Markham experience highlights a conundrum of race relations in the
United States: blacks move into previously all-white neighborhoods, but the
resulting integration does not persist and the neighborhoods eventually lose
virtually all their white residents. One analysis offers this explanation:

Given decades of history that the entry of blacks into a neighborhood
signals its transition to an all-black neighborhood; given that many neighborhoods are still closed to blacks; given the natural tendency of minority
families to seek housing in areas where they know they will be welcomed;
given the wider range of choice open to whites—all these factors push
newly integrated neighborhoods in the direction of becoming all-minority
neighborhoods. When illegal racial steering is added, the resulting transition to a resegregated neighborhood becomes almost inevitable.[7]

A village president warns members of the National League of Cities that they
must face the resegregation issue. "Inaction," he contends, "is tantamount to
support for segregation, racial change and resegregation in town after town
throughout the metropolitan areas across our nation."[8]

Small but growing numbers of integrated suburban municipalities across the
country have begun to address the resegregation issue.[9] Their efforts to maintain their racially diverse character have taken a variety of forms, including:

- Race-conscious housing counseling—a counseling service that
  encourages homeseekers to consider housing options that persons of
  their race are unlikely to consider;

- Affirmative marketing—attempts to induce or require real estate agents to inform racial groups about available housing in neighborhoods to which members of such groups are not likely to be attracted without special efforts;
- Racial record keeping—maintaining records on the racial composition and home buying and apartment seeking "traffic" of subdivisions, blocks, or other areas;
- Notification of intent to sell—attempts to require or induce owners to provide advance notice of housing to be placed on the market;
- Solicitation bans—prohibitions of real estate solicitation if property owners give notice that they do not wish to be solicited (or if other requirements are not complied with);
- Sign bans—prohibitions against the display of "for sale" or "sold" signs on residential real estate;
- Housing quality/public service standards—rigid enforcement of housing quality standards and improvement of public services in neighborhoods threatened with resegregation;
- Litigation—suits against real estate brokers for racial steering, usually based on "testing" by teams of blacks and whites who visit real estate offices and pretend to be looking for homes.[10]

These so-called "integration maintenance" activities have generated heated controversy. For example, Chicago area chapters of the NAACP and of the Southern Christian Leadership Conference (SCLC) have issued strongly critical statements. One NAACP chapter said that integration maintenance would lead to "restriction of mobility of Black people and/or abridge the civil rights of individual citizens."[11] The SCLC chapter asserted that the very concept of integration maintenance "reinforces the myth of 'White Supremacy' and Black Inferiority."[12] Testifying before a congressional committee in 1978, the general counsel of the National Association of Realtors (NAR) attacked integration maintenance ordinances as illegal "'minority scatter plans' . . . premised on the racist and biased stereotype of minority concentrations as inherently a threat to the health, safety and welfare of the community."[13]

On the other hand, a respected Chicago area fair housing organization, the Leadership Council for Metropolitan Open Communities, observed in a position paper on the subject, "We will not end the dual housing market if deliberate efforts to open communities result in resegregation." The council concluded that it would support municipal actions that "encourage choices by home seekers which will further the achievement of racial diversity, so long as the actions apply fairly to all home seekers and the right of the home seeker to make the final choice is respected."[14]

Articles on the integration maintenance issue have also begun to appear in the national and local press,[15] and scholarly analysis has commenced.[16]

Litigation too is underway. One suit led to an order invalidating antisolicitation provisions of the Bellwood, Illinois, ordinance,[17] while another attacked the integration maintenance activities of Cleveland Heights, Ohio.[18] In a Chicago area lawsuit, the National Association of Realtors is asserting that the integration maintenance ordinances and programs of nine suburbs violate fair housing laws.[19]

Even the U.S. Department of Housing and Urban Development (HUD), which long avoided serious discussion of integration maintenance questions, has begun to turn its attention to the subject. In a speech delivered to the NAR's convention in November 1983, HUD Secretary Samuel R. Pierce, Jr., offered three preliminary observations on integration maintenance:

1. He did not see the integration maintenance issue as a question of quotas. "The communities deny that their programs involve quotas or other predetermined numerical relationships. . . . The point of their programs is to expand, rather than to limit choices, and that is the basis on which we will judge them."

2. He could not ignore the fact that the integration maintenance controversy had become most pronounced in those areas that appeared to be most marked by continuing housing discrimination, or the "cruel irony" that the many communities that remained closed to minorities were "largely and directly responsible for the existence of this controversy."

3. He did not believe it useful to frame the integration maintenance issue "as a supposed conflict between free choice and integration." The issue was free choice, but restricting choice was no less real or unlawful when a white homeseeker was denied the choice of an integrated community than when a minority homeseeker was denied the choice of a nonsegregated community.[20]

In August 1984, announcing a change in its rules for determining whether the fair housing laws of state and local jurisdictions were substantially equivalent to federal fair housing laws, HUD said that, although it had not found any integration maintenance ordinance or program that in its view amounted to a quota,

> Nevertheless, the Department does not deny that it is possible for some activities purportedly undertaken in the name of racial integration to have a limiting effect on the ability of some persons to select or apply for the housing of their choice. . . . In a homeownership context, it may be possible that some elements of an "integration maintenance" program might operate to restrict the channels available to homeseekers, more than to open them, in a manner that may be considered incompatible with the prohibitions of the Fair Housing Act. Such elements, for example, might include bans on "for sale" signs or on solicitation by real estate brokers, or race-conscious counselling by municipal agencies.[21]

In light of these various developments, it is not surprising that interest in integration maintenance is growing rapidly, or that the questions it poses—to which we now turn—are complex.

The Troubling Questions

The following discussion will focus on race-conscious homeseeker counseling as carried on by a number of municipally operated or supported housing agencies. These agencies provide a counseling and referral service to homeseekers in an effort to promote and maintain racial diversity. They obtain information about racial patterns (such as homeseeker traffic) and available housing, as well as the usual information of interest to homeseekers on schools, transportation, and the like. They then try to encourage white homeseekers to consider moving to already integrated areas and black homeseekers to predominantly white neighborhoods.[22]

Such counseling, of course, involves none of the elements of a racial quota.[23] Yet race-conscious counseling is one of the most controversial, as well as one of the most important, of the integration maintenance techniques. A discussion of it is likely to illumine integration maintenance issues generally. Many other elements of a comprehensive integration maintenance strategy cause less controversy but deal only indirectly with racial transition—for example, policy statements, improved public services, and increased attention to enforcement of housing quality standards. The "direct" technique of counseling may be an essential part of any integration maintenance strategy effective enough to contend with the frequently irresistible tide of block-by-block resegregation.

Because race-conscious counseling conducted or supported by a municipality may be said to amount to government treatment of citizens differentially according to race (i.e., blacks are encouraged to consider moving to one type of area, whites to another),[24] how can such conduct survive under Title VIII of the 1968 Civil Rights Act or the Equal Protection Clause of the Constitution? Although to our knowledge no court has yet decided a counseling case, lower federal courts have determined that Title VIII proscribes "discouraging" a prospective home buyer from purchasing housing on a racial basis.[25] Race-conscious counseling may have the effect of discouraging some persons from purchasing some housing for racial reasons (indeed, in the sense that persons are counseled to consider housing options in addition to those they may have had in mind initially, that is one of its purposes).[26] Why, then, does such counseling not violate Title VIII?

The argument that it does not rests to some degree upon the asserted purpose of Title VIII to promote integration, and the judicial doctrine that a statute should not be interpreted or applied in a way that will frustrate its purpose.[27] However, whether Title VIII in fact has such a purpose—in addition to its acknowledged antidiscrimination purpose—is itself uncertain.

The stated purpose of Title VIII is "the achievement of fair housing throughout the United States," but the statute does not define the term "fair housing." And while the Supreme Court has referred to the importance and desirability of racial integration in housing in Title VIII cases,[28] no Supreme Court opinion has given us a precise meaning for that term.

There are two polar possibilities: Title VIII is designed merely to eliminate discrimination, or it is designed for that purpose and to promote integration as well. In the former view, "fair housing" means housing that is "open," that is, free from discrimination and accessible to all in free market competition, regardless of the racial residential pattern that results. In the latter view, "fair housing" means "integrated housing," racial residential diversity achieved in fact.

A third view is also possible: the law was designed to eliminate discrimination in housing and *thereby* to promote integration. That is, the legislators hoped that integration would result from the elimination of discrimination, but they did not intend specifically to authorize or validate race-conscious activities such as homeseeker counseling to achieve that result, at least not by agencies other than the federal government and its agents.[29]

The statement most often quoted in support of the integration purpose of Title VIII is that of Senator Mondale, a principal sponsor of the legislation, who said that Title VIII was intended "to replace the ghettos by truly integrated and balanced living patterns."[30] However, Senator Mondale also said, "The basic purpose of this legislation is to permit people who have the ability to do so to buy any house offered to the public if they can afford to buy it."[31] And Senator Brooke, a cosponsor of Title VIII, said:

> America's future must lie in the successful integration of all our many minorities, or there will be no future worthy of America. That future does not require imposed residential and social integration; it does require the elimination of compulsory segregation in housing, education and employment.
>
> It does not require that government dictate some master plan for massive resettlement of our population; it does require that government meet its responsibilities to assure equal opportunity for all citizens to acquire the goods and necessities of life.
>
> It does not require that government interfere with the legitimate personal preferences of individuals; it does require that government protect the freedom of individuals to choose where they wish to live.[32]

An opinion of the general counsel of HUD refers to the "twofold" purpose of Title VIII, "the provision of open housing opportunities" (presumably by prohibiting discrimination) and "the replacement of segregated housing conditions by 'truly integrated housing patterns,'" but concludes: "In summary, the two goals of [Title VIII]—integration and nondiscrimination or freedom of choice—were perceived by Congress to be complementary. Congress anticipated that the abolition of racially discriminatory housing practices would ultimately result in residential integration."[33]

An interesting argument derives from Section 809 of Title VIII, which mandates HUD to endeavor to "work out programs of voluntary compliance and enforcement" of Title VIII with, among others, persons in the housing industry. Under this provision HUD has entered into a number of voluntary affirmative marketing agreements, including one with the National Association of Realtors.[34] Pursuant to the HUD/NAR agreement, NAR has published educational and training materials for its members, including "Guidelines" respecting how Title VIII applies to the real estate industry. The Guidelines were developed in consultation with representatives of the U.S. Department of Justice and HUD, the two federal agencies responsible for the enforcement of Title VIII.[35]

The Guidelines appear quite clearly to sanction actions by real estate agents to encourage integration:

> The law does not prohibit encouragement of integration and would not be violated by such acts since they are consistent with the national housing policy.[36]

> [P]erfectly proper racial statements (in the form of encouragement of integration) take place between broker and potential buyer.[37]

Because the legal basis for the HUD/NAR voluntary affirmative action marketing agreement and its Guidelines is Section 809's directive respecting programs of voluntary "compliance and enforcement," it may be inferred that HUD has interpreted Title VIII to authorize pro-integration activities by real estate agents, at least in the context of cooperative agreements with government.[38] An argument might thus be made that HUD has interpreted Title VIII as embodying an integrative purpose independent of the hope or expectation that integration would result from the elimination of housing discrimination.

Unlike an arcane lawyers' dispute, the controversy about the meaning of Title VIII erupted in the daily newspapers in the summer of 1984. In an interview that appeared on page one of the *Washington Post*, William Bradford Reynolds, assistant U.S. attorney general for civil rights, was reported to have said that Congress intended Title VIII only to prohibit racial bias in renting or selling housing, and, as long as people are not denied free choice of housing, "I don't think any government ought to be about the business to reorder society or neighborhoods to achieve some degree of [racial] proportionality" in housing.[39]

Jane Lang McGrew, former general counsel of HUD (author of the opinion referred to above), shot back four days later in a *Los Angeles Times* column that Reynolds was engaged in "revisionist thinking" about Title VIII. There are two purposes of the law, she wrote, "to eliminate discrimination and to promote integration in housing." Stopping with the first, as Reynolds did, "doesn't go as far as Congress went, and it is nowhere close to where the courts have been," McGrew said, citing Supreme Court statements about the strong national commitment to promote integrated housing reflected in the law.[40] In an analysis entitled "Nation's Policy on Integration at Crossroads," the *Washington Post* staff writer who had interviewed Reynolds concluded that if "Rey-

nolds succeeds in greatly narrowing the interpretation of the Fair Housing Act
. . . residence patterns in the nation will be profoundly changed."[41]

A different approach to the question of whether municipal race-conscious
counseling violates Title VIII focuses on the reference to constitutional limitations in the purpose clause of Title VIII: "It is the policy of the United States
to provide, within Constitutional limitations, for fair housing throughout the
United States." The phrase "Constitutional limitations" suggests that Congress
wished constitutional principles to play a major role in determining the validity
of fair housing programs. Thus it is likely that the legality of municipal race-
conscious counseling will depend to a large extent on constitutional analysis,
to which we now turn.

The Equal Protection Clause of the Fourteenth Amendment requires government to treat similarly situated persons equally under the law. All race-
conscious actions by government are not thereby precluded; however, as the
case law has established, race-conscious actions are likely to be held unconstitu-
tional unless they further a compelling government interest and are shown to be
necessary to that end.

In addition, a recent analysis has persuasively suggested that, even if the
compelling interest and necessity tests appear to be met, the government's
interest must be found to outweigh society's strong interest in not burdening
or stigmatizing members of minority groups. Without such a balancing, no
attention would be paid to the possibility that a racial classification, necessary
to achieve a compelling interest, might impose an intolerable burden upon a
minority group.[42] What are considered "compelling," "necessary," and "burdensome" or "stigmatizing" are thus likely to be the three ultimate determinants of
the validity of race-conscious homeseeker counseling.

The Compelling Interest

The "compelling" nature of the government interest in preventing residential
segregation is strongly indicated by statements already made by the Supreme
Court. In 1979 the Court upheld the right under Title VIII of the village of
Bellwood, Illinois, to sue real estate agents who were allegedly steering prospective black home buyers toward an integrated area of Bellwood, while
steering white customers away from it. Bellwood contended that these practices were affecting the village's racial composition, replacing an integrated
neighborhood with a segregated one. Asserting that the "adverse consequences
attendant upon a 'changing' neighborhood can be profound," the Court said
that, if the alleged steering practices significantly reduced the number of buyers
in the Bellwood housing market, prices could be deflected downward, a phenomenon the Court said would be exacerbated if increases in the minority
population attributable to racial steering precipitated white flight.[43] The Court
concluded:

A significant reduction in property values directly injures a municipality by diminishing its tax base, thus threatening its ability to bear the costs of local government and to provide services. Other harms flowing from the realities of a racially segregated community are not unlikely. [Footnote omitted.] As we have said before, "[t]here can be no question about the importance" to a community of "promoting stable, racially integrated housing." *Linmark Associates, Inc. v. Willingboro* [citation omitted]. If, as alleged, petitioners' sales practices actually have begun to rob Bellwood of its racial balance and stability, the village has standing to challenge the legality of that conduct.[44]

The *Linmark* case referred to in the quotation was a 1977 decision of the Court holding that a ban on the display of "for sale" or "sold" signs on real estate violated the First Amendment and was not saved by the municipality's purpose of stemming what it perceived as the flight of white homeowners from a racially integrated community. Noting that defense of the municipality's ban relied "on the vital goal this ordinance serves: namely, promoting stable, racially integrated housing," the Court in *Linmark* said: "There can be no question about the importance of achieving this goal. This Court has expressly recognized that substantial benefits flow to both whites and blacks from interracial association and that Congress has made a strong national commitment to promote integrated housing."[45]

It is true that neither the *Bellwood* nor the *Linmark* case arose under the Equal Protection Clause. In an equal protection context, where race-conscious government action is at issue, "compelling" clearly means more than merely "important." However, with the Court viewing Congress as having made a "strong national commitment to promote integrated housing," and having itself termed that goal "vital," it seems more likely that municipal race-conscious counseling would founder—if at all—on the necessity or burden tests than that the Court would conclude that the "vital" goal of promoting integrated housing is not a "compelling" government interest.[46]

In any event, another Supreme Court case points the way to a near-certain resolution of the compelling interest issue. In 1980 the Supreme Court held that it was not a violation of the Equal Protection Clause for Congress to provide a 10 percent "set-aside" for minority businesses of federal funds granted for local public works projects. The decision, in *Fullilove v. Klutznick*, rested on Congress's determination that racial discrimination or its effects persisted in the field of government contracting, and that the minority business preference would help redress that condition.[47] In his concurring opinion, Justice Powell spoke of "the compelling government interest in redressing the discrimination that affects minority contractors."[48]

In like fashion any integration maintenance ordinance, including its counseling component, is likely to be based on a determination that discrimination or its effects persist in the housing field, and that the provisions of the ordinance are designed to redress those discriminatory conditions. Whatever difficulties may be encountered with the necessity and burden or stigma tests, such a determination, responsibly made, is likely to satisfy the compelling interest requirement.[49]

The Necessity of the Means

The necessity of employing race-conscious counseling to foster racial diversity is a more difficult issue. It is generally acknowledged that discriminatory conduct, particularly by persons in the real estate business, has been a major cause of residential segregation.[50] Yet pervasive discriminatory conduct persists,[51] arguably in part at least because enforcement of our laws against housing discrimination has been less than vigorous,[52] and the enforcement structure itself is weak.[53]

Under these circumstances, it could be asserted, Title VIII should be enforced more vigorously, and with more resources. Its enforcement provisions should be strengthened. And such steps should be taken not only at the federal level, to which the bulk of the criticism has been directed, but also at the state and local levels. The full potential of state licensing and regulation of real estate brokers as an antidiscrimination tool has not been realized. On the model of Bellwood, a municipality that was truly concerned about preserving racial diversity could engage in massive testing and litigation to stop further segregative steering within its borders.

Beyond this, the argument would run, other techniques could be employed, such as vigorous property maintenance code enforcement, equity assurance plans, and public relations, that do not pose a risk of differential treatment of the races. Finally, additional steps that have not been tried—for example, a well-publicized metropolitan-wide information service on housing opportunities—might be undertaken.[54] Without a demonstration that these measures had been tried and found wanting, it could be contended that the case has not been made for the necessity of employing a technique, such as race-conscious counseling, that may be viewed as treating persons differentially by race.

Persuasive counterarguments can be mounted. Housing discrimination may be "too pervasive and subtle to be eliminated through any enforcement effort."[55] Against the background of established attitudes and priorities, even effective enforcement efforts may take a long time to change resegregation dynamics. Meanwhile, more municipalities may suffer resegregation. One unit of government (municipal) should not be "penalized" because another (federal or state) fails to act effectively.

Moreover, because of the fragmentation of the real estate market, some segregative steering may be carried on without violation of law and would not be affected by antidiscrimination enforcement efforts. Many brokers may specialize in—that is, have listings only in—white areas, black areas, or transitional areas. "[W]hile the market as a whole functions to steer blacks to one set of neighborhoods and whites to others, we do not necessarily have violations of the law by particular persons or firms." [56]

Finally, if the "tipping" point theory of resegregation has validity,[57] the entire resegregation process may be largely immune to antidiscrimination enforcement techniques:

> The *principle* of equal housing opportunity now enjoys rather substantial public support. The force of law is on the side of the right of any person to have equal access to any housing that is on the market. A majority of whites no longer have objections to having *some* black neighbors. However, a majority of whites still become panicky and will attempt to escape if they find themselves a racial minority.

> Blacks do not share precisely equivalent feelings but it is clear that except for a courageous, pioneering few, most blacks, given a choice, will elect *not* to be the first to integrate a neighborhood. Rather, they tend to search for homes where a degree of racial balance has been established. These two sets of behavior patterns practically insure that racially balanced neighborhoods will become all or predominantly black in time.[58]

If the foregoing is correct, a race-conscious housing counseling plan able to continually adjust to racial changes might be an essential element of any effective program to prevent the (otherwise) inevitable resegregation.[59]

These arguments suggest that the case for the necessity of employing race-conscious counseling is complex, but that it *can* be made.

The Burdening Consequences

We turn lastly to the issue of burdening or stigmatizing members of minority groups. First, at least some blacks who need better housing may arguably be deterred from finding it by race-conscious counseling. Though this is not an inevitable result of such counseling, it is a possible one. Given the dynamics of the resegregation process, it is in the communities to which some blacks have already moved that other blacks, in increasing numbers, are likely to seek housing. Most black homeseekers do not perceive themselves to have realistic access to most suburban communities—if for no other reason (though there are, of course, other reasons) than that most such communities have few black residents and most blacks will elect not to be among the first to integrate a neighborhood. Yet it is communities to which blacks have already moved that have an interest in encouraging blacks to consider moving to communities that do not yet have significant numbers of blacks. Race-conscious counseling by the former communities may thus have the effect of discouraging some blacks from looking for housing where they wish to find it, while failing to provide them with what are perceived to be equally satisfactory alternative housing possibilities. Such a result would burden the very persons who should be helped.[60] With rare exceptions, however, race-conscious government action has been sustained by the Supreme Court only when it is designed to benefit minorities and does not entail the imposition of burdens upon them.[61]

Second, any race-conscious counseling program presents a risk of appearing to stigmatize blacks. Given the minority status of blacks in the population at large, and the disinclination of most whites to remain in communities that have a majority black population, race-conscious counseling may understandably be viewed as an effort to keep the black population below a specific percentage. As some of the statements quoted above demonstrate, such a view would lead some blacks to perceive race-conscious counseling to be predicated upon an assumption of the undesirability of a black majority community.[62]

Third, race-conscious counseling programs are likely to come at some cost in divisiveness. The intensity of the rhetoric in several of the statements referred to above reflects this reality. The Shaker Heights integration maintenance program erupted into public controversy even among those who supported race-conscious counseling.[63] To some degree such counseling may be perceived as restricting the mobility of minorities because of white fear or prejudice. If "no issue since the Vietnam War had produced such bitter divisions among Americans as had the issue of racial preferences,"[64] widespread race-conscious counseling in metropolitan areas across the country may well possess the potential for generating comparable divisions.

There are, of course, counterarguments. The risk that race-conscious counseling might deter or discourage some blacks from finding needed housing appears much more serious if one assumes—as do many discussions of race-conscious counseling, indeed of integration maintenance activities of any sort—that the issue is freedom of choice versus coercion.[65] Yet it is obvious that some forms of race-conscious activity do not involve coercion, as, for example, HUD's affirmative marketing regulations illustrate.[66] Moreover, the risk of deterrence coexists with the potential of race-conscious counseling to expand the options of black homeseekers, thereby helping to remedy one of the persisting effects of housing discrimination. Choice-expansion should be particularly effective if counseling is conducted on a regional basis. Coordinated region-wide race-conscious counseling should be able to offer black homeseekers at least as many comparable housing opportunities in predominantly white communities as are available to them in already well-integrated communities.[67] It would be ironic if such efforts to *expand* choice (by encouraging homeseekers to consider areas they have traditionally assumed to be "off limits") were to be treated as steering, which is said to violate Title VIII because it *limits* freedom of choice.[68]

This dual impact of race-conscious counseling—a risk of deterrence and a possibility for choice-expansion—suggests that the issue of burden or stigma may be framed helpfully in terms of "fundamental fairness," a formulation Justice Powell used in discussing the minority business set-aside in the *Fulli-*

love case referred to above. "[T]he effect of the set-aside is limited and so widely dispersed that its use is consistent with fundamental fairness." [69] It may be inferred from another of Justice Powell's opinions that the kind of race-conscious action least likely to survive under the Equal Protection Clause is a classification that "denies an individual opportunities or benefits enjoyed by others," or under which "some individuals are excluded from enjoyment of a state-provided benefit." [70] More likely to survive are actions that do "not result in the denial of the relevant benefit," or "[e]xclude individuals . . . enjoyment of the relevant opportunity." [71] Race-conscious counseling neither denies benefits nor excludes individuals, and its risk of deterrence coexists with a choice-expansion potential. If the "marginal unfairness" (as Justice Powell termed it) to innocent nonminority contractors in *Fullilove* [72] — *which did* result in excluding nonminority contractors from competition for a portion of a state-provided benefit — was not significant enough to place the minority business set-aside in the former category, it seems doubtful that race-conscious counseling would be placed there either.

Of course, the burden in *Fullilove* fell upon whites. In race-conscious counseling the burden may be said to fall upon blacks, an important difference notwithstanding the coexisting benefit possibility of choice-expansion. It may be helpful in considering this aspect of race-conscious counseling to refer back to the earlier discussion about the purposes of Title VIII, particularly to the position of William Bradford Reynolds that government should not be in the business of trying to bring about integration, and to statements made in that regard by HUD's general counsel, John Knapp, that he saw no conflict between HUD's requirements for site selection and affirmative marketing plans, which are clearly race-conscious actions, and the Justice Department's position. [73]

Like race-conscious counseling, HUD's site selection criteria and affirmative marketing regulations are race-conscious steps having dual impacts. Under its site selection criteria HUD considers the racial composition of areas proposed for subsidized housing for the purpose (consistent with other policy considerations) of avoiding concentrations of subsidized housing in racially impacted areas. [74] The affirmative marketing regulations require suppliers of federally assisted housing to market their housing "affirmatively" by taking special steps to make its availability known to those racial groups least likely to apply for it because of, among other reasons, neighborhood racial patterns. [75] In each case there are dual impacts.

Under the site selection criteria, minority areas may not get needed housing, but housing opportunities for minorities in nontraditional neighborhoods may be provided. In affirmative marketing, special efforts in addition to normal marketing may be undertaken with respect to blacks (but not whites) or whites (but not blacks) to assure that the racial group least likely to apply is informed about available housing. Though both techniques are race-conscious actions, the burden of which to some extent may be said to fall upon blacks, both would seem clearly to be on the safe side of Justice Powell's line as steps that do not exclude identified individuals from the enjoyment of benefits, and whose "negative" effects are therefore limited and dispersed. When the choice-expansion benefits are included in the calculation, it is easy to conclude that both are consistent with fundamental fairness. Though counseling involves identified individuals and site selection criteria and affirmative marketing do not, the absence of exclusion and the choice-expansion benefits that characterize counseling should lead to the same result.[76]

Finally, the risks of appearing to stigmatize blacks and of generating divisiveness, serious though they may be, should arguably not preclude responsible, fair programs designed to foster as compelling a value as racial diversity. Surely the answer lies in sensitivity of conduct and statement, and better communication,[77] not in eschewing an activity that may be an important element in achieving what the Supreme Court in *Linmark* called the "vital goal . . . [of] promoting stable, racially integrated housing."

How, then, does one strike an ultimate balance when the interest is compelling, the means pretty clearly necessary, yet the "costs" considerable? The example of *Linmark* is a reminder that countervailing constitutional values (there the First Amendment, here the Fourteenth) will not necessarily be pushed aside by the force of a compelling governmental interest. In *Linmark*, Willingboro's nonwhite population had grown from .005 to 11.7 percent during the 1960s, and had jumped to 18.2 percent by 1973. Although the evidence was conflicting, there was testimony about "panic selling" by whites who feared the township was becoming all black. And though the Court called the promotion of stable, racially integrated housing a "vital goal" and an "important governmental objective," it nonetheless struck down Willingboro's ban on "for sale" signs. Because it prevented residents from obtaining information about real estate activity, the ban was viewed as violating the First Amendment's protection of the free flow of information.

Yet one cannot read the *Linmark* case without sensing an important distinction between Willingboro's absolute ban on a means of communication, which had the effect of *limiting* homeseekers' knowledge of available housing, and noncoercive race-conscious counseling where clients may choose to ignore the views and information provided through counseling, or indeed may decline to use counseling services at all. When coordinated region-wide counseling which should have the effect of *increasing* homeseekers' options is included in the calculus, municipal race-conscious counseling should involve no inherent restrictions on the housing choices of black homeseekers. The result in fact should be choice-expansion; the risks, those of program abuse only.

On balance these arguments suggest that in the proper factual context — particularly in a regional geographic framework providing ample opportunity to open wider (predominantly white) market areas to black homeseekers — the Supreme Court would uphold the constitutionality of municipal race-conscious counseling.[78]

A Procedural Note

It is a truism that many of the difficult social issues in our society are ultimately resolved by the courts.[79] Within the judicial forum the care with which an issue is formulated and presented frequently determines the result. The integration maintenance issue is a rich mixture of complex legal and policy questions. Thorough analysis of these questions is likely to aid decision making in the ultimate judicial resolution.

One procedural issue is of particular importance. Few of the integration maintenance ordinances passed to date have derived from a comprehensive legislative fact-finding process. Such a process is not the norm in legislation at the municipal level, but it is what integration maintenance ordinances may require. Courts are likely to pay greater deference to legislation adopted after formal fact-finding than otherwise. A carefully laid factual foundation would enhance the prospects for municipal race-conscious counseling in the courts.[80]

The list of issues that could and should be explored in a legislative hearing is lengthy. They include:

1. Residential segregation patterns in both the local community and the metropolitan area, and the evidence that discrimination or its persisting effects (rather than economics or choice) is the principle cause for such patterns.
2. The dynamics of resegregation in both the local and metropolitan contexts, including, for example, how the fragmentation of the real estate industry and its multiple listing service arrangements contribute to the resegregation problem.
3. The adequacy of measures short of race-conscious ones to combat resegregation effectively.
4. The "fairness" of a proposed integration maintenance ordinance (including particularly the extent to which efforts are to be made to encourage black families to consider white areas, and to provide realistically available alternative housing opportunities to black families in such areas).

This list is intended merely to suggest types of issues that would merit inquiry in a legislative hearing. To conduct a thorough legislative inquiry into the need for a comprehensive integration maintenance ordinance in any community would itself be a significant task, but it may be a crucial next stage in the unfolding integration maintenance story.

It is likely that the integration maintenance controversy will grow more intense before it is finally resolved, either by circumscribing legal or policy determinations, or by validation of integration maintenance activities in the courts or administrative agencies and acceptance of them by the body politic. The extent to which our increasingly pluralistic nation either works out modes for accommodating and maintaining residential diversity, or succumbs to racial and cultural separatism, is obviously of great significance for the future course of the American experience.[81]

NOTES AND REFERENCES

1. See, for example, Joint Center for Political Studies, *Blacks on the Move: A Decade of Demographic Change* (Washington, D.C.: Joint Center for Political Studies, 1982); Harold M. Rose, *Black Suburbanization: Access to Improved Quality of Life or Maintenance of the Status Quo?* (Cambridge, Mass.: Ballinger, 1976).

2. In October 1984, some 289 persons from 56 communities in 14 states attended the seventh annual Oak Park (Illinois) Exchange Congress. Begun in 1977, and now hosted in alternate years by other cities, the congress has become a major forum for the consideration of racial diversity issues. This chapter discusses the racial diversity issue only in a black-white context, though of course the issue also arises with respect to Hispanics and Asians.

3. For example, here is the policy statement of the Oak Park, Illinois, Housing Center:

> The policy of the Oak Park Housing Center is to assist in stabilizing integration in the village. To this end, there will be encouragement of white clients to move into buildings or areas that are already integrated, and the encouragement of black clients to move into buildings or areas which are not substantially integrated. Listings will be provided in keeping with this policy, with the understanding that under both local and federal laws, all clients are free to pursue the housing of their choice. (Quoted in Carole Goodwin, *The Oak Park Strategy* [Chicago: The University of Chicago Press, 1979], p. 174)

For a detailed description of the operation of the Oak Park Housing Center, see Goodwin, *The Oak Park Strategy*, pp. 167–79. The center is a private, nongovernmental organization which, however, has substantial contacts with and support from the village government. Other such centers, for example, that of Bellwood, Illinois, are government agencies.

4. Markham Commission on Human Relations, *The Extension of Urban Patterns of Racial Transition to the Suburbs* (24 January 1967), p. 1, quoted in Peter W. Colby and Larry McClellan, *Can Public Policy Decisions Prevent Suburban Racial Resegregation?* Institute for Public Policy and Administration (Park Forest South, Ill.: Governors State University, 1980), p. 25.

5. Id., quoted in Colby and McClellan, *Can Public Policy Decisions Prevent Suburban Racial Resegregation?* p. 18.

6. Discussions of racial diversity, or "resegregation" or "integration maintenance," other frequently used terms, sometimes founder on the definition of "integration." Any numerical definition is obviously arbitrary, and no single definition or concept of integration is likely to be satisfactory for all conceivable circumstances. In general, it seems preferable to focus on the dynamics of the housing market rather than occupancy statistics. For example, integration might be defined as a condition in which, within the area in question, consumers of housing (buyers and renters) continue to include substantial percentages of both blacks and whites.

7. Kale Williams, Donald DeMarco, and Dudley Onderdonk, *Affirmative Action in Housing—An Emerging Public Issue*, Institute for Public Policy and Administration (Park Forest South, Ill.: Governors State University, 1980), p. 4.

8. Mayer Singerman, "We Must Avoid Turning Integration into Apartheid," *Nation's Cities Weekly*, 20 October 1980.

9. Integration may have developed because of proximity to areas of black residence in the central city, expansion of a historical black "enclave" within the municipality, or receptivity of present residents to black entry for social justice reasons.

10. Actions taken by Oak Park, Illinois, include the following:

- Enactment in 1968 of a Fair Housing Ordinance that outlawed panic peddling and regulated solicitation
- Promulgation of a "Policy Statement on Residential Diversity" as official village policy
- Formation in 1971 of a fully staffed and funded Department of Community Relations designed to centralize integration maintenance activities within the village management
- Institution of a counseling program for homeseekers
- Careful record keeping on racial occupancy
- Institution of a "testing" program to monitor real estate practices
- Licensing of apartments, with requirements for mandatory annual inspections and reporting on the race of occupants
- Affirmative marketing of property in an integrated area to white buyers and property in other areas to minority buyers
- Legislation to maintain housing quality, enforced by routine inspection of home exteriors and of apartments
- Special attention to garbage collection, police protection, and other measures
- Institution of an "equity assurance plan" guaranteeing homeowners against loss of property values due to racial change in the neighborhood

Municipal strategies to maintain racial diversity may be generally categorized as efforts (1) to maintain or enhance the attractiveness of residential and adjacent commercial areas, (2) to obtain accurate information on racial residential patterns (occupancy and "traffic"), (3) to control real estate practices seen as adverse to racial diversity, and (4) to inform and encourage homeseekers respecting pro-integration moves. See Kermit J. Lind, "Maintaining Residential Integration: Municipal Practices and the Law," *Cleveland State Law Review* 31 (1982): 603, 629–45.

For a comprehensive proposed model fair housing ordinance with an "affirmative marketing" option, see Northeastern Illinois Planning Commission, *A Suggested Fair Housing Ordinance: A Guide for Local Officials* (draft), revised 9 February 1981. A more recent ordinance, drafted with racial diversity concerns in mind, has been prepared by BPI (unpublished draft, 13 February 1984).

11. "Resolution Pertaining to the Attempted Control of the Mobility of the Black Population in a Free Market System" (n.d.), p. 1, of the Far South Suburban Chapter, NAACP. However, the NAACP's national director of research, policy, and plans has written:

Some communities that already are racially integrated have taken steps— through local ordinances, fair housing councils and private actions—to . . . [reverse] the illegal practice of steering blacks only to black or integrated areas.

Ironically, the National Association of Realtors, a johnny-come-lately to fair housing, attacks such efforts as illegal racial steering. But Samuel Pierce, Secretary of Housing and Urban Development, favors "integration maintenance" guidelines that will genuinely preserve racial diversity in neighborhoods. . . .

The NAACP, which stalwartly supports integration, has counseled that affirmative marketing techniques that do not use hard-and-fast, exclusionary quotas to prevent resegregation are valid, indeed compelling. (*Chicago Tribune,* 4 February 1984)

12. Position Paper, *Integration Maintenance/Management* (n.d.), p. 5, Chicago-Suburban Chapter, SCLC.

13. Statement of William D. North on behalf of the National Association of Realtors before the House Judiciary Committee, Subcommittee on Civil and Constitutional Rights, 11 May 1978, p. 10.

14. Leadership Council for Metropolitan Open Communities Position Paper, *Affirmative Action for Racial Diversity in Housing,* 21 December 1978, pp. 4, 6.

15. "Some Integrated Towns Draw Fire for Efforts to Keep Racial Balance," *Wall Street Journal,* 8 January 1979, p. 1; "Integrated Suburbs Now Fearful of Not Drawing Enough Whites," *New York Times,* 9 April 1979, p. 1; "Racial 'Steering' Big Suburban Issue of the '80s," *Chicago Tribune,* 6 May 1979; "Fighting Segregation" (editorial), *Chicago Sun-Times,* 16 September 1983. See also *The Chicago Reporter* 8, nos. 5, 6 (May, June 1979). In 1984 the Gund and Cleveland foundations in Cleveland, Ohio, were reported to have given $250,000 to the East Suburban Council for Open Communities to promote integrated housing in Cleveland's eastern suburbs. *Cleveland Plain Dealer,* 20 December 1984.

16. Williams, DeMarco, and Onderdonk, *Affirmative Action for Housing.* See also Note, "Benign Steering and Benign Quotas: The Validity of Race-Conscious Government Policies to Promote Residential Integration," *Harvard Law Review* 93 (1980): 938–65 (hereafter cited as "Benign Steering"); Rodney A. Smolla, "Integration Maintenance: The Unconstitutionality of Benign Programs that Discourage Black Entry to Prevent White Flight," *Duke Law Journal* (1981): 891–939; Lind, "Maintaining Residential Integration," n. 10 above.

17. *Illinois Association of Realtors v. Bellwood,* 516 F.Supp. 1067 (N.D. Ill. 1981). The provisions were stricken on First Amendment (prior restraint, overbreadth, and vagueness) grounds.

18. *William Smith v. City of Cleveland Heights,* C 80-1695, in the U.S. District Court for the Northern District of Ohio, Eastern Division (12 September 1980). The plaintiff, a black resident of an integrated neighborhood, could show no injury to himself caused by the Cleveland Heights ordinances and was therefore held to lack standing to bring the suit.

19. *South Suburban Housing Center v. Greater South Suburban Board of Realtors and National Association of Realtors,* no. 83 C 8149, in the U.S. District Court for the Northern District of Illinois, Eastern Division (14 November 1983). The lawsuit was begun by the Housing Center over another integration maintenance technique, affirmative marketing—that is, employing special efforts (e.g., advertising) to make the availability of housing known to those racial groups least likely to apply for it. As owner of three rehabilitated homes in a predominantly black section—having little white traffic—of Park Forest, Illinois, the Housing Center entered into an affirmative mar-

keting listing agreement with a local broker that called for affirmative advertising efforts to be directed to whites (in addition to normal marketing). The local multiple listing service refused the listings on the ground that such advertising amounted to racial steering in violation of fair housing laws. See 24 C.F.R. ¶200.600 et seq. for HUD's Affirmative Fair Housing Marketing Regulations applicable to federally assisted housing, and HUD Handbook 8021.1, *Voluntary Affirmative Marketing Handbook* (November 1979), for information on HUD's voluntary affirmative marketing agreements relating to nonfederally assisted housing.

20. Remarks prepared for delivery by Samuel R. Pierce, Jr., before the National Association of Realtors, 14 November 1983.

21. 49 Fed. Reg. 32042, 9 August 1984.

22. Race-conscious counseling may include provision of (1) information about the amenities and policies of municipalities, and the housing market in general, including segregatory patterns, with the aim of persuading the counselee to consider and—if persuaded—choose a pro-integration housing location; (2) information about specific listings of currently available housing; and (3) additional services, such as direct referrals to landlords and/or cooperating real estate agents, and assistance in inspecting available housing and negotiating with landlords. See Lind, "Maintaining Residential Integration," p. 641 ("What they [housing information services] aim to provide is information about types of housing opportunities and an enthusiastic introduction to the community in which those opportunities exist, in accordance with their mission to encourage racial diversity").

23. The essence of a quota is that on racial grounds it excludes persons from receiving, or forecloses persons from competing for, an available benefit or opportunity. Race-conscious counseling involves no such exclusion or foreclosure. See the discussion in the text accompanying nn. 65–76 below. See also *Burney v. Housing Authority of County of Beaver*, 551 F.Supp. 746, 758 (W.D. Pa. 1982).

In a notable recent action against quotas, the Justice Department moved to oppose a settlement authorizing continuation of a quota arrangement in a lawsuit brought by a local chapter of the NAACP against the Starrett City housing development in New York City. (See *Housing and Development Reporter*, 30 July 1984, p. 195.) Ironically, the lawyer representing Starrett City is Morris B. Abram, whom President Reagan recently appointed to the U.S. Commission on Civil Rights in part because of his longtime opposition to quotas. For a discussion of Abram's dilemma, see Jefferson Morely, "Double Reverse Discrimination," *The New Republic*, 9 July 1984.

24. Equality of services and listings provided black and white clients is, of course, assumed. It can be argued that black and white clients are not treated "differentially" because both are urged to consider areas they would not otherwise (i.e., but for the counseling) have been likely to give serious thought to as possible housing options. A nice question of differential treatment arises if the counseling agency—concerned about the most effective use of its limited resources—chooses not to make its services available to clients unwilling to consider pro-integration housing locations. The experience of the South Suburban Housing Center (SSHC) in this regard is reflected in the following:

> SSHC's procedures apply equally to majority and minority groups—based on demand or market information all are encouraged to consider applications they would not otherwise have been expected to make. . . . Initially SSHC's formal

policy was to provide information respecting particular locations only to clients willing to consider "non-traditional" locations. In practice very few clients—none in recent years—have been unwilling to consider such locations. SSHC's current policy is . . . *all* clients are to receive available SSHC information as they may request.

From January 1 through December 31, 1977, SSHC counseled a total of 477 clients, 160 of whom were majority and 317 of whom were minority families. Of 129 clients with whom SSHC maintained contact beyond the first interview, 70 chose to move to non-traditional locations, 38 majority and 32 minority families. After considering non-traditional locations, the remaining 59 clients (22 majority and 37 minority families) moved to traditional locations. (Statement of South Suburban Housing Center filed with HUD, November 1978, p. 8)

See also n. 66 below and accompanying text.

25. Section 804 of Title VIII makes it unlawful to refuse to sell or rent, "or otherwise make unavailable or deny," a dwelling to any person because of race. The courts have interpreted this prohibition to apply to the practice of "steering"—any action by a real estate agent "which in any way impedes, delays or discourages a prospective homebuyer from purchasing housing on a racial basis" (*Zuch v. Hussey*, 366 F.Supp. 553, 557 [E.D. Mich. 1973]; see also *Zuch v. Hussey*, 394 F.Supp. 1028, 1047 [E.D. Mich 1975], *aff'd and remanded*, 547 F.2d 1168 [6th Cir. 1977]). It has been suggested that the reason steering is unlawful is that it interferes with "the freedom of choice for the purchaser which the Fair Housing Act prohibits" (*Zuch v. Hussey*, 394 F.Supp. at 1047).

In *Havens Realty Corp. v. Coleman*, 455 U.S. 363, 366 n. 1 (1982), the Supreme Court quoted the following definition of racial steering from the complaint: "[a] practice by which real estate brokers and agents preserve and encourage patterns of racial segregation in available housing by steering members of racial and ethnic groups to buildings occupied primarily by members of such racial and ethnic groups and away from buildings and neighborhoods inhabited primarily by members of other races or groups."

"Steering" is described and defined as follows in James A. Kushner, *Fair Housing* (Colorado Springs, Colo.: Shepard's/McGraw Hill, 1983), p. 220:

It has long been a practice of real estate brokers to discourage integration and maintain racially, and often ethnically or religiously, homogeneous neighborhoods. Until 1950, such a requirement was part of the Code of Ethics of the National Association of Real Estate Boards. When discrimination in housing was finally prohibited, real estate brokers and agents, partly to serve the express or assumed preferences of their clientele and partly based on their own perception that racial change affects property values, almost universally continued the practice of *steering*; the direction of potential buyers or renters to specific neighborhoods on the basis of race. Typically, blacks are shown housing in all-black or racially integrated neighborhoods while whites are shown listings only in all-white neighborhoods. [Footnotes omitted.]

Cases holding that steering violates Title VIII are collected in ibid., p. 221, n. 89.

26. But see n. 24.

27. For example, in an employee training program context the Supreme Court upheld a minority preference clearly based on race because of its view that the purpose of

the relevant statute was to prevent employment discrimination against minorities, and that to preclude minority preference arrangements would frustrate efforts to remedy the effects of just such discrimination. *United Steelworkers of America v. Weber*, 443 U.S. 193 (1979).

28. For example, *Trafficante v. Metropolitan Life Insurance Co.*, 409 U.S. 205 (1972), and *Gladstone, Realtors v. Village of Bellwood*, 441 U.S. 91 (1979).

29. See Leonard Rubinowitz and Elizabeth Trosman, "Affirmative Action and the American Dream: Implementing Fair Housing Policies in Federal Homeownership Programs," *Northwestern University Law Review* 74 (1979): 491 at 533–65.

The reason for the qualification stated in the text is that a separate provision of Title VIII (42 USC §3608(d)) imposes upon executive departments and agencies of the federal government the duty to administer their programs relating to housing and urban development "affirmatively" to further Title VIII's purposes. In particular contexts— for example, site selection for subsidized housing (*Shannon v. HUD*, 364 F.2d 809 [3rd Cir. 1970]) and selection of tenants for a subsidized housing development (*Otero v. New York City Housing Authority*, 484 F.2d 1122 [2d Cir. 1973])—lower federal courts have upheld race-conscious activity by the federal government or its agents to achieve or maintain integration in a neighborhood or in a housing development. However, because Section 3608(d) is directed only to executive departments and agencies, it is questionable whether the Supreme Court would view this section as validating race-conscious counseling by municipalities even though they were recipients of HUD funds (e.g., Community Development Block Grant funds). See discussion in *Burney v. Housing Authority* (n. 23 above), 551 F.Supp. at 769. See also Rubinowitz and Trosman, "Affirmative Action," pp. 539–40, n. 183.

Moreover, *Shannon* cautioned that desegregation is not the only goal of national housing policy (346 F.2d at 822), and *Otero* was limited on its facts to the effect of a housing authority's admission policies on former occupants of the project site (i.e., no question of ongoing occupancy quotas was involved). Occupancy quotas *have* been upheld in a "remedial" context, that is, where necessary to remedy prior adjudicated discrimination by a particular agency—for example, *Gautreaux v. CHA*, 304 F.Supp. 907 (1969). Cf. the discussion in *Burney*, 551 F.Supp. at 763.

30. 114 Cong. Rec. 3422.

31. 114 Cong. Rec. 3421.

32. 114 Cong. Rec. 2525.

33. Jane McGrew to Lawrence B. Simons, HUD Memorandum, 16 January 1981, pp. 1, 4. Rubinowitz and Trosman's "Affirmative Action" explores the meaning of the affirmative duty imposed upon HUD by Title VIII. In this context two alternative interpretations of the affirmative mandate are suggested: policies to actually achieve integration, and policies to ensure that minority homeseekers have a realistic choice of all neighborhoods throughout a metropolitan area. The authors opt for the latter interpretation. Rubinowitz and Trosman, "Affirmative Action," pp. 533–34, 565.

34. Affirmative Marketing Agreement for Voluntary Use by Boards of Realtors, jointly approved by HUD and the NAR on 16 December 1975. The agreement was amended in 1978 and 1981, and revised in 1982. (It is printed at 49 Fed. Reg. 12319, 29 March 1984.) Among other things, the agreement provides that its goal is "to provide information that will enable minority buyers to make a free choice of housing location."

HUD also entered into an affirmative marketing agreement with the National Association of Real Estate Brokers (14 May 1976, revised 12 August 1982), the goal of which is "to provide information that will enable all buyers to make a free choice of housing location." In addition, HUD has entered into voluntary affirmative marketing agreements with other groups—for example, home builders and apartment managers. HUD's most recent agreement with the National Association of Home Builders provides: "Each *Builder* shall direct a substantial part of its marketing activity to those groups which are not likely to seek housing marketed by the *Builder* without special outreach: *i.e.*, to racial minority groups for housing in predominantly non-minority areas, and to racial majority groups for housing in integrated areas" (HUD voluntary affirmative marketing agreement with the National Association of Home Builders, 17 April 1984, p. 4).

35. National Association of Realtors, *Realtors Guide to Practice Equal Opportunity in Housing* (1976), p. 41 (hereafter cited as *Realtors Guide*).

36. Ibid., p. 45. The Guidelines also advise brokers to "take all reasonable steps to see to it that their agents' inability to show and inform prospects of all available listings does not restrict the prospect to selecting among homes located only in neighborhoods where the prospect's race is predominant." Ibid., p. 44.

37. Ibid., p. 46. The Guidelines also permit a broker to cooperate with "neighborhood stabilization" groups if he is satisfied that the "legitimate goal of maintaining neighborhood integration is being furthered," but only by "being completely open and honest with his minority prospects who are interested in the area." The broker is advised, "He may explain the goal sought, offer the prospect comparable listings anywhere else, but never refuse to show the specific home in question." The Guidelines also state that such involvement with "neighborhood stabilization" groups should take place "preferably only after having secured appropriate approval of those governmental agencies concerned." Ibid.

38. A letter written by a deputy general counsel of HUD after publication of the NAR Guidelines suggests that for-profit real estate agents may not unilaterally engage in such pro-integration activities. The letter does not address the inference drawn in the text, but it does indicate that Title VIII permits such for-profit agents to refer clients to nonprofit fair housing centers carrying on race-conscious counseling. S. Leigh Curry, Jr., to Werner E. Petterson, 26 February 1981.

39. *Washington Post*, 11 July 1984, p. 1.

40. Jane Lang McGrew, "Integration *Is* Goal of Housing Policy," *Los Angeles Times*, 15 July 1984.

41. Ann Mariano, "Nation's Policy on Integration at Crossroads," *Washington Post*, 21 July 1984.

42. "Benign Steering" (n. 16 above), p. 952. In *Regents of the University of California v. Bakke*, 438 U.S. 265, 361–62 (1978), Justice Brennan—not writing for the Court—said: "[A]ny statute must be stricken that stigmatizes any group or that singles out those least well represented in the political process to bear the brunt of a benign program."

43. *Gladstone, Realtors v. Village of Bellwood*, 441 U.S. 91, 110–11 (1979).

44. Ibid.

45. *Linmark Associates v. Willingboro*, 431 U.S. 85, 94–95 (1977). The "express recognition" referred to is the Court's language in *Trafficante v. Metropolitan Life Insurance Co.*, 409 U.S. 205 (1972). In that case, black and white tenants of a large apartment complex alleged that the owner-operator was engaged in discriminatory housing practices (manipulating the waiting list on a racial basis, among others), main-

tained the complexes as a "white ghetto," and thus deprived the plaintiffs of their right to live in a racially integrated community. In upholding the tenants' right to bring suit under Title VIII to stop such practices the Court said: "The person on the landlord's black list is not the only victim of discriminatory housing practices; it is, as Senator Javits said in supporting the bill, 'the whole community,' . . . and as Senator Mondale . . . said, the reach of the proposed law was to replace the ghettos 'by truly integrated and balanced living patterns'" (409 U.S. at 211).

46. The issue of the legitimacy of government promotion of integration has reverberations that reach back to *Brown v. Board of Education*. In a thoughtful review of the arguments made in *Brown* and the "legacy" of the decision over the ensuing three decades, Diane Ravitch asserts that "the group-based concepts of the present are in conflict with the historic efforts of the civil rights movement to remove group classifications from public policy." She reminds us that in *Brown* the NAACP argued for the "total exclusion of race and color" from governmental conduct, and her article sometimes sets color-consciousness in opposition to individual rights as if the two were wholly antithetical. Yet Ravitch says, "Somewhere between the Scylla of color-blindness and the Charybdis of color-consciousness must be a reconciliation of democratic values," and she concludes by appearing to recommend a "creative interweaving of color-conscious and racially neutral approaches." Diane Ravitch, "The Ambiguous Legacy of *Brown v. Board of Education*," *New Perspectives*, U.S. Commission on Civil Rights (Summer 1984), p. 6.

Some seventeen years after *Brown*, the Supreme Court (again unanimously) said: "School authorities are traditionally charged with broad power to formulate and implement educational policy and might well conclude, for example, that in order to prepare students to live in a pluralistic society each school should have a prescribed ratio of Negro to white students reflecting the proportion for the district as a whole. To do this as an educational policy is within the broad discretionary powers of school authorities" (*Swann v. Charlotte-Mecklenberg Bd. of Ed.*, 402 U.S. 1, 16 [1971]). Little appears to have been made of this dictum in the fifteen years since it was pronounced.

More recently, *Regents of the University of California v. Bakke*, 438 U.S. 265 (1978), dealt with an admissions program of the medical school of the University of California at Davis under which 16 places were reserved for minority students. Whereas blacks were able to compete for all 100 available seats, whites were able to compete for only 84 places. The admissions program was defended on the ground, among others, that it helped to attain a diverse student body. A majority of the Court held that the program's racial classification violated the Equal Protection Clause. Because of divided views there was no opinion for the entire Court; Justice Powell announced the Court's judgment. Though concluding that the university's admission program failed to meet the necessity test (438 U.S. at 320), Justice Powell did say that the interest of diversity was "compelling in the context of a university's admissions program" (438 U.S. at 314). But he relied heavily on the educational context (which involves considerations—e.g., academic freedom—not present in the residential context). Moreover, he said, "[T]he nature of the state interest that would justify consideration of race or ethnic background . . . is not an interest in simple ethnic diversity. . . . The diversity that furthers a compelling state interest encompasses a far broader array of qualifications and characteristics of which racial or ethnic origin is but a single though important element" (438 U.S. at 315).

47. 448 U.S. 448, 480, 481 (1980).

48. Id., 448 U.S. at 515.

49. Evidence that pervasive discrimination in fact persists in American housing markets is referred to in n. 51. The determination would of course embrace discrimination against whites as well as blacks. As Secretary Pierce has said (see the text accompanying n. 20), restricting choice is no less unlawful when a white homeseeker is denied the choice of an integrated community than when a minority homeseeker is denied the choice of a nonsegregated one.

Fullilove rested heavily on congressional power to determine that discrimination exists and select remedial means, but state and local legislatures, subject to the Constitution, have similar powers.

50. Even the real estate industry acknowledges this now, although it emphasizes the role of government: "The inescapable fact is that it took nearly 102 years for the Supreme Court to recognize the full Constitutional guarantee of equal opportunity in housing contemplated by the 13th and 14th Amendments. During those one hundred two years, the decisions of the Supreme Court and the policies of the federal, state and local government affirmatively created, or at least countenanced, a segregated and discriminatory housing market." *Realtors Guide* (n. 35 above), p. 21.

The literature includes many descriptions of the history of housing discrimination in America. For several brief ones, see *Twenty Years After Brown*, A Report of the U.S. Commission on Civil Rights (Washington, D.C.: Government Printing Office, 1975), pp. 1–5; Alexander Polikoff, *Housing the Poor: The Case for Heroism* (Cambridge, Mass.: Ballinger, 1978), pp. 3–30; Gary Orfield, *Must We Bus?* (Washington, D.C.: The Brookings Institution, 1978), pp. 78–85; Citizens' Commission on Civil Rights, *A Decent Home* (1983), pp. 2–54.

In the last analysis, of course, we are all responsible for housing discrimination and its effects: "The many services which collectively constitute the housing market— brokers, agents, property owners, property managers, rental agents, and lending institutions—have indeed, through the decades, served as the instruments for limiting housing choices for blacks and other minorities and creating and reinforcing the dual market. However, they were doing so primarily because the larger consuming public and for many years the federal, state and local governments expected them to function in precisely the manner they did." George Schermer, *Steering: Realtors as Gate Keepers* (Michigan Advisory Committee to U.S. Commission on Civil Rights, 9 July 1979), p. 31.

51. Secretary of HUD Pierce said, "The evidence clearly shows that discrimination is pervasive in American housing markets." Recent Evidence on Discrimination in Housing, HUD–PD&R–786, April 1984, p. i. See also U.S. Department of Housing and Urban Development, *Measuring Racial Discrimination in American Housing Markets* (Washington, D.C.: Government Printing Office, 1979), and *Analysis for South Suburban Housing Center* (Park Forest South, Ill.: Governors State University, February 1981).

52. U.S. Commission on Civil Rights, *The Federal Fair Housing Enforcement Effort* (1979), pp. 230–35.

53. Recent efforts to strengthen the enforcement provisions of Title VIII have failed to pass the Congress.

54. See Lawrence Rosser and Elizabeth White, "An Answer to Housing Discrimination: The Need for a Unitary Marketing System," *Civil Rights Digest* 7 (1975): 10–19.

55. "Benign Steering" (n. 16 above), p. 956; and see generally pp. 955–58.

56. Schermer, *Realtors as Gate Keepers*, p. 17. Some real estate firms appear to be "transition specialists" who seek out and become especially active in the real estate market in racially changing neighborhoods. These firms are likely to be engaged in segregative steering.

57. See Rubinowitz and Trosman, "Affirmative Action," pp. 536–37, n. 174. For a review of social science evidence on the tipping phenomenon, see John Goering, "Neighborhood Tipping and Racial Transition: A Review of Social Science Evidence," *Journal of the American Institute of Planners* 44 (1978): 68. It is frequently pointed out that tipping is a conceptually imprecise concept. This does not mean that tipping is not a real-life phenomenon. The *Burney* opinion contains an interesting treatment of evidentiary aspects of a tipping argument (551 F.Supp. at 765–67).

58. Schermer, *Realtors as Gate Keepers*, pp. 31–32.

59. "Benign Steering" (n. 16 above), pp. 940–44. The discussion assumes a counseling program as part of a total racial diversity effort. Counseling alone might easily fail the necessity test on the ground that it alone would have little chance of success.

60. Controversy over an alleged failure to treat black home buyers equally with whites in the Shaker Heights, Ohio, housing counseling program erupted in public charges, countercharges, and staff resignations. See the *Sun Press*, Beachwood, Ohio, 12 April 1979, p. 1. As one observer has argued, "[I]t is unfair to place the burden of enforcing the law upon the shoulders of the black homeseekers. Whites have an equal responsibility to (a) affirmatively welcome black neighbors and to resist the impulse to flee when the ratio of blacks increases and (b) to themselves seek for housing in areas where they can contribute most to assuring racial balance." Schermer, *Realtors as Gate Keepers*, p. 32.

However, it may be inappropriate to focus exclusively on black homeseekers affected by a race-conscious housing service and ignore the interests of black residents of integrated neighborhoods who may consider themselves to be negatively affected by resegregation. In a recent opinion survey conducted in Shaker Heights, black residents were more supportive than whites of the view that city programs should encourage the continued movement of white families into areas of Shaker Heights in which black families predominate. "Community Opinion Survey" (Report prepared for Shaker Heights by the New England Municipal Center, Durham, Mass., January 1983).

61. In a few instances, lower courts have held that minorities may be subjected to burdens or disadvantages in the interest of advancing a compelling societal goal. See, for example, *Parent Association v. Ambach*, 598 F.2d 705 (2d Cir. 1979) (school integration); *Otero v. New York City Housing Authority*, 484 F.2d 1122 (2d Cir. 1973) (public housing integration). See also the discussion in *Burney*, 551 F.Supp. at 763. The only such modern decisions of the Supreme Court appear to be the Japanese exclusion cases of World War II, *Hirabayashi v. United States* (320 U.S. 81 [1942]) and *Korematsu v. United States* (323 U.S. 214 [1944]).

62. That the perceived need to keep the black population below 50 percent may be explained as a response to the "white flight" phenomenon (see "Benign Steering" [n. 16 above], p. 959) is not likely to lessen (indeed, may intensify) the stigmatic effect.

63. See n. 60 above.

64. Kenneth Karst and Harold Horowitz, "The *Bakke* Opinions and Equal Protection Doctrine," *Harvard Civil Rights–Civil Liberties Law Review* 14 (1979): 6–29 at 28.

65. For example, with little analysis of race-conscious counseling or other integra-

tion maintenance techniques in real-life operation, one discussion is sprinkled with such phrases as "constraint on choice," "race-based restrictions on access," and "restricting black residential choice." Robert W. Lake and Jessica Winslow, "Integration Management: Municipal Constraints on Residential Mobility," *Urban Geography* (1981): 311.

66. 24 C.F.R. §200.620 *et seq.* Race-conscious counseling may be conducted in a manner consistent with ultimate, informed decision making by the individual homeseeker. A description of one such program (of the South Suburban Housing Center) states: "SSHC makes it clear that it is the client's right to pursue the housing of his or her choice. In all cases SSHC provides its clients with general information on the total south suburban area as well as more specific information . . . about particular locations as requested." Statement of South Suburban Housing Center, filed with HUD, November 1978, pp. 7–8.

The statement, responding to several complaints against SSHC for allegedly violating Title VIII by its race-conscious practices, goes on to say:

> Families seeking homes to buy or apartments to rent are presented with four possibilities:
>
> 1. White neighborhoods (all or nearly all white).
> 2. Black neighborhoods (all or nearly all black).
> 3. Changing neighborhoods (in rapid transition from white to black).
> 4. Stably integrated neighborhoods.
>
> For families, white or black, who wish to live in neighborhoods of the first three types, some choice exists. However, choice for families seeking housing in the fourth type of neighborhood is severely constrained.
>
> This reality in effect denies housing choice to what may be a significant portion of our population. Polls indicate that substantial numbers of both white and black families desire to live in stably integrated neighborhoods. The counseling activities of SSHC are designed to assist in the maintenance of such neighborhoods where they exist and to help bring about their creation where they do not. In this important sense the counseling activities of SSHC are designed to increase housing choice. (Statement of South Suburban Housing Center, pp. 12–13)

67. For example, in the Cook County suburbs south of Chicago the South Suburban Housing Center operates in a 36-municipality area, in which there are a number of integrated and many predominantly white neighborhoods. See Rubinowitz and Trosman, "Affirmative Action," p. 552, n. 234, for a discussion of what constitutes a "comparable" housing opportunity (however, in the context of a quota, not a counseling, arrangement).

68. See n. 25 above and the NAR Guidelines quoted in the text at nn. 36, 37 above. In his speech to the National Association of Realtors (see text accompanying n. 20 above), Secretary Pierce said: "The point of their programs [communities' integration maintenance programs] is to expand, rather than to limit choices." Yet it may be argued that—because of the special weight of *government* authority—race-conscious counseling by government is likely to be *inherently* coercive to some persons, regardless of how clear it may be made that it is the client's right to pursue housing of his or her choice. For this reason the potential for coercion may be greater when such counseling is carried on by a government rather than a private agency.

69. *Fullilove v. Klutznick*, 448 U.S. 448, 515 (Justice Powell concurring).

70. *Bakke* (n. 46 above), 438 U.S. at 305.

71. Id. at 304, 305.

72. 448 U.S. at 515.

73. See n. 41 above.

74. See 24 C.F.R. §§880.112 and 881.112.

75. 24 C.F.R. §200.620 *et seq.*

76. The text accompanying nn. 47–49 above suggests a way of reconciling the apparent difference of views between Knapp of HUD and Reynolds of the Justice Department. Because HUD's project selection criteria and affirmative marketing requirements can presumably each pass muster as steps designed to combat the persisting effects of racial discrimination in housing markets, and need not be characterized simply as the promotion of integration, Reynolds might agree with Knapp that the HUD techniques were proper.

The ultimate "philosophic" issue between Knapp and Reynolds might be posed by the following hypothetical situation. Assume a community in which all vestiges of past discrimination had been eradicated, in which a truly open, "unitary" housing market existed, and in which integration characterized all residential neighborhoods. Assume also that racial concentration begins to develop in one neighborhood. (By hypothesis, the developing concentration is *not* the result of discrimination.) In such a situation, would HUD be free under Title VIII to utilize its techniques of site selection criteria and affirmative marketing to forestall resegregation, or would it be barred from doing so because the developing racial concentration is not the result of discrimination? Would the community even be free to spend tax funds on a public statement extolling racial diversity and warning of the developing threat to it in one of its neighborhoods? Perhaps Reynolds and Knapp would indeed disagree on the answers to these questions.

77. For example, integration maintenance is to be pursued not because a black majority community is undesirable but because a racially diverse one *is* desirable.

78. Nonetheless, in any governmental counseling program the risk of "inherent coercion" and a heightened risk of program abuse remain (see n. 67 above). For these reasons it would seem preferable for race-conscious counseling to be carried on by private agencies rather than governmental ones.

The author of *The Oak Park Strategy* (n. 3 above), p. 222, strikes the balance between costs and benefits this way:

> As long as a dual housing market exists, the primary way that additional housing units will become available to black people is by total transition of neighborhoods on the edge of the black ghetto. The more the movement of black people into these fringe areas is restricted, the lower is their supply of housing, the more limited their choices, and by simple supply and demand, the more they will end up paying for shelter.
>
> Oak Park's strategy does result in such restriction and theoretically has those effects, although the practical significance of this case is limited by Oak Park's tiny share of the total metropolitan housing stock.
>
> However, given the prevailing dual housing market and Oak Park's geographical location, completely open housing and stable racial integration are mutually exclusive goals. Ultimately the choice must be made for one of these ends over the

other. Oak Park has value as a model that may contribute to lessening the kind of discrimination that results in total exclusion of blacks from white neighborhoods, while white people in fringe neighborhoods bear along with black people the cost of maintaining the dual market. In my estimation this overrides the immediate deleterious effect of the Oak Park strategy on black housing supply.

But given the personal nature of constitutional rights—see *Regents of the University of California v. Bakke*, 438 U.S. 265, 299 (Opinion of Justice Powell)—this Oak Park analysis is troublesome. Restricting the movement of homeseekers, if that is in fact the result of the Oak Park "strategy," would be impermissible notwithstanding the ultimate choice-expansion goal. Even within Oak Park, however, there may be sufficient housing opportunities in predominantly white portions of the village so that there need be no "restrictions" on blacks seeking housing in Oak Park who receive counseling from the housing center there. In any event, the restrictions, if any, in the Oak Park situation may stem from the efforts of an "island" municipality to foster racial diversity in a sea of closed communities. Region-wide counseling as discussed in the text should offer a way to substitute choice-expansion for restriction.

79. School textbooks are already describing integration maintenance as just such an issue. A recent social science text says: "Attempts by some suburbs to maintain racial diversity have raised a debate that will probably be settled only by the Supreme Court. The eventual outcome will have profound effects on the racial makeup of metropolitan areas for decades to come." J. John Palen, *The Urban World*, 2d ed. (New York: McGraw-Hill Book Company, 1980), p. 178.

80. Much of the discussion in the opinions of Chief Justice Burger and Justice Powell in *Fullilove* is about the congressional "findings" underlying the legislation at issue in that case. Justice Powell said it is "important that the legislative record supporting race-conscious remedies contain evidence that satisfies fair-minded people that the congressional action is just" (448 U.S. at 506, n. 8).

Municipal officials may be apprehensive about such a legislative hearing, fearing that public exploration of the threat of resegregation might induce white flight and deter white move-ins. Nonetheless, in one case, after a searching review of a voluntary "benign discrimination" school plan that established racial quotas to maintain racially diverse schools, and after concluding that the goal of the plan passed constitutional muster, the court decided it required detailed "evidence of a factual nature . . . to support the particular details of the Plan." *Parent Assn. v. Ambach*, 598 F.2d 705, 720 (2d Cir. 1979). And see *Burney* in which the court concluded that government agencies "have failed to meet their burden of proof" with respect to the necessity and precise "tailoring" of a quota arrangement in public housing projects. 551 F.Supp. at 764.

In this regard, one may contrast the discussions of integration maintenance in the *Harvard Law Review* and *Duke Law Journal* articles cited in n. 16 above. Each begins with a very different perspective on the causes of racial and ethnic separation and re-segregation. According to the Harvard note, the principal cause is discrimination and the principal discriminators are to be found in the real estate industry. The Duke article on the other hand, while acknowledging that discrimination plays a role, appears to attribute residential separation primarily to the desire of Americans to group themselves on an ethnic basis. Given these different starting assumptions, the authors reach very different conclusions about integration maintenance programs. To Harvard, they are option expanding; to Duke they interfere with individual freedom.

81. "Every time a community resegregates, the pattern of racial separation and hostility is reinforced, thereby increasing barriers to black entry in the remaining white communities and making stable integration more difficult once black entry has begun. The movement toward racial equality will continue to languish until some communities break out of the cycle of resegregation by creating a stable interracial environment which demonstrates that racial harmony is not merely desirable but also attainable." "Benign Steering" (n. 16 above), pp. 960–61. See also ibid., pp. 953–55.

In 1978 John Goering said: "None of the research or modeling of the process of racial succession provides any reason for optimism about the future of neighborhood racial integration in American cities" (Goering, "Neighborhood Tipping," p. 76). In a recent study of neighborhood change and integration in Metropolitan Chicago from 1970 to 1980, Gary Orfield concludes: "What has happened is that real residential choices have expanded for a small fraction of the black population while most blacks are experiencing even greater residential segregation. There is nothing in this data that suggests that this problem will cure itself without much stronger residential integration policies" (Gary Orfield, Albert Woolbright, and Helene Kim, "Neighborhood Change and Integration in Metropolitan Chicago," A Report of the Leadership Council for Metropolitan Open Communities, July 1984, p. 29).

Section II
Segregation and Discrimination in Housing

Introduction

JOHN M. GOERING

Efforts to formulate clearsighted policies and programs to promote housing desegregation must be built on an accurate understanding of the legal and social, malleable and intractable aspects of residential segregation. Only through such an assessment can policymakers avoid creating more folly and frustration than planned change. Such assessments should also provide evidence of how well existing legislation and programs have served to reduce the extent of discrimination in cities. Segregation and discrimination, however they are measured, are the racial backdrop against which all federal and nonfederal desegregation efforts are played out.

Social scientists have assisted in two major ways in this process of assessment. First, they have developed and tested a variety of measures of residential segregation that provide relatively clear standards for measuring changes and trends. They have also offered assessments of the determinants of segregation, including the role of discrimination.

Karl and Alma Taeuber (1965), two decades ago, provided a now classic description of the extent of and variations in segregation in American cities. Others have offered criticisms and refinements of this early research that now suggest the need for multiple measures of segregation (Lieberson 1981; Lieberson and Carter 1982; Sakoda 1981; White 1983; Morgan 1983). James and Tynan in this section reflect the consensus that no single measure of segregation can adequately express its level, patterns, fluctuations, and impacts.

One clear, and to many unexpected, finding based on Taeuber's index of dissimilarity is that the level of segregation declined in cities and metropolitan areas between 1970 and 1980. The "trajectory of change," which Taeuber had predicted from his analysis of 1970 data, an average level of 75, did in fact come about. He finds a value of 76 for the 109 cities he originally examined using 1970 data. For a smaller subset of 28 cities, there has been a decline in segregation of 6 points—from 87 to 81—with some cities experiencing declines of up to 10 points over the decade (Taeuber 1983).

Explaining why these declines have occurred for black Americans is complicated by the absence of causal models in which all relevant variables can be plugged in, evaluated, and weighted for specific regions, cities, and suburbs. Taeuber (1983) speculates about, but does not measure, the probable role of a number of causal influences. The passage of federal, state, and local fair housing laws is seen as one probable influence on the declines registered between 1970 and 1980. The declining growth of black inner-city populations, growth of the black middle class, school desegregation, and regional factors are all of apparent importance. The overall "dynamics of urban growth and change" is, however, a controlling influence according to Taeuber. The power of these ecological forces is such that the pace of "natural" desegregation, as measured by Taeuber's index, is very slow. "If a similar rate of decline were to occur each decade for the next 50 years," Taeuber remarks, "the average score for these (28) cities would still be above 50" (ibid.: 4).

If some change for black Americans is now occurring in many cities, it does not appear to be shared by the Hispanic populations of the three sunbelt cities studied by James and Tynan. They too note the declines in segregation for blacks, but find little or no change for Hispanics. Despite the minimal changes for Hispanics, their data from Denver and Houston nevertheless reveal that Hispanics were in 1970 and still are, in the 1980s, less segregated than black residents of these cities. In Phoenix, however, Hispanics appeared to be slightly more segregated than blacks as of 1980.

The second arena in which social scientists have contributed to the understanding of housing desegregation is in their analyses of causal influences of the level of segregation in specific cities and metropolitan areas. Research over the past two decades makes it clear that economic and housing factors, racial discrimination, and preferences for self-segregation are among the most plausible factors promoting segregation (Myrdal 1944; Taeuber and Taeuber 1965; Roof 1972; Yinger et al. 1979). Socioeconomic and housing factors such as dwelling quality, value, and tenure appear to explain from 15 to 60 percent of the variance in measures of segregation (Darden 1976:89; Smith 1977). In a detailed regression analysis of hundreds of categories of possible demographic and housing influences, Kain, in this section, shows the powerful role of racial constraints in limiting the housing choice of economically qualified blacks. Housing market discrimination, he argues, is the major force concentrating blacks within the central cities of both Cleveland and Chicago. There is no parallel between the housing choices of nationality groups and black Americans, nor does self-segregation appear to Kain as a plausible explanation for the substantial gap between the expected and actual distribution of blacks.

Kain, James and Tynan, and Galster, in this section, all utilize evidence gained by means of audits or tests to document the powerful role of racial discrimination. They refer to or use the Housing Market Practices Survey of the U.S. Department of Housing and Urban Development (HUD) (Office of Policy Development and Research 1979a, 1979b), which found upward of 2 million instances of discriminatory treatment against blacks in 1977, with more recent studies in Columbus (Ohio), Boston, Denver, and Baltimore also documenting high levels of differential treatment of blacks (White 1979; Pearce 1970; Feins, Bratt, and Hollister 1981; Jacobson 1983; Baltimore Neighborhoods 1983). Galster's analysis directly links the audit measures of discrimination gathered in HUD's study of discrimination in 40 metropolitan areas to measures of black segregation and centralization. His findings are dramatic. Cities that had high levels of measured discrimination had roughly one-quarter more black centralization, with lower levels of exposure of blacks to whites.

Income factors, he notes, continue to be influential with the prospect that higher median incomes for blacks could decrease their centralization. Galster's analysis raises many questions paralleling his analytic insights. He finds it probable that there may need to be a "threshold level" of discrimination in a city before it has a measurable impact on black segregation, a finding unreported by others and one clearly in need of further examination. He was also frustrated by his inability to adequately predict the degree of housing market discrimination and he argues for closer attention to regional factors.

Without exception, however, the four analysts in this section agree that stronger enforcement of fair housing laws would significantly reduce the levels of discrimination and consequent segregation in cities and their surrounding suburbs. James and Tynan, in fact, support new fair housing amendments in an effort to give federal agencies stronger authority than that currently provided in Title VIII. But this conclusion is only made inferentially. None of the authors has incorporated direct measures of federal, state, local, or private fair housing enforcement in the effort to explain variations and reductions in segregation. The incorporation of such measures would no doubt involve a substantial number of novel methodological and data gathering problems. Future efforts at analysis and predictions must, however, soon move from speculation to the actual measurement of legislative and judicial impacts on segregation and discrimination (Darden 1973; Schechter 1973; Bullard and Tryman 1979).

One clear finding emerging from both Kain and Galster's analyses is that class and income factors remain inextricably linked to the problem of desegregating American cities. To a degree, the desegregation or decentralization of blacks and Hispanics can only be influenced by addressing the high concentrations of poverty in these communities.[1] Increasing the employment or purchasing power of minority households remains a fundamental part of the problem of creating effective housing desegregation. It is, of course, also true that residential segregation negatively affects opportunities for economic advancement (Langendorf and Silvers 1976; Marston and Van Valey 1979:20–21). There are presumably better chances for occupational advancement, all things being equal, in a city with less residential segregation.

The contentiousness over residential integration is interwoven with deep distrust of programs aimed at economic and school integration. The mixture of poorer, subsidized households with those better off can lead to chain reactions of concerns among potential neighbors that may have little to do with racial fears. The inseparability of racial and economic pathologies is at the root of much of the congressional discontent over programs aimed at deconcentrating the minority poor (see Section IV). Socioeconomic factors and racial discrimination will continue to interact, as both cause and effect with desegregation policies and programs (Hermalin and Farley 1973; Orfield 1978; Wilson 1980; Hawley et al. 1982).

The analysis of the changes and determinants of residential segregation is therefore crucial to unscrambling our understanding of what it will take to promote faster, more widespread desegregation. Analyses of segregation have an important limitation, however. Segregation indices are not designed to be sensitive to the issue of housing integration, a fact noted for some time (Cortese, Falk, and Cohen 1976). They tend to mask, indeed overwhelm, evidence concerning the existence of modest levels of housing integration. Only analyses of within-city, neighborhood-by-neighborhood changes are likely to reveal the slowing or reversal of the "normal" patterns of rapid racial change.

A small number of stably integrated neighborhoods were shown to exist in a handful of cities in the 1940s and 1950s, surviving best when the overall rate of black population growth was low (Taeuber and Taeuber 1965:120–21). Measures of the turnover of housing units from whites to blacks in the 1960s also revealed small numbers of integrating moves. Although over 90 percent of all city and suburban housing transactions went from white to white or black to black; 46 out of every 1,000 "replacement moves" in cities and 15 in the suburbs involved a transfer from white to black occupancy. During the period from 1967 to 1971, about 3 percent of white households were replaced by blacks, and nearly 30 percent of all black households "moving into a previously occupied housing unit were replacing whites" (Long and Spain 1978:9; Spain, Reid, and Long 1980).

Annual Housing Survey data provide more recent evidence of a national trend toward black movement to predominantly white suburbs. In the mid–1970s, "approximately 40 percent of Blacks moved to tracts which had been less than ten percent Black in 1970; another 27 percent moved to tracts which were between ten and forty percent Black. Thus, nearly 70 percent of all Black movers to tracts in the balance of SMSA's selected tracts that were more white than Black" (Spain and Long 1981). A small number of better-off black households appear, therefore, to be moving in increasing numbers to white suburban neighborhoods.[2]

Many of the moves of blacks to suburbs were, however, to spill-over ghetto areas (Grier and Grier 1983; Lake and Cutter 1980; Farley 1983). There has been a partial cloning of racial ghettos in many parts of American suburbs. At the same time, however, the steamroller pattern of inevitable racial transition found in the 1950s and 1960s in cities has not been as predictable in all suburbs (Aldrich 1975:335; Obermanns 1980; Long and DeAre 1983). Suburbs of Washington, D.C., as well as some in New Jersey have modest levels of racial stability (Zehner and Chapin 1974; Lake and Cutter 1980). And in St. Louis the process of racial and socioeconomic change "stabilized and even reversed itself without massive public intervention" in at least two suburbs (Little 1980: 148).

Even in a city like Chicago, which is plagued with interracial violence and has the highest level of segregation in the United States, interracial living occurs. Orfield, in the preceding section, refers to his recent analysis of 1980 census tract data for the city of Chicago which found that 3 percent of Chicago's white population and 4 percent of its blacks lived in stably integrated census tracts (Orfield, Woolbright, and Kim 1984:17). These areas generally have economically better-off residents, illustrating a well-known fact that integration—if it is to succeed—succeeds among those better educated and financially well off.

The existence of high levels of segregation and discrimination does not, therefore, preclude the coexistence of modest levels of residential integration. Regional variations in attitudes, the economic resources of minorities, the enforcement of fair housing laws, or the presence of vigorous community organizations dedicated to housing integration may all help to explain the fact that there is some residential integration in many American cities.

The contributors in Section III examine some of the principle attitudinal and sociological factors that help to explain the emergence and survival of housing integration in various parts of the United States.

NOTES

1. In 1947, black median income was 51 percent that of whites and by 1979 this ratio had improved to only 57 percent of whites (U.S. Bureau of the Census 1980). And whereas the proportion of white persons living in poverty declined roughly 40 percent from 1959 to 1979, the decline for blacks was only roughly half of this. The proportion of blacks living in poverty has remained roughly 30 percent from 1969 to 1979, whereas the proportion for whites declined slightly from 9.5 percent to 8.7 percent.

Poorer black families are also becoming more heavily concentrated in central cities; between 1969 and 1976, for example, there was a 12 percent increase in the number of black poor living in central cities at the same time that there was a 5 percent decline in the number of poor whites. Thus, although blacks make up roughly 22 percent of the nation's central city population, they constitute 45 percent of the central city poor (*President's National Urban Policy Report* 1980:4.3). Between 1970 and 1982, the number of persons living in poverty in central cities increased 22 percent, with a doubling of the number of black female-headed families living in cities. Nearly half of all black female-headed households lived in poverty in central cities in 1982; the comparable figure for whites was 22 percent (*President's National Urban Policy Report* 1984:40–41).

2. Studies of the residential integration of Hispanics reveal important differences, as well as some similarities, to patterns of black integration. Rosenberg and Lake (1976), for example, found Puerto Ricans competing for housing with blacks, occasionally acting as a "buffer" between blacks and whites, with a variety of pressures preventing longer-term residential stability. Massey (1981:22) found that residential turnover was slower in areas of Hispanic succession: "the transition from Anglo to black occurs at four to five times the rate of turnover from Anglo to Hispanic. Moreover, the succession process does not seem to proceed as far in Hispanic areas, accounting for the dearth of established Hispanic areas. In Hispanic areas, the succession process apparently stabilizes at a lower percentage minority than in black areas." Socioeconomic and regional factors also appear to be of considerable importance in explaining variations in the segregation of Hispanics (Lopez 1982).

REFERENCES

Aldrich, Howard. 1975. "Ecological Succession in Racially Changing Neighborhoods: A Review of the Literature." *Urban Affairs Quarterly* 10 (March): 327–48.

Baltimore Neighborhoods. 1983. "Apartment Discrimination in Baltimore County and City." Baltimore Neighborhoods, Inc., Baltimore, March.

Bullard, Robert, and D. Tryman. 1979. "Discrimination in a Southwestern City: A Study of Conciliated Complaints." *Housing and Society.* Proceedings, pp. 65–66.

Cortese, Charles, R. Frank Falk, and Jack Cohen. 1976. "Further Considerations on the Methodological Analysis of Segregation Indices." *American Sociological Review* 41 (August): 630–37.

Darden, Joe. 1973. *Afro-Americans in Pittsburgh.* Lexington, Mass.: Lexington Books.

———. 1976. "The Residential Segregation of Blacks in Detroit, 1960–70." *The International Journal of Comparative Studies* 17 (June): 84–91.

Farley, John. 1983. "Metropolitan Housing Segregation in 1980: The St. Louis Case." *Urban Affairs Quarterly* 13 (March): 347–59.

Feins, Judith D., Rachel Bratt, and Robert Hollister. 1981. *Final Report—A Study of Racial Discrimination in the Boston Housing Market.* Cambridge, Mass.: Abt Associates, November.

Grier, George, and Eunice Grier. 1983. "Black Suburbanization in the 1970's: An Analysis of Census Results." The Grier Partnership, Bethesda, Md., June.

Hawley, Willis, et al. 1982. "Using School Desegregation to Effect Housing Desegregation." In *Strategies for Effective Desegregation: Lessons from Research,* by Willis Hawley et al., pp. 61–71. Lexington, Mass.: Lexington Books.

Hermalin, Albert, and Reynolds Farley. 1973. "The Potential for Residential Integration in Cities and Suburbs: Implications for the Busing Controversy." *American Sociological Review* 30 (October): 595–610.

Jacobson, Joan. 1983. "Race Bias Cited in Apartment Rentals." *The Evening Sun,* 21 March, p. 1.

Lake, Robert, and Susan Cutter. 1980. "A Typology of Black Suburbanization since 1970." *The Geographical Review* 70 (April): 167–81.

Langendorf, Richard, and Arthur Silvers. 1976. "Residential Segregation and Economic Opportunity in Metropolitan Areas." University of Miami, Coral Gables, Fla.

Lieberson, Stanley. 1981. "Residential Segregation." In *A Piece of the Pie: Blacks and White Immigrants since 1880,* by Stanley Lieberson, pp. 253–91. Berkeley: University of California Press.

———, and Donna Carter. 1982. "Temporal Changes and Urban Differences in Residential Segregation: A Reconsideration." *American Journal of Sociology* 88 (September): 296–310.

Little, James. 1980. "Contemporary Housing Markets and Neighborhood Change." In *Residential Mobility and Public Policy,* edited by W. A. V. Clark and Eric Moore, pp. 126–49. Beverly Hills: Sage.

Long, Larry, and Diana DeAre. 1983. "The Slowing of Urbanization in the U.S." *Scientific American* 249 (July): 33–41.

———, and Daphne Spain. 1978. "Racial Succession in Individual Housing Units."

Current Population Reports, Special Studies, Series P–23, No. 71. Washington, D.C.: U.S. Government Printing Office, September.

Lopez, Manual. 1982. "Housing Characteristics and Residential Segregation: Mexican Americans in the Urban Southwest." *Housing and Society* 9, no. 3: 16–28.

Marston, Wilfred, and Thomas Van Valey. 1979. "The Role of Residential Segregation in the Assimilation Process." *The Annals* 441 (January): 13–25.

Massey, Douglas. 1981. "Residential Succession and Segregation: The Hispanic Case." Paper presented at the Population Association of America meetings, Washington, D.C., March.

Morgan, Barrie. 1983. "An Alternative Approach to the Development of a Distance-Based Measure of Racial Segregation." *American Journal of Sociology* 88 (May): 1237–49.

Myrdal, Gunnar. 1944. *An American Dilemma*. New York: Harper.

Obermanns, Richard. 1980. "Stability and Change in Racially Diverse Suburbs, 1970–1978." Unpublished report. Heights Community Congress, Cleveland Heights, Ohio, October.

Office of Policy Development and Research. 1979a. "Measuring Racial Discrimination in American Housing Markets: The Housing Market Practices Survey." Division of Evaluation, U.S. Department of Housing and Urban Development, Washington, D.C.

————. 1979b. "Discrimination against Chicanos in the Dallas Rental Housing Market: An Experimental Extension of the Housing Market Practices Survey." Division of Evaluation, U.S. Department of Housing and Urban Development, Washington, D.C.

Orfield, Gary. 1978. "If Wishes Were Houses Then Busing Could Stop: Demographic Trends and Desegregation Policy." *The Urban Review* 10 (Summer): 108–24.

————, Albert Woolbright, and Helene Kim. 1984. "Neighborhood Change and Integration in Chicago." Leadership Council for Metropolitan Open Communities, Chicago, July.

Pearce, Diana. 1979. "Gatekeepers and Homeseekers: Institutional Patterns in Racial Steering." *Social Problems* 26 (February): 325–42.

President's National Urban Policy Report. 1980. U.S. Department of Housing and Urban Development. HUD 583–1–CPD. Washington, D.C.: U.S. Government Printing Office, August.

————. 1984. U.S. Department of Housing and Urban Development. HUD–909–PDR. Washington, D.C.: U.S. Government Printing Office, August.

Roof, W. Clark. 1972. "Residential Segregation of Blacks and Racial Inequality in Southern Cities: Toward a Causal Model." *Social Problems* 19: 393–407.

Rosenberg, Terry, and Robert Lake. 1976. "Toward a Revised Model of Residential Segregation and Succession: Puerto Ricans in New York." *American Journal of Sociology* 8 (March): 142–50.

Sakoda, James. 1981. "A Generalized Index of Dissimilarity." *Demography* 18 (May): 245–50.

Schechter, Alan. 1973. "Impact of Open Housing Laws on Suburban Realtors." *Urban Affairs Quarterly* 8 (June): 439–63.

Smith, Barton. 1977. "Separating Discriminatory Segregation from De Facto

Segregation." Unpublished paper. Office of Policy Development and Research, U.S. Department of Housing and Urban Development, Washington, D.C., December.

Spain, Daphne, and Larry Long. 1981. "Black Movers to the Suburbs: Are They Moving to Predominantly White Neighborhoods?" Special Demographic Analyses, CDS–80–4. U.S. Bureau of the Census, Washington, D.C., December.

————, John Reid, and Larry Long. 1980. "Housing Successions among Blacks and Whites in Cities and Suburbs." *Current Population Reports*, Series P–23, No. 101. Washington, D.C.: U.S. Government Printing Office, January.

Taeuber, Karl. 1983. "Racial Residential Segregation, 1980." In *A Decent Home*, by the Citizens Commission on Civil Rights. Washington, D.C.: National Center for Policy Review, April.

————, and Alma Taeuber. 1965. *Negroes in Cities*. Chicago: Aldine.

U.S. Bureau of the Census. 1980. "Money Income and Poverty Status of Families and Persons in the United States: 1979." *Current Population Reports*, Series P–60, No. 125. Washington, D.C.: U.S. Government Printing Office.

White, Carl. 1979. "A Survey of Marketing Practices in Real Estate Offices within the City of Columbus, Ohio and Franklin County." Unpublished report to the City of Columbus, Ohio. Housing Opportunity Center of Columbus, Ohio, 30 August.

White, Michael. 1983. "The Measurement of Spatial Segregation." *American Journal of Sociology* 88 (March): 1008–18.

Wilson, William. 1980. *The Declining Significance of Race*. Chicago: University of Chicago Press.

Yinger, John, George Galster, Barton Smith, and Frederick Eggers. 1979. "The Status of Research into Racial Discrimination and Segregation in American Housing Markets: A Research Agenda for the Department of Housing and Urban Development." *Occasional Papers in Housing and Community Development* 6 (December). Office of Policy Development and Research. Washington, D.C.: U.S. Department of Housing and Urban Development.

Zehner, Robert, and F. Stuart Chapin. 1974. *Across the City Line: A White Community in Transition*. Lexington, Mass.: Lexington Books.

Chapter Four
Segregation and Discrimination of Hispanic Americans
An Exploratory Analysis

FRANKLIN J. JAMES*

EILEEN A. TYNAN

A great deal of research has measured the discrimination and segregation experienced by blacks in urban housing markets.[1] Audit-based evidence summarized by Newburger (1984) also shows that discrimination remains a significant problem for blacks seeking either rental or owner-occupied housing in most metropolitan areas. Very little research has examined these problems as they are encountered by Hispanics.[2]

Hispanics in 1980 comprised 6.4 percent of the U.S. population; they are growing in number far more rapidly than blacks.[3] Previous evidence on the residential segregation of Hispanics, based largely on Hispanic experiences during the 1960s, suggested that Hispanics were moving rapidly toward racial and social integration (Massey and Mullen 1984). Progress toward residential integration appeared more rapid among Hispanics than among blacks between 1960 and 1970. The "ultimate probability of residential contact with Anglos" was judged to be "much lower for blacks than for Hispanics" (ibid., p. 836).

However, two recent audit studies measuring discrimination against Hispanics have found that Hispanics encounter more serious discrimination than blacks. One study, which measured discrimination against Chicanos in rental housing in Dallas (Hakken 1979), found that discrimination in Dallas against Chicanos was at least as severe as that against blacks. In fact, discrimination against dark-skinned Chicanos was found to be more severe than the discrimination encountered by blacks.[4] A second study measuring discrimination against Hispanics, blacks, and Southeast Asians in Boston also suggests that discrimination against Hispanics was as, or more, severe than that experienced by blacks (Feins, Bratt, and Hollister 1981; Feins and Holshouser 1984).

Optimistic evidence from the 1960s regarding lessened Hispanic segregation appears inconsistent with observations of severe discrimination currently experienced by Hispanics in urban housing markets. Have Hispanics continued to make rapid progress toward integration despite such severe discrimination? The recent audit studies may be signaling that Hispanics are encountering

*This research was funded by the Colorado Civil Rights Division and by the Office of Fair Housing and Equal Opportunity of the U.S. Department of Housing and Urban Development (HUD). Responsibility for the findings and analysis lies entirely with the authors. The views and opinions in this chapter do not represent those of HUD or the U.S. government.

tougher barriers to fair housing and equal opportunity than they did in the past.

To be sure, interrelationships between housing segregation and discrimination are not clearly understood. For instance, Galster, in this section, concludes that segregation is significantly increased by discrimination only when it is prevalent on a *metropolitan* scale in *both* rental and for sale housing. The audit studies of discrimination against Hispanics cited above focused on central cities, not metropolitan areas. The Dallas study also did not examine discrimination in the sales market. Thus, if one accepts Galster's conclusion, severe discrimination could conceivably be accompanied by modest, declining segregation of Hispanics.[5]

This chapter provides preliminary evidence describing changes in Hispanic segregation in three metropolitan areas during the 1970s: Denver, Houston, and Phoenix. For the purpose of comparison, the study also examines trends in the segregation of blacks in these same metropolitan areas.[6] Events in Denver, Houston, and Phoenix suggest larger patterns—inasmuch as two-thirds of the nation's Hispanic population lives in the sunbelt states.

The chapter also presents the results of a new, comprehensive audit of discrimination encountered by blacks and Hispanics seeking to rent or purchase housing in the Denver metropolitan area. The audit utilizes methods and techniques developed in HUD's national Housing Market Practices Survey and in the audit of discrimination in Boston (U.S. Department of Housing and Urban Development 1979; Feins and Bratt 1983). The audit had as its primary goal the measurement of the overall severity of discrimination against blacks and Hispanics. A subsidiary objective was to gather more information on exactly how discrimination and segregation are linked. To meet this second objective, the audit measured patterns and severity of discrimination in three types of neighborhoods:

1. Largely Hispanic (and black) census tracts within the city of Denver, termed "minority city neighborhoods";
2. Predominantly Anglo neighborhoods within the city of Denver, termed "Anglo city neighborhoods"; and
3. Predominantly Anglo census tracts in suburban counties surrounding Denver, termed "Anglo suburban neighborhoods."[7]

As will be seen, important spatial differences exist in the severity of discrimination in Denver among these types of neighborhoods. Although these differences are complex, they are a likely influence contributing to maintaining segregation among Hispanics.

The Segregation of Hispanics

The extent of neighborhood segregation of Hispanics is in part a function of how Hispanics are defined.[8] The definition used here—persons of Spanish origin—includes all persons who retain some cultural or ethnic identification with Spanish-speaking nations. A definition that focused on recent immigrants from such nations would likely show greater segregation, as would a measure that focused on Hispanics of lower socioeconomic status (Grebler, Moore, and Guzman 1970; Massey and Mullen 1984).

Keeping this in mind, evidence from the 1970 and 1980 censuses for Denver, Houston, and Phoenix shows that:

- Hispanics were markedly segregated from *both* Anglos and blacks in 1970 and 1980;
- The extent of Hispanic segregation did not diminish markedly in any of the three cities during the 1970s, and increased significantly in one; and
- By contrast, blacks made considerable progress toward integration in Denver and Phoenix, though not in Houston.[9]

The Pattern of Segregation

Because so little research has focused on the neighborhood segregation of Hispanics, it is useful to begin with simple descriptions. Figures 1 and 2 describe patterns of residence of Hispanics and blacks in Denver in 1980. It is apparent that Hispanics were more dispersed among Denver census tracts than were blacks. In particular, significant numbers of Hispanics lived in northern and southwestern portions of the Denver metropolitan area, areas with hardly any black population. More importantly, a close comparison of the two figures suggests a significant degree of segregation of both blacks and Hispanics from one another. Blacks were very highly concentrated in inner-city neighborhoods extending east from the downtown to the edge of the city of Denver. A number of these tracts were 50 percent or more black. By contrast, census tracts in which the population was predominantly Hispanic were located to the *west* of Denver's downtown extending in a band from north to south along major transportation lines.

These general patterns of residence of Hispanics and blacks were similar to those that had prevailed in Denver in 1970. Figure 3 maps neighborhood patterns of Hispanics in 1970. A comparison with Figure 1 shows that the primary change during the decade was an extension of Hispanics into low density suburban areas. Comparable maps show similar trends in Houston and Phoenix: that is, relatively dispersed patterns of residence of Hispanics compared to blacks, marked spreading out of both groups among neighborhoods, and significant segregation of blacks and Hispanics from one another, in both 1970 and 1980 (see James, McCummings, and Tynan 1984).

Exposure rates provide a simple quantitative indicator of trends in the degree to which various racial or ethnic groups share urban neighborhoods. The exposure rate is the average representation of various racial or ethnic groups in the neighborhoods of the group being studied (James, McCummings, and

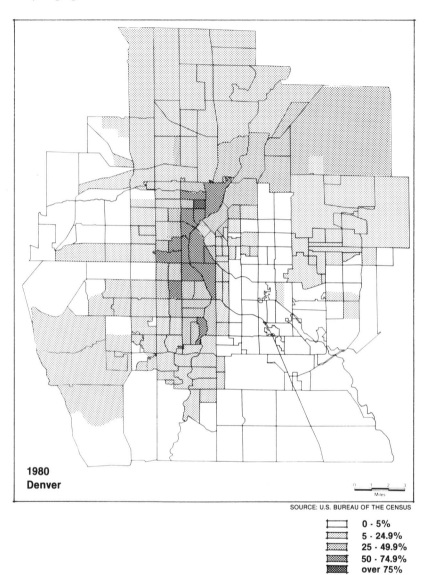

1980
Denver

SOURCE: U.S. BUREAU OF THE CENSUS

0 - 5%
5 - 24.9%
25 - 49.9%
50 - 74.9%
over 75%

Figure 1. Hispanic Composition of Neighborhoods (Percentage of Population of Spanish Origin)

Tynan 1984). Such rates strongly suggest that the spreading out of Hispanics among census tracts in Denver, Houston, and Phoenix was not a symptom of greater neighborhood integration of Hispanics, but rather of simple growth in the overall Hispanic populations of the three areas (Table 1). As can be seen, the racial and ethnic compositions of the neighborhoods of the average His-

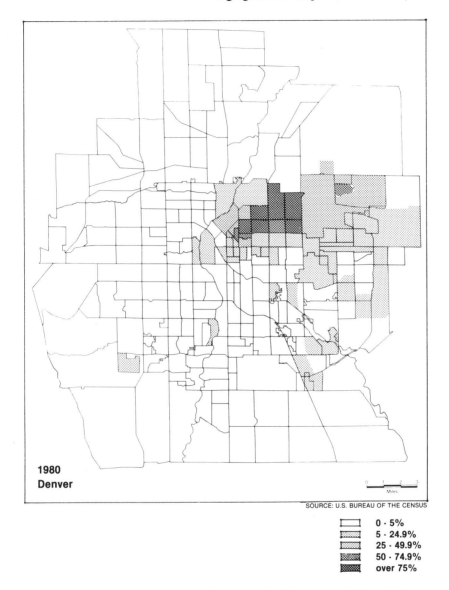

SOURCE: U.S. BUREAU OF THE CENSUS

	0 - 5%
	5 - 24.9%
	25 - 49.9%
	50 - 74.9%
	over 75%

Figure 2. Racial Composition of Neighborhoods (Percentage of Population Black)

panic hardly changed in any of the three metropolitan areas during the 1970s. Indeed, Hispanic exposure to Anglos *fell* slightly in Houston (from .55 to .51), and held substantially constant in Denver and Phoenix.

Exposure rates are sensitive to the overall racial and ethnic composition of the metropolitan area. A number of quantitative indicators are available to

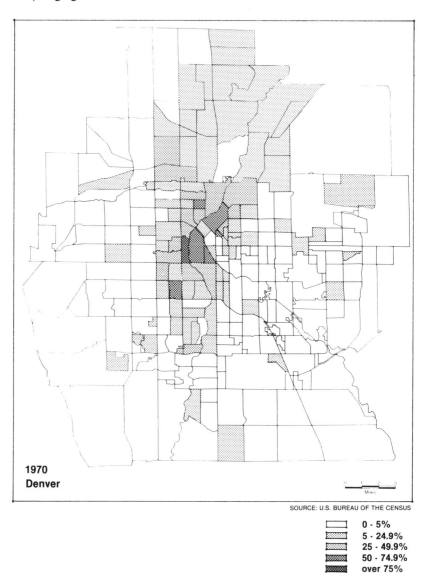

SOURCE: U.S. BUREAU OF THE CENSUS

1970
Denver

☐	0 - 5%
▦	5 - 24.9%
▦	25 - 49.9%
▦	50 - 74.9%
■	over 75%

Figure 3. Hispanic Composition of Neighborhoods (Percentage of
Population of Spanish Origin)

measure neighborhood segregation, controlling for overall population mix.
These segregation indexes thus permit comparisons of residential patterns
among areas and over time.[10]

Table 1 also presents estimates of the segregation indexes for the various
ethnic and racial groups in Denver, Houston, and Phoenix metropolitan areas

Table 1. Exposure Rates and Segregation Indexes of Hispanics in Denver, Houston, and Phoenix, 1970 and 1980

	Denver 1970	Denver 1980	Houston 1970	Houston 1980	Phoenix 1970	Phoenix 1980
Exposure Rate[a]						
Hispanics	.285	.276	.278	.351	.331	.329
Anglos	.637	.646	.551	.509	.563	.567
Blacks	.059	.049	.160	.118	.075	.064
Others	.020	.030	.011	.021	.030	.030
Segregation Index[b]						
Hispanics	.218	.189	.203	.240	.241	.228
Anglos	.380	.262	.517	.421	.041	.206
Blacks	.592	.393	.611	.586	.359	.210
Others	.012	.009	.009	.031	.106	.108

[a]Exposure rates indicate the weighted average racial or ethnic composition of the census tracts inhabited by Hispanics.

[b]The segregation index is defined as:

$$S_j = \frac{_jP^*_j - \frac{N_j}{N}}{1 - \frac{N_j}{N}}$$

, where $_jP^*_j$ is the exposure rate of group j to itself, and (N_j/N) is the proportion of the area population comprised of group j.

Source: U.S. Bureau of the Census, Fourth Count Data File, 1970; and Summary Tape file 1, 1980.

for 1970 and 1980. As can be seen, the segregation indexes verify that progress toward integration was quite limited for Hispanics. In Denver and Phoenix, Hispanic segregation declined, but only slightly. The segregation index actually rose by 20 percent for Hispanics in the Houston metropolitan area. Overall, these measures of Hispanic segregation were very similar across the three cities and changed little during the 1970s. In contrast, although blacks were more segregated in 1970 than Hispanics, they experienced a greater movement toward integration.

Of course, it should be emphasized that evidence from three metropolitan areas cannot establish national patterns during the 1970s. More work needs to be done in more metropolitan areas. Nevertheless, it appears that optimistic predictions of progress for Hispanics toward integration may have been proven wrong during the 1970s.

Patterns of Housing Discrimination

In order to provide evidence on the role of discrimination in fostering Hispanic segregation, 134 audits or tests of the treatment accorded Hispanics in housing markets were conducted in the Denver metropolitan area during the summer of 1982. In these audits, pairs of Anglo and Hispanic testers responded to advertisements of housing units for sale and rent in Denver's two major newspapers. Auditors were matched by sex and general age and assigned similar family and economic identities. Thorough records were made by both auditors of the treatment they received from the real estate agents (James, McCummings, and Tynan 1984). To provide a benchmark against which to interpret the Hispanic audits, precisely comparable audits were performed at the same time and in the same manner to measure the discrimination encountered by blacks seeking housing in Denver.[11]

In line with earlier audits, three types of discrimination by real estate professionals were measured in Denver:

1. Differential amounts or qualities of information provided Anglo and minority testers regarding the number and characteristics of housing units available for rent or purchase.

2. Differences in the terms and conditions on which housing was said to be available to Anglo and minority auditors. (Examples of such terms and conditions include sales prices or rents, financing or lease requirements, and application procedures and requirements.)

3. Salesmanship or steering practiced by real estate professionals. (Accurate information provided begrudgingly or incompletely can deter minority persons from obtaining housing that meets their needs. Whether subtle or blatant, practices that encourage minorities to choose housing in minority or integrated neighborhoods can forestall progress toward neighborhood integration and limit minority housing options.)

As noted above, audits were performed in the three types of neighborhoods: minority city neighborhoods, Anglo city neighborhoods, and Anglo suburban neighborhoods.[12]

Audit Findings: Housing for Sale

Concealment of information regarding available housing can be a potent constraint on minority housing choices, and is extremely difficult for individuals to detect. Auditors were directed to first inquire about the availability of the advertised home and then request information on other comparable units in the same neighborhood. If agents failed to identify several such units, the auditors were directed to request information on similar housing in other neighborhoods, and on alternative types of housing that might meet their needs.

On average, in the Denver metropolitan area, Anglo auditors were given the same information as Hispanics about the availability of the advertised house (Table 2). However, Anglo auditors were given more information about other houses available for purchase than were the Hispanic auditors. Overall, real estate agents volunteered an average of 1.7 houses to Hispanic auditors as serious possibilities as opposed to 2.1 houses volunteered to Anglo auditors.

Table 2. Amount and Quality of Information Given Hispanic and Anglo Auditors in Sales Market, by Neighborhood Type, Denver and Suburbs, 1982

Indicators	Neighborhood Type							
	Hispanic City Neighborhoods		Anglo City Neighborhoods		Anglo Suburban Neighborhoods		Metro Area	
	Hispanic Auditors	Anglo Auditors	Hispanic Auditors	Anglo Auditors	Hispanic Auditors	Anglo Auditors	Hispanic Auditors	Anglo Auditors
Percentage of Auditors Told That								
Advertised unit available for immediate inspection	100	95	95	81	68	80	86	85
More than two similar units available in same neighborhood	29	19	19	48	47*	60*	33**	44**
One or more similar houses available in different neighborhoods	29	52	29*	57*	19*	48*	25*	51*
One or more housing units available with different characteristics	48	52	48	52	30*	57*	40	54
Offered use of multiple list or similar directory	24	38	29	29	19	38	23*	35*
Average Number of Homes								
Suggested as "serious possibilities"	1.5	1.7	1.6	1.9	1.9	2.6	1.7	2.1
Invited to inspect	1.3	1.4	1.5	1.5	2.0	2.1	1.7	1.7
Actually inspected	0.9	1.1	1.0	1.3	1.0	1.4	1.0	1.3

*Statistically signficant difference at .01 level.
**Statistically signficant difference at .05 level.

The results imply that Hispanic home buyers would have to visit four agents in order to get as much information as Anglos can get by visiting three agents.[13]

The auditors were instructed to make every effort to actually inspect at least one of the houses identified by the agents as a serious possibility. Discrimination by agents had the effect of limiting Hispanics to the *advertised* unit. Three-fourths of the Hispanic auditors inspected the advertised unit. Only 55 percent of the Anglo auditors inspected the advertised unit; fully 40 percent of the Anglo auditors inspected other units they or the agents considered more likely to meet their needs.

No evidence was found suggesting that agents reported different home sales prices or down payment requirements to the Hispanic and Anglo auditors. However, significant evidence was found that some agents offered Hispanics less assistance with home financing arrangements. Because mortgage rates were extremely high during the audit period, the sales market was a buyer's market and a lot of "creative financing" was taking place. Real estate agents suggested various forms of creative financing to 39 percent of the Anglo auditors as opposed to 27 percent of the Hispanic auditors.

Racial steering is often very difficult to detect because it can take so many forms. One technique that has been alleged to exist in Denver revolves around concerns about the quality of inner-city schools and the busing issue. It has been alleged that negative comments about the city school system have often been used to steer Anglo home buyers to Anglo suburban neighborhoods (Orfield 1980).

The audit teams requested the same information about the advertised house, the neighborhood surrounding the advertised house, and the public schools. Compared to the Hispanics, Anglo auditors received significantly more positive comments about the advertised homes and the public schools. This was true in all types of neighborhoods. They also received more negative comments. These findings suggest that real estate agents exerted more effort to sell homes to Anglo auditors than they did to Hispanics. Real estate agents often requested information on how the auditor could be reached in the future; 80 percent of the Anglo auditors were requested to give their phone number as opposed to 64 percent of the Hispanics.[14]

A close review of Table 2 shows that these overall metropolitan indicators of discrimination understate by a considerable margin the possibility that a Hispanic seeking "for sale" housing outside an established Hispanic neighborhood would be discriminated against. Discrimination is shown to have been far more common and severe in Anglo suburban neighborhoods than in Hispanic city neighborhoods (Table 2). The data also suggest, but do not prove, that discrimination is more severe in Anglo *city* neighborhoods than in Hispanic city areas. The audits did not detect significant discrimination against Hispanic home buyers in terms of housing availability in Denver's Hispanic neighborhoods.

The fact that discrimination against Hispanic home buyers is more common and more severe in Denver's Anglo neighborhoods than in Hispanic areas has the straightforward implication that discrimination exacerbates segregation among Hispanic homeowners in Denver. When it actually is encountered by Hispanics, it limits information and access to homes in Anglo neighborhoods. Fears of discrimination doubtlessly also lead some Hispanic home buyers to focus their housing searches in Hispanic areas where they are less likely to encounter it.

Table 3 presents several indicators of metropolitan discrimination encountered by Hispanics and blacks seeking for sale housing. As can be seen, the data suggest that Hispanics encountered more severe discrimination than did

Table 3. Audit Indicators of Discrimination in Housing Availability
Encountered by Hispanics and Blacks, Denver Metro Area

Indicators (percent of auditors told that:)	Hispanic Audits		Black Audits	
	Hispanic	Anglo	Black	Anglo
Advertised unit available for immediate inspection	86	85	90	94
More than two similar units available in same neighborhood	33***	44**	27	43
One or more similar houses availabe in different neighborhoods	25*	51*	31	35
One or more housing units availabe with different characteristics	40***	54***	35	35

*Statistically significant differences, .01 level.

**Statistically significant differences, .05 level.

***Statistically significant differences, .10 level.

blacks. Indeed, none of the indicators presented in the table suggests statistically significant discrimination measures for blacks.[15]

Findings: Housing for Rent

Patterns of discrimination in Denver's rental housing market are quite different than in the sales market. Discrimination against Hispanics regarding housing availability was not found to be as widespread in the rental housing market as in the sales market. Hispanic auditors were twice as likely as Anglo auditors to be told that the advertised units were unavailable. Hispanic auditors were also twice as likely not to be told of serious rental housing possibilities that might meet their needs. In neither case, however, were the differences statistically significant in the metropolitan area as a whole.[16]

The major explanation for the apparent lack of evidence for discrimination is that discrimination against Hispanic renters was concentrated in Denver's Hispanic neighborhoods. In Hispanic neighborhoods, agents for rental housing commonly concealed the availability of units to Hispanic auditors, were less likely to identify any units that might meet the needs of the Hispanic auditors, failed to offer Hispanics a place on waiting lists, and invited significantly fewer Hispanics to inspect units than they did Anglos. By contrast, most of the indicators suggest that agents in Anglo neighborhoods offered much the same basic information on rental housing availability to Hispanic and Anglo auditors. As was found for home buyers, there is little evidence that agents skewed the qualitative information on housing and schools to attract Hispanics to Hispanic neighborhoods, or to steer Anglos away from these areas. In general, Anglo auditors were given more information, positive and negative, in all types of neighborhoods.

These findings appear to imply that discrimination is not a strong force for segregation in Denver's rental housing market. This finding, however, requires more research and verification before it is accepted. It could result from specific housing market conditions prevailing at the time of the study. This was a time of rapid housing inflation and economic recession, with intense demand for lower cost rental housing. Excess demand among Anglos for lower cost housing could have led landlords in Hispanic areas to seek out Anglos in the hope of securing more stable tenants or higher rents. However, no evidence was found in the audits to suggest rent premiums were paid by either Hispanic or Anglo auditors.

Alternatively, the findings could be a result of inherent biases in the characteristics of units approached in the audits: that is, units advertised in local newspapers as for sale or for rent. Advertised units from minority neighborhoods are likely to be the higher cost and quality units in the areas. Landlords from such housing may seek to enforce racial or ethnic "quotas" on tenant composition in order to maintain the attractiveness of the units to Anglos as well as Hispanics.

Conclusions

The evidence from Denver, Houston, and Phoenix suggests that the housing options of Hispanics are curtailed by segregation and discrimination as much as are those of blacks. Housing discrimination per se appears to be at least as frequent against Denver's Hispanics as against that city's blacks. Overall, Hispanics are somewhat less segregated than blacks. However, Hispanic segregation does not appear to have diminished during the 1970s, whereas the segregation of blacks frequently did.

The findings suggest that Hispanics are encountering more stringent barriers to equal housing opportunity than they did during the 1960s. After examining 1960s data, one researcher concluded:

> If there is an underclass in the United States, Hispanics cannot be considered "permanent" members of it in the same way as blacks. Our results point consistently to an ongoing process of assimilation among Hispanics circa 1970. Unlike blacks, they are able to translate social mobility into residential mobility. Hispanics are simply not trapped in the barrio in the same way that blacks are trapped in the ghetto. (Massey and Mullen 1984:870)

Trends during the 1970s in Denver, Houston, and Phoenix imply a much more pessimistic diagnosis.

It is apparent that far too little research and public attention has been placed on understanding and ameliorating the unique housing problems of Hispanics. The major research priority is to establish that findings from Denver, Houston, and Phoenix are applicable to other places, by extension to other metropolitan areas of the research methodologies reported here. If further research supports the conclusions of this chapter, one important question will be why the experience of Hispanics was so different in the 1970s and the 1960s and what the difference implies about likely future trends. A second important issue will be appropriate policy responses.

With respect to the first issue, growing international in-migration is a likely contributor to segregation and discrimination against the Hispanic community. Growing numbers of migrants are boosting Hispanic populations markedly in areas receiving these migrant flows, such as New York, Miami, Houston, and Los Angeles. New migrants may be contributing to wider average cultural and language differences between Hispanics and Anglos. The result could be a "circle the wagons" mentality among Anglos and among native Hispanic Americans.

With respect to policy issues, the evidence clearly supports stronger efforts to curtail housing discrimination against Hispanics. If effective, such efforts are likely both to improve Hispanic housing standards and to increase Hispanic integration. At a minimum, fair housing agencies at HUD and in the states should mount effective outreach efforts into the Hispanic community. Hispanics do not seek the help of such agencies nearly as frequently as do blacks (James, McCummings, and Tynan 1984). Why this is true is unknown. However, this behavior attenuates the already generally weak protections of civil rights laws for victims of discrimination.

NOTES

1. This research is well summarized in Kain and Quigley 1975; Yinger 1979.

2. Examples of the fragmentary previous research on Hispanic housing conditions are provided by deLeeuw, Schnare, and Struyk 1976; Yezer 1980; Hakken 1983.

3. For purposes of this report, Hispanics are defined as nonblack persons of Spanish origin. The research on which this chapter is based is presented in more detail in James, McCummings, and Tynan 1984.

4. For example, dark-skinned Hispanics were 43 percent more likely than non-Hispanic whites to be given inferior information about the availability of rental units. Light-skinned Hispanics were 16 percent more likely to encounter this form of discrimination than were non-Hispanic whites. For purposes of comparison, blacks in Dallas were 17 percent more likely to encounter this type of discrimination than were Anglos. Hakken 1979.

5. However, theoretical and empirical research has shown that the severity of *black*

segregation can be attributed to actual or feared experiences of blacks with discrimination (Kain and Quigley 1975; Yinger 1979; Bianchi, Farley, and Spain 1982). Moreover, Galster's empirical evidence is highly suspect. His conclusions are based on observed weak relationships between discrimination as measured in 1977 and segregation prevailing almost a decade earlier, in 1970. It would be surprising to find a strong relationship given the wide time interval separating the two measurements.

6. A limited budget dictated the focus on only three metropolitan areas.

7. Anglos are defined as whites not of Spanish origin. Largely minority tracts are those in which minorities comprise at least 30 percent of the population. Predominantly Anglo tracts are those in which Anglos comprise at least 93 percent of the population.

8. Quantitative research on the characteristics and circumstances of Hispanics has been impeded by uncertainty regarding who should be counted as Hispanic. For example, the U.S. Census Bureau utilized several different definitions of Hispanics in reports of the 1970 census, causing needless confusion. Fortunately, there is increasing consensus among researchers on how best to define Hispanics. Most statistics now reflect the concept of "Spanish origin." Under the current procedures of the U.S. Bureau of the Census (1983), a person was counted as of Spanish origin in the 1980 census if he or she answered "yes" to the following question: "Is this person of Spanish/Hispanic origin or descent?" Much the same question was asked of a sample of persons in the 1970 census.

9. Because so little research has focused on the neighborhood segregation of Hispanics, it is useful to describe patterns of residence of Hispanics and blacks in the Denver metropolitan area in 1980. Hispanics were more dispersed among Denver census tracts than blacks. In particular, significant numbers of Hispanics lived in northern or southwestern portions of the metropolitan area, areas with hardly any black population. Blacks were highly concentrated in inner-city neighborhoods extending east from the central business district to the edge of the city of Denver. A number of these tracts were 50 percent or more black. By contrast, census tracts in which the population was predominantly Hispanic were located to the west of Denver's downtown. These patterns of residence of the two groups were similar to those that had prevailed in Denver in 1970. The primary change during the decade was an extension of Hispanics into low density suburban areas to the west and north of downtown.

10. These indexes have been used primarily to measure the degree of segregation of blacks from whites (Lieberson 1980; deLeeuw, Schnare, and Struyk 1976). A segregation index of 1.0 indicates complete segregation, that is, racial and ethnic groups live in neighborhoods comprised totally of their own group. A value of 0 indicates perfect integration—for example, a situation in which groups live in neighborhoods where the percentage of blacks, Anglos, and others is the same as in the metropolitan-wide percentage.

11. These audit methodologies were used in three previous research studies, the Housing Market Practices Survey (U.S. Department of Housing and Urban Development 1979), the Chicano Dallas Audit (Hakken 1979), and a study of discrimination against blacks in Boston (Feins and Bratt 1983). The instruments used to record the treatment of auditors were based on the instruments developed for the Boston audit. Or course, audits only measure discrimination that occurs early in a real estate transaction. Discrimination at later stages (e.g., in credit checks, mortgage applications, and insurance arrangements) cannot be estimated using audit methodologies (Kain 1980; Feins and Bratt 1983).

12. The obvious drawback of the neighborhood typology is that a number of neighborhoods in which Hispanics comprised between 7 and 29 percent of the population were not included in the tests. Budget constraints made it impossible to treat these areas as a fourth neighborhood type.

13. The audits also show that agents did not encourage Hispanics to identify housing opportunities on their own. A multiple listing book or similar directory of homes for sale was offered twice as frequently to Anglo auditors as to Hispanic auditors.

14. There was evidence of less intense "salesmanship" efforts by agents for Hispanics than for Anglos, even in Hispanic city neighborhoods. There was also evidence that agents volunteered more help in arranging financing for Anglo auditors in these neighborhoods. These types of discrimination were found to be significant throughout the metropolitan area. James, McCummings, and Tynan 1984.

15. A number of other indicators did demonstrate significant discrimination against blacks. Ibid.

16. Hispanics were more likely than Anglos to be offered to be entered on waiting lists. This difference, however, could reflect either favorable or unfavorable treatment.

REFERENCES

Bianchi, Suzanne M., Reynolds Farley, and Daphne Spain. 1982. "Racial Inequalities in Housing: An Examination of Recent Trends." *Demography*.

Feins, Judith D., and Rachel G. Bratt. 1983. "Barred in Boston: Racial Discrimination in Housing." *Journal of the American Planning Association* 49 (Summer): 344–55.

———, Rachel Bratt, and Robert Hollister. 1981. *Final Report—A Study of Racial Discrimination in the Boston Housing Market*. Cambridge, Mass.: Abt Associates, November.

———, and William Holshouser, Jr. 1984. "The Multiple Uses of Audit-Based Research Evidence from Boston." Paper presented at the HUD Conference on Fair Housing Testing, Washington, D.C., 6–7 December.

Grebler, Leo, Joan Moore, and Ralph Guzman. 1970. *The Mexican American People: The Nation's Second Largest Minority*. New York: The Free Press.

Hakken, Jon. 1979. "Discrimination against Chicanos in the Dallas Rental Housing Market: An Experimental Extension of the Housing Market Practices Survey." Division of Evaluation, Office of Policy Development and Research, U.S. Department of Housing and Urban Development, Washington, D.C.

———. 1983. "Housing the Hispanic Population: Are Special Programs and Policies Needed?" Unpublished report, Office of Policy Development and Research, U.S. Department of Housing and Urban Development, Washington, D.C., March.

James, Franklin J., Betty McCummings, and Eileen A Tynan. 1984. *Minorities in the Sunbelt: Segregation, Discrimination and Housing Conditions of Hispanics and Blacks*. New Brunswick, N.J.: Rutgers University Center for Urban Policy Research.

Kain, John F. 1980. *National Urban Policy Paper on the Impacts of Housing Market Discrimination and Segregation on the Welfare of Minorities*. Cambridge: Harvard University Press, April.

———, and John M. Quigley. 1975. *Housing Markets and Racial Discrimination*. New York: National Bureau of Economic Research.

deLeeuw, Frank, Ann B. Schnare, and Raymond J. Struyk. 1976. "Housing." In *The Urban Predicament*, edited by Nathan Glazer and William Gorham. Washington, D.C.: The Urban Institute.

Lieberson, Stanley. 1980. *A Piece of the Pie.* Berkeley: University of California Press.

Massey, Douglas S., and Brendan P. Mullen. 1984. "Processes of Hispanic and Black Spatial Assimilation." *American Journal of Psychology* 89 (January): 836–73.

Newburger, Harriet. 1984. "Recent Evidence on Discrimination in Housing." HUD–PDR–786. Office of Policy Development and Research, U.S. Department of Housing and Urban Development, Washington, D.C., April.

Orfield, Gary. 1980. "Housing and School Integration in Three Metropolitan Areas: A Policy Analysis of Denver, Columbus and Phoenix." Office of Economic Planning and Development, U.S. Department of Housing and Urban Development, Washington, D.C.

U.S. Bureau of the Census. 1983. *Public-Use Microdata Samples Technical Documentation.* Washington, D.C.: U.S. Department of Commerce.

U.S. Department of Housing and Urban Development. 1979. *Measuring Racial Discrimination in American Housing Markets: The Housing Market Practices Survey.* Office of Policy Development and Research. Washington, D.C.: U.S. Department of Housing and Urban Development, April.

Yezer, Anthony. 1980. "How Well Are We Housed? 1. Hispanics." HUD–PPD–33393. Office of Policy Development and Research, U.S. Department of Housing and Urban Development, Washington, D.C., July.

Yinger, John. 1979. "Prejudice and Discrimination in the Urban Housing Market." In *Current Issues in Urban Economics*, edited by Peter Mieskowski and Mahlon Straszheim. Baltimore: The Johns Hopkins University Press.

Chapter Five
The Influence of Race and Income on Racial Segregation and Housing Policy
JOHN F. KAIN

Black Americans have been largely excluded from the rapid suburbanization that has occurred since World War II: despite a 42 percent increase in the black population in suburban areas between 1970 and 1980, blacks in 1980 accounted for only 6.1 percent of the suburban ring population, as compared to 22.5 percent of the central city residents in U.S. metropolitan areas.[1] Moreover, although growing numbers of black households are buying and renting in previously all-white neighborhoods, most of the recent increase in the suburban black population appears to be accounted for by the expansion of central city ghettos into adjacent suburban communities.

These trends have not gone unnoticed. Scholars and policymakers alike have shown concern and have argued for programs and policies that would reverse them. The Kerner Commission, for example, in analyzing the causes of the riots that swept American cities during the summers of 1966 and 1967, found that "Discrimination and segregation have long permeated much of American life" and that "they now threaten the future of every American."[2] Contrasting the experience of black Americans with that of earlier immigrant groups, the commission noted:

Thousands of Negro families have attained incomes, living standards, and cultural levels matching or surpassing those of whites who have "upgraded" themselves from distinctly ethnic neighbors. Yet most Negro families have remained within predominantly Negro neighborhoods, primarily because they have been effectively excluded from white residential areas.

Their exclusion has been accomplished through various discriminatory practices, some obvious and overt, others subtle and hidden. Deliberate efforts are sometimes made to discourage Negro families from purchasing or renting homes in all-white neighborhoods. Intimidation and threats of violence have ranged from throwing garbage on lawns and making threatening phone calls to burning crosses in yards and even dynamiting property. More often, real estate agents simply refuse to show homes to Negro buyers.

Many middle-class Negro families, therefore, cease looking for homes beyond all-Negro areas or nearby "changing" neighborhoods. For them, trying to move into all-white neighborhoods is not worth the psychological efforts and costs required.[3]

The Kerner Commission and other critics, moreover, strongly implicated government in initially creating and then supporting segregated living patterns. The U.S. Department of Housing and Urban Development (HUD), for example, was held responsible for first allowing public housing authorities to operate racially segregated projects and then with permitting them to build new, all-black projects in ghetto areas.

During the Carter administration, HUD implemented three small pilot programs that were widely interpreted as efforts to offer minority participants in public housing and other subsidized housing programs the opportunity to obtain housing outside of ghetto neighborhoods. However, all three programs— the Areawide Housing Opportunity Program (AHOP), the Regional Housing Mobility Program (RHMP), and the Section 8 Existing-Mobility Demonstration—had as their stated objective the provision of additional housing opportunities for low-income *and* minority households outside of areas of racial *and* low-income concentration.[4] Nevertheless, in the minds of many advocates of integration the goal of providing low-income and minority households with housing outside of areas of low-income and minority concentration is synonymous with providing black, inner-city residents with housing opportunities in white or predominantly white communities. As discussed below, however, this notion is simply incorrect.

The myth that black-white differences in income is a major, if not the principal, explanation of racial segregation persists in the face of large numbers of systematic analyses that show otherwise. In combination with a desire to minimize the politically sensitive racial implications of policies, this belief has caused policy analysts, policymakers, and politicians to avoid programs aimed at reducing racial segregation, in favor of programs that would reduce racial and income segregation. Yet income and class integration has much less legal and political acceptance as a goal than racial integration. Not surprisingly, the unwillingness or inability to distinguish between race and income as causes of racial segregation, and the massive concentration of black households in American cities, produces programs that yield disappointing results when evaluated in terms of their success in reducing racial segregation.

This chapter seeks to clarify these issues by documenting the extent of racial segregation in American cities; by evaluating its causes, particularly the role of black-white income differences; and, finally, by identifying appropriate policies to reduce racial segregation.

The Extent of Segregation

Although a full understanding of the extent and nature of recent black suburbanization will have to await detailed analyses of the 1980 census, special

Table 1. Black Percentage of Total Population and School Enrollment, by Type of School, Geographic Area, and Year, Cleveland SMSA, 1970–1978

| Type and Year | Elementary Schools Central City | | | All Grades | | | | | |
| | All | East | West | Central City | Suburban | | | Cuyahoga | Rest of Urban Area |
					All	East	West		
Public Schools									
1970	NA	NA	NA	57.1%	6.3%	13.0%	0.3%	29.1%	NA
1974	56.3%	4.2%	84.1%	57.6	9.4	19.7	0.3	30.1	NA
1977	NA	NA	NA	60.9	12.3	26.1	0.5	33.5	NA
1978	63.9	7.5	88.9	63.4	13.6	28.1	0.6	34.4	1.9
Other Schools									
1978	17.4	NA	NA	16.2	3.8	NA	NA	8.5	NA
Public and Catholic Schools	NA	NA	NA	55.2	11.6	NA	NA	29.6	NA
Other Church and Private Schools	NA	NA	NA	NA	NA	NA	NA	10.7	NA

Source: H. Richard Obermans, "Racial School Enrollment Patterns in Cuyahoga County, 1970-78," The Cuyahoga Plan of Ohio, Inc., Cleveland, Ohio, August 1974.

studies for a few metropolitan areas and early findings from the 1980 census provide fragmentary evidence. Public school enrollments are among the most useful data because they indicate the racial composition of individual suburban communities and, in those cities without busing, the racial composition of central city neighborhoods.[5]

Shown in Table 1 are statistics on the racial composition of public, parochial, and private schools for several years in various parts of the Cleveland standard metropolitan statistical area (SMSA). In 1970, 92 percent of all blacks lived within the central city and east of the Cuyahoga River; this general pattern persists, except that the ghetto has expanded into the adjacent suburbs to the east and south. Indeed, East Cleveland and Warrensville Heights, whose public school enrollments were 98.9 and 92.7 percent black in 1978, had merged into the central city ghetto by that year.[6]

The number of blacks in Cleveland's public schools increased from 57.1 percent in 1970 to 63.4 percent in 1978. As the east-west breakdown indicates, however, the city's schools remain intensely segregated, mirroring the pattern of housing segregation.[7] Similarly, whereas the black percentage of suburban public school enrollments increased from 6.5 percent in 1970 to 13.6 percent in 1978, nearly all of this growth occurred in the eastern suburbs bordering the central city ghetto. In 1978, 97.8 percent of the black students enrolled in suburban Cuyahoga County schools were attending schools located east of the Cuyahoga River and 91.7 percent were concentrated in six eastside districts that were more than 10 percent black.

Housing market segregation does not end with the exclusion of blacks from suburban areas. Segregation indexes calculated from census block and tract statistics for the period 1940–70 quantify the intensity of racial segregation in American cities and its changes over time.[8] These indexes, which assume values between 0 and 100, measure the extent to which observed patterns of residence location by race differ from proportional representation. The higher the value of the index, the higher the degree of residential segregation. Index values in 1970 for the 109 cities that contained more than 1,000 nonwhite households in 1940 ranged from 61.4 (East Orange, New Jersey) to 97.8 (Shreveport, Louisiana), with only 6 cities having values below 75.[9]

Determinants of Segregation

One of the most common explanations for the intense segregation of blacks is that they are poor, spend too little on housing, or differ systematically from the majority white population in terms of other characteristics affecting their choice of residence.[10] Although many tests of this socioeconomic hypothesis rely on elaborate statistical methods, even simple analyses illustrate its inadequacy. If low incomes explain the concentration of black residences in central cities, we would expect to find that most low-income whites also live in central cities and that most high-income blacks live in the suburbs. The data in Table 2 demonstrate, however, that almost as many low-income whites live in the suburban rings of the largest metropolitan areas as reside in their central cities. For example, 52 percent of Detroit's poor white families lived in suburban areas in 1970, as compared to 75 percent of all white families and 78 percent of high-income white families. In contrast, in all eleven SMSAs the percentage of high-income blacks living in suburban areas was considerably less than even the percentage of low-income whites.

Another "explanation" for residential segregation is that blacks wish "to live with their own kind," something the proponents of this view argue is a normal and healthy manifestation of a pluralistic society. The immigrant colonies that exist today in many cities are offered as evidence of the normality of this behavior. Nathan Kantrowitz argues this position on the basis of an analysis of racial and ethnic segregation in Boston: "Residential segregation in Boston between European ethnic populations has declined little during the 19th and

Table 2. Percentage of White and Black Families Living in Suburban Ring of Eleven Large SMSAs, 1970

SMSA	**** White Families **** Percent			**** Black Families **** Percent		
	Percent Total	Income <$3,000	Income >$10,000	Percent Total	Income <$3,000	Income >$10,000
New York	36.2%	16.6%	40.0%	11.5%	7.7%	14.5%
Los Angeles–Long Beach	58.3	45.9	58.1	31.5	24.6	37.5
Chicago	61.1	36.4	64.6	10.4	6.1	12.3
Philadelphia–Camden	67.6	47.8	71.7	22.6	16.9	23.4
Detroit	75.5	51.5	78.3	12.8	10.6	11.7
San Francisco–Oakland	71.9	47.4	72.8	33.1	26.5	35.2
Boston	79.8	65.9	84.5	17.6	13.3	27.1
Washington, D.C.	90.2	73.1	89.3	23.6	14.2	25.6
Pittsburgh	81.5	72.2	82.9	38.2	32.7	40.7
Cleveland	73.4	66.2	80.0	13.5	5.8	20.1
St. Louis	69.4	61.2	85.6	32.9	31.5	36.8

Notes: For New York and Chicago the suburban ring is the difference between the Standard Consolidated Area and the Central City. For St. Louis the ring is the difference between the SMSA and both East St. Louis, Ill. and St. Louis, MO. For all other cities it is the difference between the SMSA and the central city or cities.

Sources: U.S. Bureau of the Census, "Census of Housing, 1970; Metropolitan Housing Characteristics, Final Report," HC(2), Parts 30, 44, 60, 120, 149, 165, 168, 187, 195, and 232 (GPO, 1972); U.S. Bureau of the Census, "1970 Census of Population and Housing. United States Summary. General Demographic Trends for Metropolitan Areas, 1960 to 1970," Final Report, PHC (2) – 1. (GPO, 1970), Table 10, pp. 1–34.

early 20th century. Racial segregation rose during the 19th and early 20th century, but has remained stable since about 1940. . . . These conclusions indicate that racial segregation is but an extension of ethnic separation, especially since Asian and Latin ethnics show similar patterns in the contemporary city."[11]

Kantrowitz's findings are strongly disputed by Hershberg et al., who conclude from a comparative analysis of three waves of immigrants to Philadelphia that "analysis of the city's changing opportunity, structure and ecological form, and the racial discrimination encountered shows the black experience to be unique in kind and degree."[12]

Hershberg et al.'s findings for Philadelphia are supported by virtually every other study of racial and ethnic segregation. These studies have determined that the intensity of black residential segregation tends to be greater than that documented for other identifiable subgroups and that the segregation of other groups has declined over time whereas black segregation has remained at a high level or even increased.[13] It is also well to keep in mind that metropolitan areas are far less compact and employment much more dispersed than 30 to 50 years ago when the immigrant colonies flourished. Thus, Hershberg et al. observe that "today's blacks inherit the oldest stock of deteriorated housing once inhabited by two earlier waves of immigrants, but the jobs which once were nearby . . . are gone."[14]

The next section of this chapter examines the roles of income and other socioeconomic variables in explaining the residence patterns of both blacks and several nationality groups.

Income and Other Socioeconomic Determinants

Analyses of 1970 census tract and Public Use Sample data for Cleveland and of 1975 Annual Housing Survey data for Chicago provide evidence on the roles of income and other socioeconomic variables in creating and maintaining the high levels of racial segregation that characterize the nation's cities and metropolitan areas. These analyses predict the numbers and percentages of blacks that would reside in each of several subareas of Cleveland and Chicago if black households had the same probability of living in each area as whites possessing the same socioeconomic characteristics. The methods used are similar to those employed in a number of studies for other cities and earlier time periods and yield similar results.[15]

Using information on family type, family size, age of head, and income, the Cleveland analysis defines 384 household categories for black and white households as well as for nine ethnic groups and for all foreign-born whites.[16] The analysis then calculates the fraction of blacks, total foreign stock, and nine separate nationality groups that would live in the 23 geographic areas shown in Figure 1 if neither race nor national origin were factors in residential location decisions. More specifically, the predicted number of blacks, of foreign stock, or of each of the nine nationality groups living in each census tract was obtained by multiplying a_{ik}^e, the areawide proportion each racial-nationality group comprised of each household type, times H_{ik}, the total number of households of that type residing in each tract. The total predicted black, foreign stock, and nationality group population of each tract in 1970, H_j^e, was then obtained by summing over the 384 household types.

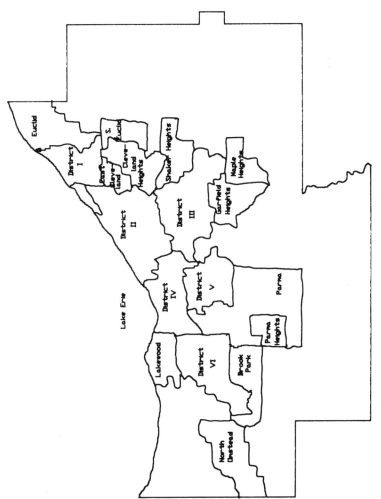

Figure 1. Central City Districts and Cuyahoga County Communities of More Than 25,000 Population, 1970

Table 3. Actual and Predicted Percentage of Foreign Stock and Black
Population, Selected Geographic Areas

Area	Percent Black Actual	Percent Black Predicted	Percent Foreign Stock Actual	Percent Foreign Stock Model I	Percent Foreign Stock Model II
Brook Park	0.3%	13.3%	20.8%	19.0%	21.7%
District 1	10.9	16.7	35.4	27.1	29.4
District 2	78.4	31.2	8.5	21.6	7.6
District 3	54.2	20.8	20.1	24.7	15.8
District 4	1.4	20.2	27.8	24.0	29.2
District 5	0.2	15.8	37.5	27.0	31.6
District 6	2.7	14.3	31.1	25.9	29.3
Cleveland Hgts.	2.5	11.4	36.7	28.8	31.6
East Cleveland	58.6	19.3	15.9	24.4	15.6
Euclid	0.4	18.1	33.1	27.2	30.9
Garfield Hgts.	4.3	13.7	35.9	26.7	29.6
Lakewood	a	13.0	28.3	27.9	31.8
Maple Hgts.	2.0	13.6	33.3	25.8	29.2
North Olmstead	a	12.6	24.0	22.6	25.8
Parma	a	12.7	36.1	25.7	29.3
Parma Hgts.	a	12.1	32.6	26.2	29.6
Shaker Hgts.	14.4	8.5	28.3	30.4	29.1
South Euclid	0.1	11.2	45.8	30.0	33.4
Balance of Cuyahog	2.6	14.9	39.9	35.4	38.9
Mentor	0.5	13.7	14.4	22.8	26.1
Geauga County	1.2	13.8	20.4	21.7	24.7
Balance of Lake Ct	1.6	14.0	21.7	23.1	26.2
Medina County	0.8	14.7	12.8	22.9	26.5
Mean	10.3	15.0	27.8	25.7	27.1
Standard Deviation	21.3	4.4	9.5	3.4	6.5
Mean Error	–	15.7	–	6.4	4.5

a = less than .1 percent

Two predictions were obtained for both the total foreign stock and individual nationality groups. Model I predicts the residence patterns of Cleveland's foreign stock ignoring the reality of racial segregation; Model II, in
contrast, predicts the residential location decisions of both total foreign stock
and individual nationality groups assuming that members of these groups (virtually all of whom are white) do not reside in the ghetto. In essence, the predictions for Model II involve revising the prediction model by multiplying the
proportion a^e_{ik} for foreign-born whites and for each of the nine nationality
groups times the total number of white households of each k type residing in
each area i in 1970, H^w_{ik}, and finally summing the predicted number of each
nationality group over the k household types.

Acknowledging the effect of racial segregation on the residential choices of
white nationality groups significantly increases the accuracy with which the
residential location patterns of both all ethnics and the nine individual nation-

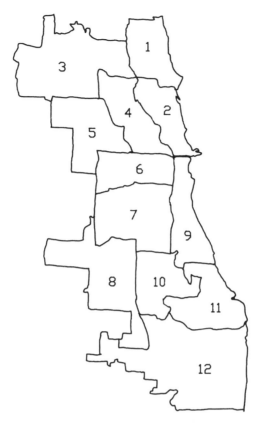

Figure 2. Annual Housing Survey Analysis Districts, City of Chicago, 1975

ality groups can be predicted. The mean prediction error for the 23 Cleveland analysis zones, for example, declines from 29 percent for Model I to 19 percent for Model II. The largest improvements, not surprisingly, occur for Cleveland's District II and East Cleveland, the areas that were mostly black in 1970.

The results for both black households and total foreign stock, shown in Table 3, clearly illustrate two aspects of their residential location patterns. First, whereas the concentrations of both all foreign born and individual nationality groups may exceed the levels that would be predicted solely from a knowledge of socioeconomic characteristics, Cleveland's foreign stock and individual nationality groups reside in significant numbers in all parts of the SMSA. Indeed, the ghetto is the only area where Cleveland's ethnics are significantly underrepresented. And second, socioeconomic characteristics explain a large part of the residence choices of Cleveland's nationality groups. Cleveland's blacks, in contrast, live in the ghetto regardless of their income or other socioeconomic characteristics; the 11,028 percent mean prediction error for blacks is the most vivid indicator of how racial discrimination dominates their residence choices.

Table 4. Actual and Predicted Numbers of Nonwhite Households and Actual and Predicted Black by Subarea, Chicago SMSA, 1975

| | 324725.316 | | Percent Black | |
| | Number of Black Households | | of Total Households | |
Area	Actual	Predicted	Actual	Predicted
Chicago				
District 1	11,328	23,852	9.1%	19.1%
District 2	13,498	24,020	10.8	19.2
District 3	1,722	14,346	1.7	14.5
District 4	3,797	13,181	3.8	23.0
District 5	26,126	20,795	29.6	23.5
District 6	50,196	23,315	87.9	40.8
District 7	4,664	17,312	6.2	22.9
District 8	1,710	13,696	2.0	16.0
District 9	68,962	26,407	81.7	31.3
District 10	68,854	22,266	96.6	31.3
District 11	74,234	23,520	86.7	27.5
District 12	45,600	16,661	64.6	23.6
Entire City	370,691	249,371	34.6	23.3
Rest of Cook County	34,856	102,043	4.9	14.3
Dupage County	2,668	22,127	1.6	13.1
Lake County	3,515	13,585	4.0	15.6
Kane County	6,371	17,275	5.5	15.0
Will & McHenry County	5,199	18,899	4.3	15.6
Entire SMSA	423,300	423,300	18.5	18.5

Source: John F. Kain, "National Urban Policy Paper on the Impacts of Housing Market Discrimination and Segregation on the Welfare of Minorities," Paper prepared for the Assistant Secretary for Community Planning and Development, U.S. Department of Housing and Urban Development, Cambridge, MA., April 1980.

As noted above, the comparable mean prediction errors for the total foreign stock are 29 percentage points using Model I and 19 percentage points using Model II. Although the small size of each of the nine individual nationality groups makes it exceedingly difficult to predict their residential locations, the mean percentage errors for Model I only range from 34 percent for Austrian-Americans to 123 percent for Italian-Americans.[17]

The Chicago analysis uses the same methodology as the Cleveland analysis except that each black and white household is assigned to one of 216 household categories defined in terms of family type, family size, age of head, and household income.[18] The geographic areas used for the Chicago SMSA include the 12 central city districts shown in Figure 2, the balance of Cook County, and the five other counties comprising the SMSA in 1975. Statistics presented in Table 4 indicate that nearly 9 out of every 10 black households (87.6 percent) in the Chicago SMSA reside in the central city and 73 percent reside in the five districts that were more than 65 percent black in 1975. If 1975 data were available for smaller geographic areas, racial segregation would be even more pronounced.

As in the Cleveland analysis, the predicted distribution of Chicago's black households differs markedly from the actual. Estimates in Table 4 indicate that the number of black households residing in the central city in 1975 is nearly 50 percent greater than the number that would choose to live in the city in the absence of housing market discrimination. Similarly, the actual number of black households residing in the rest of Cook County is only about a third as large as if racial discrimination did not exist. Comparison of actual and predicted percentages of black households even more clearly demonstrates the effect of housing market discrimination. None of the districts are predicted to be more than 14 percent black. In 1975 the predicted percentage of blacks for District 6, the subarea with the highest predicted black share, for example, was 40.8 percent or less than half the actual black share of 87.9 percent. District 10, which was 96.6 percent black in 1975, had a predicted black share of only 31.3 percent or less than one-third the actual number.

Analyses by Ann Schnare of actual and predicted distributions of black households in 76 large SMSAs (all SMSAs in excess of 250,000 population and those with a significant number of blacks) in 1970 demonstrate that the results for Cleveland and Chicago described in this chapter apply to all U.S. metropolitan areas.[19] Schnare uses a methodology similar to those discussed above for Cleveland and Chicago, except that in her analysis the predictions of black residence patterns are based solely on household income. The use of additional household characteristics would undoubtedly affect the details of Schnare's findings, but the overall conclusion would be the same.

As Figure 3 illustrates, 74 percent of black households in the 76 large SMSAs included in Schnare's study lived in tracts that were more than 50 percent black in 1970; Schnare estimates this proportion would be less than one if their location patterns depended only on household incomes. Similarly, Schnare finds that in the absence of racial discrimination over 87 percent of the sample's blacks would live in tracts in the 5 to 30 percent range, whereas the actual percentage was only 12.[20]

Self-segregation and Exclusion

Although there are difficulties of interpretation, attitudinal surveys provide little support for the view that most blacks prefer to live in segregated neighborhoods. A paper by Thomas Pettigrew provides a highly useful compilation of the findings of eleven different surveys conducted between 1958 and 1969 by seven polling organizations. In summarizing these results, Pettigrew concludes that, "when presented with a meaningful choice between an all-black neighborhood and a mixed neighborhood, black residents overwhelmingly

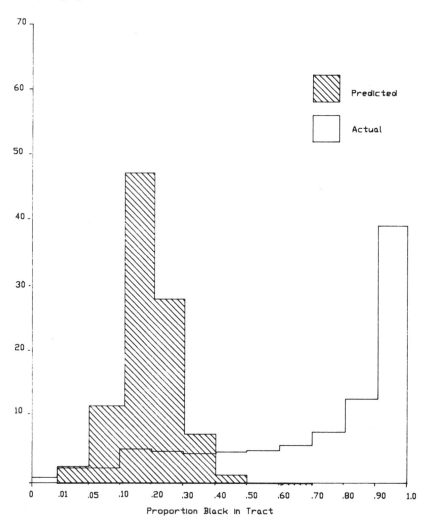

Figure 3. Actual and Predicted Distribution of Urban Blacks, by Proportion Black in Tract, 1970

favored the latter. . . . Those who favored desegregated residential areas made it clear that they did so for positive reasons of racial harmony even more than for the obvious advantages of good neighborhoods."[21] Thus, 74 percent of a random sample of black Americans interviewed in a 1969 *Newsweek* poll responded that they would rather live in a neighborhood that had both whites and blacks than in a neighborhood with all black families; only 16 percent chose an all-black neighborhood.[22] Moreover, the percentages preferring all-black neighborhoods declined whereas the percentages preferring integrated neighborhoods increased between 1963 and 1969. More blacks in the North and West preferred integrated neighborhoods than those residing in the South, while the percentage of middle-income blacks preferring integrated neighborhoods was greater than the percentage of low-income blacks.

Pettigrew also provides survey findings that indicate an increasing racial tolerance among whites. In particular, he presents the responses to identical questions included on seven National Opinion Research Center (NORC) polls administered between 1942 and 1968, and a second set of identical questions included in five Gallup polls conducted between 1958 and 1967. In the NORC surveys, the percentage of whites indicating that it would make a difference to them if a black—with just as much income and education as the respondent—moved onto their block declined from 62 percent in 1942, to 46 percent in 1956, to 35 percent in 1963, and to 21 percent in 1968.[23] Similarly, in 1958, 48 percent of whites interviewed by Gallup stated they definitely would or might move "if colored people came to live next door"; nine years later, in 1978, the percentage had declined to 35 percent. An even more recent Gallup survey reveals that the fraction of white households who said they would move if a black family lived next door had declined to only 13 percent in 1978.[24]

At first glance the evidence above appears encouraging to efforts to promote racial integration. A more probing examination by Reynolds Farley et al., however, illustrates that the underlying attitudes of blacks and whites toward integration are considerably more complex.[25] The authors surveyed a sample of 743 white and 400 black households in Detroit to determine the willingness of blacks and whites to live in or move into neigborhoods of varying racial composition. Black respondents were asked to indicate their preferences for each of five types of neighborhoods defined by the percentage black. For the blacks who expressed an unwillingness to live in an all-black or all-white neighborhood, follow-up questions were included to determine their reasons. Farley et al. also asked white respondents if they would be uncomfortable in each of four types of neighborhoods defined by racial composition and, if so, would they move away and why? The authors also attempted to determine the willingness of whites to purchase a home in a racially mixed neighborhood.

Table 5 summarizes Farley et al.'s findings concerning the attitudes of blacks and whites toward moving into neighborhoods of various racial compositions. As these data reveal, 82 percent of blacks selected a 45 percent black neighborhood as their first or second choice, and only 5 percent listed a predominantly white (7 percent) neighborhood as their first or second choice; the completely black neighborhood was the first or second choice of only 17 percent of black households. When questioned about their willingness to move into each type of neighborhood provided they found a nice house they could afford, however, fully 38 percent of black respondents answered that they would be willing to be the first black to enter an all-white neighborhood.

Of the large number of blacks (62 percent) who would be unwilling to move into an all-white area, only a few gave the desire to live with other blacks as the reason; most—about 90 percent—"expressed an opinion that whites in

Table 5. Black and White Attitudes Toward Neighborhoods of Varying Racial Composition

Percent Black	Percent of Blacks		Percent of Whites		
	Neigh 1 or 2 Choice	Willing to Move In	Uncom-fortable	Try Move Out	Would Not Move In
100	17.0%	69.0%	NA	NA	NA
80	68.0	99.0	NA	NA	NA
60	NA	NA	72.0%	64.0%	84.0%
45	82.0	99.0	NA	NA	NA
30	NA	NA	57.0	41.0	73.0
20	24.0	95.0	42.0	24.0	50.0
7	5.0	38.0	24.0	7.0	27.0

Source: Reynolds Farley, Howard Schuman, Suzanne Bianchi, Diane Colasanto, and Shirley Hatfield, "Chocolate City, Vanilla Suburbs Will the Trend Toward Racially Separate Communities Continue?" Social Science Research 7 (1978), pp. 330 and 332.

white areas would not welcome them."[26] About one-sixth of the black respondents stated that "I might get burned out or never wake up," or, "They would probably blow my house up." Farley et al. concluded that "freed of the fear of racial hostility, we believe that most Detroit area blacks would select neighborhoods which are about one-half white and one-half black."[27]

Data on the attitudes of whites, summarized in Table 5, in contrast, indicate that large fractions of whites would feel uncomfortable in a neighborhood with equal numbers of whites and blacks, that if they lived in a neighborhood with this racial composition they would try to move out, and that they would be unwilling to move into such a neighborhood. Indeed, only 50 percent of white respondents stated they would be willing to move into a neighborhood with as few as three blacks out of fifteen households (20 percent black). Forty percent of the whites who said they would move away from an integrated neighborhood gave anticipated declines in property values as their reason. From these analyses, Farley et al. conclude: "When we consider the residential preferences of whites in the Detroit area, the prospects for residential integration seem quite slim." They add: "While the neighborhood preferences of blacks are considerably more favorable to residential integration than the preferences of whites—the overwhelming majority of blacks choose an integrated neighborhood as the one most attractive to them—even these data must be interpreted with a certain amount of pessimism."[28]

Farley's findings suggest that even though more blacks would prefer to live in integrated neighborhoods, and although whites appear to have a growing tolerance for black neighbors, significant progress in achieving desegregation and integration will be difficult. Long memories and strongly held, though often incorrect, beliefs markedly affect the behavior of both blacks and whites, and powerful incentives will be needed to offset these deep-seated attitudes. At the same time, it is well to keep in mind that the attitudes of both blacks and

Table 6. Composite Indexes of Housing Availability for Sales and Rental Housing, for the Entire U.S. and by Region and SMSA Size

Type and Location	No Difference	White Favored	Black Favored	Discriminatory Treatment
Rental Housing				
National	31%	48%	21%	27%
Northeast	32	44	24	20
North Central	34	50	17	33
South	27	52	21	31
West	34	49	17	32
Large SMSA's	30	49	21	28
Small SMSA's	35	43	22	21
Sales Housing				
National	37%	39%	24%	15%
Northeast	33	39	29	10
North Central	23	55	22	33
South	46	33	22	11
West	34	39	27	12
Large SMSA's	37	40	23	17
Small SMSA's	36	36	28	7

Source: Wienk, et. al., "Measuring Racial Discrimination in American Housing Markets: The Housing Market Practices Survey," Tables 3, 5, 26, and 28; pp. 58, 66, 124, and 129.

whites are strongly conditioned by existing patterns of segregation. Because the demand for black housing at the periphery of the ghetto is typically so great, whites are usually correct in their perception that the entry of a few blacks into a neighborhood is the first step in a rapid shift to all-black occupancy. If market forces or a combination of market forces and public policy begin to make these outcomes less certain, both black and white attitudes and behavior could change dramatically.

Despite the lack of any systematic evidence for the self-segregation hypothesis, it is impossible to fully assess its role as long as significant majority (white) antagonism remains toward black efforts to leave the ghetto. Although the obstacles to moving into white neighborhoods are probably less today than in the past, many subtle and indirect forms of intimidation and discouragement still exist.[29] A recent HUD-sponsored study demonstrates both that racial discrimination is still commonplace in urban housing markets and that a persistent black can probably find a place to buy or rent in all-white areas.[30]

In HUD's Housing Market Practices Survey, pairs of black and white testers—matched in terms of age, general appearance, income, and family size—conducted 3,264 sales and rental audits in 40 metropolitan areas. The audit data were used to construct several indexes of discriminatory treatment including the index of housing availability shown in Table 6. Nationwide, HUD analysts found that there were no differences in rental housing availability in 31 percent of the cases; that whites were favored 48 percent of the time; and that blacks were favored 21 percent of the time. Blacks were thus less favorably treated in 27 percent of the rental audits. Discriminatory treatment was found less often in the sales audits. Even higher levels of discrimination were detected in audits conducted in the city of Boston in 1980 and in Cleveland Heights, Ohio, in 1978.[31]

Although the authors of the HUD study define the difference in black and white treatment as their index of discrimination, it is noteworthy that the white testers received more favorable treatment in nearly half of the audits. Moreover, the HUD audits and similar studies generally understate the extent of housing market discrimination. Audits address only the initial phase of the search process and thus cannot detect discriminatory practices that often occur at later stages—for example, at the time security deposits are required or financing is sought. In addition, the preliminary analyses of the HUD study did not consider steering, one of the most common and pernicious techniques used by brokers to maintain segregated residence patterns. Most importantly, however, the education and other socioeconomic characteristics of the auditors were higher than those of the general population and especially of most black housing seekers.

Concluding Remarks

Efforts to formulate public policies to eliminate or reduce racial discrimination in urban housing markets have suffered from a confusion about the roles of discrimination and socioeconomic determinants of segregation. Although virtually every systematic study has concluded that black and white differences in income and other socioeconomic variables account for very little of current and past patterns of racial residential segregation, the belief that income is a major, if not the principal, determinant of racial segregation stubbornly persists and has prompted policymakers to emphasize policies aimed at reducing the concentration of low-income and minority households rather than policies that would combat discriminatory practices in private housing markets.

In spite of the limited governmental efforts to combat discrimination in private housing markets, preliminary analyses of the 1980 census for the Cleveland SMSA, at least, indicate that increasing numbers of individual minority households are managing to acquire sale and rental housing in formerly all-white residential areas. These early indications may signal a fundamental change in America's patterns of residence by race and reflect important qualitative changes in the forces that have maintained segregated living patterns over the past half century or more.

Analyses of the 1980 census for Cuyahoga County, Ohio, reveal that 18 suburban communities had more than 100 black households in 1980. These

18, however, included three suburban communities that were more than 50 percent black in 1980—East Cleveland (82.2 percent), Warrensville Heights (69.6 percent), and Warrensville Township (69.6 percent).[32] East Cleveland, which was 48 percent black in 1970, is located adjacent to Cleveland and to its massive central city black ghetto (Figure 1). Indeed, by 1980 East Cleveland had for all practical purposes become part of the Cleveland ghetto. Warrensville Heights and Warrensville Township, which were 43 and 48 percent black in 1970, are located adjacent to Cleveland's District II, south of Shaker Heights and north of Maple Heights (Figure 1).

All but one of the remaining Cuyahoga County suburbs with more than 100 black households in 1980 are also located either east or south of the central city black ghetto, but several are located some distance from its periphery. Moreover, the black populations of all 18 communities increased between 1970 and 1980; excluding the three black suburbs, the remaining 15 suburban communities with 100 or more households in 1980 had an average of 953 black households in 1980 as contrasted with an average of 218 in 1970.

In addition to the 18 Cuyahoga County communities with more than 100 black households in 1980, 10 others had 25 or more black households in 1980 and an additional 8 had 10 or more. None of the 10 Cuyahoga County suburbs with 25 or more black households in 1980 had more than 10 or more black households in 1970, and none of the 8 suburbs with 10 or more black households in 1980 had as many as 10 in 1970. Although the number of black households residing in these predominantly white suburban communities in 1980 is still quite small (black residents of the 33 Cuyahoga suburbs with more than 10 black households in 1980, but excluding the 3 that were more than 50 percent black in 1980, accounted for only 12.4 percent of Cuyahoga County's black households in 1980), the growth of the black population in these formerly all-white suburban communities during 1970–80 is a highly significant development.

If careful analyses of 1980 census data for other metropolitan areas reveal similar developments, there may be some basis for optimism. The emergence of these more dispersed residence patterns by minority households could mark a turning point, and one that may reflect a significant weakening of the forces that have previously maintained segregated living patterns. Although recent audits demonstrate that steering and other forms of discriminatory practices are still prevalent, the 1980 census data for Cleveland and earlier school enrollment data for Cleveland and a number of other metropolitan areas suggest that the nearly absolute barriers to black entry into most suburban communities may have been breached.[33] Whether these new suburban black households reside in widely dispersed patterns or in small clusters, their appearance in so many formerly all-white communities creates a base for further black population growth. Their success should provide proof to dubious black households that, given sufficient effort, blacks are able to obtain rental and ownership housing in communities that were previously closed to them. If these new black settlement patterns, by still token numbers of minority households, are carefully nurtured and encouraged by public policy, they could be the basis for a significant and rapid dispersal of minority households and a rapid breakdown of the current massive concentrations of minority populations in American cities.

Elimination of racial discrimination and concentration, however, will require aggressive enforcement of existing laws, enactment of even stronger laws, and further incentives for integration. A first step is for citizens and policymakers to come to understand the respective roles of income and race as causes of past and current patterns of racial segregation. Although policies to reduce the level of racial segregation in federally subsidized programs will contribute to the goal of reducing racial segregation, public policy needs to give more emphasis to eliminating discriminatory practices in private housing markets. This means the vigorous enforcement of existing antidiscrimination laws (too few white Americans, for example, understand that it is illegal for them to refuse to show or sell their home to a black or Hispanic person), audits of the practices of real estate brokers and rental agents, and the strict monitoring of affirmative marketing programs by the U.S. Department of Housing and Urban Development.

NOTES AND REFERENCES

1. U.S. Bureau of the Census, *Statistical Abstract, 1981* (Washington, D.C.: U.S. Government Printing Office, 1982), table 19, p. 16.

2. National Advisory Commission on Civil Disorders, *Report of the National Advisory Commission on Civil Disorders* (New York: Bantam Books, 1978).

3. Ibid., p. 244.

4. Trudy P. McFall, "Voluntary Agreements among PHAs Can Increase Low Income Housing Choices," *Journal of Housing* (May 1981): 251–55.

5. Because black immigrants tend to be younger and many whites attend parochial or private schools, however, these statistics often exaggerate the black share of the population by as much as 2 to 1 in many integrated neighborhoods. H. Richard Obermans, "Racial School Enrollment Patterns in Cuyahoga County, 1970–78" (The Cuyahoga Plan of Ohio, Inc., August 1979).

6. Ibid., table 12.

7. Cleveland implemented a housing plan to foster integration of its public schools in September 1979. Thus, the black percentage of schools in East and West Cleveland would presumably be quite different today.

8. Karl Taeuber and Alma Taeuber, *Negroes in Cities: Residential Segregation and Neighborhood Change* (Chicago: Aldine Publishing Co., 1965).

9. Annemette Sørensen, Karl E. Taeuber, and Leslie J. Hollingsworth, Jr., "Indexes of Racial Residential Segregation for 109 Cities in the United States, 1940 to 1970," *Sociological Focus*, April 1975, pp. 125–42. The Sorensen, Taeuber, and Hollingsworth study reveals a decline in the indexes of residential segregation between whites and nonwhites between 1960 and 1970. If the indexes had been calculated for entire metropolitan areas, however, the opposite would be true (pp. 131–32).

10. For a discussion and tests of this socioeconomic hypothesis, see Taeuber and Taeuber, *Negroes in Cities*; A. H. Pascal, "The Economics of Housing Segregation" (The Rand Corporation, 1967); John R. Meyer, John F. Kain, and Martin Wohl, *The Urban Transportation Problem* (Cambridge: Harvard University Press, 1965), chap. 7; Davis McEntire, *Residence and Race* (Berkeley: University of California Press, 1960); Karl E. Taeuber, "The Effect of Income Redistribution on Racial Residential Segregation," *Urban Affairs Quarterly* 4 (September 1978): 5–15; Ann B. Schnare, "Residential Segregation by Race in U.S. Metropolitan Areas: An Analysis across Cities and over Time" (The Urban Institute Working Paper 246–2, Washington, D.C., February 1977).

11. Nathan Kantrowitz, "Racial and Ethnic Residential Segregation in Boston 1830–1970," *The Annals of the American Academy of Political and Social Science* 441 (January 1979): 41.

12. Theodore Hershberg, Alan Burstein, E. Ericksen, S. Greenberg, and W. Yancey, "A Tale of Three Cities: Blacks and Immigrants in Philadelphia: 1850–1880, 1930, and 1970," *The Annals of the American Academy of Political and Social Science* 441 (January 1979): 55.

13. Stanley Lieberson, *Ethnic Patterns in American Cities* (New York: The Free Press of Glencoe, 1963); Karl E. Taeuber and Alma F. Taeuber, "The Negro as an Immigrant Group," *American Journal of Sociology* 64 (January 1964): 374–82.

14. Hershberg et al., "A Tale of Three Cities," p. 73.

15. Pascal, "Economics of Housing Segregation"; Taeuber, "Effect of Income Redistribution."

16. See John F. Kain, "Race, Ethnicity, and Residential Location," in *Public and Urban Economics*, ed. Ronald E. Grieson (Lexington, Mass.: D. C. Heath and Company, 1977).

17. Austrian-Americans comprise only 1.5 percent of the Cleveland SMSA population, whereas Italian-Americans and Polish-Americans each represent 3.0 percent. Kain, "Race, Ethnicity, and Residential Location," table 3, p. 21.

18. The categories used to define household types are as follows: two family types (husband-wife and other), three age of head categories (less than 35 years, 35–65 years, and more than 65 years), six family sizes (1, 2, 3, 4, 5, and 6 or more), and six income categories (less than $5,000, $5,000, $5,000–6,999, $7,000–9,999, $10,000–14,999, $15,000–24,999, and more than $25,000).

19. Schnare, "Residential Segregation by Race."

20. Ibid., p. 35.

21. Thomas Pettigrew, "Attitudes on Race and Housing: A Socio-Psychological View," in *Segregation in Residential Areas*, ed. A. H. Hawley and V. P. Rock (Washington, D.C.: National Academy of Sciences, 1973).

22. The exact question of the *Newsweek* poll was, "In living in a neighborhood, if you could find the housing you want and like, would you rather live in a neighborhood with Negro families, or in a neighborhood that had both whites and Negroes?" Pettigrew, "Attitudes on Race and Housing," p. 44.

23. Ibid., p. 93.

24. American Institute of Public Opinion, *The Gallup Opinion Index* (Princeton, N.J.: American Institute of Public Opinion, November 1978), p. 93.

25. Reynolds Farley, H. Schuman, S. Bianchi, D. Colsanto, and S. Hatchett, "Chocolate City, Vanilla Suburbs: Will the Trend Towards Racially Separate Communities

Continue?" *Social Science Research* 7 (1978): 319–44; Reynolds Farley, S. Bianchi, and D. Colasanto, "Barriers to the Racial Integration of Neighborhoods in the Detroit Case," *The Annals of the American Academy of Political and Social Science* 441 (January 1979): 97–113.

26. Farley et al., "Chocolate City, Vanilla Suburbs," p. 331.

27. Ibid.

28. Ibid., p. 334. For a discussion of the problems that arise from the contradictory preferences of blacks and whites for neighborhoods of varying racial composition, see Thomas Schelling, "A Process of Residential Segregation: Neighborhood Tipping," in *Racial Discrimination in Economic Life*, ed. Anthony H. Pascal (Lexington, Mass.: Lexington Books of D. C. Heath and Co., 1972); Thomas C. Schelling, "Modes of Segregation," *American Economic Review* (May 1969): 169–85; Ann B. Schnare and Duncan C. MacRae, "A Model of Neighborhood Change" (Contract Report no. 225–4, The Urban Institute, Washington, D.C., 1975).

29. Until very recently, the devices used to enforce segregation could hardly be called subtle. Among the most important were deed restrictions (racial covenants), the appraisal practices of the Federal Housing Administration and private lending institutions, the actions of local officials, and the practices of real estate agents. See Charles Abrams, *Forbidden Neighbors: A Study of Prejudice in Housing* (New York: Harper and Brothers, 1955); Davis McEntire, *Residence and Race*; National Committee Against Discrimination in Housing, *Jobs and Housing: A Study of Employment and Housing Opportunities for Racial Minorities in Suburban Areas of the New York Metropolitan Region* (New York: National Committee Against Discrimination in Housing, Inc., March 1970); U.S. Commission on Civil Rights, *Federal Civil Rights Enforcement Effort* (Washington, D.C.: U.S. Government Printing Office, 1974), and *Housing* (Washington, D.C.: U.S. Government Printing Office, 1961).

30. Ronald Wienk, Clifford E. Reid, John C. Simonson, and Frederick J. Eggers, *Measuring Discrimination in American Housing Markets: The Housing Market Practices Survey* (Office of Policy Development and Research, U.S. Department of Housing and Urban Development, April 1979).

31. Juliet Saltman, "Cleveland Heights: Housing Availability Survey, February–June 1978, Final Report" (Cleveland Heights Community Congress, n.d.); Judith D. Feins, Rachel Bratt, and Robert Hollister, *Final Report—A Study of Racial Discrimination in the Boston Housing Market* (Cambridge, Mass.: Abt Associates, November 1981); John Yinger, "Evaluation of the Final Report of a Study of Racial Discrimination in the Boston Housing Market" (Cambridge, Mass., November 1982, Mimeographed).

32. The Cuyahoga Plan of Ohio, Inc., "Black Ownership in the Cleveland Area: Patterns of Residence in 1970 and 1980" (Cleveland, Ohio, October 1982).

33. Ibid.

Chapter Six

More than Skin Deep

The Effect of Housing Discrimination on the Extent
and Pattern of Racial Residential Segregation
in the United States

GEORGE C. GALSTER *

The purpose of this chapter is to estimate empirically the degree to which variations in the extent and pattern of black residential segregation result from housing discrimination. The key advance offered by the research beyond existing studies is that it employs the measures of housing discrimination obtained by the U.S. Department of Housing and Urban Development (HUD) in its 1977 Housing Market Practices Survey (HMPS). Thus, for the first time, it is possible to perform direct statistical tests on cross-sectional data of the relationship between residential segregation and discriminatory activities.

The chapter first discusses the extent and pattern of segregation and its three distinct causes. Next, the data and empirical specification are described. The final section reports the results of empirical tests and draws conclusions.

The Phenomenon of Racial Segregation in the United States

Segregation of blacks and whites in U.S. metropolitan areas is characterized both by the large *extent* of residential racial separation within and between neighborhoods and by the *pattern* of black concentration in central city areas. The extent of segregation in 1970 was such that, on average, 80 percent of urban black households would need to move into white areas in order to achieve complete integration (Sorensen, Taeuber, and Hollingsworth 1974; Farley 1977). Further, another study has shown that the residential contact or "exposure" of blacks to whites has been decreasing at the metropolitan level, even during the supposedly "enlightened" 1960s (Schnare 1980).[1] In 1974, 77 percent of urban blacks lived in central cities, whereas only 38 percent of whites did so, and this black centralization also has been increasing (Schnare 1977:chap. 1).[2]

Three competing theories have been forwarded to explain this phenomenon: the "class" theory, the "prejudice" theory, and the "discrimination" theory.

*This research was supported by a grant from the Ford Foundation. Opinions expressed are those of the author and do not necessarily reflect those of the Ford Foundation.

The author gratefully acknowledges the research assistance of Vassilios Fourlis, Daniel Harkins, Carol Murdock, Vasiliki Tsiliopolos, Anastasia Tzavaras, and Robert Yopko. The comments offered on earlier drafts by Johnny Yinger are appreciated.

The class (or "ecological segregation") theory attempts to explain racial segregation as the "natural" ecological segregation of groups according to socioeconomic class. Given the segregation of housing and the fact that blacks are disproportionately represented in the lower income classes, one would expect to find that relatively few blacks can afford to live in higher quality (white suburban) neighborhoods. (For a more complete discussion of the class theory, see Duncan and Duncan 1955; Lieberson 1963; Park 1967; Marshall and Jiobu 1975.) This theory has received some empirical support,[3] but the evidence shows that in most cases "class" grounds explain only a small fraction of the observed extent of racial segregation (Taeuber and Taeuber 1965; Hermalin and Farley 1973; Schnare 1977:chap. 3; Farley 1977), although Smith (1977) has shown that the proportion varies significantly from one city to the next. Similarly, relatively low socioeconomic status explains only a small part of the centralized pattern of black residences. In the eleven largest standard metropolitan statistical areas (SMSAs) in 1970, a higher proportion of whites with incomes below $3,000 than of blacks with incomes above $10,000 lived in the suburbs (Kain and Quigley 1975).

The prejudice (or "voluntary segregation") theory holds that whites prefer to live "with their own kind" in predominantly white areas, because they perceive either something undesirable about other races or something positive in their own culture that is worthy of preserving. Downs (1973) and Pettigrew (1975) cite opinion poll evidence of white perceptions that blacks hold different (and less desirable) values and norms. Leven et al. (1976) and Pettigrew (1975) also note that whites often view integration as a harbinger of declining neighborhood status. A corollary sees blacks similarly wanting to segregate voluntarily so as to foster a "black identity" or to develop distinct, supportive institutions (see Lieberson 1963; Yinger 1979). The weight of the evidence for blacks, however, suggests that they typically would prefer neighborhoods with approximately equal racial proportions to all-black ones (Pettigrew 1973, 1975; Schuman and Hatchett 1974; Farley et al. 1978; Galster 1982).[4] Theoretical models have shown that even mild white preferences for racially homogeneous neighborhoods can lead to a large extent of segregation through a dynamic process of "tipping" (Schelling 1972). However, as Yinger has demonstrated (1976, 1979), the centralized pattern is not consistent with a model based on prejudice alone, especially if blacks desire to integrate. If class and preference were the only operative segregating forces, one would expect to find rings of alternating race/class groups, with higher income blacks more suburbanized than lower income whites, and with blacks tending to attempt to integrate the borders of the adjacent white group of comparable status. This does not represent the ecology of the typical American metropolitan area.

The major premise of the third theory, discrimination (or "involuntary segregation"), is that blacks are barred from moving into areas that their incomes and preferences might otherwise allow because of a host of discriminatory barriers in the housing market. Numerous statistical studies have documented indirectly the existence of such barriers by uncovering their results: higher prices and lower quality levels for black-occupied dwellings compared to identical white-occupied ones (Straszheim 1974; Kain and Quigley 1975; Galster 1977; Yinger 1979). Important direct evidence for 40 metropolitan areas came from the 1977 Housing Market Practices Survey (Wienk et al. 1979). These data revealed that, on average, blacks were likely to confront some sort of discrimination in 27 percent of their attempts to find rental units and 15 percent of their attempts to find units for sale. It has been proven theoretically that such discrimination provides the only explanation for the observed pattern of racial residential location, given relative black-white incomes and preferences (Yinger 1976, 1979). However, no one has performed direct tests of the correlation between the intensity of discrimination and the pattern (and extent) of segregation.

With two exceptions, previous studies have analyzed empirically these three theories of segregation separately, and only for individual cities. Marshall and Jiobu (1975) constructed a path model of segregation embodying both "class" and "prejudice" theories. The former was operationalized by racial dissimilarity indices of occupation and income. The latter was operationalized by percent of nonwhite, number of nonwhite, and nonwhite-white growth differentials, so as to proxy for white perceptions of "threat" and/or the "critical mass" present for distinct minority institutional development. Using a sample of 149 central cities in 1960, Marshall and Jiobu found that in both southern and nonsouthern cities the occupational and income dissimilarity indices were the strongest predictors of Taeuber's "dissimilarity" index of segregation. The other variables dealing with the black population's size, proportion, and growth demonstrated lower correlations with the extent of segregation, and the direction of the relationships often varied among regions. No correlates of the pattern of segregation were investigated.

Schnare (1977) tried to explain variations in a metropolitan "racial exposure" index of residential segregation through the use of multivariate analysis for a sample of 112 SMSAs in both 1960 and 1970. The "class" variables of median housing costs as a percentage of median family income, black-white ratio of white-collar workers, and black-white median income ratio were all significantly and positively correlated with black exposure to whites in both years. The "prejudice" proxies of number, proportion, and relative growth of black population were significantly, negatively correlated with exposure in both years. Finally, regional dummy variables were used to "reflect a host of unmeasurable differences in attitudes, policies, and practices, as well as in the historical pattern of development" (ibid.: 50). Southern and north central SMSAs showed less interracial exposure, *ceteris paribus*, than those in the West, while those in the northeast region indicated comparatively more exposure.

As suggestive as these two studies are, they unfortunately suffer from the specification error of omitted variables (Wonnacott and Wonnacott 1979:413–19). Empirical estimates of the relationship between segregation, class and prejudice are likely to be biased when the effects of a third force—discrimination —are not controlled for and this third force is correlated with the first two. The present study adds the crucial empirical dimension that up to this time has been unavailable: a cross-sectional measure of the intensity of housing market discrimination as measured by the HMPS. This will make it possible to assess directly the contribution that this factor makes to both the degree and the pattern of segregation in metropolitan areas, as well as to obtain unbiased estimates of the contributions made by the other two elements. The statistical technique used is path analysis.

Data and Model Specification

Data

Data for this analysis came from a sample of 40 SMSAs that HUD selected for the HMPS. These were chosen from a universe of 117 SMSAs containing central city populations of more than 11 percent black. These 117 were, in turn, divided into "large" (central cities above 100,000 population) and "small" SMSA groups. Thirty-two of the former and eight of the latter were chosen on the basis of a controlled selection procedure. SMSAs of various sizes were represented within each regional subsample.[5] All other social, economic, and demographic data used in this chapter were obtained from the *1970 Census of Population and Housing*.

Specification of Dependent Variables

To measure the *extent* of segregation two variables are used: the exposure of blacks to whites (EXPBW) and the exposure of whites to blacks (EXPWB). (A glossary of these and all other variable names is provided in an appendix to this chapter.) The exposure of race X to those of another race Y is defined as the proportion of Y in the average X's census tract:

$$EXPXY = (100/X) \sum_{i}^{n} X_i(Y_i/T_i)$$

where X_i, Y_i are numbers of race X, Y in the ith tract, respectively; T_i is the total population of the tract; X is the total population of race X in the SMSA; and n is the number of tracts. The maximum value of EXPXY is the proportion of race Y in the SMSA; the minimum value is zero. The exposure rates calculated by Schnare for individual SMSAs (1977:table B.1) are used in the present study.

The exposure rate is used to measure the extent of segregation instead of the conventional "dissimilarity" (D) index, because the latter's value depends only on the distribution of races among neighborhoods with above-average

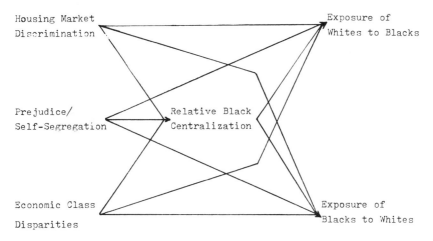

Figure 1. Path Model for Causes of Segregation

proportions of blacks and those with below-average proportions of blacks, but does not depend on the distribution of blacks and whites within each neighborhood type (Zoloth 1974). Schnare (1980) has found that significant changes of the latter type occurred during the 1960s—changes that were reflected in exposure indexes but not in dissimilarity indexes. For the types of residential distributional alterations now occurring, it thus appears that exposure rates are a more sensitive measure.[6]

The *pattern* of segregation was measured by Redick's (1956) "index of centralization of black population with respect to white population" (BCINDEX):

$$BCINDEX = (100) \left(\sum_i^n \bar{B}_{i-1} \bar{W}_i - \sum_i^n \bar{B}_i \bar{W}_{i-1} \right)$$

where i is one of n concentric rings centered on the SMSA's central business district ($i = 0$ is the CBD); $\bar{B}_i$, $\bar{W}_i$ are the cumulative proportions of blacks and whites, respectively, moving from $i = 0$ to $i = n$. BCINDEX ranges from a possible value of -100 if all whites were in the most central ring(s) and all blacks were in more decentralized rings, to a value of $+100$ when the reverse was true.[7] This index of relative black centralization is chosen instead of the more conventional proportion of blacks in central cities versus suburbs (see Hermalin and Farley 1973; Schnare 1977) because the latter is insensitive to variations in location of blacks within either central cities or suburbs.

In the model, black centralization is specified as an "intervening variable" in a "path model" of residential segregation (see Figure 1). That is, the pattern of segregation is believed to influence the extent of segregation. The more centralized a given number or proportion of blacks, the lower the ratio of the sum of the (black-white border) perimeter(s) of the predominantly black neighborhoods to the sum of their areas. Thus, for geometric reasons the centralization index should be inversely related to interracial exposure if most of such exposure occurs in neighborhoods bordering the "ghetto."

Specification of Independent Variables

As outlined above, the causes of both the extent and the pattern of segregation can be conceptually grouped in three categories. Variables proxying for components of each of these categories are considered as independent variables in a larger "path model" (see Figure 1). The variables are defined and expected relationships described below.

Discrimination. A measure of the "discrimination" component of segregation is derived from the HMPS described above. For each of the 40 SMSAs a sample of real estate agencies and apartment rental complexes to be audited was selected from classified newspaper advertisements. During May and June 1977, matched pairs of black and white auditors separately visited the sampled agencies and complexes and requested the housing listed in the advertisement.[8] Both auditors kept careful reports of their experiences and organized them within the following categories: housing availability, courtesy, terms and conditions, and information requested and volunteered.

The first category, housing availability, was considered by HUD as the most fundamental component of potentially discriminatory behavior (Wienk et al. 1979:51). Not only does differential treatment concerning housing availability clearly violate Title VIII of the 1968 Civil Rights Act, but also such items as courtesy and terms become largely irrelevant if false information on the availability of housing is provided. To assess whether such differential treatment occurred during an audit, experiences of each auditor pair were compared for the series of items comprising the housing availability category. If the white auditor was favored on at least one item and the black was not, the observation was coded "white favored." Opposite situations were coded "black favored." Observations where whites were favored on some item(s) and blacks on other(s), and those where both were treated identically, were coded "no difference." The number of "white favored" minus the number of "black favored" observations provided HUD's estimate of "net discriminatory treatment." These measures were computed separately by tenure and by SMSA, and in each case a sign test was conducted to assess whether the measure was (statistically) significantly different from zero (see Wienk et al.:chaps. 2–4).

Several preliminary trial specifications involving different formulations of the discrimination variable were undertaken. They revealed that the absolute value of net discriminatory treatment in an SMSA (an average weighted by the housing stock proportions in the two tenures) was only modestly (positively) correlated with segregation. Experimentation with various "dummy variables" indicated that the impact of net discriminatory treatment is either nonlinear or discontinuous. More specifically, the final measure of discrimination employed, which is reported in this chapter, is a dummy variable taking the value "one," if the SMSA demonstrated net discriminatory treatment levels that were significantly greater than zero at the 5 percent level in *both* owner and rental submarkets, and the value "zero otherwise" (BDISCRIM).[9] In other words, it indicates the SMSAs where we have great confidence that discrimination exists to a considerable degree. Theory would predict that this measure of housing discrimination should be inversely related to interracial exposure rates and directly related to relative black centralization.[10]

An unavoidable temporal inconsistency occurs between the discrimination variable (measured for 1977) and all other variables in the model (measured for 1970). Although it need not be assumed that the absolute magnitude of discrimination occurring in 1970 was identical to that observed in 1977, to avoid bias the model does assume that the inter-SMSA variation in the measure of discrimination was identical in both years.[11]

Class. The variable employed as a proxy for "class" segregation is the ratio of black/white median incomes of families and unrelated individuals in the SMSA (BWMEDIN). It is expected that the higher the relative economic position of blacks, the greater will be the likelihood that more blacks will have the financial means to live in higher quality housing. Such housing generally is located in neighborhoods that are farther from the central city and have higher proportions of white residents. Thus, BWMEDIN should be directly related to exposure of blacks to whites and vice versa, and inversely related to the relative centralization of blacks.[12]

Prejudice. The "prejudice" dimensions of the phenomenon would be most directly captured by measures of black and white racial attitudes. Unfortunately, no such comparable cross-sectional data exist for the SMSA sample here. A set of five variables are thus employed as "second-best" proxies for these racial attitudes: the number, proportion, and relative growth rate of the black population, and the proportions of the white population that are college-educated and age 45 or older.

The absolute number of blacks in the SMSA (BSMSA) proxies for attitudes and perceptions on the part of both races. From the whites' perspective, higher numbers of blacks would increase their "visibility" and, perhaps, the potential "competition" or "threat" they might hold for whites (Roof 1972; Marshall and Jiobu 1975; Schnare 1977). Bradburn, Sudman, and Gockel (1970: 103–18) have found that white hostility to neighborhood integration and the likelihood of "white flight" from these integrating neighborhoods are directly related to whites' perceptions of the strength of black housing demands. From the blacks' perspective, larger numbers of blacks are the prerequisite for the formation of a variety of institutions that serve to both aid and unify the black residential community. Black desires to "self-segregate" may be present in such situations. Thus, black population size should be inversely related to interracial exposure rates. It should be directly related to black centralization, because the pull of black self-segregation would likely be "inward" toward traditional central city "ports of entry" for black immigrants, and the push of white flight would likely be "outward" toward predominantly white suburban neighborhoods.

The ratio of black and white populations in the SMSA (BWSMSA) is, like BSMSA, also seen as a proxy for white perceptions of black "threat" (Marshall and Jiobu 1975; Schnare 1977) and the likelihood of white prejudice and self-segregation. On this basis, one could predict an inverse relationship between the proportion black and interracial exposure, although no a priori predictions about the relationship with black centralization can be made.

In addition to the behavioral arguments given, the two variables just specified are likely to be related to interracial exposure rates purely on the basis of geometric arguments. First, the greater the absolute number of blacks in an SMSA, the less likely the exposure of blacks to whites, independent of any racial attitudes, incomes, or relative population sizes. Schnare (1977:20–22) has shown this in the archetypical situation where most blacks live in the central city, predominantly black ghettos, and most interracial exposure occurs in neighborhoods bordering the ghetto. As the absolute size of the ghetto population rises, the average black will have a lower percentage of white neighbors simply because the perimeter of the ghetto will grow less rapidly than its area. Second, given the definition of exposure rates as the average percentage of one race living in the tracts occupied by the other, higher proportions of blacks in an SMSA must result in lower black-white exposure and higher white-black exposure, *ceteris paribus*.

The absolute difference in the rate of growth of the black population versus white population during the preceding decade (BWCHNG) can also be viewed as a proxy for white fear and self-segregation tendencies (Morrill 1965; Marshall and Jiobu 1975; Schnare 1977). From the black perspective, high black population growth could mean the presence of many new in-migrants to the urban milieu who would be especially in need of the supportive institutional structures available only in predominantly black areas (Duncan and Lieberson 1959; Lieberson 1963). Both these arguments imply that BWCHNG would be inversely related to exposure and directly related to black centralization.

Finally, the proportion of whites who have college degrees (PWCOLEG) and the proportion of whites who are 45 years or older (PW45P) are included as demographic proxies for racial attitudes. Opinion surveys have shown consistently that attitudes about neighborhood integration sharply differ between less versus better educated and younger versus older white groups (Campbell and Schuman 1968:104–5; Bradburn, Sudman, and Gockel 1970:chap. 8; Pettigrew 1975:92–126; Middleton 1976; Galster 1980). The proportion of college-educated (presumably less prejudiced) whites should be directly related to interracial exposure and inversely related to black centralization. For the proportion of older whites, the opposite would be expected. Of course, interpretation of these two variables is especially problematic because they likely proxy for a variety of unspecified factors besides racial attitudes.

Table 1. Means, Standard Deviations, and Zero-Order Correlations of Variables

Variable	Mean	Std. Dev.	1	2	3	4	5	6	7	8	9	10	11	12
1. BWMEDIN	59.0	8.64												
2. BWSMSA	13.6	10.5	-.52											
3. BWCHNG	.194	.271	.34	-.47										
4. BSMSA	149	326	.12	.18	.24									
5. LBSMSA	4.78	.518	-.02	.32	.11	.77								
6. PWCOLEG	3.89	1.40	-.44	.47	-.21	.04	.19							
7. PW45P	30.8	4.77	.05	-.15	-.08	.14	.12	.08						
8. COSTCCR	87.9	20.7	-.14	-.09	-.10	-.15	-.24	-.01	-.34					
9. PCCJOBS	57.0	16.5	-.32	.38	-.31	.10	.20	.14	-.11	.04				
10. BDISCRIM	.175	.389	.08	-.07	.05	.17	.24	-.08	.21	.11	-.06			
11. BCINDEX	46.8	19.7	-.20	-.10	.21	-.12	.03	-.24	-.03	-.33	.11	.10		
12. EXPBW	40.5	16.9	-.28	-.50	.30	-.24	-.56	-.20	-.04	.05	.49	-.29	-.21	
13. EXPWB	4.62	3.09	-.39	.80	-.40	.11	.08	.60	-.19	.01	.19	-.27	-.30	-.03

Table 2. Unstandardized Regression Coefficients, Dependent Variables
(Standard Errors in Parentheses)

Independent Variables	EXPBW	EXPWB		BCINDEX
BWMEDIN	-.004 (.301)	.039 (.039)		-.124 (.385)[a]
BWSMSA	-.334 (.277)[d]	.222 (.036)[a]		-.380 (.393)
BWCHNG	20.0 (8.8)[b]	.284 (1.17)		18.1 (12.6)[c]
LBSMSA	-16.5 (4.9)[a]	-1.06 (.58)[b]	BSMSA	-.011 (.009)[d]
BCINDEX	-.231 (.112)[b]	-.018 (.015)[d]		NA
PWCOLEG	-.327 (1.73)	.661 (.229)[a]		-4.60 (2.18)[b]
PW45P	.183 (.434)	-.034 (.057)		-.706 (.665)
BDISCRIM	-8.34 (5.23)[c]	-1.13 (.69)[c]		11.1 (7.0)[c]
COSTCCR	NA	NA		-.493 (.144)[a]
PCCJOBS	NA	NA		.209 (.173)[d]
CONSTANT	128.1 (29.4)[a]	3.80 (3.89)		192.2 (46.4)
R^2	.61	.80		.50
N	40	40		40

a,b,c,d = t-test of coefficient significantly different
from zero at 1%, 5%, 10%, 15% levels, respectively.
(one-tail test)

NA = Not Applicable

Control Variables. Two final independent control variables are specified as predictors of the relative black centralization index: the ratio of housing costs in the central city versus the suburban ring (COSTCCR),[13] and the proportion of SMSA employment located in the central city (PCCJOBS). Given the larger proportion of lower income blacks, housing costs are more likely to constrain their residential choices than those of whites. Higher suburban versus central city housing prices should thus lead to more relative centralization for blacks than whites. Along a similar line, comparatively few blacks would be

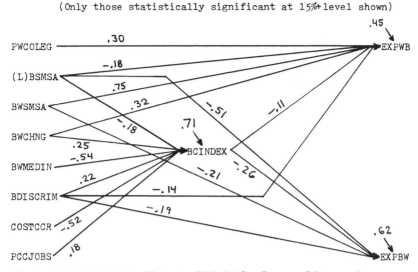

(Only those statistically significant at 15%+ level shown)

Figure 2. Path (beta) Coefficients of Model for Causes of Segregation

willing and able to make long commutes: whence the greater the proportion of jobs in the central city, the greater the BCINDEX.

The means, standard deviations, and zero-order correlations for all variables are shown in Table 1.

Empirical Results

The unstandardized coefficients estimated by multiple regression analysis for the model specified above are presented in Table 2. To facilitate comparing magnitudes of relationships among variables that are measured along different scales, the standardized (beta) coefficients are portrayed diagrammatically in Figure 2. Only path coefficients significantly different from zero at the 15 percent level of significance or better are shown. The total, direct, and indirect effects of variables on segregation are shown in Table 3, presuming that the path coefficients estimated are indicative of causal relationships.

The discrimination variable proved to be negatively correlated with both types of interracial exposure and positively correlated with relative black centralization, as predicted. Because centralization, in turn, was negatively correlated with exposure, the impacts of discrimination appear to be twofold.[14] SMSAs having significant amounts of discrimination in both housing tenures (BDISCRIM = 1) had, *ceteris paribus*, 24 percent higher relative black centralization (computed at the mean) compared to those that did not. This more centralized pattern of segregation, plus the direct impact of discrimination,

Table 3. Comparative Effects of Variables on Segregation

	Total[a]	EXPBW Direct	Indirect	Total[a]	EXPWB Direct	Indirect	Total[a]	BCINDEX Direct
BDISCRIM	-.29	-.19	-.06	-.27	-.14	-.02	.10	.22
(L)BSMSA	-.56	-.51	-.09	.08	-.18	-.01	-.12	-.18
BWSMSA	-.50	-.21	-.06*	.80	.75	-.03	-.10	-.20*
BWCHNG	.30	.32	-.07	-.40	.03*	-.03	.21	.25
PWCOLEG	-.20	-.03*	-.03	.60	.30	-.01	-.24	-.13
BWMEDIN	.28	.00*	.14	-.39	.11*	.06	-.20	-.54
BCINDEX	-.21	-.26	NA	-.30	-.11	NA	NA	NA

[a]Defined as the zero-order correlation. Note the direct plus indirect effects do not sum to the total due to spurious and joint effects.

*Coefficient of path(s) not statistically significant at 15% level or better.

NA = Not Applicable

means that the extent of segregation was much higher in SMSAs having discrimination: 26 percent lower white exposure to blacks and 36 percent lower black exposure to whites (computed at the sample means).

The "class" segregation proxy of black-white median income ratios proved statistically significant only in the equation predicting black centralization. The effect of economic disparity on the extent of segregation thus appears to be only indirect, being mediated by its effect on centralization. This aspect of the phenomenon has not been investigated by earlier studies of income differential and segregation (Marshall and Jiobu 1975; Schnare 1977). Here it indicates that, if the median income ratio was raised from its present average .59 to, say, .65, one would predict a decrease in black centralization of 8 points, or 17 percent. This, in turn, should lead to a predicted 3 percent increase in exposure of whites to blacks and a 5 percent increase in exposure of blacks to whites.

In the set of five variables proxying for "prejudice" segregation forces, all consistently demonstrated statistically significant relationships with segregation except the proportion of whites age 45 or older. Because there were no clear theoretical guidelines for specifying linear or log-transformations of the black population size, proportion, and relative growth variables, both forms were tried, and the superior form reported here. There was no marked sensitivity of results to the different specifications, except for the absolute size of the black population. Here the log-transformed variable (LBSMSA) was much more strongly correlated to both exposure indexes than the linear form.[15] The signs of the direct paths indicated that an SMSA with more blacks than another would be expected to have less interracial exposure but also less black centralization, which tends to offset the former effect somewhat.

In order to comprehend the net effect of these countervailing relationships, consider two SMSAs that have all characteristics equal to the sample mean, except that one has twice as many blacks as the other. The net result would be that the one with the larger black population would be expected to have 6 percent less exposure of whites to blacks, 11 percent less exposure of blacks to whites, and 3.5 percent less centralization of blacks.

The ratio of blacks to whites in the SMSA (BWSMSA) proved positively correlated with white-black exposure and negatively correlated with black-white exposure. The magnitudes of these statistically significant coefficients were such that an SMSA with a .10 higher proportion black would be expected to have a 48 percent higher exposure of whites to blacks and an 8 percent lower exposure of blacks to whites (measured at sample means).

The difference between the decadal black and white population growth rates (BWCHNG) was significantly, positively correlated with black-white exposure and black centralization. The coefficients indicated that one would predict that an SMSA with a .10 higher comparative black-white growth rate would have a 49 percent higher exposure of blacks to whites and a 39 percent greater degree of black centralization.

The proportion of whites who have college degrees (PWCOLEG) demonstrated a significant positive correlation with white-black exposure and was negatively correlated with black centralization. Coefficient magnitudes were such that an SMSA with a one percentage point higher proportion of white college graduates would be expected to have 14 percent greater white exposure to blacks and 10 percent less black centralization.

The control variables used as additional predictors of black centralization— the relative cost of housing in the central city versus suburb (COSTCCR) and the proportion of jobs in the central city (PCCJOBS)—demonstrated the expected signs. All else equal, if COSTCCR was .10 higher, black centralization should be 11 percent less; if PCCJOBS was .10 higher, it should be 5 percent greater.

Conclusions and Policy Implications

The model presented in this chapter was based on the theoretical proposition that three conceptually distinct causes of the extent and pattern of segregation —class, prejudice, and discrimination—could be identified. Empirical tests demonstrated the veracity of this approach. They also suggest that previous empirical studies in this area suffer from serious specification errors in that they omit controls for the crucial component of discrimination.

As for the "class" component, black-white differentials in median incomes proved to be by far the most significant correlate of black centralization. Through this correlation, it had a somewhat less important relationship with interracial exposure rates. The combined beta coefficients for the median income ratio variable's direct and indirect paths to exposure are of the same order of magnitude as the coefficient for the discrimination variable, but are considerably smaller than most of those for the three black demographic variables. This latter result contrasts with that obtained by Marshall and Jiobu (1975), who found that interracial income differentiation was the most important predictor of Taeuber's block-based segregation index for both northern and southern central cities in 1960, although they did not distinguish the pattern from the extent of segregation. The current results should not, however, be interpreted as clear evidence that the "class" component of exposure is an insignificant dimension. First, the measured impacts of class are likely biased downward in the present study compared to those of Marshall and Jiobu. Here a census tract is used as the basis for computing exposure, whereas a block-based index has been shown to be more sensitive to income differentials (Roof and Van Valey 1972). Second, there is likely some simultaneity bias in the "class" estimate, as explained below.

Support for the "prejudice" dimension is provided by results for the variables measuring the size, proportion, and relative growth of the black population and white educational levels. The absolute size of the black population was the strongest predictor of black exposure to whites. The fact that the log-transformation of this variable fit the exposure data far better suggests that the decreases in black exposure to whites are sizable as the black population grows from a small base, but are tempered as the black population continues to grow larger. This is consistent with self-segregation forces generated by both races. As the black population grows toward some "critical mass," black supportive institutions should begin to spring up in rapid succession, thus encouraging blacks to congregate in predominantly black communities. Once these key institutions are in place, further increases in the black population have comparatively smaller self-segregating effects. From a white perspective, the apparent black "threat" associated with a somewhat larger black population may be greater when the black population first starts to become visible, as compared to when a significant black presence already has been established.[16]

The proportion of blacks in the SMSA was positively correlated with the exposure of whites to blacks. This was clearly the result of (aforementioned) geometric factors, as the argument based on white prejudice would have predicted the opposite relationship. The negative correlation between the proportion black and exposure of blacks to whites is consistent with both geometric and self-segregation explanations, and there is no way to discern their relative contributions.

The relative growth of black versus white populations over the previous decade was positively correlated with exposure of blacks to whites yet also to black centralization. This apparent anomaly can be explained by disequilibrium processes of neighborhood transition. Larger black population growth would likely generate a good deal of black expansion on the periphery of the ghetto, setting in motion the process of neighborhood transition and white flight in many areas. Thus, at any given moment one would observe relatively fewer whites in central neighborhoods and more blacks living in substantially (if temporarily) white neighborhoods.[17]

The importance of the "discrimination" component of segregation is clearly demonstrated by the results. The strongest correlations with segregation were generated in situations where discrimination (measured as statistically significant amounts of "net discriminatory treatment" of HUD's auditors) was present in *both* owner and renter markets.[18] This finding suggests either that HUD's methodology is not accurately measuring discrimination, or that its impact operates in a nonlinear fashion. That is, it appears that black residential choices may not become noticeably constrained until discrimination reaches some critical "threshold level." Given the magnitudes of net discriminatory treatment in the SMSAs where BDISCRIM = 1, this threshold appears to be when blacks can expect to face discrimination from one out of every three housing agents they will confront.

The model and the results suggest several directions for further research. First, it is reasonable to specify discrimination as an intervening variable between prejudice and segregation in the path model. However, an attempt to predict adequately the existence and degree of housing discrimination in SMSAs was disappointing. Clearly more work is needed here to gain a better understanding of the origins and forms of such activity. Second, although Marshall and Jiobu (1975) have shown there are likely structural differences in relationships between various regions, the paucity of sample size here precluded any sample stratifications.[19] The desirability of obtaining a broader sample of cities for which housing discrimination is measured is manifest. Third, the model presented here is recursive, yet various elements are likely simultaneously determined (Yinger et al. 1979:114–17; Galster 1981). For example, housing discrimination and segregation could influence interracial economic differentials by (1) intensifying interracial competition and the likelihood of labor market discrimination (Franklin 1968; Roof 1972) and (2) reducing black access to jobs and superior educational systems (Masters 1975; Yinger et al. 1979:96–118). The demographic and economic characteristics of the black population itself may also be endogenous if black migration is responsive to variations in discrimination and economic inequality (Marshall and Jiobu 1975; Masters 1975:chap. 4). What the foregoing means is that the estimated path coefficients may be subject to simultaneous equation bias. In particular, the current model likely understates the correlation of median income differentials with segregation.

In spite of these shortcomings, the empirical results reported here hold great importance for public policy if one assumes that the estimated coefficients are indicative of causal relationships. Despite 1968 federal civil rights law, housing discrimination clearly persisted in 1977, and was likely responsible for a significant portion of the extent and pattern of racial segregation observed in metropolitan areas where it was present. If, for example, housing discrimination were eliminated in SMSAs where it was present in both housing tenure markets, the results lead one to predict that, *ceteris paribus*, white exposure to blacks would increase by 45 percent, black exposure to whites would increase by 38 percent, and relative black centralization would decrease by 26 percent in these areas.[20] The potential payoffs for effectively enforced fair housing policies are thus manifest.

APPENDIX
Glossary of Variable Definitions

BCINDEX	Index of centralization of blacks relative to whites, scaled $-100 - +100$[a]
BDISCRIM	"One" = statistically significant levels of housing discrimination in both rental and sales markets; "zero" otherwise[b]
BWCHNG	Difference in proportional changes in black population-white population, 1960–70[a]
BWMEDIN	Ratio of black-white median income for families and individuals $\times$ 100[a]
BWSMSA	Ratio of black-white populations in SMSA $\times$ 100[a]
COSTCCR	Weighted average of ratios of median house values and median rents in central city vs. ring $\times$ 100[a]
EXPBW	Index of exposure of blacks to whites, scaled 0–99.9[c]
EXPWB	Index of exposure of whites to blacks, scaled 0–99.9[c]
(L)BSMSA	(Common log of) number of blacks in SMSA[a]
PCCJOBS	Proportion of SMSA employment located in central city $\times$100[a]
PWCOLEG	Proportion of whites in SMSA with college degrees[a]
PWSTP	Proportion of whites in SMSA age 45 or older[a]

a. From *1970 Census of Population and Housing*, calculated by author.
b. From Housing Market Practices Survey (Wienk et al. 1979).
c. From Schnare (1977:table app. B1).

NOTES

1. The "dissimilarity" index of segregation (see Taeuber and Taeuber 1965; Sorensen, Taeuber, and Hollingsworth 1974) for central cities dropped slightly for most cities during the 1960s. This is misleading, however, because it does not include segregation in noncentral city jurisdictions. Schnare's (1980) exposure measures do include the latter in their computation.

2. For a complete review of the empirical literature, see Yinger et al. 1979:71–75; Yinger 1979:446–49. The social harms of segregation have been documented in Yinger et al. 1979:96–118.

3. Marshall and Jiobu (1975) found that interracial dissimilarity indexes for both income and occupation were significantly correlated with Taeuber's residential dissimilarity (segregation) index in 1960. A comprehensive summary of findings is contained in Yinger et al. 1979:76–79 and Yinger 1979:448–49.

4. For a thorough review and critique of empirical studies of preference for neigh-

borhood racial composition based on multiple regression analyses of housing price data, see Yinger 1979 and Mieszkowski 1979.

5. A more complete description of the sampling technique and a list of sampled SMSAs is given in Wienk et al. 1979:20–30.

6. Dissimilarity indices have been employed by Taeuber and Taeuber (1965) and Sorensen, Taeuber, and Hollingsworth (1974). Another reason for not using the D index was that published values were not available for 14 SMSAs in the HMPS sample.

7. Seven rings were used for each of the calculations for this study with population figures for tracts obtained from the 1970 *Census*. The innermost three rings were scaled with radii = .05R, .10R, .15R, respectively, where R is the longest radius from CBD to edge of SMSA. The next two rings had radii = .25R and .35R. The final two rings had radii = .67R and R. Calculations of the BCINDEX are available from the author on request.

8. For details, see Wienk et al. 1979:30–37, chaps. 2, 3. A minimum of 30 rental and 30 sales units were audited in each SMSA. For a critique of the methodology, see National Commission Against Discrimination in Housing 1979 and Yinger 1982.

9. In this sample, 23 SMSAs had significant discrimination in the rental market, 15 had it in the sales market, 7 had it in both, and 9 had it in neither. The 7 SMSAs where BDISCRIM = 1 were Detroit, Fort Lauderdale-Hollywood (Fla.), Indianapolis, Los Angeles, Milwaukee, Tulsa, and York (Pa.).

10. It could be reasonably argued that discrimination should be modeled as an intervening variable, that is, prejudice and class differences themselves contribute to discrimination as well as to segregation (see Marshall and Jiobu 1975; Schnare 1977; Yinger 1979). Such a specification was estimated, but only one variable (the log of the absolute number of blacks in an SMSA) proved statistically significant. Further, for no trial did the F-test allow one to reject the hypothesis that coefficients of all variables were zero. In the results presented, BDISCRIM is thus modeled as exogenous.

11. This may not be a fair assumption, especially because the migration patterns of blacks during the 1970s were very different from those witnessed in previous decades.

12. This measure admittedly provides little information about the disparity between races at various points of the income distribution. Nevertheless, when interracial "dissimilarity" indices for both income and occupation were tested in the model, they proved far less statistically significant than BWMEDIN. This contrasts sharply with the findings of Marshall and Jiobu (1975). Ideally, one would also have a variable measuring the distribution of housing qualities over space in an SMSA. It was beyond the scope of the present study to construct such a variable.

13. COSTCCR is defined as the average of central city/ring median values of owner-occupied homes plus the ratio of median rents, weighted by proportions of the two stock types in the SMSA.

14. The combined effect of BDISCRIM on exposure is the sum of the direct path plus the product of the indirect paths via BCINDEX. For EXPWB it is −.16; for EXPBW it is −.25. See Table 3.

15. This is consistent with the findings of Marshall and Jiobu (1975), who used 1960 data and Taeuber's segregation index. LBSMSA is used in both exposure index equations; BSMSA, in the centralization equation.

16. These nonlinearities in the apparent "threat" represented by the black population have been found elsewhere by Galster (1982).

17. A similar argument has been used to explain the Taeubers' (1965) finding of an inverse relationship between the degree of segregation and black growth rates from 1940 to 1950 and from 1950 to 1960.

18. Various specifications (not reported here) hinted that there may, however, be important differences between the two tenures. Discrimination in the rental market alone was associated with nearly as low a level of exposure of whites to blacks as was discrimination in both markets. This implies that the houses in white areas that most likely would be occupied by blacks in the absence of discrimination would be of rental tenure. Discrimination in owner markets was associated with as high a level of black centralization as discrimination in both. This could be expected, because the typical ecological pattern of owned versus rented dwellings is such that the former are more decentralized.

19. The use of regional dummy variables in the model was eschewed here due to the difficulty in interpreting the myriad of unspecified effects that might be proxied for.

20. The means of EXPWB, EXPBW, and BCINDEX for SMSAs where BDISCRIM = 1 are 2.76, 28.6, and 51.7, respectively.

REFERENCES

Blalock, Herbert. 1956. "Economic Discrimination and Negro Increase." *American Sociological Review* 21 (October): 584–88.
———. 1957. "Percent Nonwhite and Discrimination in the South." *American Sociological Review* 22 (December): 677–82.
Bradburn, Norman, Seymour Sudman, and Galen Gockel. 1970. *Racial Integration in American Neighborhoods.* Chicago: National Opinion Research Center.
Campbell, A., and H. Schuman. 1968. "Racial Attitudes in 15 American Cities." In *Supplemental Studies for the National Advisory Commission on Civil Disorders.* Washington, D.C.: U.S. Government Printing Office.
Downs, Anthony. 1973. *Opening Up the Suburbs.* New Haven: Yale University Press.
Duncan, Otis, and Beverly Duncan. 1955. "Residential Distribution and Occupational Stratification." *American Journal of Sociology* 60 (March): 493–503.
Farley, Reynolds. 1977. "Residential Segregation in Urbanized Areas of the U.S. in 1970." *Demography* 14 (November): 497–518.
———, H. Schuman, S. Bianchi, D. Colsanto, and S. Hatchett. 1978. "Chocolate City, Vanilla Suburbs: Will the Trend toward Racially Separate Communities Continue?" *Social Science Research* 7 (December): 319–44.
Franklin, Raymond. 1968. "A Framework for the Analysis of Interurban Negro-White Economic Differentials." *Industrial and Labor Relations Review* 21 (April): 367–74.
Galster, George. 1977. "A Bid-Rent Analysis of Housing Market Discrimination." *American Economic Review* 67 (March): 144–55.
———. 1980. "Class and Segregationist Attitudes." Unpublished paper, Urban Studies Program, College of Wooster.
———. 1981. "Subjectivity, Systems, and the Underclass." Unpublished paper, Urban Studies Program, College of Wooster.

————. 1982. "Black and White Preferences for Neighborhood Racial Composition." *American Real Estate and Urban Economics Association Journal* 10 (Spring): 39–66.

Haugen, Robert, and James Heins. 1969. "A Market Separation Theory of Rent Differentials in Metropolitan Areas." *Quarterly Journal of Economics* 83 (November): 660–72.

Hermalin, Albert, and Reynolds Farley. 1973. "The Potential for Racial Integration in Cities and Suburbs." *American Sociological Review* 38 (October): 595–610.

Kain, John, and John Quigley. 1975. *Housing Markets and Racial Discrimination.* New York: National Bureau of Economic Research.

Leven, Charles, James Little, Hugh Nourse, and R. Read. 1976. *Neighborhood Change.* New York: Praeger.

Lieberson, Stanley. 1963. *Ethnic Patterns in American Cities.* New York: The Free Press.

Marshall, Harvey, and Robert Jiobu. 1971. "Urban Structure and the Differentiation between Blacks and Whites." *American Sociological Review* 36 (August): 638–49.

————. 1975. "Residential Segregation in U.S. Cities: A Causal Analysis." *Social Forces* 53 (March): 449–60.

Masters, Stanley. 1975. *Black-White Income Differentials.* Madison: Institute for Research on Poverty, University of Wisconsin.

Middleton, Russell. 1976. "Regional Differences in Prejudice." *American Sociological Review* 41 (February): 94–117.

Mieszkowski, Peter. 1979. *Studies of Prejudice and Discrimination in Urban Housing Markets.* Boston: Federal Reserve Bank.

Morrill, Robert. 1965. "The Negro Ghetto." *Geographical Review* 55 (July): 339–61.

National Commission Against Discrimination in Housing. 1979. *The HMPS Survey: Another Perspective on the Analysis.* Washington, D.C.: National Commission Against Discrimination in Housing.

Park, Robert. 1967. "The Urban Community as a Spatial Pattern and Moral Order." In *Robert Park: On Social Control and Collective Behavior*, edited by Ralph Turner. Chicago: University of Chicago Press.

Pettigrew, Thomas. 1973. "Attitudes on Race and Housing." In *Segregation in Residential Areas*, edited by Amos Hawly and Vincent Rock. Washington, D.C.: National Academy of Sciences, 21–84.

————, ed. 1975. *Racial Discrimination in the U.S.* New York: Harper and Row.

Redick, Richard. 1956. "Population Growth and Redistribution in Central Cities." *American Sociological Review* 21 (February): 38–43.

Roof, Clark. 1972. "Residential Segregation of Blacks and Racial Inequality in Southern Cities." *Social Problems* 19 (Winter): 393–407.

————, and Thomas Van Valey. 1972. "Residential Segregation and Social Differentiation in American Urban Areas." *Social Forces* 51 (September): 87–91.

Schelling, Thomas. 1972. "A Process of Residential Segregation: Neighborhood Tipping." In *Racial Discrimination in Economic Life*, edited by Anthony Pascal. Lexington, Mass.: Lexington Books.

Schnare, Ann. 1977. *Residential Segregation by Race in U.S. Metropolitan Areas.* Washington, D.C.: The Urban Institute.

————. 1980. "Trends in Residential Segregation by Race: 1960–70." *Journal of Urban Economics* 7 (May): 293–301.

Schuman, H., and S. Hatchett. 1974. *Black Racial Attitudes*. Ann Arbor: Survey Research Center, University of Michigan.

Smith, Barton. 1977. *Separating Discriminatory Segregation from De Facto Segregation*. Washington, D.C.: U.S. Department of Housing and Urban Development.

Sorensen, Annemette, Karl Taeuber, and Leslie Hollingsworth. 1974. *Indices of Racial Residential Segregation for 109 Cities in the U.S., 1940–1970*. Madison: Institute for Research on Poverty, University of Wisconsin.

Straszheim, Mahlon. 1974. "Housing Market Discrimination and Black Housing Consumption." *Quarterly Journal of Economics* 88 (February): 19–43.

Taeuber, Karl, and Alma Taeuber. 1965. *Negroes in Cities*. Chicago: Aldine.

Wienk, Ron, Cliff Reid, John Simonson, and Fred Eggers. 1979. *Measuring Racial Discrimination in American Housing Markets: The Housing Market Practices Survey*. Washington, D.C.: U.S. Department of Housing and Urban Development.

Wonnacott, Ronald, and Thomas Wonnacott. 1979. *Econometrics*. 2nd ed. New York: John Wiley and Sons.

Yinger, John. 1976. "Racial Prejudice and Racial Residential Segregation in an Urban Model." *Journal of Urban Economics* 3 (July): 383–406.

————. 1979. "Prejudice and Discrimination in the Urban Housing Market." In *Current Issues in Urban Economics*, edited by P. Mieszkowski and M. Straszheim, pp. 430–68. Baltimore: Johns Hopkins.

————. 1982. "Measuring Racial and Ethnic Discrimination with Fair Housing Audits." Unpublished paper, Program in City and Regional Planning, Harvard University.

————, George Galster, Barton Smith, and Fred Eggers. 1979. "The Status of Research into Racial Discrimination and Segregation in American Housing Markets." *HUD Occasional Papers* 6 (December): 55–175.

Zoloth, Barbara. 1974. *An Investigation of Alternative Measures of School Segregation*. Madison: Institute for Research on Poverty, University of Wisconsin.

Section III
Social and Attitudinal Factors
Affecting Housing Integration

Introduction

JOHN M. GOERING

The severest critics of the movement toward housing integration charge that public and private housing desegregation programs involve the forced, artificial merging of races that would rather be left alone to determine who their neighbors will be. Integration and desegregation programs are seen as inequitable and unfair—as a violation of the integrity of local communities. A New York journalist typified many of these attitudes in his description of residents' reactions to a proposed subsidized high-rise housing project for one New York neighborhood:

> Scatter-site housing. Preach it from the pulpit Sunday morning. Speak of it from a lectern at Yale or Berkeley. Advocate it to old classmates over coffee at Gracie Mansion. But don't take the subject to the people because they will roar against you through meetings in the night. And if you ever dare to try to build scatter-site housing, the people—ordinary people, people who have lived sedentary lives, who have never done much of anything physical in their lives—will rush into the streets and they will picket and fight policemen and throw themselves in front of trucks and attempt to attack a mayor. And from the dark recesses of the American Soul, little men will appear, men you have never heard of, and they will stand in front of the crowd to harangue and the television lights will turn on them and the despair for the American Soul will rise with the sound of their voices." (Breslin 1974:vii)[1]

Such communities often angrily reject accusations that they are prejudiced. One suburban Chicago mayor "bristled" at the suggestion that his community was segregated: "Berwyn has been integrated for the 40 years that I've lived here. We've got Czechs, Poles, Italians, Irish. We've got Dutch, Asians, Hispanics, Greeks" (Wiessler and Bosc 1983:28). Others, after close examination of such communities, have found racial fears and anxiety deeply interwoven with residents' rejection of planned or natural racial change. Andrew Greeley, assessing racial fears in one Chicago neighborhood, argues that reactions are not pure prejudice or bigotry, but derive from fears and insecurity based on others' experiences with racial change:

> An increase in the amount of murder, rape, and burglary in the neighborhood may not be something that is accepted as just punishment for the sins of the white race. To tell the Beverlyites that most blacks are not criminal would be to state something they would not deny, but it only takes one to two stabbing murders such as occurred in Beverly's sister neighborhood South Shore to create an atmosphere of intense fear that

no community can long survive. The terror in white neighborhoods at the time of black immigration may very well be excessive, but again, terror has never been known to decrease in the human population simply because pious liberals arrive on the scene to announce that terror is excessive. (Berry 1979:245)

Such anxieties related to expected changes in the racial composition of local housing markets are a well-known, deeply entrenched fact frustrating efforts at promoting or maintaining housing integration.

Race-related tensions in neighborhoods of large cities like New York and Chicago generally dominate the public's perceptions of the probable outcome of housing desegregation. Generally lost from sight are the modest number of successfully integrated communities whose integrated status survives, in part, because it is unheralded (Hunt 1959). Recent research also suggests that scattered-site housing in a large number of cities has been more successfully accepted by local residents than the "worst cases" lead one to believe (Hogan 1984; "Most of Dispersed Housing" 1984).

Is the virulent opposition to housing, or school, desegregation only the visible tip of an iceberg of racial resentment? Or do the examples of successful desegregation reveal contrary evidence of more tolerant racial attitudes? The chapters in this section explore the many shades and possible interpretations of the attitudes of Americans toward racial integration. These analyses synthesize much of what is known about the concurrence of racial intolerance as well as racial residential stability. The extent to which Americans prefer racially homogeneous, segregated neighborhoods is the first piece of attitudinal puzzle necessary to assess the strength and directions for racial residential harmony.

In the late 1960s, survey researchers found that nearly 20 percent of all Americans reported living in stably integrated areas, although the average number of blacks living in these areas was quite low — 3 percent or less (Bradburn, Sudman, and Gockel 1970: 30, 84).[2] Roughly ten years later, a nationwide survey of over 7,000 white, black, and Hispanic households found substantially more respondents expressing a willingness to live in integrated areas. These data reveal that 60 percent of whites would accept some form of residential integration, although only 17 percent would select a substantially integrated area. Roughly two-thirds of all blacks indicated their willingness to live in an integrated or all-white community, although only 2.5 percent said they were willing to be racial pioneers. The remaining blacks, one-third, stated a preference for predominantly or all-black residential areas. Hispanics appeared less hesitant than blacks to become pioneers in white areas, with 9 percent willing to move to all-white neighborhoods, and nearly 80 percent willing to accept life in a mainly white community (Office of Policy Development and Research 1978). These attitudes are congruent with the patterns of residential concentration for Hispanics reported earlier by James and Tynan (see Chapter 4).

A major part of the explanation for the difference between Americans' expressed preferences and the actual racial composition of neighborhoods is the gap between what Americans believe in principle and what they will accept in practice. In a careful assessment of changing racial attitudes over the last several decades, Bobo, Schuman, and Steeh, in this section, find a pronounced, systematic gap between attitudes toward *principles* of racial equity and reactions to the *means* used to implement the principles. Whites, more so than blacks, are much less supportive of various modes of civil rights implementation, including fair housing laws, than they are of the basic principle of racial integration. The substantial increases in the expressed willingness of white Americans to live near modest numbers of blacks parallel, therefore, the responses reported in the 1978 HUD Survey. Bobo, Schuman, and Steeh, advancing the analysis of racial attitudes, also find a rejection of full-scale integration, with more than half of all Americans saying they would move if "great numbers" of blacks moved into their communities.[3] And although there has been a substantial increase in support for an open housing law, less than half of whites, and roughly three-quarters of blacks, support such laws.

Part of the explanation of the changes in attitudes toward programs for racial equity relates to shifting personal priorities in areas unrelated to race. Survey research concerning the general aspirations and hopes of Americans reveals that only 7 percent of respondents in 1974 felt that social justice and the elimination of discrimination were what they most wanted in their lives. A better standard of living, good health, a happy family life, owning a home, employment, and peace in the world were values that were judged to be of higher priority—of greater salience. By 1981, discrimination and social justice were not even listed among the items judged by whites to be of greatest personal importance (Setlow 1976a:1448; Watts 1981:40).

Many other issues can also cause "slippage" between an integrative or prejudicial attitude and the actual movement to another community (Speare, Goldstein, and Frey 1975; Goodman 1978; Goodman and Streitwieser 1983). Rose Helper, in this section, provides an assessment of many of the allied sociological, organizational, and attitudinal factors that need to be in place in order for some level of racial residential mixing to succeed. Institutional pressures in real estate, mortgage lending, and schooling are identified as crucial parts of the context for resisting or succeeding at integration. Based on a variety of case studies and her own research, she lists key factors that are likely to be associated with successful integration, whether singly or, more likely, in combination. She in particular focuses on the role of community organizations that have helped to foster racial stabilization in a number of cities. Helper, like other students of racial attitudes, is aware of the substantial levels of racial hostility and conflict that occur when blacks arrive. There is also enough evidence of cooperation and goodwill, she finds, to suggest that more racially mixed communities will emerge.

Helper's report is one of only a handful of attempts to synthesize research evidence on interracial housing into general principles and policy recommendations (Social Science Panel 1972; Downs 1973; Millen 1973; McFall 1974; Beach 1975; Pedone 1976; Brennan 1977; Orfield 1979). Most of these assessments are based on case studies conducted at widely different times, in different cities, and with differing research objectives, perspectives, and methodological rigor (Grier and Grier 1960; Rosen and Rosen 1962; Schermer and Levin 1968; Alfred and Marcoux 1970; Bradburn, Sudman, and Gockel 1970:29-63; Molotch 1972; Gruen and Gruen 1979:119-45; Heumann 1973, 1979; Ginsberg 1975; Tobin 1976; Goodwin 1979; Berry 1979; Varady 1979; Weinberg 1980; Lake and Winslow 1981; Saltman 1983).

Such case studies have generated differing assessments of the relative utility of neighborhood organizations in fostering stable neighborhood integration. A wide range of legal and illegal activities have been undertaken by such organizations with varying levels of support from residents and local officials. At times such organizing efforts have been too late to be of any use in creating accepting attitudes, increased cohesion, and biracial strategies, or in developing remedial programs. In some instances, organized efforts have spotlighted the neighborhoods' problems and increased white flight. The strength of organized or informal neighborhood ties could be of considerable importance in encouraging, or shaming, people to remain. Such cohesion could operate in an informal, nonorganized fashion to stabilize housing patterns, but would likely eventually succumb to the weakened structural or economic underpinnings of many of these older, ethnic neighborhoods (Yancey and Erikson 1979; Berry 1979).

Neighborhoods, formally organized or not, may experience acts of racial violence that may intimidate blacks as well as potential white inmovers. Such actions may symbolize the frustration and inability of residents and local leaders to develop an acceptable, organized response to racial newcomers and, in turn, serve as an opening for more militant antiblack organizations to become involved in local affairs (Aldrich 1975:336; Berry 1979:191). Such occurrences, limited evidence suggests, only exacerbate the tendency for whites to flee and discourage other households from replacing them (Bradburn, Sudman, and Gockel 1970:61, 95; Farley, Richards, and Wurdock 1980; Lake 1981:94-95).[4]

One factor deeply implicated in the frustrations of neighborhood groups to achieve integration is the association of blacks with status loss. "From the perspective of the American cultural context . . . 'black' carries the imputation of status inferiority and a black or integrated neighborhood is considered low status" (Berry et al. 1976:247; Marston and Van Valey 1979:22; Krefetz 1979; Conrad 1980). More educated, cosmopolitan or accepting whites may, under certain conditions, not oppose racial mixing and may even adopt a more positive attitude toward integration (Deutsch and Collins 1951; Gans 1967; Hamilton and Bishop 1976). How long-standing or stable such changes are, however, is unknown given the normal turnover of residents. Better-off residents in expensive homes, located at a distance from the ghetto, with few concerns about municipal services will think twice about moving. They may wait months or years before deciding to leave for "racial" reasons.

One of the major obstacles to the placement of HUD-assisted housing in many communities is indeed the interlocked fear of blacks and status decline (Berry et al. 1976; Conrad 1980; McGrew 1981). The prospect that low- and moderate-income housing would be placed in Dayton, Ohio, for example, generated fears of declining property values, a loss in neighborhood status, less stability, and a perceived decline in law and order as well as in the quality of schools (Gruen and Gruen 1972:64; Ford 1972). Race was not stated as an important reason for their opposition to federal housing, but the interconnection between the two appears inescapable in most other jurisdictions.

Few case studies or analyses of housing integration have, however, focused in detail on federal or local housing desegregation, although school desegregation figures prominently in many studies. Local community leaders can play an important role in determining the location and type of assisted housing for specific neighborhoods. There is some evidence, however, that public officials are relatively unconcerned with the problems of housing segregation and discrimination. A survey of roughly 125 state and 250 local housing officials conducted in 1973 revealed that the need for more housing for low-income groups was at the top of their list of priorities, whereas only 2 percent of officials were concerned about bias in public housing. But public officials were acutely sensitive to public opposition to the siting of low- and moderate-income housing, with the greatest concerns expressed by suburban officials. When asked about the low-rent public housing program, the biggest concerns of local officials were not with its racial makeup but with its condition, maintenance, and the shortage of funds (Setlow 1976b:1326–52).

A more recent survey of attitudes of mayors of large cities indicates that the main barriers to an effective housing policy in their cities are still seen as the low income of residents and inadequate housing, with discrimination viewed as the least pressing concern (United States Conference of Mayors 1984:23). The majority of elected officials surveyed believe, in fact, that, although problems of poverty have greatly increased, problems of discrimination and segregation have remained unchanged or improved. Public officials, at least those in larger cities, appear distracted from the issues of desegregation and discrimination as they focus on addressing the housing needs of the poor. This priority has been, as will be seen in Section IV, of considerable importance in the evolution of federal housing desegregation policy.

Both citizens and public officials appear, therefore, to have other choices and preferences in their schemes of personal and public priorities. Neighborhoods searching for assistance in stabilizing their housing stock may find public disinterest as well as political resistance. The needs of communities at or near the point of racial transition may be so pressing, however, that they may not be able to wait while other citizens, voters, and public officials notice their needs. Apathy, fear, and out-migration may result as residents realize the huge obstacles in the path to neighborhood racial stability (Winerip 1985:B1).

Officials and other neighborhood groups may also be aware that, if one community succeeds in slowing or stopping the process of racial change, other nearby areas may feel the ripple effects of deflected black housing demand. Many may realize the social science axiom that by solving the problem of racial change in one area one may accelerate it in others (Downs 1981:99; Winerip 1985). Neither social scientists nor policymakers are, however, knowledgeable or shrewd enough to be able to predict how much stabilization or exclusion in one submarket will impact what type of similar or contiguous markets.

Case studies and survey research have taught us much of what we know about how specific contextual and historical factors shape and accelerate the attitudes and choices of black and white neighbors. All too often, however, case studies are a very limited basis upon which to build national programs or to draw implications for national policy. Case studies have generally not provided the careful quantification of local and regional, social, economic, fiscal, and political pressures needed by policymakers.

There are, therefore, some notable handicaps in developing a model or even a catalog of factors promoting residential integration and in being certain that conclusions are sound, replicable, and policy relevant. The following is a summary of these limitations, the blank research spaces, which others will hopefully fill building on the work of Bobo, Schuman, and Steeh; Helper; and others:

• Relatively few of the determinants of racial change or stability have been rigorously tested for their importance; thus, it is not clear what order of importance to attach to the determinants identified, or to specify how they interact with each other. The evidence justifying the inclusion of some items is often impressionistic and judgmental.

• It is unclear how the determinants vary in importance over time within, as well as between, neighborhoods and cities.

• There is no reason to believe that the current list of determinants is exhaustive or immutable. The interaction of macro- and micro-level contextual influences in specific settings has been poorly examined and may produce new effects and determinants.

• It is unclear whether the conditions for long-term stability are the same as those for short-term success. It is also not clear what long-term racial stability means—whether ten years or forty years is a reasonable standard for neighborhood change.

• Although recommendations for policy action or intervention are made by researchers, there is no way to know what unintended effects could arise from implementing them in another city or neighborhood. What works in one area may backfire in another, or simply have no effect at all. Most of the recommendations are also made in hindsight, offering what the author feels could have made a difference had they been tried in time. That is, it is not really clear which variables are intractable and which are amenable to some degree of positive policy intervention.

- A substantial number of the case studies referred to above are based on research on racial succession and efforts to thwart it, rather than on integration per se. There has been more careful research done to explain how and why neighborhoods change racially than to explain the more unusual event of racial stability. It is hazardous to suggest that by simply reversing the findings in studies of racial succession a cure can be found that will promote stability. Much of what the National Academy of Sciences wrote over a decade ago still applies: "Where these situations have been studied, their small scale and diversity inhibit generalization. Furthermore, what has been written is often descriptive, impressionistic, and strongly committed to particular policies" (Millen 1973:150). The reason why some areas with comparable housing remain stably integrated while similar areas do not remains a question that will only be answered with careful, long-term comparative research and program evaluation.

NOTES

1. I am indebted to Professor William Hanna for pointing out this quotation to me.

2. The Bradburn data were gathered in 1967, a year before the passage of the Fair Housing Act. Attitude surveys reported that, in 1974, 42 percent of whites reported black neighbors; a year later the proportion dropped to 33 percent (Pettigrew 1980:70–71). Variations in the questions used to determine integration, as well as other survey or sampling design factors, are most likely responsible for these shifts in responses. There is no way to assess the role of publicity surrounding the debate and passage of the Fair Housing Act in fostering these shifting responses.

3. No attempt is made to review all of the sociological and social-psychological literature on racial tipping that relates to this finding. For more details on this, see Schelling 1972; Farley et al. 1978; Farley, Bianchi, and Colosanto 1979; Goering 1978. The sometimes dramatic shifts in pro- and anti-integration attitudes of older and younger, urban and rural blacks are also not explored here (Paige 1970; Apostle and Glock 1983).

4. There are often substantial disagreements among analysts of interracial neighborhood organizing about its effectiveness. Heumann (1979:6), for example, believes that "effective neighborhood organizations can either counter or redirect institutional actions that encourage racial segregation." He notes the important role of the rate of black population pressure but argues that strong public commitment by neighborhood organizations is a necessary and, in some instances, sufficient condition for racial stabilization (Heumann 1973). Others are considerably less sanguine about the prospects that neighborhood groups can address in a sustained, legal, nonracist manner all the forces impacting areas experiencing racial transition. The commitment and amenities found by Heumann in West Mt. Airy are indeed quite "rare." The exclusion of renters from his analysis (as having "very little input into the evolution of stable integration") is not an option all neighborhoods can afford, especially because many public policy levers are designed to address the rehabilitation or construction of rental housing. Heumann also only examines public policies, such as housing rehabilitation, from the perspective

of local organizations whereas national or federal policies and programs, which may then be utilized by local organizations, are constrained in ways that fundamentally alter the options for neighborhood groups.

REFERENCES

Aldrich, Howard. 1975. "Ecological Succession in Racially Changing Neighborhoods: A Review of the Literature." *Urban Affairs Quarterly* 10 (March): 327–48.

Alfred, Stephen, and Charles Marcoux. 1970. "Impact of a Community Association on Integrated Suburban Housing Patterns." *Cleveland State Law Review* 19 (January): 90–99.

Apostle, Richard, and Charles Glock. 1983. *The Anatomy of Racial Attitudes.* Berkeley: University of California Press.

Beach, Mark. 1975. "Desegregated Housing and Interracial Neighborhoods: A Bibliographic Guide." National Neighbors, Philadelphia.

Berry, Brian. 1979. *The Open Housing Question: Race and Housing in Chicago, 1966–1976.* Chicago: University of Chicago Press.

———, C. Goodwin, R. Lake, and K. Smith. 1976. "Attitudes towards Integration: The Role of Status in Community Response to Racial Change." In *The Changing Face of the Suburbs*, edited by Barry Schwartz, pp. 221–64. Chicago: University of Chicago Press.

Bradburn, Norman, Seymour Sudman, and Galen Gockel. 1970. *Racial Integration in American Neighborhoods.* Chicago: National Opinion Research Center.

Brennan, Mary Lou. 1977. "The Characteristics of Integrated Neighborhoods: A Review of Existing Research." Working Paper 246–3, The Urban Institute, Washington, D.C., April.

Breslin, Jimmy. 1974. Preface to *Forest Hills Diary*, by Mario Cuomo, pp. iii–xii. New York: Random House.

Conrad, Dorothy. 1980. "Low Income Housing and Neighborhood Resistance." In *Reinvestment and Housing Equality in Michigan: Local Decisions and Federal Funds*, pp. 51–57. Washington, D.C.: U.S. Commission on Civil Rights, September.

Deutsch, Morton, and Mary Collins. 1951. *Interracial Housing: A Psychological Evaluation of a Social Experiment.* Minneapolis: University of Minnesota Press.

Downs, Anthony. 1973. *Opening Up the Suburbs.* New Haven: Yale University Press.

———. 1981. *Neighborhoods and Urban Development.* Washington, D.C.: The Brookings Institution.

Farley, Reynolds, H. Schuman, S. Bianchi, D. Colosanto, and S. Hatchett. 1978. "Chocolate City, Vanilla Suburbs: Will the Trend toward Racially Separate Communities Continue?" *Social Science Research* 7 (December): 319–44.

———, S. Bianchi, and D. Colasanto. 1979. "Barriers to the Racial Integration of Neighborhoods: The Detroit Case." *The Annals* 441 (January): 97–113.

———, T. Richards, and C. Wurdock. 1980. "School Desegregation and White Flight: An Investigation of Competing Models and Their Discrepant Findings." *Sociology of Education* 53 (July): 123–39.

Ford, W. Scott. 1972. *Interracial Public Housing in Border City: A Situational Analysis of the Contact Hypothesis.* Lexington, Mass.: Lexington Books.

Gans, Herbert. 1967. *The Levittowners*. New York: Random.

Ginsberg, Yona. 1975. *Jews in a Changing Neighborhood*. New York: The Free Press.

Goering, John M. 1978. "Neighborhood Tipping and Racial Transition: A Review of Social Science Evidence." *Journal of the American Institute of Planners* 44 (January): 68–78.

Goodman, John L. 1978. "Urban Residential Mobility: Places, People and Policy." The Urban Institute, Washington, D.C.

————, and Mary Streitwieser. 1983. "Explaining Racial Differences: A Study of City-to-Suburb Residential Mobility." *Urban Affairs Quarterly* 18 (March): 301–25.

Goodwin, Carole. 1979. *The Oak Park Strategy: Community Control of Racial Change*. Chicago: University of Chicago Press.

Grier, George, and Eunice Grier. 1960. *Privately Developed Interracial Housing: An Analysis of Experience*. Berkeley: University of California Press.

Gruen, Nina, and Claude Gruen. 1972. *Low and Moderate Income Housing in the Suburbs: An Analysis for the Dayton, Ohio Region*. New York: Praeger.

Hamilton, David, and George Bishop. 1976. "Attitudinal and Behavioral Effects of Initial Integration of White Suburban Neighborhoods." *Journal of Social Issues* 32: 46–67.

Heumann, Leonard. 1973. "The Role of Urban Housing as a Physical, Social and Economic System in Existing and Maintaining Stable Racial and Socio-Economic Integration." In *Urban Housing*, edited by Vasily Kouskoulas, pp. 120–28. Detroit: Wayne State University Press.

————. 1979. "Racial Integration in Residential Neighborhoods: Toward More Precise Measures and Analysis." *Evaluation Quarterly* 3 (February): 59–79.

Hogan, James. 1984. "Scattered-Site Housing—A Success Story" and "The Scattered-Site Alternative." Unpublished papers. Department of Political Science, Seattle University, Washington.

Hunt, Chester. 1959. "Private Integrated Housing in a Medium Size Northern City." *Social Problems* 7: 195–209.

Krefetz, Sharon. 1979. "Low- and Moderate-Income Housing in the Suburbs: The Massachusetts Anti-Snob Zoning Law Experience." *Policy Studies Journal* 8 (Special #1): 288–99.

Lake, Robert. 1981. *The New Suburbanites: Race and Housing in the Suburbs*. New Brunswick, N.J.: Center for Urban Policy Research.

————, and Jessica Winslow. 1981. "Integration Management: Municipal Constraints on Residential Mobility." *Urban Geography* 2: 311–26.

McFall, Trudy. 1974. "Racially and Economically Integrated Housing: Can It Work? Under What Conditions?" Unpublished paper. Metropolitan Council, St. Paul, Minnesota.

McGrew, Jane. 1981. "Resistance to Change Continues to Restrict Public Housing Choices." *Journal of Housing* 38 (July): 375–80.

Marston, Wilfred, and Thomas Van Valey. 1979. "The Role of Residential Segregation in the Assimilation Process." *The Annals* 441 (January): 13–25.

Millen, James. 1973. "Factors Affecting Racial Mixing in Residential Areas." In *Segregation in Residential Areas*, edited by Amos Hawley and Vincent Rock, pp. 148–71. Washington, D.C.: National Academy of Sciences.

Molotch, Harvey. 1972. *Managed Integration*. Berkeley: University of California Press.

"Most of Dispersed Housing Projects in 87 Cities Are Said to Be Successes." 1984. *New York Times*, 30 September, p. 32.

Office of Policy Development and Research. 1978. "The 1978 HUD Survey on the Quality of Community Life: A Data Book." HUD–PDR–350. U.S. Department of Housing and Urban Development, Washington, D.C., November.

Orfield, Gary. 1979. "Federal Agencies and Urban Segregation: Steps Toward Coordinated Action." In *Racial Segregation: Two Policy Views*, pp. 6–44. New York: The Ford Foundation.

Paige, Jeffrey. 1970. "Changing Patterns of Anti-White Attitudes among Blacks." *Journal of Social Issues* 26 (Autumn): 69–86.

Pedone, Carla. 1976. "Neighborhood Dynamics: A Review of Previous Studies and Some Strategies for New Empirical Research." Working Paper 243–2. The Urban Institute, Washington, D.C., November.

Pettigrew, Thomas. 1980. "Racial Change and Intrametropolitan Distribution of Black Americans." In *The Prospective City*, edited by Arthur Solomon, pp. 52–79. Cambridge, Mass.: The MIT Press.

Rosen, Harry, and David Rosen. 1962. *But Not Next Door*. New York: Ivan Obolensky, Inc.

Saltman, Juliet. 1983. "Neighborhood Change: Theories, Realities, Prospects." Unpublished report. National Neighbors, Washington, D.C.

Schelling, Thomas. 1972. "A Process of Residential Segregation: Neighborhood Tipping." In *Racial Discrimination in Economic Life*, edited by Anthony Pascal. Lexington, Mass.: Lexington Books.

Schermer, George, and Arthur Levin. 1968. *Housing Guide to Equal Opportunity: Affirmative Practices for Integrated Housing*. Washington, D.C.: The Potomac Institute.

Setlow, Carolyn. 1976a. "A Study of Public Attitudes toward Federal Government Assistance for Housing for Low Income and Moderate Income Families." In *Housing in the Seventies Working Papers 2*, National Housing Policy Review, pp. 1433–81. Washington, D.C.: U.S. Government Printing Office.

————. 1976b. "A Survey of the Attitudes and Experience of State and Local Government Officials with Federal Housing Programs." In *Housing in the Seventies Working Papers 2*, pp. 1326–82. Washington, D.C.: U.S. Government Printing Office.

Social Science Panel. 1972. *Freedom of Choice in Housing: Opportunities and Constraints*. Washington, D.C.: National Academy of Sciences.

Speare, Alden, Sidney Goldstein, and William Frey. 1975. *Residential Mobility, Migration, and Metropolitan Change*. Cambridge, Mass.: Ballinger.

Tobin, Gary. 1976. "An Analysis of Attitudinal Responses of Movers in Transition Neighborhoods." Working Paper HMS 7. Institute for Urban and Regional Studies, Washington University, St. Louis.

United States Conference of Mayors. 1984. "Housing Needs and Conditions in America's Cities: A Survey of the Nation's Principal Cities." Joint Hearing on Housing Needs — Mayor's Perspective. Subcommittee on Housing and Community Development, Washington, D.C., 2 October.

Varady, David. 1979. *Ethnic Minorities in Urban Areas: A Case Study of Racially Changing Communities*. Boston, Mass.: Martinus Nijhoiff Publishing.

Watts, William. 1981. "The Future Can Fend for Itself." *Psychology Today* 15 (September): 36–48.

Weinberg, Meyer. 1980. "Integrating Neighborhoods: An Examination of Housing and School Desegregation." *Journal of Housing* 37 (December): 630–36.

Wiessler, David, and M. Bosc. 1983. "Ghettos That People Don't Want to Get Out Of." *U.S. News and World Report*, 25 April, pp. 28–30.

Winerip, Michael. 1985. "L.I. School District Torn Over Issue of Integration." *New York Times*, 6 February, pp. B1, B4.

Yancey, William, and Eugene Erickson. 1979. "The Antecedents of Community: The Economic and Institutional Structure of Urban Neighborhoods." *American Sociological Review* 44 (April): 253–62.

Chapter Seven
Changing Racial Attitudes toward Residential Integration

LAWRENCE BOBO*

HOWARD SCHUMAN

CHARLOTTE STEEH

The separation of blacks and whites into different residential neighborhoods has been labeled the "structural linchpin" of American race relations (Pettigrew 1979). It is a key factor shaping the character of interaction between the races, and it greatly affects other matters like the potential for school integration and the type of job opportunities open to blacks. As compared to progress in the legal and economic status and general treatment of blacks, change in the racially segregated makeup of communities has come much more slowly. To what extent is residential segregation a reflection of public attitudes and preferences? Do Americans, white or black, hold attitudes that impede progress in this domain?

In an effort to shed light on these questions, this chapter reports trend results of cross-sectional national surveys of racial attitudes toward residential integration, utilizing data gathered over the last several decades. We are not the first to report such over-time changes (see Pettigrew 1973; Taylor 1979), but this analysis is unique in its connection to a larger study of changes in attitudes on a wide range of racial issues. Thus, we will regularly refer to the ways in which attitudes on residential integration resemble or differ from patterns observed for other racial issues. In addition, we report data on the attitudes of blacks and make several illuminating comparisons to the attitudes of whites.

Attitudes on residential integration are not neatly separable from attitudes in other domains of race relations. In our larger study of such attitudes—only a small part of which is reported here—two patterns emerged that tended to crosscut issue domains. First, we found recurring differences in the overall levels of support and extent of positive change depending on a key conceptual distinction between racial principles and the implementation of such principles (see also Jackman 1978; Pettigrew 1979). Attitude questions concerned with racial principles ask respondents whether they endorse broad ideals of nondiscrimination and integration, but make no reference to how such ideals might be put into practice. Implementation questions deal with steps the government

* This chapter was prepared with the help of John M. Goering. The collection and analysis of data were supported by an NIMH grant (MH 34116), with supplementary assistance from the Social Science Research Council. Related methodological research was supported by the National Science Foundation (SES-8016136).

(usually but not always meaning the federal government) might take to reduce discrimination or segregation. As shown below, principle questions generally achieve a higher level of pro-integration or pro-equal treatment response and have moved more steadily in a positive direction over time than comparable implementation questions.

Second, the degree of integration mentioned in a question influences responses. A number of questions we examined concern social distance preferences. This type of question asks the respondent how he or she would react in particular situations involving differing degrees of integration at a personal level. Such questions deal with the principle of integration, but they do so not in an abstract way, nor in terms of government enforcement, but rather at the level of the individual's behavior or feelings about being personally a part of the change. The questions can be considered abstract in another sense, however, for they ask people to *predict* how they would react in the hypothetical situation described. Importantly, whether the concern was with schools or housing, the number of blacks mentioned as being involved in the proposed integration influenced white responses.

Trends in White Racial Attitudes: The Principle of Residential Integration

Table 1 presents two questions that we classify as exclusively or primarily concerned with broad principles toward residential integration and choice. Results are given for all available time points for samples intended to represent the total white adult population 21 years of age or older. Percentages are given only for the more positive or pro-integration responses.

One of the two questions comes from the National Opinion Research Center (NORC) with data beginning in 1963; the other comes from the Institute for Social Research (ISR) with the series beginning in 1964.[1] Both of these questions are somewhat "loaded" in the sense that they emphasize individual rights, and this is especially true for the NORC item that speaks only of white rights. Perhaps for this reason, the two questions behave rather differently. The ISR question indicates that the level of acceptance of black rights approached 90 percent by 1976 and might well have exceeded that point had the question been asked since that time. The NORC question presents a somewhat different picture. Starting at a much lower level of acceptance of the right of blacks to choose any residential neighborhood they wish, the acceptance—which involves disagreeing with the item—shows signs of leveling off after 1972, though perhaps resuming a small upward slope in the last two years. However, if the break on the four-point scale for this item is made between "agree strongly" and the other three choices, the absolute level and the overall trend are more similar to the ISR version. We believe that the difference in absolute levels between the ISR and NORC versions is due to the more one-sided wording of the NORC

Table 1. Questions Concerning Principles

Questions	Year of Survey																					Last Minus First
	63	64	65	66	67	68	69	70	71	72	73	74	75	76	77	78	79	80	81	82	83	
Residential Choice 1 alt (NORC)																						
% Agree slightly	21					25		18		15				18	21			17		15		-6
% Disagree slightly	20					25		19		23				26	29			29		32		+12
% Disagree strongly	19					19		34		40				34	28			38		39		+20
Residential Choice 2 alt (ISR)																						
% Blacks have rights	65					73		76		80				87	88							+23

Question Wordings and Variants

Residential Choice 1 alternative (NORC)
"Here are some opinions other people have expressed in connection with Black-White relations. Which statement on the card comes closest to how you yourself feel? White people have a right to keep Blacks out of their neighborhoods if they want to, and Blacks should respect that right."
1. Agree strongly
2. Agree slightly
3. Disagree slightly
4. Disagree strongly

Residential Choice 2 alternatives (ISR)
"Which of these statements would you agree with: White people have a right to keep Black people out of their neighborhoods if they want to, or, Black people have a right to live wherever they can afford to, just like anybody else?"
1. Keep Blacks out
2. Blacks have rights
(Variant: In 1964 replace "anybody else" with "white people.")

question, a phenomenon noted in other research (Schuman and Presser 1981: chap. 7), and one that indicates that adherence to principles at the abstract level is somewhat a function of how the principles are stated.

More puzzling is the partial difference in trends: although it may be due also to the question wording difference, the provision of a scale of four choices, with two degrees on each side of the issue, may play a role as well. It is possible that the movement of attitudes is not so much clearly toward acceptance of integrated housing as it appears to be when a dichotomized choice is forced, but rather is away from strong adherence ("agree strongly") to the principle of segregated housing.

Both of these questions are clearly related to a respondent's level of education. For example, in 1964, 53 percent of those with 11 or fewer years of education supported free residential choice for blacks when asked the ISR version of the question. This compares with 70 percent of those with 12 years of education (high school graduates), and 76 percent of those with 13 or more years of education (at least some college) who supported free choice. The last point at which this question was asked, 1976, reveals substantial change for all three educational levels. The percentage of whites supporting free residential choice for blacks was 80, 89, and 94 percent, respectively, for those with less than a high school education, high school graduates, and those with at least some college. These figures reflect an average change over the period covered of about +20 percent.

More recent data are available for the NORC residential choice question. The 1982 results for this question show that 82 percent of those with at least some college are opposed ("disagree slightly" + "disagree strongly") to allowing whites to "keep blacks out of their neighborhoods." In contrast, only 56 percent of those with less than a high school education favored blacks' rights, as did 61 percent of those who were high school graduates. On the whole, the effect of education on the residential choice questions is similar to that found with other racial principle questions.

In addition, responses to these questions are influenced by region. In 1964 only 38 percent of southern whites supported free residential choice for blacks when asked the ISR version of the question.[2] This compares with 74 percent of northern whites taking such a position, a difference of 36 percent. Similarly, when NORC first asked its residential choice question in 1963, 25 percent more northern than southern whites gave the pro-integration response, 46 versus 21 percent. These regional differences diminished over time. Thus, the difference between northerners and southerners on the ISR question dropped to only 9 percent in 1976, with 90 percent of whites in the North and 81 percent of whites in the South supporting free residential choice. But the difference between the regions undergoes less dramatic reduction for the NORC question. Although support for the pro-integration response among southern whites had risen to 57 percent by 1982, northern white support had risen to 76 percent, leaving a difference of 19 percent.

Table 2. Implementation Question

Questions	Year of Survey 73|74|75|76|77|78|79|80|81|82|83	Last Minus First
Open Housing (NORC)		
% No discrimination	34| |34|35| |37| |40| | |46|	+12

Question Wordings and Variants

Open Housing (NORC)

"Suppose there is a community-wide vote on the general housing issue. There are two possible laws to vote on. One law says that a homeowner can decide for himself who to sell his house to, even if he prefers not to sell to Blacks. The second law says that a homeowner cannot refuse to sell to someone because of their race or color. Which law would you vote for?"

    1. Homeowner can decide
    2. No discrimination

The difference between the two questions in the amount of regional convergence is, again, probably a result of differences in question wording and response levels (northern response to the ISR item having nearly reached a ceiling). There is less convergence on the NORC item with its more one-sided wording, which does not explicitly mention the rights of blacks and therefore results in lower overall support for nondiscrimination. All in all, the movement toward regional convergence, especially that observed in the ISR item, is typical of our results for most principle questions. This general pattern of convergence, where the North nears a ceiling and the South progressively catches up, includes questions concerning equal job opportunities, access to public accommodations and to public transportation, and school integration.

Attitudes toward Implementing Residential Integration

Attitudes toward implementation deal with approval or disapproval of steps that might be taken by the government to end housing discrimination or segregation. Ideally, it would be useful if the questions exactly paralleled the principle questions in both content and dates, but this is not always the case. Trend data are available for one implementation-type question concerning the issue of residential integration.

The implementation question deals with open housing laws, with results presented for the white adult population as a whole. This question, shown in Table 2, gives an indication of the extent of white willingness to enforce free choice for black homeseekers. The question also has the advantage of referring to a "community-wide vote" to prevent housing discrimination, so that concern over federal intrusion into local affairs is not relevant to the results.

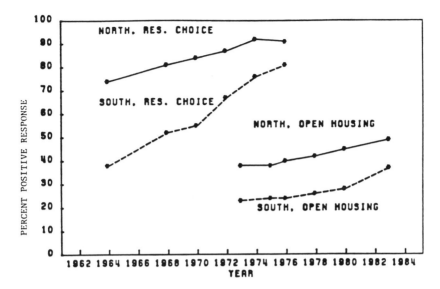

Residential Choice: 2 alternatives (ISR)
"Which of these statements would you agree with: White people have
a right to keep black people out of their neighborhoods if they
want to, or, black people have a right to live wherever they can
afford to, just like anybody else?" 1. Keep blacks out 2. blacks have
right

Open Housing (NORC)
"Suppose there is a community-wide vote on the general housing issue.
There are two possible laws to vote on. One law says that a homeowner
can decide for himself who to sell his house to, even if he prefers not
to sell to blacks. The second law says that a homeowner cannot refuse
to sell to someone because of their race or color. Which law would you
vote for?" 1. Homeowner can decide 2. No discrimination

Figure 1. Attitudes Toward Free Residential Choice and Open-Housing
Laws

Table 2 and Figure 1 show that support for open housing legislation is not
strong, reaching only 46 percent at the peak. This is in contrast to the upper
levels reached in support of the *principle* that blacks have a right to live in
white neighborhoods if they wish: 88 percent on the ISR version of the question (shown in Figure 1) and 71 percent on the NORC version. (The ISR
question on residential choice seems the more appropriate one for comparison,
because it, like the open housing question, presents a dichotomous choice between two alternatives that are balanced in the sense that each alternative
offers an appealing rationale.) This gap between support for the principle of
free residential choice and laws to implement the principle is consistent with
the results for other principle-implementation pairings on such issues as school
integration and equal job opportunities. Although we do not place heavy emphasis on isolated instances of differences in marginal percentages, we cannot

disregard them when they occur repeatedly and consistently in comparisons of principle and implementation questions.

The difference in levels of support notwithstanding, there is a positive trend ($p < .001$) on the open housing question, although during the comparable time period when both were asked (1972–73 to 1976), the residential choice question showed a clear positive change (+8%), whereas the open housing question showed virtually none at all (+1%). In addition, there are regional differences with regard to open housing laws, as there are for residential choice. And there are clear monotonic differences by educational category: the more education, the more support for opening housing. The differences are somewhat smaller, however, than for the principle itself. The positive effect of increasing education on the open housing question sets it apart from implementation questions on other issues, which usually have only a negligible relation to educational levels.

In sum, the results for the open housing implementation question appear to resemble, though on a reduced scale, the results for the residential choice question. There is some support for open housing legislation, but it is more limited than is support for the principle of residential integration; there is some definite increase in that support, but it is less sharp. It is important to note, however, that support for an open housing law has continued to grow over the recent past, and it is at least possible that in this area of life attitudes toward implementation will parallel, with some degree of lag, attitudes toward principle. It will be especially important to follow future time points for this trend.

We should be cautious, however, before concluding that there is a deepening commitment to enforce open housing laws. Our examination of other principle-implementation pairings suggests that reversals in public sentiment can occur. For example, a sizable drop in the willingness of whites to endorse federal efforts to implement school desegregation occurred between 1972 and 1978. This decline occurred despite high and increasing support for the principle of integrated schooling (see Schuman, Steeh, and Bobo 1985:chap. 3).

Furthermore, in order to better understand the generally low levels of support for implementation items, we conducted an experiment using different questions. The results of this experiment indicate considerable reluctance to enforce free residential choice for blacks. An ISR national telephone survey in November 1983 included two forms of a question we prepared on enforcing nondiscrimination in housing, with each form administered to a random half of the sample. Our experimental manipulation of wording distinguished between enforcement by the "government" and enforcement by "laws," the latter presumably suggesting a more orderly and judicious procedure than the former. In addition, both forms of the question speak of "a black family" (i.e., a single family) in order to reduce the possible fear by white respondents of a mass influx of blacks and thus to concentrate on the issue of legal enforcement as such. Finally, in order to avoid pressuring respondents to fit into either alternative of a simplistic dichotomy, we instructed interviewers to accept (and

Table 3. Experiments on Support for Enforcement of Non-Discrimination in Housing

Government Version		Laws Version	
On another subject, suppose a black family plans to move into a house in an all-white neighborhood, and some white people in the neighborhood want to stop them from moving in. Do you think the government should enforce the black family's right to live where ever they can afford to, or that it should be left entirely up to the white neighborhood residents to decide? (IF "OTHER" VOLUNTEERED, ACCEPT AND RECORD.)		On another subject, suppose a black family plans to move into a house in an all-white neighborhood, and some white people in the neighborhood want to stop them from moving in. Do you think there should be laws to enforce the black family's right to live where ever they can afford to, or that it should be left entirely up to the white neighborhood residents to decide? (IF "OTHER" VOLUNTEERED, ACCEPT AND RECORD.)	
1. GOVERNMENT ENFORCE	52.2%	1. LAWS TO ENFORCE	56.1%
2. LEAVE IT UP TO WHITE NEIGHBORS	15.9	2. LEAVE IT UP TO WHITE NEIGHBORS	4.9
3. OTHER TYPES OF RESPONSE		3. OTHER TYPES OF RESPONSE	
a. Says laws already exist	0.7	a. Says laws already exists	4.1
b. Favors non-discrimination but does not support enforcement	21.7	b. Favors non-discrimination but does not support enforcement	23.6
c. Opposes enforcement no other comments	2.9	c. Opposes enforcement, no other comments	1.6
d. Other vague responses "depends, don't know"	6.5	d. Other vague responses "depends, don't know"	9.8
	100		100
	(138)		(123)

record) volunteered "other" responses, which in fact more than a third of the respondents did offer. In the end we classified most of the "other" responses as implying rejection of legal or government enforcement, despite the frequent affirmation of support for the *principle* of nondiscrimination.

The experimental results shown in Table 3 suggest that specification of laws rather than government may make it easier for respondents to support implementation but the difference does not reach significance for the most crucial test and, in any case, is not very large. Furthermore, although the proportion supporting "laws to enforce" nondiscrimination in housing is higher than most figures for implementation items, it is considerably below the 88 percent that supported nondiscrimination in housing in principle in 1976 (the ISR residential choice item), and even below the 66 percent that in 1974 supported government intervention to prevent discrimination in access to hotels and restaurants (data not shown; see Schuman, Steeh, and Bobo 1985:chap. 3). It seems evident that an important segment of the population upholds the right of black people to live wherever they wish *but* is unwilling to see legal means used to enforce that right. Unfortunately, our experiment did not probe further to discover how this apparent inconsistency is best explained.

Social Distance

The third substantial set of trend questions that are available asks white respondents how they personally would feel with regard to particular situations

Table 4. Social Distance Questions

Questions	42	43	44	45	46	48	50	56	57	58	59	60	61	62	63	64	65	66	67	68	69	70	71	72	73	74	75	76	77	78	79	80	81	82	83	Last Minus First
Next Door (Gallup)																																				
% Might										23					24	23	21	24														10				-13
% No										56					55	63	66	63														86				+30
Great Numbers (Gallup)																																				
% Might										29					28	30	31	32														33				+4
% No										20					23	28	30	28														46				+26
Same Block (NORC)																																				
% No	36							53							63	64	69	71	77				85													+49

Question Wordings and Variants

Next Door (Gallup)
"If Black people came to live next door, would you move?"
1. Yes, definitely
2. Might
3. No

Great Numbers (Gallup)
"Would you move if Black people came to live in great numbers in your neighborhood?"
1. Yes, definitely
2. Might
3. No

Same Block (NORC)
"If a Negro with the same income and education as you have moved into your block, would it make any difference to you?"
1. Yes
2. No

involving racial integration. Thus the questions, shown in Table 4, concern practical situations, but with the focus not on government or other political forms of implementation, but on predicting one's own behavior in such situations. For most respondents, of course, the situations are hypothetical and we are not here directly concerned with whether the predictions would turn out to be valid. Instead, we consider the predictions informative in their own right and especially useful because they differentiate rather clearly among several degrees of integration acceptable to whites at a personal level.

The first two questions in Table 4 asked whether respondents would themselves move if, at one extreme, blacks came to live "next door," and at the other extreme, "great numbers" of blacks came into the neighborhood. (Although the "next door" question is not wholly unambiguous, it is probably taken to refer to a single black family considered in isolation from other changes.) These two questions were always asked together (by Gallup) in that sequence at different points between 1958 and 1978. The third question by NORC more clearly involves a single black person or black family, specifies that income and education are the same as the respondent's, and speaks of the same block rather than next door—all of which might elicit more white acceptance. On the other hand, the inquiry has to do with this making "any difference" to the respondent (rather than with actually moving), which might more easily allow a negative answer. The time period is also different for this item (1942 to 1972) from the Gallup period, but there is enough overlap to allow close comparison.

Such a comparison, presented graphically for the total population in Figure 2, indicates that the "same block" and "next door" questions yield quite similar results, despite their several differences in wording, and both show much higher support than the "great numbers" question. All of the questions show a clear upward trend. By the end of the time periods (late seventies in one case, mid-seventies in the other), northern respondents approach 90 percent positive answers with regard to a black family moving "next door" or onto the "same block," and 48 percent for "great numbers of black people moving into the neighborhood." Separate analysis shows that southern respondents are definitely less positive, paralleling the North at a lower level over the entire period, but with some convergence in more recent years.

On the two questions about single black families, college-educated respondents in the North give more positive responses than do other educational groups, but the difference is not large and it does not hold as clearly for southern respondents. In the case of the "great numbers" question, there are no clear educational differences in either region, just as there were no clear educational differences for a question concerning the acceptability of school integration where "more than half" of the children were black (data not shown; see Schuman, Steeh, and Bobo 1985:chap. 3). In other words, respondent education is positively associated with personal acceptance of a small number of blacks, but this effect of education disappears when the degree of integration posed by a question is so great as to put whites in the minority. Acceptance of

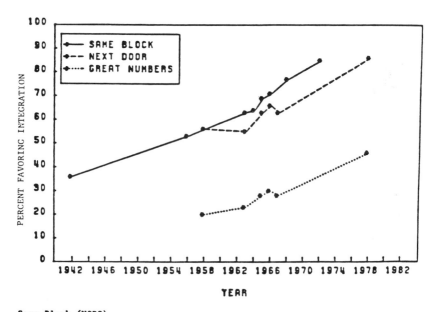

Same Block (NORC)
"If a Negro with the same income and education as you have moved into your block, would it make any difference to you?" 1. Yes   2. No

Next Door (Gallup)
"If black people came to live next door, would you move?" 1. Yes, definitely 2. Might   3. No

Great Numbers (Gallup)
"Would you move if black people came to live in great numbers in your neighborhood?" 1. Yes, definitely 2. Might   3. No

Figure 2. Attitudes Toward Different Levels of Neighborhood Integration

a single black family into one's immediate neighborhood starts at a much lower level than other social distance questions, but shows a sharp climb over the time period available. The upward slope for the housing questions thus represents the increasing acceptance in the past four decades of such small-scale neighborhood residential integration.

Despite some puzzles, the social distance questions form a generally meaningful pattern both internally and in relation to the principle and implementation questions considered earlier. The major change in the past several decades has involved rejection of absolute racial segregation and acceptance of the principle of movement by blacks into previously all-white spheres of life. This is supported by the claim by most whites that they personally have no objection and would not mind if a particular black adult, family, or child moved into their neighborhood, school, or other area of life. Moreover, this acceptance of integration goes beyond the single black individual, and similar answers would be given if the questions involved almost any number of blacks, so long as the number represented a clear minority.

But as soon as questions indicate that blacks might constitute a sizable proportion of the neighborhood (or school) open white objection becomes more pronounced. In addition, a large proportion of whites object to any governmental action that might facilitate such a change from white preponderance, and, so far as we can tell, this opposition has decreased very little over the past four decades. In sum, the change over the past four decades has been away from both the principle and, to an extent, the practice of absolute segregation —and in this sense it has been a genuine and large change—but it has not been clearly toward full integration in the sense of complete acceptance of blacks into white society.

Trends in Black Racial Attitudes: Principles and Implementation

Trend data on black racial attitudes are much sparser than for whites. There are several reasons for this. During the 1940s and 1950s, survey investigators interested in racial issues saw the racial problem as almost entirely one of white acceptance of equal treatment across racial lines. After all, laws and administrative rules upheld racial segregation during much of that period, and large parts of the white population still supported segregation as a general principle. As one of the major initiators of research in this area has commented: "It never occurred to us when we wrote questions in the Forties and Fifties to ask them of blacks because Myrdal's dilemma was a white dilemma and it was white attitudes that demanded study" (Paul Sheatsley, personal communication, 1984).

With the rise of new and diverse forms of political ideology, action, and organization among blacks in the 1960s, it became clear to survey investigators (who were almost always white) that blacks were not merely passive players in the rapidly changing racial scene and that black attitudes should not be assumed to be either self-evident or fixed. Beginning in the 1960s, a few questions on racial issues began to be asked of blacks as well as whites on a regular basis by the major survey organizations. But here the problem becomes one of small numbers of cases, for a typical national sample of 1,500 to 2,000 Americans yields only 150 to 200 black respondents, except in a few instances where supplements were added. These black sample sizes mean that even overall distributions of answers lack the sampling reliability we were able to count on in the analysis of white attitudes. Moreover, there are additional problems of possible race-of-interviewer effects and also because in some instances questions originally designed for white respondents are less appropriate or less clear in meaning when asked of black respondents.

Despite these limitations, the available data from national surveys on black attitudes are of considerable value. Comparisons between black and white

Table 5. Trends in Black Racial Attitudes

Questions	Year of Survey																										Last Minus First
	58	59	60	61	62	63	64	65	66	67	68	69	70	71	72	73	74	75	76	77	78	79	80	81	82	83	
Residential (ISR) Choice 2																											
% Blacks rights						98					98	98	98		99	99	99		99								+1
Open Housing (NORC)																											
% No Discrimination																				71		71				75	+4

answers to the same item turn out to be illuminating, and additional light is cast on certain of the findings for whites when we learn the extent to which blacks show similar or different trends. Therefore, with the necessary caution that smaller sample sizes for the black data make it important to avoid fixation on a single point in a time series, results will be presented for those time lines of sufficient length to allow conclusions about trends in black racial attitudes.

In Table 5 we present the record of black trends for one of the questions dealing with principles and for the open housing question. Responses to the residential choice principle question in Table 5 are very close to 100 percent in one direction at all time points. Similarly high levels of support for the principles of equal treatment and integration were found on the issues of school integration and politics (data not shown; see Schuman, Steeh, and Bobo 1985: chap. 4).

Do blacks respond differently than whites to questions concerning the implementation of principles? Responses concerning the implementation of principles have always received considerably less support from whites than do the principles themselves. It is rather natural to interpret this difference as due to a failure of whites to live up in practice to what they claim to subscribe to in abstract credo. It is important at this point to recognize that blacks also show something of the same disjunction. Black responses on most implementation items (not shown) are always below—and sometimes well below—the near-100 percent levels reached on several principle items.

Table 5, for example, always registers 98 or 99 percent black support for "blacks have the right to live wherever they can afford to." Results presented in Table 5 for the open housing laws question are limited to too short a time span to establish any clear trend, but they do allow us to examine differences in levels of support for principle and implementation. During the 1978–83 period for which black data were collected by NORC, black support for a "no discrimination" law on the open housing item averaged 73 percent; that is, 25 percent less than the 98+ percent supporting black rights to free residential choice in principle. This 25 percent gap for blacks compares with a 53 percent gap for whites in 1976, the most recent year in which whites were asked both questions (one by ISR and one by NORC). Thus the gap for blacks is only half as large as the gap for whites, but both differences are substantial in absolute magnitude. Both blacks and whites find it easier to support the general principle of freedom of residential choice than they do the implementation of the principle by means of an open housing law.

Interpretation and Conclusions

The findings reported here defy simple summary or simple interpretation. On the one hand, there is evidence of a steady progressive trend toward acceptance of the goal of residential integration and toward support for enforcement of blacks' housing rights. These changes are lent further credence by expressed white willingness to take part in integrated living situations that involve more than a token black presence. On th other hand, support for enforcing blacks' rights to free residential choice is well below that for the principle itself. Indeed, respondents proved to be quite willing to endorse the principle and express reluctance to enforce it. Also, whites were sufficiently color conscious to reject participation in integrated settings where blacks were in the majority. What is more, there are other complexities concerning the varying impact of education and region on attitudes, and concerning the attitudes of blacks themselves. If a general label had to be applied to these findings, especially with regard to white attitudes, then perhaps the phrase "meaningful patterns of progress and resistance" would be most appropriate. Several motives or factors may serve to create the mixture of progress and resistance we have described.

One reason for the gap between principle and implementation may be that constraint of any kind is disliked and that the extent to which constraint is accepted is heavily influenced by the *degree* to which a particular policy goal is supported. When there is a strong commitment to a policy goal, support for the use of government authority to reach that goal will usually be expressed as well. This does not mean that those who support a principle but not its legal implementation are without any real commitment to the principle. Such an attempt to separate people into the truly committed and the truly noncommitted is an oversimplification, far removed from the realities of life. Thus, many of those who support residential integration in principle and oppose government implementation of such integration show their modest commitment to the principle by positive answers to social distance items. Both commitment to a principle and commitment to its implementation must be seen as continuous dimensions, and the exact balance between them is always problematic for each member of the population at each point in time. In particular, Taylor (forthcoming) has suggested that one of the prominent cultural motifs in American race relations has been the idea of voluntary, not mandatory, compliance with racial change.

A useful way to view implementation questions is in terms of the psychological forces supporting or opposing a particular response. Because there are some legitimate reasons for questioning almost any nonvoluntary change— whether it is a step to promote racial integration or some other required action —one must ask what are the forces that support implementation in each case. One force in the case of laws promoting equal treatment is a strong commitment to the principle being implemented, and another force is a personal stake in the success of implementation. Blacks tend to have both of these to a high degree where, for example, implementing free residential choice by means of open housing laws is the issue. Therefore, *most* blacks should support such steps toward implementation when asked, although enough do not to create small but significant "gaps" between principle and implementation. White persons, never having been denied freedom of residential choice on the basis of race, do not see any personal interest at stake, and the principle itself is probably so much taken for granted in their own case that commitment to it as a necessary bulwark is not deeply felt.

Thus the reasons for black and white attitudes on residential integration can in good part be the same, yet the balance of forces can be different enough to lead to quite different proportions that finally support or oppose a particular form of implementation. This is not the whole story, for many whites also appear to react as a group to what they perceive as an intruding group threat posed by blacks (Bobo 1983), a point we raised earlier in discussing white objections to situations where they lose majority status (see also Smith 1981).

In addition, it must be admitted that persons answering the question on the principle of residential integration probably run the full gamut from those deeply committed to the idea to those who feel quite otherwise but are embarrassed to admit it to a survey interviewer. We have no way of knowing exactly what the distribution along this continuum is, but quite likely most people fall somewhere in the middle: they feel some genuine belief in the norm but also have other beliefs that leave them conflicted on the issue. One reason to think that outright lying is probably rare in these data is the fact that there is compelling evidence that most people assume that others—in this case, white interviewers—agree with their own views, so there is little reason to expect a felt need for deception on the part of the respondents (Schuman and Kalton forthcoming). On the other hand, it is clear from other trend questions and from trends in actual behavior that many white respondents do feel conflicted about important aspects of integration and that their responses in support of integration in principle are unlikely to be translated directly into action. It is therefore essential that future research try to understand the sources of these conflicts.

One way to do this would be to pose more real-life value and preference conflicts in survey questions. As we suggested earlier, support for the principle of residential integration surely carries some force, but it may lose out when in conflict with other principles (e.g., "individualism"), or with personal preferences (e.g., to live in a largely white neighborhood). This does not mean that integrationist principles are without any efficacy, but rather that in race relations, as in other areas of life, a single principle is not the only or even the major determinant of behavior. For example, a respondent might believe that blacks should be able to live wherever they wish, but so should whites, with the latter meaning the "right" of a white family to leave a changing neighborhood in favor of a largely white neighborhood. Unfortunately, most survey questions do not simulate such real-life conflicts between one principle and another, or between principles and personal preferences, and this leads to results that are more limited to the abstract plane than need be (Schuman 1972).

This suggests that part of the task for the future, in addition to regular monitoring of these important trends, is to develop ways of achieving better under-standing of the intraindividual conflicts, ambivalences, and compartmentalized inconsistencies that are present among most whites and perhaps blacks as well (cf., Katz 1981). Simple questions that assume that people are either for *or* against integration can be very misleading when employed to deal with the psychological and sociological complexities of the relations between blacks and whites in the United States. Any attempt to sketch broad trends using survey data must necessarily simplify the real situation somewhat, but present incon-sistencies in the trend data would almost certainly become more understand-able with additions and improvements in the available set of questions.

In terms of the larger social implications of these results, it would appear that the normative definition of appropriate relations between blacks and whites has changed. Whereas discrimination against, and enforced segregation of, blacks was taken for granted as reasonable and appropriate behavior by most white Americans as recently as the 1940s, today the dominant belief is that blacks deserve the same treatment and respect as whites, and that some degree of racial integration is a positive thing.

For the future, the strong and still growing commitment to equalitarian prin-ciples by whites, and yet the serious inconsistencies when these are applied, indicate the importance of strategic choices and actions by leaders who favor implementation of such principles. Public attitudes are certainly malleable, and unless crystallized in a politically relevant way they are often ineffective; yet once aroused and pervasive, they must be viewed seriously, which is not to say that they are merely to be accepted. A leadership that sees positive racial change as desirable will need to combine clear emphasis on principled ends with carefully chosen means that can win majority support when challenged. When means not likely to win substantial support become necessary, efforts at implementation must be accompanied by equal efforts at persuasion.

NOTES

1. Most of the NORC data prior to 1972 and all of the Gallup data were obtained through the Roper Center, which provided us with specific cross-tabulations. NORC data from 1972 to 1983 were taken from the General Social Survey (GSS) cumulative tape. Most of the ISR data were taken from the National Election Study surveys, data for which were made available through the Interuniversity Consortium for Political and Social Research. A more detailed discussion of data sources, coding, and analysis is provided in Schuman, Steeh, and Bobo 1985.

2. We employ the U.S. Census definition of the South: Alabama, Arkansas, Dela-ware, Florida, Georgia, Kentucky, Louisiana, Maryland, Mississippi, North Carolina, Oklahoma, South Carolina, Tennessee, Texas, Virginia, West Virginia, and the District of Columbia. All other states are defined as "North" except Alaska and Hawaii, which are not included in national survey samples.

REFERENCES

Bobo, Lawrence. 1983. "Whites' Opposition to Busing: Symbolic Racism or Realistic Group Conflict?" *Journal of Personality and Social Psychology* 45: 1196–1210.

Jackman, Mary R. 1978. "General and Applied Tolerance: Does Education Increase Commitment to Racial Integration?" *American Journal of Political Science* 22: 302–24.

Katz, Irwin. 1981. *Stigma: A Social Psychological Analysis.* Hillsdale, N.J.: Lawrence Erlbaum Associates.

Pettigrew, Thomas F. 1973. "Attitudes on Race and Housing: A Social-Psychological View." In *Segregation in Residential Areas*, edited by Amos Hawley and V. Rock. Washington, D.C.: National Academy of Science.

———. 1979. "Racial Change and Social Policy." *The Annals of the American Academy of Political and Social Science* 441: 114–31.

Schuman, Howard. 1972. "Attitudes vs. Actions versus Attitudes vs. Attitudes." *Public Opinion Quarterly* 36: 347–54.

———, and Graham Kalton. 1985. "Survey Methods." In *The Handbook of Social Psychology*, 3rd ed., edited by Gardner Lindzey and Elliot Aronson, 1: 635–97. New York: Random House.

———, and Stanley Presser. 1981. *Questions and Answers in Attitude Surveys.* New York: Academic Press.

———, Charlotte Steeh, and Lawrence Bobo. 1985. *Racial Attitudes in America: Trends and Interpretations.* Cambridge: Harvard University Press.

Smith, A. Wade. 1981. "Racial Tolerance as a Function of Group Position." *American Sociological Review* 46: 558–73.

Taylor, D. Garth. 1979. "Housing, Neighborhoods, and Race Relations: Recent Survey Evidence." *The Annals of the American Academy of Political and Social Science* 441: 26–40.

———. Forthcoming. *Public Opinion, Collective Action and Anti-Busing Protest: The Boston School Desegregation Controversy.* Chicago: University of Chicago Press.

Chapter Eight
Success and Resistance Factors in the Maintenance of Racially Mixed Neighborhoods

ROSE HELPER

In 1979, an article was published under the title, "Social Interaction in Racially Mixed Neighborhoods" (Helper 1979:20–38). Data for this article came from a review of the literature and from four studies the author made in Chicago, three dealing with mixed neighborhoods and one with real estate brokers. The article reported that relationships between neighbors and near-neighbors are friendly, or at least peaceful, where a few black families of middle-class or better social standing are dispersed in a white area, and also where a substantial number of black families live in the area. In fact, friendly and helpful interaction occurs between blacks and whites even when whites are much in the minority, except in some reported cases. The 1979 study concluded that black and white neighbors of similar socioeconomic status generally get along well. Furthermore, the presence of children increases contact between black and white neighbors.

This chapter explores in greater detail the factors that affect the stability of a racially mixed neighborhood, and, for the sake of completeness, repeats some points covered in the previous article. The discussion begins by considering a central concept: the meaning of social integration in racially mixed neighborhoods. This is followed by an examination of first, the roadblocks (resistance factors) to racially mixed neighborhoods; and second, constructive actions (success factors) that contribute to the stability of such neighborhoods.

Of the roadblocks discussed, the first and most potent is the real estate industry with its various forms of influence. Other powerful influences considered are lending agencies, school boards, zoning boards, and other departments of municipal government. The desegregated school is seen as a factor of particular importance in maintaining a mixed neighborhood, and problems concerning it are pinpointed.

Among the factors that contribute to the stability of the mixed neighborhood, dispersal of housing for low- and moderate-income black families is seen as important, but also essential is the racial integration of the school. The slowing of black in-migration is viewed as an aid to the stability of the mixed neighborhood. That white families have for some years been buying homes in areas where black families are living is emphasized, as is the importance of equal status contact between black and white. Other success factors include a good building manager, helpful amenities such as a conveniently located shopping center, and the presence of types of housing conducive to mixed living. The helpfulness of quota systems is discussed. Also described are the useful and intensive work of racially mixed organizations to maintain mixed neighborhoods and the beneficial effects of recently introduced Integration Maintenance programs. The growing number of interracial neighborhoods and integrated public elementary schools is noted. Suggestions for needed research follow the conclusion.

The Meaning of Social Integration in Racially Mixed Neighborhoods

In this chapter the term "mixed" is used because its definition is less arbitrary than "integrated." Here, a "mixed neighborhood" means a neighborhood containing black and white residents, or blacks, whites, and residents of other racial groups. Duncan and Duncan (1957:120) view census tracts with non-white proportions of 25 to 75 percent as tracts with a "mixed" population.

The meaning of integration varies among analysts. Some stress process and/or equality as principal ingredients but with different connotations (Northwood and Barth 1965:50–55; Moore and McKeown 1968:2; Bradburn, Sudman, and Gockel 1970:4–7; Hunt and Walker 1974:8). Heumann (1973:XI–iii) presents a threefold definition, requiring first, a public moral commitment to stable racial integration by a sizable portion of neighborhood residents; second, the physical mixture of residents; and finally, an institutional commitment and related actions to defend and maintain that stable racial mix.

Social integration is here viewed as a process. At any point in the process, social integration is a matter of degree. In a mixed neighborhood, integration refers to a growing recognition of neighbors as human beings. The same sense of integration is present in Pettigrew's (1975:141) statement on school integration: "Integration . . . means not just having children together in the same building, but rather something about the quality of the contact that goes on between them. I'm talking about humanity. I am talking about cross-racial acceptance and friendship and equity and equality." Thus, it is more accurate to describe neighborhoods where both blacks and whites live as "mixed" and to apply the term "integrated" only when some degree of mutual acceptance is occurring.

Resistance Factors

The Real Estate Industry

The real estate industry is still the main cause of problems that undermine racial mixing in residential neighborhoods. Some real estate brokers try to frighten white owners into selling their property in neighborhoods that are close to black areas, attempt to persuade white people not to enter mixed areas, and guide black buyers to mixed or black areas and whites buyers to white areas. Because of blockbusting and racial steering, mixed areas often become entirely black. Several researchers view the real estate industry as the major threat to stable mixed neighborhoods. Darden (1973:46–47) concludes in his study on residential segregation in Pittsburgh that "the most influential element among the discriminating forces seems to be the white real estate broker or salesman." White owners of dwellings are second to white brokers as a force for discrimination (ibid.:49).

The Back-to-the-City Movement

A further problem for mixed neighborhoods, and one often intensified by the actions of real estate agents, is the back-to-the-city movement. In major cities members of the white middle class are returning to inner cities that are the homes of the poor. Although this resettlement is bringing a striking revival to decaying neighborhoods, most of the rehabilitation results in the eviction of poor people who cannot afford to buy or rent housing.[1]

Unequal Access to Market Information Channels

Another hindrance to the development of mixed neighborhoods is unequal access to market information channels. The growth of interracial neighborhoods probably would have received a boost if the Fair Housing Amendments Act of 1980 or 1983 had passed. Although Title VIII of the Civil Rights Act of 1968 prohibits several discriminatory practices, it does not sufficiently protect black homeseekers or home sellers. As Lake (1981:47) points out, restricted access to market information channels for both buyers and sellers raises entry costs for blacks while simultaneously reducing the eventual payoff from home ownership. Lake maintains that suburban black home buyers spend substantially more time in searching than whites, but look at fewer units in.fewer communities.

Other Hurtful Outside Influences

The real estate industry is not the only problem for racially mixed neighborhoods. Heumann (1973:2–3, Abstract) describes other barriers: "The experiences of mixed neighborhoods indicate that any neighborhood which becomes obviously interracial is subject to institutional actions that accelerate transition to a new state of segregation. (These actions are taken by realtors, banks, insurance companies, school boards, zoning boards, peer groups, and many others.)."

In one case, the board of education seemed to be the main force contributing to the end of a mixed neighborhood. The first black family moved into North Beverly View, part of a community area in southwest Chicago with a population of fewer than 600, mostly middle-class people, in 1973. The white children had been attending school just outside the school district in which the area lies. When black parents were told their children could not attend, they protested. The white children started school, but after three days they were told they could not attend either. The Chicago Board of Education had denied admission to both groups. The school situation brought the two groups into communication and helped them to work together on other problems with more success. As for the children, some enrolled in a largely black school about a mile away, while the majority entered private schools.

In October 1974, residents organized the United Association of North Beverly View to hold the neighborhood together as a united community, establishing block clubs and committees to serve community needs. Interracial cooperation occurred on the organizational, community, individual, and family levels and in the association. Black and white residents joined in community gatherings, talked together on the streets, invited one another for dinner, and became acquainted on a first-name basis. By July 1975, the area was 60 percent black and 40 percent white and seemed to be stabilizing (Wysocki 1975).[2]

This neighborhood, it seems, could have continued as a mixed area meeting the needs of the residents if it had not been for the school problem. Early in 1976, because of the continuing inability of the parents to send their children to the nearby school, white residents began moving away, and the neighborhood was rapidly becoming predominantly black.

The school board is not the only municipal body that, at times, has hindered interracial associations in their efforts to maintain mixed neighborhoods. Law courts and judges may also be involved. In 1957, when blacks expressed interest in moving into a small neighborhood on the far southwestern side of Chicago (Helper 1962; 1965:135–40), white residents organized the Winneconna Lakes Area Improvement Association. When blacks moved into the neighborhood in 1958, the association elected a mixed leadership and tried to promote good community relations. By 1961, the area was 50 to 60 percent black, but the association continued to work hard to keep the area mixed. Nevertheless, other factors hindered these efforts. Crime increased and residents found it impossible to obtain more police protection. The association spent two years getting a landlord, guilty of serious violations, to court; the judge fined him $25 and then suspended the fine. Other cases of flagrant official neglect occurred. Absentee landlords exploited buildings. Real estate brokers incited white people to sell their property. Real estate blockbusters, both white and black, undermined the goals of the improvement association, and even "legitimate" real estate firms offered little cooperation.

One factor that may have contributed to the relatively rapid racial change was the difference in status levels among the previously all-white population. Although some were white-collar business executives and professionals, most were blue-collar workers, and leaders found it difficult to unite the two groups behind common goals. This lack of unity among the white residents undermined the sense of community and added to the difficulties of the association.

Yet, in all this change, painful to many whites who felt they had to move, and to whites and blacks who saw their efforts to maintain a mixed neighborhood fail, examples of friendship, cooperation, and solidarity between black and white were common.

Zoning laws, especially in suburbs, that prevent building for multifamily use and reduce the supply of rental housing, have been a major hindrance to the development of mixed communities. At times, after great effort, the stranglehold of the zoning law can be broken—as in the case of Black Jack, Missouri, which illegally sought to block construction of a low-income housing project to prevent blacks from moving into the community. A consent decree issued by the U.S. district court ended twelve years of litigation. "The results in this case are ideal: racially integrated housing for low income tenants has been constructed; the city is now formally committed to a nondiscriminatory housing policy; and violation of the fair housing law was shown to be costly and counterproductive to the transgressor," said Janice Cooper, general counsel of the National Committee Against Discrimination in Housing (National Committee Against Discrimination in Housing 1982:1–3).

Lending agencies—including savings and loan associations, commercial banks, mortgage houses, and insurance companies—have long been an obstacle in the path of mixed housing (Helper 1969:166–72). Lending agencies have barred real estate brokers from selling to black people by refusing to make loans or requiring more difficult terms for black buyers. Redlining or "writing off" an area, that is, refusing to make loans in an area that black people have entered or are likely to enter, or that lending agencies consider to be in a state of decline, is a well-known practice of many lending agencies.

Now a "greenlining" campaign has developed to end redlining. The Philadelphia Council of Neighborhood Organizations announced a pledge campaign called "greenlining" to respond to the continuing problem of redlining in Philadelphia's neighborhoods. Greenlining involves a pledge on the part of concerned citizens to support banks that make mortgage money available to all of the city's neighborhoods. The redlining problem has been alleviated somewhat by the Philadelphia Mortgage Plan (PMP), developed by area banks, which has brought mortgage money back into some neighborhoods. However, not all lending institutions subscribe to the PMP, not all members take the plan seriously, and the PMP itself does not operate in certain neighborhoods. Members of the Philadelphia Council of Neighborhood Organizations and cooperating groups analyze home mortgage disclosure data available by federal law. This law, the Home Mortgage Disclosure Act, requires commercial banks, savings banks, and savings and loan associations to list their mortgages by census tract. This enables those who are interested to determine whether a lending institution is lending money in the city's neighborhoods.

Darden (1973:50) has a kind word to say about white financial institutions. Although he concedes that they have the power to influence the residential location of many black homeowners in the United States, he insists that there is little evidence to support any claim that they have done so in Pittsburgh. He also points out that it is difficult to estimate adequately the role of the lending institution as a discriminating force, for it always is the second link in the chain of operation. Furthermore, financial institutions do not deal with renters. Thus, much of the black population never comes into contact with the lending agencies. Obermanns (1981), on the other hand, concludes that Cleveland's racially diverse suburbs are not well served by area financial institutions.

The Desegregated School as a Factor in the Stability of the Mixed Neighborhood

Before the Civil Rights Act of 1968 was passed, many believed that the main roadblock to achieving racially mixed neighborhoods was the exclusion of blacks and other minority groups from all-white neighborhoods. Now it is clear that open housing legislation is not enough to ensure lasting integration. Eleanor Holmes Norton, former chairman of the New York City Commission on Human Rights, and other workers for mixed neighborhoods emphasize that the most important factor in retaining white middle-class families in the city is the condition of its school system. Jean Milgram, former executive director of National Neighbors, a Philadelphia-based federation of multiracial neighborhood organizations, noted that people most frequently asked for information, first, on how to deal with real estate practices; second, on what to do about schools; and third, on how to influence city government (Kaiser 1976). Little doubt exists about the importance of the mixed school for mixed neighborhood stability.

In an insightful paper, Wegmann (1977) examines the problems of withdrawal from desegregated schools and resegregation. Wegmann maintains that white flight is a class phenomenon as well as a racial issue. He suggests a distinction between withdrawal and nonentrance. Parents who fear for the safety of their children in the mixed school will not enter the mixed neighborhood or will withdraw from it. In anticipatory nonentrance, parents anticipate future racial change and possible unwanted effects. The concerns that lead parents either not to enter the neighborhood or to withdraw their children from the mixed school are likely to be those of quality, safety, and status. Middle-class parents often are afraid that children of a lower social class will influence their children.

Wegmann asks, "To what extent is the racially mixed school truly integrated? Are the students merely physically copresent, or are they relating to one another in an environment of mutual understanding and respect?" This aspect of desegregated schooling seems to him, and to this author, to be the heart of the issue. Furthermore, Wegmann points to the scarcity of reports about programs that structure the school to foster interracial cooperation and understanding. He draws a number of conclusions, among which the following seem the most important:

Little formal research has been done on the motivations behind white withdrawal from desegregated schooling. Worries about the quality of education, student safety, and social status differences may be among the chief causes. To the extent that this is true it could be expected that, other things being equal, school integration would more likely be stable and successful when combined with programs of educational improvement, in settings where concerns about safety are adequately met, and when programs of which parents can be proud are featured. (Wegmann 1977:42)

Obstacles to Urban Integration

Orfield (1981:18–24), in his study of twelve cities, draws attention to certain serious problems regarding urban integration. He found little discussion of housing integration as a policy among elected officials, and even less about the connection between housing and school integration. Cities with delicately balanced school desegregation plans often pursue housing policies that are unintentionally but steadily undermining the school plan. Desegregation plans also frequently bus children out of residentially integrated neighborhoods. Among the districts he visited, only Louisville, Kentucky, has an order that explicitly exempts integrated neighborhoods from busing. In Charlotte, North Carolina, and Columbus, Ohio, children are bused from most integrated neighborhoods. Orfield maintains that with little change in court orders integrated neighborhood schools could be exempted from busing. He says Louisville's approach to exemptions could become a model.

How Success and Failure Factors May Change over Time
as Well as Affect One Another

Sometimes failures may contribute to success. In the back-to-the-city movement, the decline in central city neighborhoods, occurring in Washington, D.C., and other cities, resulted in large part from racial transition and particularly from the inability or unwillingness of former white owners and later the inability of black owners to keep up their property. Incoming suburbanites, benefiting from the lower housing costs in the central declining area, can build up a good, mixed neighborhood.

Success Factors

The Importance of Dispersal

The concentration of black demand on mixed areas near the ghetto fosters racial transition. Dispersal policies would decrease this pressure on mixed communities and, thus, white residents of these areas would be more hopeful about their communities remaining mixed. Also, white families who were planning to move in order to avoid living in a mixed area might decide against it if most suburban communities were also mixed.

Varady (1974:367), in his concern about enabling racially mixed fringe communities to attain some degree of stability, suggests types of neighborhood stabilization strategies that, according to his findings, are most likely to be effective. His own results do not suggest that changing communities appeal more to the young and educated, as is stressed in local stabilization policies (those implemented within mixed areas). He argues that "metropolitan-wide housing policies aimed at dispersing low- and moderate-income black families are more likely to improve the long-range prospects for stabilizing mixed communities."

Increasing Integration in a Metropolitan Area

Although a number of discouraging situations exist in regard to desegregated schools, encouraging developments have occurred. The principal findings of a study by Richard Obermanns (1982) corroborate the conclusion of Wegmann (1977), Orfield (1981), and other researchers that the racial integration of the school cannot be considered apart from the integration of the neighborhood. Obermanns reports that, in the Cleveland metropolitan area, there were more integrated suburban districts and school buildings in 1980 than in 1978 and more students than ever before were attending integrated public elementary schools. Most of the integrated districts and schools in the area also give promise of remaining racially integrated. Most integrated suburban districts voluntarily have taken steps to reduce racial imbalance among elementary schools by closing schools, redistricting, pairing, setting up magnet schools, and encouraging students to transfer voluntarily. Segregated schooling has decreased, but it still remains the norm in the metropolitan area.

The Slowing of Black In-migration

Schnare (1977:59) draws attention to the slowdown in the rate of black in-migration to metropolitan areas and concludes that this may reduce the proportion of blacks living in highly segregated neighborhoods. Schnare suggests that, if migration continues to decrease, future increments in the number of blacks may be more evenly distributed throughout the metropolitan area. Thus, the slowing of in-migration of blacks may contribute to the development of mixed neighborhoods.

The Purchase of Homes by White Families
in Areas Where Black Families Are Living

A common belief exists, especially among most real estate brokers (Helper 1969:74–75), that a white family will not buy a house for personal residence in an area where black families are living. Rapkin and Grigsby (1960) undertook to determine the demand for housing in racially mixed areas in Philadelphia, hardly expecting to find any white purchasers in the four mixed areas they selected for their study. They discovered that, in 1955, 2,017 bona fide transfers of ownership of residential property for owner occupancy occurred in these areas. Of this group of home purchasers, 443 were white and 1,574 were black. This finding, they say, "sheds doubt on the premise that once blacks enter a neighborhood, no white will purchase in the area thereafter." Some of the white purchasers lived previously in mixed areas. In one of the two study areas, where the housing was of good quality, white buyers outnumbered black buyers by two to one; for all four areas, the ratio of black to white purchasers was three to one (Rapkin and Grigsby 1960:17). The authors also learned that, contrary to previous research findings (Rose, Atelsek, and McDonald 1953), almost three-quarters of the white purchasers had children under 18 and half had children of school age. Further investigation revealed some unawareness of the presence of blacks in the area, some dissatisfaction, and a tendency to buy houses somewhat distant from black-occupied residences. The fact remains, however, that almost three-quarters of the white families bought homes on or adjacent to mixed blocks and one-fourth bought on mixed street fronts, but "less than a handful" purchased homes next to black residences.

Rapkin and Grigsby point out that, if it is true that white people will not buy a home next door to a black family, then the occupancy of a black family of a single dwelling unit on a block must eventually result in an all-black block. However, the experience of some real estate firms in Chicago discredits this hypothesis. Several real estate brokers refused to assume that they could not sell to white people in an area where blacks were living. They sold property, although at low prices, to white buyers for residences. One of these brokers said: "From a sale of perhaps one or two houses a year in this neighborhood, we have gone to twelve to fourteen sales per year to white families in an area where blacks are living frequently next door, between, or across the street. It has been our experience that a significant number of white people are willing and even eager to live in a coracial neighborhood providing it remains in all other respects a pleasant place in which to live" (Helper 1969:94).

Other researchers also have reported sales to white people in areas where blacks are living. Northwood and Barth (1965:37) say that, in most of the neighborhoods they studied, they interviewed some white residents who had moved there *after* black entry. Other reports, of a less systematic type, also noted white people moving into mixed areas (*Newsweek* 1971b; Stalvey 1963; Rosen and Nicholson 1959).

Types of Housing Conducive to Racially Mixed Living

The type of housing available is important to mixed living. Researchers have noted that rental units seem to be associated with mixed neighborhoods. Rental units often will not admit families with children, thus eliminating the problems of parents who may not want their children to attend desegregated schools. Furthermore, renting an apartment does not carry the finality and the investment burden of buying a house. Thus, childless couples who have not lived in mixed buildings before might undertake the new experience more readily (Wegmann 1977:22; Rapkin and Grigsby 1960:17; Wolf and Lebeaux 1969: 504–5). Heumann (1973:XI-v–XI-vi) hypothesizes, based on the observations of several Philadelphia realtors, that, when value among housing types is constant, resistance to black entry into very dense row housing is the most severe, and, once blacks enter, it is difficult to maintain stable integration. Some of the reasons for this are the closeness of interracial living and the possibility of life-style differences—real or imagined. Moreover, because row houses tend to be less expensive than other types of housing, and because many black families are in the lower income range, the concentration of black demand would make it difficult to stably integrate row housing.

Cooperative housing has lent itself in a considerable number of cases to mixed living (Milgram 1977:173–83; Grier and Grier 1960:28–29, 199–204, 236–40). Milgram reminds us that the basic principles of cooperatives include open membership with no restrictions on race, creed, or color.

Rochdale Village (Swados 1966) presents a unique example of black-white organizational interaction in an interracial project. This housing complex, which is next to a large black ghetto in New York City, consists of twenty 14-story apartment buildings housing nearly 6,000 families. In 1966, 15 percent of the families were black and 85 percent were mainly Jewish. Some Italian, Oriental, Puerto Rican, and WASP families also lived there.[3] The black residents were almost all middle-class professionals, civil servants, and technicians, whereas the whites were mainly working-class Jews.

Several black residents spoke of clashes between black-white values. The 15- to 18-year-old groups, because of parental pressure, were largely segregated, although the groups claimed they "got along great." There was some uneasiness among Jews at community meetings because of black militancy. Fear also existed among the whites because people from the adjacent black ghetto committed various offenses against white and some black residents despite project security. Yet Rochdale Village generally is an impressive case of black-white interaction, of relative harmony between members of two (in fact, more) minority groups.

As of 20 September 1976 (Weinstein 1976), there were more black residents, but a large proportion of whites continued to live there and the various ethnic groups were represented as before. Blacks and whites were participating in the village's many organizations although some blacks had formed the Black Society for black members only. Some mixed political clubs had also developed. Good relations generally existed between black and white residents.

New, well-constructed buildings make an important contribution to neighbors' relations in mixed communities. An example appears in Wolf and

Lebeaux's (1969:107–54) case study of Lafayette Park, a residential redevelopment area near downtown Detroit. The park contained a high-rise apartment building and 186 single, low-rise units, 10 percent and under 20 percent non-white respectively, where blacks and whites maintained friendly relations. Some white residents for the first time found themselves "inviting black friends to their parties and accepting dinner invitations from black residents who had become their personal friends." Both white and black residents were pleased with the new dwellings.

The Importance of a Good Manager

The importance of a good manager for an interracial housing development has not been fully recognized. Milgram (1977:67–68) tells of Glover Park Apartments, a 73-unit, four-story, hillside building with an elevator near Georgetown in Washington, D.C. When a limited partnership organized by Planned Communities bought the building in 1962, a study by the Social Science Research Bureau revealed that 16 percent of the residents threatened to move if the building were integrated and 10 percent said they would consider moving. However, none of the white residents left when the first black families moved into the building. By 1976, the building was about 12 percent black and "there had been no white flight and no diminution of heavy white demand."

Milgram (1977:68) says the crucial factor is the "social concern of a manager, his or her regard for others" because this alone can transform an apartment house into a truly integrated community.[4] As a result of his own experience in developing mixed communities, he maintains that it does not matter whether the manager is black or white. What does matter is the manager's concern for the welfare of every tenant.

Helpful Amenities

A good shopping center is also important in creating satisfaction among residents of a racially mixed neighborhood. Opportunities arise for greeting neighbors at the store and for eventually even shopping together (Molotch 1972:175). The convenience of a good shopping area with a parking lot nearby may override some qualms of prospective buyers in a mixed area. Carefully supervised and efficiently operated indoor and outdoor recreational facilities for adults and for adolescents—for example, a good park, playground, swimming pool, and well-stocked library—contribute to resident satisfaction.

The Importance of Equal Status Contact

Some studies have shown that equal status contact *before* moving into the neighborhood is an important factor in favorable racial attitudes. Studies by Hunt (1959), Northwood and Barth (1965), Jeffries and Ransford (1969) in relation to the Watts riot, and others support this proposition. Bradburn, Sudman, and Gockel (1970:406) concede that their data do not tell whether pro-integration attitudes were present before interracial contact or developed after such contact.

Improvement in racial attitudes *after* equal status contact in a mixed neighborhood was emphasized in the Deutsch and Collins (1951) study and elsewhere (Wilner, Walkley, and Cook 1955). More recently, the equal status contact hypothesis has met with some qualification. For example, the Meer and Freedman (1966) study, which tested this hypothesis, found no reduction of prejudice in the white neighbors of the black families studied.

Zeul and Humphrey (1971) regard the contact hypothesis as simplistic and contend that it implies that white attitudes toward blacks are initially negative. In investigating mixed upper middle-class suburban housing, they found a positive relationship between "cosmopolitanism" and positive attitudes toward blacks and living with black neighbors, and that a larger percentage of cosmopolitans than "locals" had *much* contact with black neighbors. The authors point to respondents' prior racial attitudes as a better explanation than the contact hypothesis.

In Ford's (1973) reexamination of the contact hypothesis within the context of public housing in a border-state city, his principal hypothesis was that a positive relationship exists between equal status interracial contact and racial tolerance. His results support the contact hypothesis for white respondents only. Equal status contact did not appear to be related significantly to reduced prejudice for blacks; greater awareness of dominant-subordinate relationships seemed indicated. Ford suggests the need to gain a thorough understanding of the conditions under which interracial contact occurs and the meaning of such contact for blacks.

Hamilton and Bishop (1976) undertook to explain the differences in response to a new neighbor as a function of the race of that neighbor. They held interviews in eighteen white areas in suburbs of New Haven, Connecticut, with women who were all white. In eight locations a black family, the first in the area, recently had bought a home. The results show a progression from apprehension about the black family before and right after it moved in to at least some degree of acceptance after it had lived in the area for a year. The authors cannot explain their findings by the interracial hypothesis because such interaction was infrequent. They conclude that the most important determinant of differences in racism for the respondents was the fact of having lived in an integrated setting. Changes observed over time were due to a disconfirmation of negative expectations.

Given the preceding qualifications, it is still valid to conclude that equal status is important for good interracial relations. The absence of competition also is a necessary ingredient. Wilner, Walkley, and Cook (1955:4), in their review of some thirty-six studies, conclude that these support "the general hypothesis that equal status contact between members of initially antagonistic ethnic groups under circumstances not marked by competition for limited goods or by strong social disapproval of intergroup friendliness tends to result in favorable attitude change." Allport (1954), in his concept of constructive contact, stresses the importance of equal status, common goals, interdependence, and the support of authority. Emphasis on the common goals of two groups may enhance the sense of equal status, and working together for a common goal becomes a powerful solvent of prejudice. Interracial contact also requires the explicit support of authority and the benefit of a favorable social climate (Social Science Panel 1972:14–17; McFall 1974:10).

Quota Systems

Although some believe that quota systems introduce legal uncertainty and have urged project developers to use them only under "the most compelling circumstances," in some cases such systems have helped projects or communities to retain their mixed character. Milgram (1977:56, 58, 67) describes the necessary and successful use of quotas in three of the projects he developed.

In Park Forest, Illinois, the community maintains the principle that the village and its governing body must determine when an area is overrepresented by persons of a specific race and when affirmative marketing activities are required. Nothing in the Integration Maintenance Program, as administered by Park Forest, purports to control rates of racial change. The program only purports to keep housing markets open to all seekers, to stop panic, and to encourage, through voluntary affirmative marketing, purchase or rental by persons of a race that is underrepresented in a subarea (Heumann 1981:iv). The assistant to the village manager indicated that the village considered an area underrepresented when the proportion of black residents in the area was lower than the proportion of black citizens in the greater metropolitan area at the same income level (ibid.:22).

Desirable ratios can exist and continue in projects even when there are no quotas (Milgram 1977:59–60). The U.S. Supreme Court has not, however, established the constitutionality of "benign quotas" (Social Science Panel 1972: 19; Heumann 1981:69).

The Work of Mixed Organizations
to Maintain Racially Mixed Neighborhoods

The joint efforts of residents to prevent neighborhoods from becoming completely black are now rather familiar happenings in the United States. Organizations formed for the purpose often began as white associations (Mikva 1951) with the stated goals of improving their neighborhoods. When blacks approach, major emphasis often focuses on keeping them out. When this fails, the organizations change their goal to that of maintaining their areas as mixed neighborhoods. Soon the membership and boards of such organizations become mixed.

To keep the area mixed, an association tries to prevent panic selling and white flight, to bring into the area white people of the same socioeconomic standing as those who have left (Watts et al. 1964:11), and to prevent, or correct, housing neglect. The group also tries to bring in black families of suitable social level, but the overriding concern is to maintain white occupancy (Abrahamson 1959; Leacock, Deutsch, and Fishman 1965; Helper 1965; Damerell 1968; Wolf and Lebeaux 1969; Kusner 1972). To achieve its goals, the organization sets up committees, develops block clubs, holds meetings and social gatherings, distributes information, and tries in every way it can to bolster the morale and cohesion of the residents.

Organizations established in community areas of Chicago to protect neighborhoods and to keep them mixed reveal impressive cooperation between blacks and whites with a variety of programs and procedures (Helper 1979:26–29). Organizations in many other cities also show much racial cooperation.

Two cases, each unusual in its own way, each involving a hardworking organization, illustrate what such groups can accomplish.

The Park Hill Area of Denver: A Neighborhood in Search of Itself. The Park Hill area of Denver, Colorado, has aroused doubt and conjecture about itself as a mixed entity in the minds of some of its residents and of some researchers (O'Dell 1973). The area consists of three parts, the North, the South, and the Middle. Mostly young black families live in the North, whereas mostly older white, richer families live in the South and the Middle is mixed. The Middle area is distinct in significant ways from the North and the South. O'Dell (p. 3) claims that "a potential base for a long range mixed and diverse community is now present in the middle area." However, the chairwoman of Greater Park Hill Community, Inc. (GPHC) maintained that "it's one big Park Hill," and that "what happens in one part affects the other." The Middle community may be the nucleus of the kind of community envisioned by the corporate goals of GPHC.

The future character and stability of this potentially mixed community remain, however, an open question. There are several indications that the Park Hill area may be on its way to becoming one mixed community. GPHC, which has existed since 1969, seems to draw solid support from all three geographic areas. Several realtors operating in the Park Hill area believe that the residential pattern has stabilized and have said repeatedly that the change from white to black in the Middle area has stopped. GPHC is working assiduously to make and keep Park Hill a united, mixed community.

West Mt. Airy Neighbors: The Development of the Organization and the Need for a Moral Commitment. Because a relatively high level of racial integration has been achieved in West Mt. Airy, a neighborhood in Philadelphia, it is important to examine features contributing to its success. Heumann (1973), in his study of West Mt. Airy, discusses the requisites for stable integration in a neighborhood. Because we live, he says, in a society in which residential segregation is the prevailing pattern, and because a neighborhood that becomes visibly interracial is subject to institutional actions that accelerate transition to a new state of segregation, rapid transition toward segregation will occur unless the interracial community can organize consciously to confront and defeat these pressures.

Thus, according to Heumann, a moral commitment by the residents becomes the critical dimension if a neighborhood is to attain and maintain stable integration. He examines predisposing factors in West Mt. Airy that led to a moral commitment to stable integration. Along with a great diversity of housing, West Mt. Airy has retained an open space system and has developed different recreational and cultural facilities that attract residents with a variety of life-styles. Heumann concludes that this socioeconomic heterogeneity produced four factors that fostered an atmosphere in which a moral commitment to stable integration could evolve. These factors are (1) a diversity of living arrangements providing diverse reasons for moving into and remaining in the neighborhood; (2) a more tolerant population, having had to tolerate a high level of socioeconomic diversity; (3) more likelihood of attracting blacks and whites with shared interests because the variety of living arrangements increased the chances for blacks and whites with like interests to meet; and (4) a greater likelihood of evolving an effective interracial organization. A final predisposing factor was that the blacks who sought housing on the black-white frontier in the early 1950s were willing to give integration a try. Still, he says, even with all these predisposing factors, a mixed neighborhood may succumb to total racial transition if individual moral commitments fail to evolve into institutional actions to withstand institutional pressures in the larger society for local racial homogeneity.

From its beginning in 1958–59, West Mt. Airy Neighbors (WMAN) was different from most neighborhood associations formed to prevent racial transition. The organization did not try to hold onto white people or to prevent black entry. It was a large, well-organized, mixed group with a highly coordinated and carefully planned program. WMAN did not establish racial proportions. It tried to heighten demand for West Mt. Airy as a place to live by lowering the turnover rate and raising the level of housing prices. "Above all, a single sense of community, centered around the theme that different races can live together harmoniously, was deemed necessary" (Heumann 1973:52).

WMAN viewed local real estate brokers as the greatest problem. Members felt that most of them were showing homes on a racially selective basis. WMAN asked its large membership to demand that brokers show both white and black potential buyers housing on all blocks and, through its membership, asked community residents to inform the executive secretary when they intended to sell. The association then channeled these sales to "cooperative" brokers. Most sellers did cooperate. Most brokers cooperated once WMAN became a "clearing-house" controlling local business and steering potential customers to cooperative brokers on a rotating basis. The organization asked citizens to report blockbusters to the central office and dealt effectively with these persons. WMAN also employed other methods to monitor other harmful, external threats, such as discriminatory zoning or acts that would damage the physical appearance or health of the area.

The neighborhood association developed committees for every possible need of the community, and decentralized itself to give precedence to issues surrounding interracial living on the block level. Racial integration began to coincide with a sense of community in West Mt. Airy. Membership at the time of the study amounted to more than one-third of the residents of the neighborhood, and West Mt. Airy was 58 percent white and 42 percent black. As a result of his research, Heumann concludes that WMAN is a key reason for the sense of community in West Mt. Airy: "WMAN is viewed as a guarantee of stability and a major source of community identity for many respondents. This sense of community and the WMAN role in strengthening it also seem to be an important factor in attracting both black and white residents to West Mt. Airy" (Heumann 1973). The situation in West Mt. Airy demonstrates that stable racial integration is virtually impossible without constant vigilance and careful, conscious planning.

Interracial Neighborhoods throughout the United States

Other stable interracial neighborhoods exist elsewhere in the United States. National Neighbors, founded in 1977, is an interracial, interfaith organization working for open housing (SOHI 1977). *The Directory of Interracial Neighborhoods*, 1977, assembled by National Neighbors, describes 144 interracial communities and the programs of their interracial organizations. Among these communities, many of which are suburbs or parts of large cities, are some that show substantial heterogeneity both in type of housing and in population, whereas others are quite homogeneous in both characteristics; good relations occur in both types of communities. In these communities, dispersed in 28 states of the nation, local organizations appear to be effective and to foster a sense of community. Most organizations have a wide range of activities. One example, from the program of Greater Park Hill Community, Inc., of Denver, Colorado, illustrates the diversity of their activities:

> Park Hill covers a large residential section of five hundred blocks in northeast Denver. The area as a whole contains 37,000 people. . . . Today the active citizens' organization is called Greater Park Hill Community, Incorporated (GPHC), a name selected in 1969 when the Park Hill Action Committee joined the Northeast Park Hill Civic Association to form one organization. The goals of the organizations have merged: they are to achieve and maintain an integrated community, work to eliminate prejudice and discrimination, work for better schools, cultural and recreational programs, and prevent community deterioration.
>
> The organization holds a monthly town meeting, distributes its monthly newsletter through block workers on more than four hundred of the five

hundred thirty-five blocks, and welcomes newcomers at wine and punch parties in homes three times a year. Three paid staff people and many volunteers working out of the GPHC office coordinate a multitude of programs serving the community and representing the community.

The organization also cooperates with the Colorado Heart Association in a community education campaign. . . . There is an active police-community relations committee which has sponsored Operation Identification, Neighborhood Watch programs, and provides periodic luncheons for policemen and community residents in private homes. GPHC received two major awards for pioneering human relations programs—a Human Relations Award from Beth Joseph Congregation and an award from the Cosmopolitan Club of Denver.

Many of these organizations are making strong efforts to counter the destructive actions of real estate companies and are fighting against unlawful real estate practices. Organizations report effective audits, court cases, and efforts to educate, to influence, and even to win the cooperation of real estate people.

Integration Maintenance Programs: The Park Forest Case

Integration Maintenance (IM) programs are a recent development in the United States. The village of Park Forest, Illinois, formally adopted such a program in 1973.

Park Forest is located near the southern limits of Cook County and has a population of about 27,000. The village was a "planned community," built by the American Community Builders and incorporated in 1949. Early in its history, Park Forest took an interest in open housing. A Commission on Human Relations (CHR) was created by the Village Board of Trustees in 1951 to study issues surrounding the entrance of minority families and to plan for peaceful relations in the community. Black families began to move into the village in 1959.

In 1965, Park Forest began to be concerned about the phenomenon of "clustering" of black residents caused by the tendency of real estate agencies to market homes near black residents exclusively to other black buyers. In a 1965 memorandum to real estate agencies, the village president urged brokers to encourage purchases by white buyers near black residents. The real estate agents received a similar memorandum again in 1968. In January 1968, the village formally adopted a comprehensive fair housing ordinance. By 1973, black residents comprised approximately 5 to 7 percent of the population. The increasing black population prompted concerns that clustering and eventual resegregation of parts of Park Forest might occur without affirmative actions to forestall this result. The village formally adopted an Integration Maintenance Program after advice from other municipalities (Heumann 1981:17–18).[5]

The IM Program of Park Forest involves educational programs and real estate activities, legal problems and public relations, and counseling on housing. It is also concerned with planning, commercial development, revitalization, and school desegregation. Of a total of 30 activities in which Park Forest is involved, 27 are funded by the municipality, but other funding comes from other sources.

The IM Program also monitors racial change in surrounding communities and keeps track of regional institutions that can affect the traffic in potential buyers seeking housing in Park Forest's price range. The ultimate goal of the IM Program is stable integration. More specifically, it is striving for a stable, integrated neighborhood; a unitary, open housing market; and enlistment of the real estate industry as a full partner of the program. Some adversaries have challenged the IM Program in the courts but the program has so far survived these tests.

A comparative analysis of similar suburban municipalities with IM programs throughout the country was designed to gain perspective on the Park Forest experience (Heumann 1981:1–15). Fewer than 25 suburban municipalities with IM programs were found. From this universe, 16 programs in comparable communities were identified. All 16 were located in midwestern and northeastern states. Only 3 suburban municipal IM programs were as old or older than the Park Forest program. Analysis revealed that the typical IM Program concentrates responsibility for activities on a specific implementation source, usually its own municipal staff. Park Forest, however, divides the implementation responsibility among staff, contractors, and voluntary groups with heavy emphasis on contractors. The rate of racial change is slowing in some suburbs with IM programs, including Cleveland Heights and Shaker Heights in the Cleveland area; University City, Missouri; and Oak Park, outside Chicago.

Racially Diverse Suburbs Are Stable and Increasing

Using birth rate data, Obermanns (1980) found that the number of what he terms "racially diverse" suburbs among 700 suburbs in 23 major midwestern metropolitan areas had doubled from 98 in 1970 to 204 in 1978, and that most of the 204 suburbs were stable and resisting resegregation.[6] Obermanns makes it clear that only 70 to 100 of the racially diverse suburbs were internally integrated. About 50 were internally segregated, and another 50 had nonblack minorities. The typical racially diverse suburb had a population of fewer than 25,000 (152 of 204 suburbs) and a racial composition of 5 to 39 percent nonwhite births (175 of 204 suburbs). Thus, most were small to medium in size and predominantly white in births and population.

Blacks also were found to be moving in increasing numbers into "open suburbs"—that is, those with 2 to 4 percent black births. The latter movement eased the pressure on other suburbs to resegregate. Only 30 percent of the midwestern suburbs had predominantly nonwhite births in 1978. His report also indicates that an overwhelming majority of suburban nonwhite births occurs in racially diverse or nearly all-white suburbs rather than in nearly all-black suburbs. Obermanns sees the suburbs with their small self-governing groups as better equipped than cities to make integration work.[7]

Conclusion

Among the factors that destroy the stability of racially mixed neighborhoods, some of the most damaging are indifferent, inept, or corrupt agencies of city government; irresponsible or prejudiced real estate brokers; uncooperative lending agencies, which sell property to black or white buyers who are not financially capable of maintaining it; and various fears and negative preconceptions of white people concerning black people that prompt them to move.

One finding stressed by researchers and informants is that white families with previous equal status experience with blacks more readily enter a neighborhood where some black people already are living than those lacking such experience. They also engage in more contact with black neighbors in the mixed neighborhoods.

Some factors that contribute to stable interracial neighborhoods are supportive municipal governments in all departments; truly integrated and good quality schools; well-operated recreational and cultural facilities; good quality buildings; concerned managers or managing agents; and shopping centers with plenty of parking space. Integration Maintenance programs are also proving to be an effective instrument for keeping interracial communities mixed.

Another important finding is the notable cooperation that occurs among black and white residents in organizations established to maintain racially mixed neighborhoods. Examples of friendships and solidarity are common. The evidence is clear that some blacks and whites are working well together in the struggle to achieve true integration against great odds.

In 1968, the following conclusion appeared in the *Report of the National Advisory Commission on Civil Disorders* (1968:1): "This is our basic conclusion: Our nation is moving toward two societies, one black, one white—separate and unequal." It is true that in the 1960s there was much violence and destruction in U.S. cities and that black rioters often were dissatisfied persons, extremely hostile to whites, more likely on the basis of class than of race, and almost equally hostile toward middle-class blacks (ibid.:73). However, from studies on black-white interaction in mixed neighborhoods, what emerges is not a picture of two societies growing constantly further apart, but one of members of two racial groups striving for a good, common life in common neighborhoods. Although hostility exists and racial conflict occurs, evidence of substantial cooperation and goodwill between members of the two racial groups remains.

It may be that Joseph D. Lohman's (1957:78) forecast will prove true, that "the resulting patterns for many years to come, and perhaps as long as can be imagined would be that many Negroes would live with Negroes, and many whites would live with whites, and many Negroes would live interchangeably with whites but by their own choice." It may well be that some neighborhoods will remain white, some will remain black, and others will be mixed. However, present findings indicate that it is not improbable that more and more will become mixed.

Additional Research Needed

Several issues for further research are important to expand our knowledge of how to foster interracial neighborhoods and to strengthen their maintenance. It would be helpful to be able to compare white people's conceptions of black people in the eighties with their conceptions of earlier years. It is equally important to study black people's conceptions of their white counterparts. How do members of each group respond to living next door to one another or sharing the same school and classroom? How does the blue-collar worker of a white ethnic group now view mixed neighborhoods?

Research also is needed on topics of less direct significance but of underlying importance in regard to housing. For example, Tremblay (1981:27–30) has found that we know little about the social bases of housing preferences and that, as a result, it is nearly impossible to answer accurately the question of whether different segments of the American population have divergent housing preferences. The Massachusetts Housing Finance Agency discovered the following factors to be all-important to resident satisfaction in their mixed income developments: well-designed, well-constructed, and well-maintained units were accepted by both whites and blacks despite the socioeconomic diversity of the residents (McFall 1974:15, 18). Parallel research is needed in areas that are both racially and economically mixed.

No one has probed the full significance of the varied endeavors of interracial organizations to accomplish their single purposes, especially the social-psychological aspects of these activities. In this regard, studies by Saltman (1971) and Heumann (1973) are worthy of note. Yin, in *Conserving America's Neighborhoods* (1982:xii), discusses the vitality of citizen organizations and their importance in maintaining and strengthening the neighborhood. Equally deserving of investigation are the umbrella organizations that foster community-wide cooperation among citizens.

All of these issues pose important questions for urban sociologists, students of housing, and researchers in race relations who want to take up the slack in interracial neighborhood research.

NOTES

1. The middle-class reinvestment in the cities probably had more impact in the nation's capital than anywhere else. In June 1977, the Washington Center for Metro-

politan Studies reported that Washington, with a black population of 71 percent (according to the 1970 census), had begun to show increases in its white population. Many of the newcomers, young and college educated, were settling in the Adams-Morgan section, a diverse neighborhood a mile and a half from the White House, about one-third white and two-thirds black and Hispanic. Important changes occurred in small residential streets; row houses occupied by three or four families became single-family homes (ibid.:5): "The local community group, the Adams-Morgan Organization, is engaging in a kind of legal guerilla warfare against the real estate people, encouraging tenants to resist. The group recently won a small but significant victory when it forced a developer, under threat of suit, to relinquish 9 of 26 houses that he had bought on Seaton Street. The tenants plan to buy and rehabilitate them with a combination of commercial and low-interest Federal housing loans." The Adams-Morgan Organization maintained that it did not oppose middle-class whites moving into the neighborhood, but was fighting real estate practices by which hundreds of people were evicted without help in finding new housing.

2. The three association officers interviewed (white president, black vice-president, and white treasurer) expressed satisfaction with the situation.

3. Blacks and whites participate in the many functioning organizations of the village.

4. The case of Glenclift in San Diego, California (Milgram 1977:76–77), also points to the importance of a devoted, innovative, and aggressive manager. Glenclift, a 316-unit rental development built as FHA Title 9 Defense Housing, opened in 1953 with black tenants. With vacancies and vandalism, the housing declined and was sold in 1955. Seven months later, there was 100 percent occupancy, at higher rents, and two-thirds of the residents were white. The manager, Mrs. Christine Kleponis, had discovered that many whites were willing to rent rehabilitated units next door to blacks. She proceeded to organize block parties and arranged for loans of tools and gifts of shrubs and seed to families who would use them. Because of her management capability, she was elected to the boards of directors of the local NAACP and Urban League.

5. The resolution creating the Integration Maintenance Program said, in part:

WHEREAS, the President and Board of Trustees recognize that an open community is not necessarily synonymous with a stable integrated community; and

WHEREAS, the Village of Park Forest places a positive value on its heterogeneity and ethnic integration and the maintenance of same is an implicit goal of the Village of Park Forest:

NOW, THEREFORE, BE IT RESOLVED . . . that we affirm our earlier commitments to open housing and to them add a commitment to the official policy: integration maintenance, defined as "the use of education and service programs to encourage the continuation of integration in the community," which in operation will ensure the continuance of a stable, multi-racial community.

6. Obermanns defines "racially diverse" communities as those whose births are between 4 and 94 percent nonwhite. The 204 racially diverse suburbs in 1978 had the following racial composition:

5–9% NW Births + 89	60–79% NW Births + 11
10–19% NW Births + 54	80–89% NW Births + 3
20–39% NW Births + 31	90–94% NW Births + 4
40–59% NW Births + 12	

7. Among the results of his study on "Quality of Life Indicators in Racially Diverse Communities" (Obermanns 1981), those on crime and academic performance are of particular interest. Obermanns points out that differences in the level of nonwhite composition within this group of suburbs do not usually appear related to differences in the quality of community life. He found that, except for East Cleveland and Painesville, violent crime rates in the racially diverse suburbs vary little from the average for all suburbs. Cleveland Heights and Euclid are the safest of these suburbs and, together with Berea and Bedford Heights, are below the suburban average. In academic performance, Obermanns used the National Merit Scholarship competition as a measure, because he could find no widely accepted measures of school performance that were comparable across community boundaries. His findings showed that, in a number of racially diverse suburbs and schools, continued high academic performance can be compatible with racial integration.

REFERENCES

Abrahamson, Julia. 1959. *A Neighborhood Finds Itself.* New York: Harper and Brothers.

Allport, Gordon W. 1954. *The Nature of Prejudice.* Cambridge, Mass.: Addison-Wesley Publishing Company, Inc.

Bradburn, Norman M., Seymour Sudman, and Galen L. Gockel. 1970. *Racial Integration in American Neighborhoods: A Comparative Survey.* Chicago: National Opinion Research Center, University of Chicago.

Damerell, Reginald G. 1968. *Triumph in a White Suburb: The Dramatic Story of Teaneck, N.J., The First Town in the Nation to Vote for Integrated Schools.* New York: William Morrow and Company, Inc.

Darden, Joe T. 1973. *Afro-Americans in Pittsburgh: The Residential Segregation of a People.* Lexington, Mass.: D. C. Heath and Company, Lexington Books.

Deutsch, Morton, and Mary Evans Collins. 1951. *Interracial Housing: A Psychological Evaluation of a Social Experiment.* Minneapolis: University of Minnesota Press.

Duncan, Otis D., and Beverly Duncan. 1957. *The Negro Population of Chicago: A Study of Residential Succession.* Chicago: University of Chicago Press.

Ford, W. Scott. 1973. "Interracial Public Housing in a Border City: Another Look at the Contact Hypothesis." *American Journal of Sociology* 78 (May): 1426–47.

Grier, Eunice, and George Grier. 1960. *Privately Developed Interracial Housing.* Berkeley: University of California Press.

Ham, Clifford C. 1970a. "The Impact of Non-White Movement into Previously White Suburban Residential Areas." In *Research Annual of Intergroup Relations,* no. 495, edited by Melvin M. Tumin, p. 172. Chicago: Quadrangle Books.

———. 1970b. "New Negro Neighbors in Pittsburgh Suburbs: A Study of Negro Immigration into Previously All-White Suburbs." In *Research Annual of Intergroup Relations,* no. 508, edited by Melvin M. Tumin, p. 176. Chicago: Quadrangle Books.

Hamilton, David L., and George D. Bishop. 1976. "Attitudinal and Behavioral Effects of Initial Integration of White Suburban Neighborhoods." *Journal of Social Issues* 32: 47–67.

Helper, Rose. 1962. "An Improvement Association Deals with Racial Invasion: A Case Study." Toledo, Ohio: The University of Toledo.

————. 1965. "Neighborhood Association 'Diary' Records History of Citizen Effort to Adapt to Racial Change." *Journal of Housing* 22 (March): 136–40.

————. 1969. *Racial Policies and Practices of Real Estate Brokers.* Minneapolis: University of Minnesota Press.

————. 1973. "White People's Reactions to Having Black People as Neighbors: Current Patterns." Unpublished paper presented at the Annual Meeting of the Southern Sociological Society, Atlanta, Georgia, 14 April, and at the Midwest Sociological Society, Milwaukee, 27 April.

————. 1979. "Social Interaction in Racially Mixed Neighborhoods." *Housing and Society* 6: 20–38.

Heumann, Leonard F. 1973. "The Definition and Analysis of Stable Racial Integration: The Case of West Mt. Airy, Philadelphia." Doctoral dissertation, Graduate School of Arts & Sciences, University of Pennsylvania.

————. 1981. "Integration Maintenance Program Evaluation, Part I." Report of Findings for the Village of Park Forest, Illinois, April.

Hunt, Chester L. 1959. "Private Integrated Housing in a Medium Size Northern City." *Social Problems* 7 (Winter): 195–209.

————, and Lewis Walker. 1974. *Ethnic Dynamics: Patterns of Intergroup Relations in Various Societies.* Homewood, Ill.: The Dorsey Press.

Jeffries, Vincent, and H. Edward Ransford. 1969. "Interracial Social Contact and Middle-Class White Reactions to the Watts Riot." *Social Problems* 16 (Winter): 312–24.

Kaiser, Charles. 1976. "'Resegregation' the Urban Challenge." *New York Times*, sec. 8 (Real Estate), 25 April.

Kusner, Chris. 1972. "A Look at Toledo's Housing Situation and What Is Being Done about It." *Insight, the Collegian*, 15 November, pp. 1–3.

Lake, Robert W. 1981. "The Fair Housing Act in a Discriminatory Market: The Persisting Dilemma." *Journal of the American Planning Association* 47 (January): 48–58.

Leacock, Eleanor, Martin Deutsch, and Joshuah A. Fishman. 1965. *Toward Integration in Suburban Housing: The Bridgeview Study.* New York: Anti-Defamation League of B'nai B'rith.

Lohman, Joseph D. 1957. "Top Chicago Law Officer Talks on Race Problem: Interview with Joseph D. Lohman, Sheriff of Cook County, Illinois." *U.S. News and World Report*, 29 November, pp. 72–78.

McFall, Trudy Parisa, 1974. *Racially and Economically Integrated Housing: Can It Work? Under What Conditions?* Mimeographed paper submitted for presentation at Conference in 1974. St. Paul, Minn.: Metropolitan Council.

Massachusetts Housing Finance Agency. 1974. "A Social Audit of Mixed Income Housing." Reported in *Racially and Economically Integrated Housing: Can It Work? Under What Conditions?*, by Trudy Parisa McFall.

Meer, Bernard, and Edward Freedman. 1966. "The Impact of Negro Neighbors on White Home Owners." *Social Forces* 45 (September): 11–19.

Mikva, Zorita W. 1951. "The Neighborhood Improvement Association: A Counterforce to the Expansion of Chicago's Negro Population." M.A. thesis, Department of Sociology, University of Chicago.

Milgram, Morris. 1977. *Good Neighbors: The Challenge of Open Housing.* New York: W. W. Norton and Company, Inc.

Molotch, Harvey L. 1972. *Managed Integration: Dilemmas of Doing Good in the City.* Berkeley: University of California Press.

Moore, Maurice, and James McKeown. 1968. *A Study of Integrated Living in Chicago.* Chicago: Community and Family Study Center, University of Chicago.

National Advisory Commission on Civil Disorders. 1968. *Report of the National Advisory Commission on Civil Disorders.* Washington, D.C.: U.S. Government Printing Office, 1 March.

National Committee Against Discrimination in Housing (NCDH). 1982. "Black Jack Case Ends after a Dozen Years of Litigation." *Trends* 23 (March).

Newsweek. 1971a. "The Battle of the Suburbs," 15 November, pp. 61–62, 64, 69–70.

————. 1971b. "A Suburb that Struck a Truce," 15 November, p. 63.

Northwood, L. K., and Ernest A. T. Barth. 1965. *Urban Desegregation: Negro Pioneers and Their White Neighbors.* Seattle: University of Washington Press.

Obermanns, Richard. 1980. *Stability and Change in Racially Diverse Suburbs, 1970–1978: Summary.* Cleveland Heights, Ohio: Heights Community Congress, October. Mimeographed.

————. 1981. *Quality of Life Indicators in Racially Diverse Communities.* Cleveland Heights, Ohio: Heights Community Congress, April. Mimeographed.

————. 1982. "Racial School Enrollment Patterns in Metropolitan Cleveland, 1978–1980." In *The Cuyahoga Plan's Open Housing Report*, March.

O'Dell, Doyal D. 1973. *The Park Hill Area of Denver: An Integrated Community: A Report on the Greater Park Hill Area.* Denver, Colorado: The Denver Urban Observatory, June.

Orfield, Gary. 1981. *Toward a Strategy for Urban Integration: Lessons in School and Housing Policy from Twelve Cities.* New York: The Ford Foundation.

Pettigrew, Thomas F. 1975. "The Cold Structural Inducements to Integration." *The Urban Review* 8 (Summer): 137–44.

Philadelphia Council of Neighborhood Organizations. *Greenlining: The Pledge Campaign to End Redlining.* Philadelphia. Pamphlet.

Rapkin, Chester, and William Grigsby. 1960. *The Demand for Housing in Racially Mixed Areas: A Study of the Nature of Neighborhood Change.* Berkeley: University of California Press.

Rose, Arnold M., Frank J. Atelsek, and Lawrence R. McDonald. 1953. "Neighborhood Reactions to Isolated Negro Residence: An Alternative to Invasion and Succession." *American Sociological Review* 18 (October): 497–507.

Rosen, Ellsworth E., with Arnold Nicholson. 1959. "When a Negro Moves Next Door." *Saturday Evening Post*, 4 April, pp. 32–33, 139–42.

Rosen, Harry, and David Rosen. 1962. *But Not Next Door.* New York: Avon Book Division, Hearst Corporation.

Saltman, Juliet. 1971. *Open Housing as a Social Movement: Challenge, Conflict and Change.* Lexington, Mass.: Heath Lexington Books.

Schnare, Ann B. 1977. *Residential Segregation by Race in U.S. Metropolitan Areas: An Analysis across Cities and over Time.* A report on research funded by the Office of Policy Development and Research, U.S. Department of Housing and Urban Development. Washington, D.C.: The Urban Institute, February.

Social Science Panel. 1972. *Freedom of Choice in Housing: Opportunities and*

Constraints. Washington, D.C.: National Academy of Sciences, National Academy of Engineering.

SOHI (Sponsors of Open Housing Investment, Interracial, Interfaith Organizations). 1964–Present. "Sponsors: 22,000: Works to Educate Individuals and Nonprofit Agencies to Invest Their Funds in Enterprises Creating Open Housing Opportunities." In *Encyclopedia of Associations*, vol. 1, National Organizations of the U.S.A., 11th ed., edited by Margaret Fisk, pp. 858–59. Detroit, Mich.: Gale Research Co.

Stalvey, Lois Mark. 1963. "We Moved to an Integrated Neighborhood." *Sunday Bulletin Magazine*, 19 May. Reprint.

Swados, Harvey. 1966. "When Black and White Live Together." *New York Times Magazine*, 13 November, pp. 47, 102, 104, 106, 109–10, 112, 114, 116, 119–20.

Tremblay, Kenneth R., Jr. 1981. "The Social Bases of Housing Preferences." *Housing and Society*. Proceedings of the 1981 Annual Conference of the American Association of Housing Educators, 6–10 October, pp. 27–30.

Varady, David P. 1974. "White Moving Plans in a Racially Changing Middle-Class Community." *American Institute of Planners Journal* 40 (September): 360–70.

Watts, L. G., H. E. Freeman, H. M. Hughes, R. Morris, and T. F. Pettigrew. 1964. *The Middle-Income Negro Family Faces Urban Renewal.* Waltham, Mass.: Heller Graduate School for Advanced Studies in Social Welfare, Brandeis University.

Wegmann, Robert G. 1977. "Desegregation and Resegregation: A Review of the Research on White Flight from Urban Areas." In *The Future of Big City Schools: Desegregation Policies and Magnet Alternatives*, edited by Daniel U. Levine and Robert J. Havighurst, pp. 11–54. Berkeley, Calif.: McCutchan Publishing Corporation.

Weinstein, Jules, Manager of Rochdale Village. 1976. Telephone interview, 20 September.

Wilner, Daniel M., R. P. Walkley, and S. W. Cook. 1955. *Human Relations in Interracial Housing: A Study of the Contact Hypothesis.* Minneapolis: University of Minnesota Press.

Wolf, Eleanor Paperno, and Charles N. Lebeaux. 1969. *Change and Renewal in an Urban Community.* New York: Frederick A. Praeger Publishers.

Wysocki, Walter, President, United Association of North Beverly View. 1975. Interview, 3 July.

Yin, Robert K. 1982. *Conserving America's Neighborhoods.* New York: Plenum Press.

Zeul, Carolyn R., and Craig R. Humphrey. 1971. "The Integration of Blacks in Suburban Neighborhoods: A Reexamination of the Contact Hypothesis." *Social Problems* 18 (Spring): 462–74.

Section IV
Racial Desegregation and Federal Housing Policies

Introduction

JOHN M. GOERING

"It's the first time I've ever been kicked out of my home," one elderly Texas resident recently complained. Another felt they were all being "shoved around like cattle" (*Newsweek* 1983:18, 20). Seventy-nine-year-old Iva Sewell's reaction was adamant: "no matter what happens, I'm not moving over yonder to that colored neighborhood" ("Desegregation Order" 1983). These reactions, from residents of federally subsidized public housing, arose after a federal court ordered twenty-five white and a like number of black tenants to swap apartments to achieve desegregation. The public housing authority (PHA) of Clarksville, Texas, had violated the Constitution, the federal judge stated, by creating and maintaining racially separate housing projects, flouting "the law of the land by purposefully selecting and assigning tenants by race for the purpose of segregating them by race" (*Lucille Young v. Housing Authority* 1983:6).

Such purposeful, illegal segregation is not confined solely to Clarksville. An additional sixty public housing authorities, for example, are currently the subject of intense examination as part of another federal court suit, *Young v. Pierce*. In this case, the U.S. Department of Housing and Urban Development (HUD) is accused of having "knowingly acquiesced" in the maintenance of racially segregated housing systems throughout East Texas. The plaintiffs are seeking the elimination of discrimination and the desegregation of both public and assisted housing throughout thirty-nine East Texas counties. HUD should, the plaintiffs charge, end its complacency and act to "affirmatively further" the policies of fair housing. This "affirmative" mandate includes movement toward a more racially balanced pattern of occupancy (*Young v. Pierce* 1982; *Clarence Givens v. Prairie Creek* 1985).

The *Young* case has not yet gone to trial, although the issues in the case are similar enough to the earlier *Clarksville* decision to have sparked considerable activity by HUD. These actions began with four underlying premises. First, whatever actions were taken should not involve the massive, mandatory transfer of tenants as the first or only remedy. Second, the public housing authorities must be given the responsibility of proposing effective solutions that suit the characteristics and needs of their own tenants. Third, HUD would concentrate its attention on PHAs that were already in violation, or apparent noncompliance, with Title VI. Title VI, the 1964 law prohibiting discrimination in federally assisted housing, is the specific legal tool around which remedies would be fashioned. The fourth and final premise for HUD's actions was that the Title VI enforcement process would be implemented in coordination with HUD's funding of the rehabilitation or modernization of the physical condition of the public housing stock.

The initial step in this process was a February 1984 notice by HUD's secretary ordering the "disestablishment" of racially dual public housing systems. HUD, he wrote, was beginning a "more comprehensive and intense" response to the problem of segregated public housing in East Texas than had ever been undertaken (Pierce 1984). Each PHA then submitted a plan for the relocation of tenants to achieve some level of measurable desegregation, using available vacancies and waiting list applicants. No clear record of successes or failures is yet available from this initial effort. Initial indications are that there have been varying reactions from the executive directors and tenants. In some PHAs, only lip service is given to complying with HUD's order to desegregate. Tenants provide medical exemptions that prevent their moving, there are no vacancies of the right size to accommodate desegregating moves, or there are not enough applicants for available apartments. In other resistant PHAs, white tenants leave their subsidized units and move to private market housing or to subsidized housing in other communities. Another group of PHAs has been cooperative and has achieved modest levels of desegregation in roughly two years. Whites have moved into previously all-black projects, and blacks, often the elderly, have moved into white projects. Some executive directors have gone to all available sources, including churches, clubs, nursing homes, and factories, to find new applicants to balance the racial composition of their waiting lists. There are also some PHAs where it is difficult, if not impossible, to achieve significant levels of desegregation. PHAs that have an overwhelmingly minority or all-white population in occupancy and on their waiting lists have few options to achieve system-wide desegregation.

Efforts to desegregate the nation's public housing stock were extended to the entire nation in 1985. In January, all of HUD's regional offices were instructed to begin the process of eliminating racial segregation that resulted from "official actions." PHAs are to be examined on an individual basis in order to design remedies that will be hand-tailored as well as effective. In February 1985, public housing authorities were informed that their chances of receiving a portion of fiscal year 1985 funding for the rehabilitation or modernization of public housing units would significantly increase if their modernization plans were linked to housing desegregation. A large portion of the $80 million in funding was made available in 1985 to complement efforts to desegregate authorities illegally segregating tenants. Thus, in 1985, HUD began what appears to be an aggressive effort to use its manpower and resources to reduce the level of segregation in its low-rent public and assisted housing stock.

HUD's actions, however, are likely to be constrained by the fact that there is incomplete agreement within the Executive Branch of the federal government about how federal resources should be used to promote desegregation. Questions have been raised about the legality of using race-conscious desegregation practices in the absence of a finding of purposeful or intentional discrimination. Budget officials have questioned the wisdom of using federal dollars to "reward" PHAs that have broken the law. Critics wonder why PHAs that have used HUD's funding for decades to illegally segregate their housing are to be again funded to undo these past practices. No one, indeed, is sure of whether the existing limited resources of the federal government are capable of efficiently and thoroughly reviewing the racial occupancy of nearly 3,000 PHAs and 10,000 projects in efforts to hand-tailor desegregation strategies. Monitoring these individual plans to ensure compliance will be a mountainous task, with no existing data systems in place to record transitions in racial occupancy (Rodrigue 1985).

Proposed reductions in HUD's funding for the operation and repair of the public housing stock in 1986 and 1987 will also limit its ability to promote desegregation. Scarce resources will have to be targeted on emergency repairs and the most physically inadequate housing, leaving few if any resources to use as incentives for desegregation (Kurtz 1985:A1; U.S. Department of Housing and Urban Development 1985). Congress may also elect to focus on other housing priorities, further limiting HUD's ability to desegregate or "deconcentrate" its housing.

There is indeed a long history of congressional pressures that have altered many of the original objectives of the federal low-rent public housing program, introducing numerous programmatic changes that have made it difficult to administer HUD's Title VI desegregation requirements at the same time all of its other rules and requirements are adhered to. There are, in fact, so many potentially conflicting requirements regarding the selection, or preference, systems for tenants that even well-run PHAs have difficulty understanding their multiple obligations. Conversely, skillful public housing managers can readily use HUD's myriad requirements to mask discriminatory purposes (Wood 1982:71; Struyk and Blake 1982:84–92; Kaplan 1985). That is, the long history of evolving legislative and judicial pressures on the operation of the public housing program has not produced a simple nor readily administrable program, regardless of issues of race. Incompetent public housing managers may readily mismanage all aspects of public housing, including race-related tenant selection and assignment (Miller 1985).

Congressional and Executive Branch concerns about desegregation are not the only obstacles to HUD's recent initiatives. The sheer size of the problem facing federal planners is awesome. There are nearly 10 million residents of federally assisted housing living in 3.7 million units, with a majority of them in segregated projects. Housing for the elderly is predominantly white and HUD's family projects are either racially mixed or predominantly black and Hispanic. Newer, Section 8 housing also tends to be more heavily occupied by whites whereas the older, traditional public housing stock is predominantly minority (Burke 1984, 1985).

The size of the problem would in the long run be manageable if there were cooperation from the public housing authorities and jurisdictions subject to desegregation efforts. However, the racially motivated resistance mentioned earlier is likely to be encountered in most localities. A recent, eight-day series of articles in the *Dallas Morning News*, for instance, uncovered blatant examples of racist attitudes of state and local housing officials throughout many parts of the United States. Public housing officials were openly critical of the federal court order in Clarksville, labeling it "communistic," admitted they were using "scare tactics" to keep blacks out of the predominantly white Section 8 housing program, and were unwilling to respond to HUD's new desegregation plans. One PHA board member stated: "Unless we're forced to (integrate) I don't see why we'd have to. . . . Now, if it would be absolutely necessary, if the courts and a judge said so, then we'd have to. But I don't see any point in it" (Flournoy and Rodrigue 1985:8A). Not only is there likely to be resistance to recent desegregation plans, but there is also deeply entrenched resistance to the location of low- and moderate-income rental housing for families in communities throughout the nation. Suburban jurisdictions often resist accepting housing families because of the fear of an influx of minority poor (Rodrigue and Flournoy 1985).

This opposition has been at the core of previous failures of HUD policies to promote residential desegregation or deconcentration. After the passage of major fair housing legislation in the 1960s, Congress and the courts looked for new means by which HUD programs could reduce the segregation and spatial isolation of minority poor households. The chapters in this section provide assessments of most of the major policy tools designed and implemented during the 1970s that were aimed at fostering racial "deconcentration," or more "open" patterns of racial occupancy.

Vernarelli provides a basic chronology and assessment of efforts to promote some form of racial "spatial deconcentration." A variety of internal HUD working groups struggled to provide clearer focus for the 1974 congressional requirement to reduce the spatial isolation of the minority poor. He accurately summarizes many of the judicial and legislative pressures that led to modest demonstrations, to HUD inaction, and, by 1981, to a softening of HUD's requirements related to the siting or location of assisted housing (Egan et al. 1981). The Regional Housing Mobility Program, for example, was initiated in 1979 to provide incentives to regional planning bodies to expand housing opportunities across jurisdictional boundaries, linking city to suburbs. With $2 million in initial funding for housing counseling programs, Section 8 housing certificates were to be exchanged among cooperating PHAs.

This modest effort to promote spatial deconcentration, however, quickly became the subject of intense criticism. Opponents of the program said there was a conspiracy on the part of the federal government, and others in private research centers, to forceably move black people out of central cities in order to make room for wealthier whites who wished to return (Calmore 1979). The Regional Housing Mobility Program, it was argued (De Bernardo 1979:7), was designed to move inner-city minorities from the cities to suburban "South African-style bantusans or concentration camps." Organizations that were funded to implement regional mobility plans confronted such criticisms at the local level, with the program characterized "as an experiment devised by insensitive people to toy with other people's lives" (Truslow 1982).

Black elected officials and some civil rights organizations joined in the attack on the goal of spatial deconcentration. They argued that the program would "destroy" nonwhite political and cultural ties in the city because of the broad prohibitions against building low-income housing in segregated areas (Calmore 1979). "Mayors and even some HUD officials say the policy conflicts with other HUD objectives and is restrictive and arbitrary, 'allowing housing only where it's not wanted and not putting it where the people are in dire need,' in the words of Victor Marrero, HUD's undersecretary" (Stanfield 1980:1024; McKay 1977:187).

Even a HUD-commissioned assessment of the Regional Housing Mobility Program concluded that "enabling a household to move to a greater number of jurisdictions without increasing the available supply of affordable, decent housing there merely increases the number of areas where a household may look for yet unavailable housing" (Metropolitan Action 1982:89). PHAs were reluctant to participate in interjurisdictional programs when there were insufficient resources to serve their own housing needs. The study also noted the risk that mobility programs were offering the poor fictive housing opportunities in the suburbs at the same time that white, middle-income households were gentrifying inner-city neighborhoods (ibid.:88–89).[1]

Criticisms of HUD's Regional Housing Mobility experiment reflect a long-standing concern that HUD policies place equal opportunity goals ahead of the goal of supplying adequate housing to those in need (National Housing Policy Review 1974:24; Listokin 1976:58–59). As part of the congressional debate over passage of the Housing and Community Development Act of 1980, for example, an amendment was proposed to prohibit HUD from excluding from consideration proposals for housing solely because the proposed site was located in a segregated area. Congressmen representing urban areas strongly opposed HUD's site selection criteria that resulted in housing going to areas that did not want it rather than to the areas that needed it most.[2] Congressional criticisms in 1980 were in part responsible for HUD's decision to soften its site and neighborhood standards. In January 1981, a notice was issued to all HUD field offices increasing the flexibility of their administration.

Gray and Tursky's chapter clearly reveals that there was already wide latitude in the siting of HUD-assisted housing after the initial requirements for location in "non-impacted" or less segregated areas. Programs established before 1974 clearly served more minority households and were primarily located in minority neighborhoods. More recent programs, including Section 236 and Section 8, have been less concentrated in minority areas, with a greater concentration of units in suburban areas. The occupants of suburban units are, however, more likely to be white elderly or white families. No information is available to reflect the impact of recent changes in site selection standards on the location and occupancy of HUD projects.

A major implication of the above study is that the location of a project does not ensure that it is available to house eligible minority households from central city ghettos. All too often housing built in suburban or predominantly white communities is occupied by whites, thereby limiting the effects of site selection on desegregation.[3] HUD, in fact, has relatively few tools to effectively influence the tenanting or occupancy of projects once they have been built. The major program is the Affirmative Fair Housing Marketing Program. This program, based on regulations designed to implement Title VIII, requires private developers and managers of most of HUD-assisted and subsidized housing to market to those "least likely to apply" for that housing regardless of race, ethnicity, or sex. A modest amount of research (Region IX 1974; Rubinowitz, Greenfield, and Harris 1974; Jaclyn 1976) has indicated that there are substantial problems in the consistency of HUD area office administration and monitoring of this program.

The presence of affirmative fair housing marketing plans appears to have a modest effect on projects marketing to blacks, with the clearest effect in areas outside of the central city. One study of affirmative marketing (National Capitol Systems 1983) found, however, that there was often a substantial gap between what developers stated was their racial occupancy goal and actual occupancy; indeed, the correlation between expected and actual occupancy was only .40 for blacks, .59 for Hispanics, and .32 for whites.

The results of such studies leave a large number of questions unanswered about how to bridge the gap between affirmative marketing and project integration. No data, for example, are available on what information actually reached what types of households in the eligible population, the alternatives they considered, and the role—if any—that affirmative marketing played in their decision to move to a specific project. In addition, no data are available on a control or comparison group to determine how their housing search process differed from those selecting affirmatively marketed projects. The failure of projects to reach their anticipated occupancy goals could, therefore, be the result of disinterest by those "least likely to apply," unrealistically high or low occupancy goals, some form of discrimination in tenant assignment by developers, or the fact that the projects were located in deteriorated areas unattractive to qualified households. Limited evidence, for example, suggests that affirmative marketing is more successful in reaching its goals when projects are located in racially mixed areas rather than in black neighborhoods (National Capitol Systems 1983).[4] There is, then, a long leap from programs aimed at disseminating information to minority households in the hope that this information will broaden the range of their housing choices and the actual racially balanced tenanting of a project on a more or less permanent basis (Struyk and Blake 1983).[5]

Affirmative fair housing marketing rules do not apply to HUD's current major housing assistance program, the Section 8 Existing Program. In this program, HUD's subsidy goes directly to the tenant who may then choose to use the certificate to move or to reduce the rent burden in his or her current apartment. Stucker's study, in this section, reviews evidence concerning the extent to which this program has promoted racial integration. The Section 8 program and its predecessor, the Experimental Housing Allowance Program, did encourage modest levels of desegregation. The minority families who moved went to areas in which the minority population was 7 to 8 percent lower than their former census tract. Nonminority families also experienced a slight, 3 percent increase in the minority population in their new census tracts. Despite these desegregating moves, a substantial portion of Section 8 recipients either do not move or fail to use their certificates. Minorities, often with large families, are less likely to be able to use their housing certificates than nonminorities (60 percent to 45 percent).

There is no research evidence to document Section 8 certificate holders' experience with racial discrimination in searching for and locating acceptable housing. Low vacancy rates, low levels of affordable rental housing, or discrimination could all result in these "inefficiencies" in program operation. Ongoing research on the use of housing vouchers may provide needed information on the extent of mobility generated by this current revision of the Section 8 Existing Program. This new program, however, is serving only very poor households—those whose incomes do not exceed 50 percent of the median income for the jurisdiction—rather than earlier programs, which served those having up to 80 percent of the area's median income. Limitations on the number of vouchers, plus income limits, will further circumscribe the extent to which minority households will be able to afford to move to housing in less segregated areas, when the rents are higher than covered by program standards or exceed the household's ability to add additional out-of-pocket costs (U.S. Department of Housing and Urban Development 1985:H8).

The above assessments of HUD's efforts to achieve deconcentration or desegregation of housing clearly reveal only minimal progress in the few years before the programs were altered. Because of congressional vacillation, black opposition, bureaucratic delays, and decreasing funding for costly new construction programs, there have been no long-term, coordinated, adequately funded efforts targeted on the desegregation of public and assisted housing. Before the recent intensive efforts aimed at desegregation in East Texas, there was consistent opposition to utilize limited housing resources to place families in suburban or white communities when conflict, violence, and heavy political costs were the most likely outcome. The racial prejudice and discrimination uncovered by the *Dallas Morning News* in 1984 and 1985 is strikingly similar to that reported nearly thirty years ago: "There's no question about it—our whole problem in getting a project going today is the integration, open occupancy issue. . . . Most U.S. citizens are so unready to accept Negroes as neighbors that they are exercising their sovereignty to prevent it, if possible" (Shaffer 1958:57).

The reasons why housing desegregation programs succeed or fail are not, however, solely a matter of poor program design and funding. There are a variety of contextual or macro-level forces that help to determine whether such programs succeed. The chapter by Goldstein and Yancey in this section, for example, provides a careful examination of major contextual factors responsible for the racial segregation of public housing in one city, Philadelphia. Using data relating the location of public, assisted, and scattered-site housing to the demographic and economic characteristics of the city, they search for causal relationships between racial segregation, the location of subsidized housing, and the "historical ecology" of the city. The authors relate the changing employment base of the city, real estate values, and distance from the central business district to the probability that an area has become ghettoized. They conclude that the location of public housing did not lead to its racial stigmatization and white flight. Areas selected for assisted housing after 1950 had lower property values, with less expensive land, and were located in older sections of the city where minorities were already located. Ethnic communities, close to employment, were closed to both minorities and public housing. There were, therefore, a variety of forces that influenced the "trajectory of racial transition" that were of crucial importance in fostering and maintaining the racial segregation of both private and public housing. Housing programs appear to have had little influence in establishing this trajectory.

The effectiveness of housing programs in fostering desegregation can thus be profoundly affected by the characteristics of local neighborhoods and job markets. Yinger's study concludes this section with additional insights and a critique of many of the social and public policy influences that limit the design and effectiveness of federal desegregation efforts. Racial preferences and discrimination in the private housing market, according to Yinger, powerfully influence opposition to housing integration. A small desegregation program, placing a few subsidized units inconspicuously in receptive communities, might succeed. Temporary ceiling quotas on racial occupancy might also be needed to prevent white flight. Yinger's design rules are stringent: "a program that sets unrealistic integration goals, such as a high percentage of blacks in a few suburbs is bound to fail." Without substantial, if not massive, resources a "medium" size effort at desegregation will also fail. With limited resources, he counsels, small demonstration programs would be a useful beginning to show the workability of the process and goal.

The shift of federal housing resources away from "costly" new construction programs is an important constraint on opportunities for even modest demonstration efforts. Severe resistance to regional or interjurisdictional fair share arrangements further narrows options for the use of housing vouchers for nontraditional desegregation moves (Rodrigue and Flournoy 1985). It is, however, highly likely that amendments to the Fair Housing Act will be proposed in 1986 that will significantly strengthen the federal government's ability to reduce discrimination. Modest increases in staffing for Title VI investigations and new resources to encourage desegregation by public housing authorities offer further prospects for change. It is clear, however, that the federal government, and HUD in particular, will no longer have the major housing assistance tools needed to create rapid, effective impacts on public sector housing segregation either in response to plaintiffs' requests for remedies, for demonstrations, or for major programmatic interventions.

Summary

Social science research and evaluation studies have produced a number of generalizations concerning the relationship between housing desegregation and federal policies. These generalizations, however, constitute an assessment of specific constraints rather than a heuristic model of determinants and impacts of housing desegregation. The absence of careful studies of the effectiveness of past and current federal, state, and local fair housing enforcement programs is an example of a major gap in understanding how to assess the utility and costs of such programs in reducing segregation.[6] The following is, therefore, a prescription for future policy research rather than a model for policy intervention:

• Racial segregation has been fostered and maintained by multiple influences operating at the local, regional, and even national level.

• Imperfect social science understanding of how and where to intervene in the process of desegregation and resegregation puts limitations on sensible, planned action. Policymakers are aware that attempts to intervene may exacerbate the situation, causing additional racial tensions, white flight, or litigation. Unraveling the multiple determinants of segregation will require complex negotiated solutions by multiple actors affecting both public and private sector housing and neighborhood developments. The compartmentalization of housing, transportation, education, and welfare policies, for example, may need to be selectively reintegrated to reverse the ghettoization of blacks. Such major structural alterations will only occur incrementally, if at all, with concern for the relative autonomy of states and local jurisdictions.

• Housing programs were, from the very beginning, designed to be run in collaboration with private developers and local government officials: "All of the programs administered by this agency [in 1956] rely basically upon private and local initiative and place reliance upon local responsibility in meeting housing needs. The role of the Federal Government in the housing programs is to assist, to stimulate, to lead, and sometimes to prod, but never to dictate or coerce, and never to stifle the proper exercise of private and local responsibility" (quoted in McEntire 1960:295). From their inception, federal policy actions have been vulnerable to the decisions and cooperation of local officials, developers, and residents. Congressional unwillingness to establish a centralized, powerful housing development agency has left its imprint on most HUD programs. Recent administrations have reemphasized the importance of public-private sector cooperation as well as the importance of state and local government prerogatives. These seems to be, therefore, little congressional or Executive Branch enthusiasm for asserting HUD's authority and rights over local prerogatives, making HUD's programs and civil rights obligations partially hostage to local situations and pressures.

• HUD's multiple constituencies and interests often work at cross-purposes. Neighborhood revitalization and housing rehabilitation programs, for example, often have the effect of improving conditions within ghettos whereas HUD's housing insurance (FHA) and production programs have, at least in the past, softened the market for inner-city housing. Paralleling this, some of HUD's efforts appear to be aimed at increasing household mobility whereas others are designed, indirectly, to discourage it (Clark and Moore 1980:310).

• The use of subtle, ostensibly nonracial reasons or procedures for excluding blacks by public agencies and communities is difficult to prove. Evasive practices have been in use for decades and courts are still wrestling with the means to detect racial purposes behind actions that are on the face racially neutral (Foley 1973; Fishman 1978; "Legitimate Objectives of Zoning" 1978; Krefetz 1979). This problem is continually confronted by federal agencies, such as HUD, in attempting to prove discrimination or racial segregative actions under Title VI of the Civil Rights Act of 1964.

• Some local jurisdictions have consistently evaded any responsibility to rehouse blacks in better quality, less segregated areas by simply not applying for federal funds (Krefetz 1979:299n; Tomasson 1981). Federal leverage or coercive powers are heavily linked to HUD's ability to manipulate the purse strings in order to promote more racially tolerant behavior.

• Budgetary constraints on the implementation of public policy choices are real at every level of government and will limit the degree to which public officials will prioritize their fiscal obligations to achieve desegregation. Also, Congress has been known to turn off the financial spigot for housing programs when it suspected they were being used to achieve residential desegregation (McEntire 1960:296; *Congressional Record*, 30 September 1980). Budgetary constraints will also continue to limit the amount of federal funding for much of the research needed to address the unanswered issues regarding how, and with what level of effort, to intervene to promote desegregation (Hartling 1980:277–80).

• The programs available to address housing segregation or integration fail to deal with the more fundamental black problem—high concentrations of poverty and lower average incomes. Increasing the purchasing power of black households as one key to unlock improved housing opportunities has been the concern of the Equal Employment Opportunity Commission (EEOC) and others for only roughly a decade. The absence of evaluations of EEOC's efforts makes it difficult to know how well such a tool serves what types of black households and how long it will take before such complaint-driven policies will provide a more equitable employment profile for most minorities. HUD's programs, therefore, only marginally address the problem of limited incomes, which are responsible for a varying but substantial portion of residential segregation (McGrew 1981).

• The long history of residential segregation in American cities has yielded some benefits along with its multiple costs. Segregation has fostered varying levels of political consciousness, institutional development, cohesion, and leadership within the black community. It has facilitated modest levels of control over community programs in some areas and a small but growing number of black local elected officials (Bryce, Cousar, and McCoy 1978; Karnig and Welch 1980:3-4). Opponents of desegregation assert that efforts to disperse blacks throughout a city or metropolitan area only succeed in destroying their political leverage over municipal resources, leave white political machines untouched and unthreatened, and destroy the cultural and institutional fabric of the black community.[7] High levels of racial discrimination and prejudice will continue to make it difficult to distinguish voluntary from involuntary segregation, dampening the enthusiasm of black community leaders to support programs for housing desegregation and integration.

The gloomiest forecasters need not, however, be accurate in anticipating no effects from HUD's current drive to reduce public housing segregation. A climate for change may have been fostered in which at least a portion of the nation's PHAs realize that it is better to cooperate with HUD than to risk the "worst case" of a Clarksville remedy. HUD field staff may become more effective through intraagency coordination of available information, training, and technical assistance. Local public officials, sensing an opportunity to address a pariah problem, may cooperate with PHAs and HUD in reducing the inequities in services provided to black public housing projects and in promoting the acceptance of new projects. In Chicago, for example, Mayor Harold Washington is pressing to build up to 2,000 units of scattered-site housing, after decades of local resistance and political opposition. The projects will be small, "built in conformity with existing architecture," and developed in conjunction with the enforcement of antiblockbusting legislation to allay the fears of homeowners (Henry and Thomas 1983). And in Philadelphia, local residents in the Whitman Park area reluctantly, but passively, accepted the tenanting of federally subsidized housing which they had opposed for nearly twenty-five years (Klibanoff 1982:1B). Recent research also reveals general acceptance of scattered-site housing in nearly 90 other American cities (DeMuth 1985:20-21).

No one will know for some time how well these efforts will succeed, under what conditions, at what cost, and for how long. Segregation in private sector housing will remain substantially untouched, as will its catalysts—discrimination, prejudice, and poverty. Evaluations and case studies are desperately needed to understand the effectiveness and constraints on recent judicial and administrative actions to desegregate.

NOTES

1. Limited evidence suggests that relatively few certificate holders used them to move from the city to surrounding suburbs, and in one case families moved back to the central city because of the absence of affordable rental housing in the inner suburbs (Holshouser 1983:39–A, 50).

2. Others in the House and Senate, however, were concerned that the amendment could be misinterpreted to mean that HUD no longer had to support the goal of racial integration in housing (*Congressional Record*, 30 September 1980:S–13952) or that the amendment could suggest some diminishing of HUD's authority to enforce Title VIII. As a result of these concerns, the House-Senate Conference Committee reported a modified amendment that stated: "The Secretary [of HUD] shall not exclude from consideration for financial assistance, under federally assisted housing programs proposals for housing solely because the site proposed is located within an impacted area." The committee went on to say, however, that this provision "in no way diminishes HUD's duty to promote equal opportunity and enforce the statutory and constitutional prohibitions against racial discrimination" (*Congressional Record*, 30 September 1980:H–9812).

3. Thirty years ago Robert Weaver, then serving as the administrator of New York State's Housing Rent Commission, noted that site selection was a limited means of promoting residential mixing: "Where a public housing development is located in, or contiguous to an existing, established area of nonwhite concentration, it almost invariably becomes an all minority group project. This is occasioned by the pressure of nonwhites to get into the unit and the disinclination of whites to enter and remain in a predominantly colored community. . . . Also, it is more difficult to introduce white tenants into a previously all-Negro or predominantly Negro public housing project than to bring nonwhites into a previously all-white development" (Weaver 1956:86).

4. Requirements issued in 1982 for the administration of the Affirmative Fair Housing Marketing Program may reduce the variability in the administration of this program. These requirements, however, do not establish racial residency requirements or quotas, although residency "preference" may be utilized as long as it is used in "a manner that housing opportunities will not be denied to any particular group" (U.S. Department of Housing and Urban Development 1982:2–19). HUD field staff are instructed to monitor occupancy data, applicant pool information, and the criteria for selecting tenants used by the owner, as well as demographic patterns and trends. As these requirements are implemented, it should be possible to determine whether such directives have effected the successful implementation and standardization of this program and promoted higher levels of racial mixing. The monitoring of such plans is limited because data regarding the characteristics of tenants are currently supplied on a voluntary basis by PHAs and are, therefore, notably incomplete. It is also reasonably clear that the data sent to HUD are not always accurate or verified for errors (Sadacca 1981).

5. One of the least well-researched tools available to influence the racial balancing of tenants in HUD-assisted housing is the tenant selection and assignment policy adopted by the developer or PHA manager. These policies include provisions for allocating units based on various criteria for need or merit according to preference rules established by HUD as well as by state or local authorities. Those displaced by public

slum clearance or emergencies, the handicapped, veterans, large families, or others are often given varying priorities, or weights, in assigning units to prospective tenants. There is often a long waiting list of applicants for assisted housing (from 5 to 10 years in many large housing authorities), and tenant selection policies are the basis for allocating scarce housing resources to the needy. Because of such shortages, some authorities may only be able to house emergency cases.

Where there are vacancies or modernization of units that create vacancies, tenant selection policies can exert a greater influence on the degree of dispersal or integration of family and elderly units. Limited research indicates that the managers have considerable latitude in selecting and placing white and black tenants and may use their discretion to segregate and discriminate (Luttrell 1966; Lazin 1973; Bauman 1977:125; Struyk and Blake 1983; Kaplan 1985). Struyk and Blake (1983:10), for example, note the wide range of practices employed by HUD area offices in addressing tenant selection policies of public housing authorities: "HUD area offices are providing different degrees of latitude to authorities. In effect this means there are numerous sets of regulations, not one." The lack of consistent, rational procedures in implementing these regulations is an issue that has not been systematically researched (Kaplan 1984).

6. Very little research has been done on the implementation and effectiveness of federal fair housing laws to document their utility in reducing segregation in the rental or sales markets of cities. Nationwide, federal, state, and local fair housing agencies receive less than 5,000 fair housing complaints a year. The low volume of complaint activity is the likely result of a score of factors; ineffective enforcement techniques, lack of awareness of laws, inadequate staffing, and shortages of funds have long been known as limitations of fair housing enforcement programs (Social Science Panel 1972:61; GAO 1978; U.S. Commission on Civil Rights 1979, 1983). Because of inadequate staffing and confusion over HUD's own regulations, relatively few recipients of HUD funding were examined to determine whether they were illegally segregating their tenants (GAO 1978:10-17).

There is, then, little evidence about the conditions under which Title VI or VIII enforcement techniques work best. Federal fair housing enforcement strategies have never been carefully evaluated, with no information on the effect of an administrative or court decision on the defendant or on other parties. A well-publicized case in which a discriminator is caught and punished might deter others from similar practices. The news of the victory might also sensitize minority groups to their rights to complain or sue, thereby generating additional complaints.

There is no way at present to determine the effects of local or Supreme Court decisions, Department of Justice actions, or HUD conciliations on the general level of racial discrimination either in the community affected or in those indirectly impacted by the ruling. Only by comparing areas with different levels of law enforcement, or different histories of legal action, could some insight be gained about the relationship of remedies to levels of discriminatory practices in the private and public housing markets.

7. A judgment offered nearly thirty years ago still reflects a not insignificant viewpoint within the black population: "So long as integration remains segmental and in process, Negro institutions and organizations which serve in the breach or which exist to protest or to mobilize for more participation will have a place in the Negro community" (Lewis and Hill 1956:121). Such institutions represent an adjustment to the continuing presence of community needs and discriminatory opportunities.

REFERENCES

Bauman, John F. 1977. "Safe and Sanitary without the Costly Frills: The Evolution of Public Housing in Philadelphia, 1929–1941." *The Pennsylvania Magazine of History and Biography* 51 (January): 114–28.

Bryce, Herrington, Gloria Cousar, and William McCoy. 1978. "Housing Problems of Black Mayor Cities." *The Annals* 439 (January): 80–89.

Burke, Paul. 1984. "Trends in Subsidized Housing: 1974–1981." Unpublished report. Office of Economic Affairs, U.S. Department of Housing and Urban Development, Washington, D.C., March.

———. 1985. "Trends in Racially Concentrated Projects: 1977." Unpublished report. Office of Economic Affairs, U.S. Department of Housing and Urban Development, Washington, D.C., January.

Calmore, John. 1979. "Fair Housing vs. Fair Housing: The Conflict between Providing Low-Income Housing in Impacted Areas and Providing Increased Housing Opportunities through Spatial Deconcentration." *Housing Law Bulletin* 9 (November–December): 1–12.

Clarence Givens et al. v. Prairie Creek Manor Apartments. 1985. "Post-Trial Brief on Behalf of Defendants John Wright and the United States Department of Housing and Urban Development." Civil Action No. 3–82–0985–H, Northern District of Texas, U.S. District Court, 26 January.

Clark. W. A. V., and Eric Moore. 1980. "Continuing the Debate." In *Residential Mobility and Public Policy*, edited by W. A. V. Clark and Eric Moore, pp. 308–16. Beverly Hills, Calif.: Sage.

Congressional Record. 1980. "The Fair Housing Amendments Act of 1980" (26 September; 30 September, H–9812, H–10099, S–13952; 1 December).

De Bernardo, Henry. 1979. "Analysis of HUD's Regional Housing Mobility Program." Unpublished report. Philadelphia, 31 August.

DeMuth, Jerry. 1985. "20 Years after Gautreaux." *Planning* 51 (February): 20–21.

"Desegregation Order Is Forcing Tenants to Switch." 1983. *Washington Post*, 8 December, p. A20.

Downs, Anthony. 1976. "The Successes and Failures of Federal Housing Policy." In *Housing, 1973–1974*, edited by George Sternlieb. New York: A.M.S. Press.

Egan, John, John Carr, Andrew Mott, and John Roos. 1981. "Avoiding Another Margrette Park." In *Housing and Public Policy: A Role for Mediating Structures*, edited by John Egan, John Carr, Andrew Mott, and John Roos, pp. 41–74. Cambridge, Mass.: Ballinger.

Fishman, Richard. 1978. *Housing for All under the Law: New Directions in Housing, Land Use, and Planning Law*. Cambridge, Mass.: Ballinger.

Flournoy, Craig, and George Rodrigue. 1985. "Housing Divided: Officially Sanctioned Is Rule, Not Exception, in East Texas." *Dallas Morning News*, 12 February.

Foley, Donald. 1973. "Institutional and Contextual Factors Affecting the Housing Choices of Minority Residents." In *Segregation in Residential Areas*, edited by Amos Hawley and Vincent P. Rock, pp. 85–147. Washington, D.C.: National Academy of Sciences.

GAO. 1978. "Stronger Federal Enforcement Needed to Uphold Fair Housing Laws."

Report CED-78-21. U.S. General Accounting Office, Washington, D.C., 2 February.

Hartling, James. 1980. "The Public Policy Environment: Mobility Researchers' Responsibilities." In *Residential Mobility and Public Policy*, edited by W. A. V. Clark and Eric Moore, pp. 274-82. Beverly Hills, Calif.: Sage.

Henry, Alan, and Jacqueline Thomas. 1983. "Washington's CHA Plan: The Calls for Construction Speed Up on Scattered-Site Projects." *Chicago Sun Times*, 15 April.

Holshouser, William. 1983. "An Examination of Four Boston Area Section 8 Existing Housing Mobility Programs." Unpublished report. Citizens Housing and Planning Association, Boston, 28 June.

Jaclyn, Inc. 1976. "A Study to Determine the Extent of Compliance among Developers/Sponsors with Advertising Guidelines for Fair Housing Marketing Regulations." Office of Policy Development and Research, U.S. Department of Housing and Urban Development, Washington, D.C., July.

Kaplan, Edward. 1984. *Managing the Demand for Public Housing*. Technical Report No. 183. Cambridge, Mass.: Operations Research Center, M.I.T., June.

_____. 1985. "Tenant Assignment: How PHAs Fill Their Units." *Journal of Housing* 42 (January/February): 13-20.

Karnig, Albert, and S. Welch. 1980. *Black Representatives and Urban Policy*. Chicago: University of Chicago Press.

Klibanoff, Hank. 1982. "Whitman Project Foes: No Protest, No Welcome." *Philadelphia Inquirer*, 9 October, p. 1B.

Krefetz, Sharon. 1979. "Low- and Moderate-Income Housing in the Suburbs: The Massachusetts Anti-Snob Zoning Law Experience." *Policies Studies Journal* 8 (Special #1): 288-99.

Kurtz, Howard. 1985. "Reagan Budget to Slash Housing Aid." *Washington Post*, 30 January, p. A1.

Lazin, Frederick. 1973. "The Failure of Enforcement of Civil Rights Regulations in Public Housing, 1963-1971: The Cooptation of a Federal Agency by Its Local Constituency." *Policy Sciences* 4: 263-73.

"Legitimate Objectives of Zoning." 1978. *Harvard Law Review* 91 (May): 1443-62.

Lewis, Hylan, and Mozell Hill. 1956. "Desegregation, Integration, and the Negro Community." *The Annals* 304 (March): 116-23.

Listokin, David. 1976. *Fair Share Housing Allocation*. New Brunswick, N.J.: Center for Urban Policy Research.

Lucille Young v. Housing Authority of the City of Clarksville. 1983. "Findings of Fact, Conclusions of Law and Preliminary Injunction." No. P-82-37-CA. Eastern District of Texas, U.S. District Court, 11 October.

Luttrell, Jordan. 1966. "The Public Housing Administration and Discrimination in Federally Assisted Low-Rent Housing." *Michigan Law Review* 64 (March): 871-90.

McEntire, Davis. 1960. *Residence and Race*. Berkeley: University of California Press.

McGrew, Jane. 1981. "Resistance to Change Continues to Restrict Public Housing Choices." *Journal of Housing* 38 (July): 375-80.

McKay, David. 1977. *Housing and Race in Industrial Society: Civil Rights and Urban Policy in Britain and the United States*. Totowa, N.J.: Rowman and Littlefield.

Metropolitan Action Institute. 1982. "More Places to Live: A Study of Interjurisdictional Housing Mobility Programs." Unpublished report. Metropolitan Action Institute, New York, December.

Miller, Ted. 1985. "Final Report: Feasibility Research for Public Housing Desegregation Demonstration." International Business Services, Washington, D.C., May.

National Capitol Systems. 1983. *Assessment of HUD's Affimative Fair Housing Marketing Program*. Final Report. Washington, D.C.: Office of Policy Development and Research, U.S. Department of Housing and Urban Development, April.

National Housing Policy Review. 1974. *Housing in the Seventies*. Washington, D.C.: U.S. Government Printing Office.

Newsweek. 1983. "Kicked out of My Home." 26 December, pp. 18, 20.

Pierce, Samuel. 1984. "Public Housing Desegregation." Memo to Dick Eudaly, Regional Administrator, Region VI, 18 February.

Region IX. 1974. "The Impact and Performance of Affirmative Fair Housing Marketing Regulations in Region IX." Evaluation Report. Office of Program Planning and Evaluation, U.S. Department of Housing and Urban Development, San Francisco, September.

Rodrigue, George. 1985. "Racial Data on Subsidized Housing Not Compiled." *Dallas Morning News*, 13 February.

———, and Craig Flournoy. 1985. "Stuck in the Ghettos: Failed Policies Keep Minorities in Hidden City." *Dallas Morning News*, 13 February.

Rubinowitz, Leonard, Joel Greenfield, and Jay Harris. 1974. "Affirmative Marketing of Federally Assisted Housing: Implementation in the Urban Metropolitan Area." Urban-Suburban Investment Study. Center for Urban Affairs, Northwestern University.

Sadacca, Robert. 1981. "An Analysis of PHA (Re) Certification Policies and Procedures and SHACO Tape Problems and Alternatives." Report 1279-02. The Urban Institute, Washington, D.C., June.

Shaffer, Helen. 1958. "Residential Desegregation." *Editorial Research Reports* 1 (January): 43-60.

Social Science Panel. 1972. *Freedom of Choice in Housing: Opportunities and Constraints*. Washington, D.C.: National Academy of Sciences.

Stanfield, Rochelle. 1980. "Challenge to Black Power." *National Journal* (21 June): 1024.

Struyk, Raymond, and Jennifer Blake. 1982. "Determining Who Lives in Public Housing." PR 3007-01. The Urban Institute, Washington, D.C., March.

———. 1983. "Selecting Tenants: The Law, Markets, and PHA Practices." *Journal of Housing* 40 (January/February): 8-12.

Tomasson, Robert. 1981. "Town Is Accused of Bias in Refusal of Housing Aid." *New York Times*, 25 March, p. B8.

Truslow, Jonathan. 1982. "Final Report: Regional Housing Mobility Program, Boston, Massachusetts." Metropolitan Area Planning Council, Boston, April.

U.S. Commission on Civil Rights. 1979. *The Federal Fair Housing Enforcement Effort*. Washington, D.C.: U.S. Government Printing Office, March.

———. 1983. *Federal Civil Rights Commitments: An Assessment of Enforcement*

Resources and Performance. CP #82. Washington, D.C.: U.S. Commission on Civil Rights, November.

U.S. Department of Housing and Urban Development. 1982. *Implementation of Affirmative Fair Housing Marketing Requirements Handbook.* 8025.1 Rev-1. Washington, D.C.: U.S. Government Printing Office, August.

――――. 1985. "FY 1986 Budget: Summary." U.S. Department of Housing and Urban Development, Washington, D.C., 4 February.

Weaver, Robert. 1956. "Integration in Public and Private Housing." *The Annals* 304 (March): 86–97.

Welfeld, Irving. 1977. "American Housing Policy: Perverse Programs by Prudent People." *The Public Interest* 48 (Summer): 128–44.

Wood, Elizabeth. 1982. *The Beautiful Beginnings: The Failure to Learn, Fifty Years of Public Housing in America.* Washington, D.C.: The National Center for Housing Management.

Young v. Samuel Pierce, Secretary of HUD. 1982. Civil Cause No. P-80-8CA. Eastern District, Paris Division, U.S. District Court.

Chapter Nine
Where Should HUD Locate Assisted Housing?
The Evolution of Fair Housing Policy
MICHAEL J. VERNARELLI*

Since 1968 the U.S. Department of Housing and Urban Development (HUD) has held a legislative mandate to affirmatively promote fair housing in the administration of its housing programs. Yet during the time since passage of the 1968 Civil Rights Act, the department has received little legislative direction on how to carry out its duties under Title VIII of the act. As a consequence, HUD fair housing policy has evolved in a complex process, the result of interaction among the legislative, judicial, and executive branches of the federal government. The purpose of this chapter is to chart the evolution of HUD's efforts to promote fair housing through the location of assisted housing.

The policy development process has been marked by ambiguity about the meaning of the fair housing mandate itself and the definition of key terms. Throughout the seventeen-year period since the 1968 Civil Rights Act was enacted into law, there have been a variety of interpretations of the meaning of "affirmatively promoting fair housing." A second problem has been the definition of key operational terms that have been used by the courts, Congress, and HUD. These terms include, but are not limited to, "area of minority concentration," "sufficient and comparable opportunities," and "racially mixed area." Furthermore, the societal environment and attitudes toward racial integration by minorities and nonminorities alike have provided a constantly changing milieu for policy development and implementation. Ambiguity and uncertainty have been the hallmarks of this evolutionary process. A time line or chronology of the major policy events in the executive, legislative, and judicial branches is presented in Figure 1.

This chapter begins by discussing the development of the fair housing mandate through legislative and executive actions, as well as the first HUD initiatives undertaken in the early 1970s and the development of "fair share" plans. Considered next is the interaction between federal courts and HUD in the determination of assisted housing location policy prior to the 1974 Housing and Community Development Act. Two court cases—*Gautreaux* and *Shannon*— have contributed significantly to this process. Although there obviously has

*The author would like to thank George Ferguson, Carolyn Lieberman, Feather O'Connor, and Fran White for providing information used in this research. Members of the Division of Housing Assistance Research, Kathy Peroff, and two anonymous reviewers provided comments on earlier drafts that strengthened the chapter. Special thanks are due John M. Goering for his assistance in improving the chapter. Of course, the author is solely responsible for any remaining errors or misinterpretations.

	EXECUTIVE BRANCH	LEGISLATIVE BRANCH	JUDICIAL BRANCH
1962	Executive Order: required non-discrimination in federal programs		
1964		Civil Rights Act: Title VI required non-discrimination in federal programs	
1967			Gautreaux litigation initiated
1968		Civil Rights Act: Title VIII prohibits discrimination and in its own programs required HUD to affirmatively promote fair housing	
1970			Shannon litigation initiated
1971	Executive Order: Supported the concept of fair housing		
1972	Site Selection Criteria developed by HUD		
1974		Housing and Community Development Act: gave new legislative direction to the fair housing goal	
1976	Gautreaux Housing Demonstration: metropolitan-wide housing demonstration in response to Gautreaux litigation		
1978		GAO report on HUD compliance with Fair housing goals of 1974 HCD Act	Litigation on application of HUD site selection criteria
1980		Housing and Community Development Act: Reflected changing view of application of site selection criteria	
1981	Clarification of site selection criteria published		
1983	President transmits Fair Housing Amendments to Congress		
1984	HUD acts to desegrate Public Housing		

Figure 1. A Chronology of Major Fair Housing Policy Developments

been some interdependence between the cases (early *Gautreaux* rulings were cited in the *Shannon* case), it is useful to discuss separately each case and its concomitant policy response. This is because *Gautreaux* resulted in a demonstration using the Section 8 Existing Housing Program. On the other hand, *Shannon* resulted in HUD site selection regulations designed to increase housing opportunities for minorities primarily in the Section 8 New Construction Program.

The discussion then turns to several major policy developments since passage of the 1974 Housing and Community Development Act, and reviews HUD policy decisions, recent court cases, and the results of oversight by the U.S. General Accounting Office (GAO) in the policy development process. The chapter concludes with comments assessing the current position of HUD fair housing and location policy.

Development of the Federal Fair Housing Mandate

Since the federal government became deeply involved in the housing market during the Great Depression, location policy has evolved from an essentially passive posture to active promotion of fair housing. Initially, housing policy was designed to be consistent with prevailing real estate attitudes regarding racial integration.[1] Early policies enacted for both the Federal Housing Administration (FHA) and the public housing program reinforced existing segregated housing patterns.[2]

The federal fair housing mandate began to develop in the 1960s. In 1962 President Kennedy issued Executive Order 11063, which banned discrimination in federally administered programs. This was followed by the landmark civil rights legislation. Title VI of the Civil Rights Act of 1964 required nondiscrimination in federal programs much like the earlier executive order. Title VIII of the Civil Rights Act of 1968 remains to this day the most significant piece of legislation in the area of fair housing. This act requires HUD, among its many obligations, to affirmatively promote fair housing in the administration of its housing programs. Although these legislative and executive actions required HUD to affirmatively promote fair housing, they included little direction on how to accomplish this goal. Legal scholars, in reviewing this mandate, have found that the acts do not clearly define the nature and extent of HUD's responsibility in affirmatively promoting fair housing.[3] One interpretation is that HUD is responsible for seeing that racial integration occurs through the administration of its housing programs. Another interpretation is that HUD must provide expanded housing choice both for those served by its housing programs and for the private housing market. A third interpretation is that HUD is only responsible for affirmative actions regarding its own housing programs.

In the early 1970s, under Secretary Romney, HUD attempted to induce communities to locate more assisted housing in suburban locations. The means of inducement was to make the deconcentration of assisted housing within a metropolitan area a condition for local communities' receipt of HUD housing and community development funds. HUD met stiff opposition from suburban groups but nonetheless pressed on with the policy. Secretary Romney emphasized that the alternative to voluntary desegregation was court-ordered desegregation, and that the former was more desirable. The HUD policy received a boost when President Nixon publicly endorsed HUD desegregation efforts in 1971: "By 'equal housing opportunity,' I mean the achievement of a condition in which individuals of similar income levels in the same housing market area have a like range of housing choices available to them regardless of their race, color, religion or national origin."[4]

Despite these attempts, the policy initiatives of this period appeared to have little impact: "The get-tough strategy did not succeed, mainly because HUD could not offer most communities enough of an economic reward to justify a local political confrontation over racial integration. The most conspicuous failures were in suburban communities."[5]

The early 1970s also saw the development of fair share plans implemented by area-wide planning organizations. Fair share plans have been defined as "dispersal policies for the future development of lower income units."[6] The goal of fair share plans was the balanced geographic distribution of assisted housing resources.[7] This includes placing housing where it is most needed and best suited as well as expanding the choice of housing locations for assisted families. This approach to planning represented the first metropolitan-wide attempt to increase the housing opportunities for assisted families. The fair share approach was incorporated into the HUD planning process at the federal level after passage of the 1974 Housing and Community Development Act.

The Interaction of HUD and the Courts in Determining Location Policy

Two court cases have been of particular importance in the development of HUD's location policies. Although a certain degree of interdependence exists between the cases, it is useful to discuss each separately. The *Gautreaux* case, initiated in 1967, is not completely closed. HUD's response to *Gautreaux* was to attempt voluntarily to widen housing opportunities for minorities in the Chicago metropolitan area through the Gautreaux Housing Demonstration. The *Shannon* case was adjudicated in 1970. The primary response by HUD was the promulgation of site selection criteria designed to assess the impact on minority concentration in a given area surrounding a proposed HUD construction project for low-income persons.

The plaintiffs in *Gautreaux* were a group of tenants in public housing in Chicago who filed suit against the Chicago Housing Authority (CHA).[8] They claimed that CHA and HUD had followed discriminatory practices in locating public housing projects in Chicago and in selecting tenants for given projects. Projects located in nonminority areas had virtually no black tenants whereas the reverse was true for projects in minority areas. The court found in favor of the plaintiffs, ruling that CHA had followed discriminatory practices both in site selection and in tenant selection. To remedy the situation, the court ordered that the city of Chicago be divided into two areas, a Limited Public Housing Area and a General Public Housing Area. The Limited Public Housing Area consisted of all census tracts that had minority populations of 30 percent or more and all other census tracts within one mile. The General Public Housing Area contained the remaining census tracts in Cook County. The court ordered that the first 700 new units of public housing be built in the General Public Housing Area.

After several more years of litigation, the district court entered its final judgment against HUD. The court ordered HUD to cooperate with CHA "in its best effort to increase the supply of low-rent public housing on a nondiscriminatory basis."[9] The original plaintiffs appealed this decision on the basis that metropolitan relief was required to remedy the situation. The district court's order provided limited relief only to the city of Chicago, as no other jurisdictions had been parties to the suit. The appellate court remanded the case to the district court for a metropolitan-wide relief plan.[10] HUD appealed this decision to the Supreme Court. On 20 April 1976, the Supreme Court ruled in favor of the original plaintiffs that metropolitan-wide relief was permissible.[11]

In response to the Supreme Court ruling, HUD entered into an agreement with the plaintiffs to voluntarily provide metropolitan-wide relief. This initial agreement, in June 1976, provided for several commitments on the part of HUD to expand the housing opportunities for low-income minorities in the Chicago metropolitan area. The most significant commitment was the development of the Gautreaux Demonstration. This demonstration included the use of Section 8 Existing certificates on a metropolitan-wide basis with extensive counseling and outreach services. Since the initial agreement expired, HUD has renewed modified agreements with the plaintiffs in attempting to provide relief on a metropolitan-wide basis.

The *Gautreaux* case and the Gautreaux Demonstration were significant events in the evolution of fair housing policy. First, the Gautreaux Demonstration represented the first large-scale effort on the part of HUD to redress the discriminatory effects of its past policies. Second, the Supreme Court ruled that HUD has the right to use its discretion in allocating assisted housing units to local housing agencies based on compliance with fair housing statutes and federal regulations. Finally, some thought at the time that the Gautreaux Demonstration might serve as a prototype for similar programs in other metropolitan areas. As we shall see in the discussion on fair housing policy development since 1974, below, HUD officials later decided that the Gautreaux Demonstration was not applicable on a nationwide basis.

In *Shannon v. HUD*, the courts went a long way toward defining the nature and extent of HUD's responsibility to assess proposed sites for assisted housing in accordance with the fair housing goal.[12] In the original *Shannon* case, residents (both black and white), businessmen, and representatives of local civic organizations brought suit seeking an injunction against HUD's support of an assisted rental housing project in an urban renewal area of Philadelphia. The original urban renewal plan called for owner-occupied housing to be located on the site in question, but HUD approved a change in the plan that allowed for rental housing without following official agency procedure for making such changes. In the initial complaint, the plaintiffs argued that they had made substantial investments in the area based on the urban renewal plan that called for owner-occupied housing. The plaintiffs maintained that rental housing on the site would increase the minority population in a predominantly minority area. The district court denied the request for an injunction and the plaintiffs appealed the case.

Upon appeal in 1970 the plaintiffs maintained that, in reviewing project proposals of this type, HUD had no procedures to assess the impact of the proposed project on the racial concentration in the neighborhood. The appellate court overturned the lower court decision, finding in favor of the plaintiffs. The court found that HUD had not fulfilled its obligation to affirmatively promote fair housing. Specifically, the court said the undue concentration of people of a given race, or socioeconomic group, in a given neighborhood could subject persons to discrimination, "defeating or substantially impairing accomplishment of the objectives of the program or activity as respect persons of a particular race."[13]

The court directed HUD to formulate standards for sites and neighborhoods with respect to racial and economic concentration: "We hold ... that the Agency must utilize some institutionalized method whereby, in considering site selection or type selection, it has before it the relevant racial and socio-economic information necessary for compliance with its duties under the 1964 and 1968 Civil Rights Acts."[14] The court went on to suggest examples of criteria that might be used to review proposed project sites. Although the court identified affirmative fair housing as an important goal of national housing policy, it recognized the existence of other important, competing goals: "There may be instances where a pressing case may be made for the rebuilding of a racial ghetto. We hold only that the agency's judgment must be an informed one; one which weighs the alternatives and finds that the need for physical rehabilitation or additional minority housing at the site in question clearly outweighs the disadvantage of increasing or perpetuating racial concentration."[15]

HUD's response to this ruling was expedited publication of project selection criteria in January 1972. Project selection criteria vary from program to program but the basic message is the same. The standards for the Section 8 New Construction Program adopted after passage of the Housing and Community Development Act of 1974 are a good example:

The site and neighborhood shall be suitable from the standpoint of facilitating and furthering full compliance with the applicable provisions of Title VI of the Civil Rights Act of 1964, Title VIII of the Civil Rights Act of 1968, Executive Order 11063, and HUD regulations issued pursuant thereto.

The site shall not be located in an area of minority concentration unless (i) sufficient comparable opportunities exist for housing for minority families, in the income range to be served by the proposed project, outside areas of minority concentration, or (ii) the project is necessary to meet overriding housing needs which cannot otherwise feasibly be met in that housing market area. An "overriding need" may not serve as the basis for determining that a site is acceptable if the only reason the need cannot otherwise feasibly be met is that discrimination on the basis of race, color, religion, creed, sex, or national origin renders sites outside areas of minority concentration unavailable; or a racially mixed area if the project will cause a significant increase in the proportion of minority to nonminority residents in the area.

The site must promote choice of housing opportunities and avoid undue concentration of assisted persons in areas containing a high proportion of low-income persons.[16]

Thus, these standards explicitly recognize the department's responsibility under the civil rights statutes. The regulations state that projects are not to be located in areas of minority concentration unless comparable opportunities exist in nonminority areas or the project is necessary to meet overriding needs in the minority areas.

The regulations, though consistent with the *Shannon* ruling, are ambiguous about the definitions of minority concentration, area of minority concentration, overriding housing needs, and sufficient, comparable housing opportunities. This ambiguity has become obvious through a series of cases in which the courts have wrestled with the definitions.

Further, the regulations prohibit the location of a project in a racially mixed area, if doing so would cause a significant increase in the minority percentage of total residents. This regulation, too, is fraught with definitional ambiguity. It attempts to address the problem of tipping, where a HUD action might upset the racial balance of a mixed area and the area eventually would become predominantly minority. The determination of this eventuality is, of course, an extremely difficult, if not impossible, task in many instances. Not surprisingly, a number of cases regarding this determination have come before the courts. A discussion of several representative cases is presented below.

Fair Housing Policy Development since 1974

Since 1974, fair housing policy has evolved in a number of interrelated areas. The passage of the Housing and Community Development (HCD) Act in 1974 provided HUD with a new, if somewhat ambiguous, legislative direction. In the wake of the Gautreaux Housing Demonstration, HUD policymakers attempted to recommend modifications to regulations governing the administration of assisted housing programs by public housing authorities (PHAs) to promote fair housing. These efforts, and the U.S. General Accounting Office oversight regarding HUD's fulfillment of fair housing goals stipulated in the 1974 HCD Act, are discussed in the second part of this section. The third part of this section deals with HUD's implementation of site selection criteria, while simultaneously attempting to reduce the ambiguity in the wording through the issuance of Clarification Notices. Concern with site selection criteria reflected the continuing debate regarding the efficacy and appropriateness of using site selection criteria to promote fair housing. Attempts by HUD to clarify site selection criteria, and a number of important court cases brought against HUD for its application of existing site selection criteria, are discussed in the final part of this section.

Passage of the HCD Act in 1974 led to renewed departmental interest in the fair housing goal and further emphasized HUD's duty. Under Title I, the act specified the following goals: "the reduction of the isolation of income groups within communities and geographical areas and the promotion of an increase in the diversity and vitality of neighborhoods through the spatial deconcentration of housing opportunities for persons of lower income and the revitalization of deteriorating or deteriorated neighborhoods to attract persons of higher incomes." [17] These goals, rather than helping to clarify the fair housing mandate, only added more ambiguity and uncertainty to already clouded legislative directions. The meaning of the term "deconcentration" was unclear. Also, the goals of revitalizing deteriorating neighborhoods and promoting spatial deconcentration may, in some instances, be mutually incompatible.

Under provisions of the act, communities applying for Community Development Block Grants (CDBGs) must complete a Housing Assistance Plan (HAP). The HAP is the document that surveys the condition of housing in the community and specifies a strategy to conserve or expand the housing stock, principally for lower income persons. One purpose of the HAP is to identify proposed locations for assisted projects that will avoid concentrations of assisted families and provide lower income families, especially minority households, with greater choice of housing opportunities.

The HCD Act of 1974 created the Section 8 Existing, New Construction, and Substantial Rehabilitation programs.[18] These programs have served, in part, as vehicles to meet the fair housing goal, although the fair housing goal itself was not directly referenced in the section of the act (Title II) that created the Section 8 program.

Patricia Harris took office as secretary of HUD in 1977 with a commitment to increase mobility and housing opportunities for minorities; she also inherited prior legislative and judicial mandates in this area. In May 1977, Secretary Harris established the Gautreaux Task Force. The purpose of this interdepartmental group was to analyze HUD housing policies in the light of the *Gautreaux* litigation. Initially, the task force targeted site selection and marketing policies as areas for inquiry. However, the group spent much of its effort trying to determine the applicability of the Gautreaux Demonstration for formulating national policy. After meeting for about a year, subcommittees of the task force issued draft recommendations dealing with the Section 8 Existing Program. They recommended removing geographic restrictions on the use of certificates within a metropolitan area, providing special outreach and counseling for minorities, and establishing goals for PHAs in providing certificates to those outside their jurisdictions. The secretary never formally acted on these recommendations, in part because it was felt that the Gautreaux Demonstration experience could not be replicated on a nationwide basis.[19] In the summer of 1978, Secretary Harris established an Assisted Housing Mobility Task Force to make specific recommendations to promote mobility and deconcentration in the Section 8 Existing and other assisted housing programs.

Departmental concern was refocused in October 1978 when Henry Eschwege, director of the U.S. General Accounting Office, sent a letter to Secretary Harris summarizing the results of a GAO review of HUD's efforts to avoid undue concentrations of lower income persons in its Section 8 housing assistance program. The 1974 HCD Act mandated the goal of avoiding undue concentrations of lower income households. In essence, the GAO review (CED-78-181) criticized HUD's efforts to comply with the legislation.

In general, GAO felt that the Section 8 program had not been sufficiently coordinated with the deconcentration objective. Specifically, the GAO letter outlined three major findings: (1) that key housing personnel in Washington and the field offices were unsure of how the deconcentration objective related to the administration of Section 8, (2) that HUD had provided little guidance on how to achieve deconcentration, and (3) that HUD had not assessed the degree of success in achieving the deconcentration objective. Based on its findings, GAO made three recommendations:

1. HUD should clearly define how deconcentration relates to Section 8;
2. HUD should issue guidelines to field offices on how to achieve the deconcentration objective; and
3. HUD should develop measures to assess deconcentration efforts.

The effect of the GAO letter was to accelerate the ongoing work of the Assisted Housing Mobility Task Force. In January 1979, the task force reported its recommendations to Secretary Harris. The task force focused on the Section 8 Existing Program, the vehicle used in the Gautreaux Demonstration, and consequently did not consider site and neighborhood standards. The task force considered means of increasing mobility both within and between jurisdictions.

With regard to interjurisdictional mobility, the task force noted that current regulations contained provisions for funding preferences for those PHAs that provide families with the broadest geographic choice of housing.[20] The task force also made several recommendations regarding program operation. Many of these recommendations were already listed as optional in the Section 8 Existing Housing Program Handbook, but few PHAs had exercised the options. The task force recommended the development of metropolitan-wide resource information exchanges to assist minority households wishing to lease units in nonminority areas. Along with this recommendation, the task force proposed that a portion of the secretary's Discretionary Fund be distributed for grants to develop the metropolitan-wide information clearinghouses.[21] A third recommendation in this area was that PHAs provide more specific briefings of participants to apprise them of mobility options and resources. Further, the task force proposed that HUD issue guidelines regarding the nature and extent of personalized counseling given to program participants by field offices.

Although the task force concentrated on the Section 8 Existing Program, it also suggested other policy initiatives (e.g., that the secretary issue a policy statement to emphasize the importance of the mobility goal). In addition, there were several proposals that did not gain consensus from representatives of the program offices.

Secretary Harris accepted all the proposals that gained a consensus and issued a policy statement to that effect on 17 January 1979. She assigned the Office of Policy Development and Research the responsibility to monitor implementation of the recommendations.

In March 1979, Secretary Harris issued her response to the GAO letter of 20 October 1978, as stipulated by law, to the House Committee on Governmental Operations and the Senate Committee on Governmental Affairs. She emphasized the department's and her personal commitment to the goals of deconcentration and expansion of housing choice for lower income people, particularly minorities. In essence, Secretary Harris agreed to implement the three major recommendations of the GAO report. In addition, she made several comments regarding the GAO findings. First, she expressed concern over GAO's apparent overemphasis of the deconcentration objective. Deconcentration, although rightfully a major objective of HUD, must be balanced with other, equally important legislative goals such as revitalization of neighborhoods. These goals may at times be in conflict with one another. Second, the secretary noted that the locations of Section 8 New Construction and Substantial Rehabilitation units are in part determined by a community's HAP. Third, she criticized the GAO conclusion that HUD had paid little attention to deconcentration, pointing out that the department had given substantial financial support to metropolitan-wide housing opportunities since FY 1976.

About the same time as the Supreme Court decision on *Gautreaux*, in 1976, modifications to project selection criteria were being developed within HUD. In January 1977 these proposed site and neighborhood standards were published for comment in the *Federal Register*. The preamble to the proposed regulations stated that, although site and neighborhood standards were developed in 1972, application of the standards had varied across area offices: "The lack of a simple set of uniform criteria applicable to all federally assisted housing programs, and the ambiguity of present requirements have resulted in inconsistent and uneven application of the current standards."[22]

A major issue addressed by the proposed standards was clarification of the meaning of comparable housing opportunities inside and outside areas of minority concentration. An area of minority concentration was defined as an area with 40 percent or more minority population or an area where minority residents constitute "a significantly greater proportion of the residents than the proportion of minority residents of the locality as a whole."[23] Although this provision eliminated some of the ambiguity surrounding the definition of area of minority concentration, it by no means eliminated it totally. Moreover, this section of the proposed regulations allowed for selection of sites inside areas of minority concentration "if sites outside such areas cannot feasibly be made available for assisted housing."[24]

The proposed regulations also defined a racially mixed area as one with less than 40 percent minority residents, and one that displayed a trend of racial transition. Further, the proposed regulations considered the issue of multiple, often conflicting, national housing goals: "The goals of rehabilitating blighted, abandoned or substandard dwellings in central city areas where low income families live must be weighed against the goal of expanding housing opportunities outside of areas of minority or assisted housing concentration."[25] Thus, the proposed regulations recognized goals other than increasing housing opportunities, a point recognized earlier by Congress and the courts.

The proposed regulations represented an attempt to clarify the procedures HUD field offices should follow in site selection. Although some clarification would have been accomplished, it can easily be argued that the proposed regulations would have introduced as much ambiguity as they would have eliminated. After publication in the *Federal Register*, the proposed regulations received diverse comments. The interested parties failed to reach consensus and the department never issued the proposed regulations in final form; field offices continued to use the 1972 regulations.

In the past several years, HUD site selection procedures for Section 8 New Construction projects have been called into question in a number of cases. These cases have revolved primarily around two issues. One issue has been the definition of appropriate neighborhood boundaries. This definition is crucial to the determination of whether a proposed site is located in a minority, racially mixed, or nonminority area. When the Section 8 New Construction Program was first implemented, field offices were instructed to define the neighborhood as the census tract containing the proposed site. Opponents of this procedure attacked it in suits they filed against HUD. The plaintiffs argued that census tract boundaries are inappropriate and that the use of such boundaries in lieu of the actual neighborhood boundaries is arbitrary and capricious. The courts have accepted this argument, reasoning that neighborhood boundaries must be determined by considering all relevant data. In cases where HUD demonstrated that all relevant data had been considered in the determination of the neighborhood boundaries, the courts supported HUD's site and neighborhood assessments.

Another related, sensitive issue has been the determination of whether placement of a project will lead to the tipping of a neighborhood's racial occupancy.[26] This is an extremely complex issue, in which neighborhood occupancy trends over several years must be assessed. Courts have not, however, given HUD a clear direction as to how to determine the question of neighborhood tipping.

In *King v. Harris*, a group comprised of neighborhood residents and community organizations brought suit to enjoin HUD from supporting the building of a Section 8 New Construction project in a racially integrated neighborhood on Staten Island.[27] The plaintiffs contended that development of the project would upset the neighborhood's racial balance, and that the neighborhood eventually would tip to all-black occupancy.

A key issue in this case was the determination of the relevant boundaries of the neighborhood. HUD defined the neighborhood as the census tract in which the proposed site was located. The plaintiffs contended that this definition was inappropriate because the proposed site was located at the edge of a census tract and other assisted projects across the street were in other census tracts. The neighborhood defined by the plaintiffs contained excessive concentrations of low-income minority residents and low-income assisted housing.

The court was persuaded by the plaintiffs' argument regarding the appropriate definition of the neighborhood, and rejected HUD's reliance on the boundaries of the census tract: "In general, a neighborhood represents any section of a region or city, having indefinite boundaries, and which is drawn together by the shared perceptions of its residents as to what constitutes their neighborhood, by the facilities generally available for their use, by their social and economic status, and by natural or man-made boundaries."[28] The court also found that the proposed project would have a "tipping" effect on the neighborhood and would cause an undue concentration of low-income persons. Consequently, the court enjoined construction of the project.

This case had implications for field office site selection procedures. The field office should not look at the census tract in isolation but should consider all relevant indicators of neighborhood boundaries.

In *Dalzell v. Harris*, departmental site selection procedures were once again called into question.[29] The plaintiffs sought to enjoin the construction of an assisted housing project in Abilene, Texas. They claimed that the site selection for the project was the result of an arbitrary and capricious act that would result in the tipping of an integrated neighborhood to a segregated neighborhood. The plaintiffs argued that the HUD definition of the neighborhood (the census tract that contained the proposed site) was inappropriate and that HUD had excluded from consideration all relevant data except for the 1970 census data.

The court found that the appropriate definition of the neighborhood was neither the one used by HUD nor the one asserted by the plaintiffs. The court also found that HUD had not considered all the relevant data in assessing the ethnic makeup of the neighborhood and should have taken into account more recent data that were available. Although the court found that the department had acted arbitrarily and capriciously in site selection, it did not grant the plaintiffs the relief they sought: "But the fact that HUD refused to consider all relevant factors is not alone sufficient to afford relief to the plaintiffs on the basis of arbitrary and capricious agency action. There must be clear and convincing evidence in the case showing that HUD made a clear error in its judgment."[30] Because the plaintiffs had not offered any evidence to demonstrate that HUD would have reached a different conclusion had it considered all relevant data, the court ruled in favor of HUD.

Langham v. Landrieu is another case in which the plaintiffs alleged that HUD site selection for an assisted housing project would result in the tipping of the neighborhood.[31] The plaintiffs—biracial residents of Forsyth County, North Carolina—sought to enjoin the construction of a Section 8 New Construction project, arguing that the project would upset the racial balance in an integrated neighborhood. The plaintiffs argued that HUD's definition of the neighborhood was inappropriate. During the trial, seven different definitions of the neighborhood were offered. The court found in favor of the plaintiffs, ruling that the proposed site was located in an area of minority concentration. The court also found that HUD made a wholly inadequate evaluation of the site under its regulations. The court issued an injunction against construction of the project.

These court cases point to the need for more appropriate neighborhood definitions that account for all relevant factors when the proposed site is in a racially mixed area. Although these cases have appeared to widen the scope of judicial oversight, a recent Supreme Court decision has served to limit the extent of judicial review.

In *Karlen v. Harris*, the appellants sought to reverse a judgment of the district court that upheld the department's decision to fund an assisted housing project in New York City.[32] The appellate court reversed the district court's ruling. The appellate court found that, although HUD had not acted arbitrarily and capriciously, the department failed to assign a sufficiently negative weight to the environmental effect of the proposed project on the surrounding area and thus violated the National Environmental Policy Act (NEPA).

In *Secretary of HUD v. Karlen*, the Supreme Court reversed the decision of the appellate court.[33] The Court ruled that, although the legislation in question —the NEPA—established goals for the nation, it "imposes upon agencies duties that are 'essentially procedural.' As we stressed in that case [*Vermont Yankee Nuclear Power Corp. v. NRDC*, 435 U.S. 519, 1978] NEPA was designed to insure a fully-informed and well-considered decision, 'but not necessarily' a decision the judges of the Court of Appeals or of this court would have reached had they been members of the decision making unit of the agency."[34] Thus, although the court must determine whether an agency has acted arbitrarily and capriciously, the court cannot substitute its judgment for the carefully deliberated judgment of the agency when complying with a statute that is essentially procedural.

In *Business Association of University City v. Moon Landrieu*, the plaintiffs sought a preliminary injunction to enjoin the construction of a Section 8 New Construction project in the University City section of Philadelphia.[35] The plaintiffs alleged that the defendants (HUD, the City of Philadelphia, and the Redevelopment Authority) had violated Title VIII of the Civil Rights Act of 1968 by attempting to place the project in an area of minority concentration without applying the appropriate criteria for site selection. The plaintiffs also alleged that placement of the project in the University City site was in contravention of HUD's duties under the Housing and Community Development Act of 1974 "to promote economically viable communities and a greater choice of housing opportunities for low-income persons, and to avoid undue concentrations of assisted persons in areas containing a high portion of low-income persons."[36] The plaintiffs also claimed that HUD had abused its discretion of requiring the city to place Section 8 New Construction housing in nonminority census tracts.

The court denied the motion for a preliminary injunction. It ruled that the plaintiffs had not demonstrated unequivocally that the proposed site was located in an area of minority concentration. The field office personnel had considered all relevant data in arriving at an assessment of the degree of minority concentration. The court noted that placement of federally assisted housing in minority areas is not prohibited per se by statute. The court also rejected the plaintiffs' claim that the defendants' actions violated the HCD Act of 1974 because of the proximity of the proposed site to existing assisted housing. This assessment could only be made, the court reasoned, by considering the status of citywide housing. Third, the court ruled that HUD's conditioning of CDBG funds on placement of federally assisted housing in nonminority areas had not been demonstrated by the plaintiffs to be an abuse of discretion.

The significance of this case is that, because HUD field office personnel had made a thorough investigation of the site in question, and because HUD had demonstrated that it had followed its own procedure in site selection, the court ruled that a challenge to the site selection process was invalid. This ruling was consistent with the Supreme Court ruling on *Karlen*.

Since the time the proposed regulations were published for comment in 1977 and in response to the increasing amount of litigation regarding application of existing site selection criteria, HUD officials have tried to clarify their regulations. In 1979 the Office of Housing issued a Notice on site and neighborhood standards. The clarification directed the Fair Housing and Equal Opportunity field office staff to assess the racial occupancy characteristics of assisted housing to determine whether sufficient opportunities for minority households exist outside minority areas. In general, the clarification granted the field offices a good deal of latitude in determining sufficiency:

"Sufficient" should not in every case be interpreted to require a one to one ratio but rather should be based upon a consideration of (i) the overall racial occupancy pattern in the locality, (ii) the previous experience with the locality in terms of promoting increased housing opportunities, and (iii) an assessment of what is reasonably possible in a particular community. It should be clear that the deliberate and continuous placement of housing in areas of minority concentration to avoid placement in nonminority areas is unacceptable.[37]

The Notice also identified Section 8 Existing units occupied by minority families who moved into nonminority areas as housing opportunities. Also, Section 8 Substantial Rehabilitation units in minority areas were exempted from the "comparable and sufficient opportunities" criterion.

This clarification was primarily the result of growing dissatisfaction with existing site selection criteria. Black politicians expressed a fear that application of the criteria would lead to dilution of recently acquired black political power. Others argued that minorities should have the option to live in minority areas, if they so choose. Both within and outside HUD, concerns were expressed that application of the criteria was hindering housing production. Suburban resistance was limiting the placement of projects in nonminority areas, while the regulations themselves had the effect of depriving minority areas of federal housing assistance for the needy.

These concerns were expressed on the floor of Congress during 1980. As a consequence, the 1980 Housing and Community Development Act contained the following passage: "The Secretary of Housing and Urban Development shall not exclude from consideration for financial assistance under federally assisted housing programs proposals for housing projects solely because the site proposed is located within an impacted (minority) area."[38] In January 1981, HUD issued a clarification of site and neighborhood standards for new assisted housing projects in areas of minority concentration. This clarification superseded the previous Notice, and continued the trend of encouraging flexibility in the determination of where assisted housing should be located.

The current Notice was the result of consultations with local officials and public interest groups at HUD-sponsored forums. The Notice took into account Section 216 of the 1980 HCD Act, which prohibited excluding a proposed site from consideration solely because of its location in an area of minority concentration. The major themes of the Notice are to reduce the ambiguity surrounding the definition of key terms in the site and neighborhood standards, while at the same time allowing for local variations in the assessment of housing choice for minorities.

Field offices must now review proposed sites on a case-by-case basis to determine whether a proposed site in an area of minority concentration is acceptable according to the site and neighborhood standards. The result of requiring a case-by-case analysis is to provide more flexibility in the location of assisted housing. The definitions of key terms in the standards vary depending on local conditions. For example, an area of minority concentration is defined as an area where the proportion of minority residents substantially exceeds, or as a result of placement of the project on the proposed site would substantially exceed, the proportion of minority residents in the jurisdiction as a whole. This may be contrasted with the previous definition, which used 40 percent minority as the threshold level.

The Notice further defines "sufficient and comparable" housing opportunities outside areas of minority concentration: "application of this standard should produce a reasonable distribution of units each fiscal year which *over a period of several years* [italics mine] will approach an appropriate balance of housing opportunities within and outside areas of minority concentration."[39] The Notice also clarified the definition of an overriding need to allow placement of the project in an area of minority concentration in the absence of sufficient and comparable housing opportunities outside the area of minority concentration. An overriding need was defined as a situation where the proposed housing is an integral part of the municipality's preservation and restoration program or is located in a revitalizing neighborhood that is experiencing significant private investment. Also, a project site may be approved if the area manager determines that no available sites exist outside of areas of minority concentration, with the caveat that circumventing department policy on providing expanded housing choices is unacceptable.

The clarification entailed in the Notice reflects the debate over site and neighborhood standards that has continued both within and outside HUD. The Notice reflects a consensus view that HUD must achieve a balance between its duty to create expanded housing opportunities for minorities and direct a fair share of housing resources to minority areas to serve families who voluntarily choose or need to live there. The determination of whether minority families really have "expanded opportunities" presents greater uncertainty in already muddied waters.

Samuel Pierce became secretary of HUD in early 1981. One of his major actions in the area of fair housing was to prepare the Fair Housing Amendments Act of 1983, which was submitted to Congress in July 1983. These amendments, if enacted, would strengthen fair housing enforcement practices nationwide. Additionally, Mr. Pierce has supported funding of approximately $4 million a year for state and local fair housing enforcement agencies and nearly $2 million a year for local voluntary compliance programs. In 1984, HUD began an initiative aimed more directly at housing desegregation. Secretary Pierce, in February, began actions in the state of Texas to "disestablish" racially dual public housing systems. These actions were taken immediately after a Texas federal court ordered black and white public housing tenants to make cross-racial moves or face eviction.[40] HUD's efforts to desegregate public housing agencies violating fair housing laws were expanded to another eight deep South states in April 1984.[41] At present, the department is revising and approving plans submitted by dozens of PHAs to desegregate their projects.

HUD's attempts to amend the federal fair housing law and to desegregate public housing have not been without their critics. The American Civil Liberties Union, the Leadership Conference on Civil Rights, the National Committee Against Discrimination in Housing, the (old) U.S. Commission on Civil Rights, and the Citizens' Commission on Civil Rights have issued strong criticism of current federal fair housing policy specifically, and the civil rights performance of the Reagan administration in general.[42] One assessment concluded that the current administration "is systematically assaulting the very structure of the federal civil rights machinery."[43] Part of the alleged assault focuses on the reconstitution of the U.S. Commission on Civil Rights to include members more sympathetic to the Reagan administration.[44] Whatever the future of the Civil Rights Commission, it seems clear that there will be strong differences of opinion *within* the current administration, as well as without, about the appropriate means to enforce fair housing guarantees. HUD's efforts to strengthen fair housing and attack public housing segregation may find little support by other parts of the Executive Branch and may continue to experience significant judicial challenges.

Summary and Conclusions

The development of HUD policy to promote fair housing through the location of assisted housing has been complex, with interaction among all three branches of the federal government in shaping policy. Seventeen years after the passage of Title VIII there is still uncertainty as to the precise meaning of HUD's fair housing mandate. Many equally viable interpretations abound. Is it HUD's duty to ensure that integration takes place through the administration of its programs or is HUD merely required to expand housing opportunities, even if virtually no minority families avail themselves of the opportunities? The ambiguities inherent in Title VIII have influenced the entire policy development process.

Significant interaction has occurred between HUD and the courts. Two early cases are particularly prominent. The *Gautreaux* litigation resulted in the Gautreaux Housing Demonstration, HUD's first large-scale effort to redress earlier discriminatory practices on a metropolitan-wide basis. The *Shannon* case resulted in the development of site selection criteria. The wording of the existing regulations, first developed in 1972, is still fraught with definitional ambiguity. Nevertheless, the site selection criteria represent the first attempt on the part of HUD to assess the impact of its housing programs on the racial and ethnic makeup of the population surrounding a proposed project site.

The Housing and Community Development Act of 1974 helped renew the spirit of Title VIII and gave HUD new, although ambiguous goals regarding the "fair housing" mandate. Among other things, the act reaffirmed HUD's duty to avoid the undue concentration of lower income persons through its placement of assisted housing. What constitutes an undue concentration of low-income persons is subject to conjecture, but it is a determination that the act requires HUD to make.

Since passage of the 1974 HCD Act, HUD has attempted to reduce the ambiguity in the wording of its site selection criteria while changing other housing program regulations to promote fair housing. The attempts to clarify site selection criteria reflect the changing social milieu in which policy has been evolving. Beginning in the late 1970s, numerous groups expressed concerns regarding the efficacy and appropriateness of HUD's application of site selection criteria. Combined with the litigation over HUD's use of site selection criteria and congressional concern expressed in the 1980 HCD Act, changing societal attitudes manifested themselves in HUD's current posture: a balance between its duty to create expanded housing opportunities for minorities and to direct a fair share of housing resources to minority areas to serve the families who voluntarily choose to live there.

Today the ambiguities remain and the picture is still clouded. The goals mandated by Congress are subject to various interpretations. In some ways fair housing policy has come full circle. The 1972 site selection criteria were designed initially to prevent placement of assisted housing projects where the effect would be to limit the housing choice of minority assisted housing recipients. Discussions both inside and outside the government raised concerns about the efficacy and appropriateness of the site selection criteria. In response, the interpretation of the regulations was modified to allow placement of assisted housing projects in minority areas, as well as discretionary allocation of units to nonminority areas.

The site selection issue will likely be less critical in the future because HUD is allocating fewer resources to new housing construction. The Section 8 Existing and Rehabilitation programs will continue, in conjunction with a Housing Voucher Demonstration, to suggest new issues and problems in achieving desegregation with only demand-side programs. The monitoring of civil rights enforcement of such programs is considerably more difficult, with few tools currently in place.

Regardless of any shift in the assisted housing delivery system, basic questions remain. Does the fair housing mandate include an explicit provision aimed at promoting housing integration? Can HUD maintain an adequate supply of housing for households in need while also promoting housing desegregation? These tensions, inherent in the drafting of HUD's civil rights responsibilities, will continue to confound fair housing policymakers.

NOTES AND REFERENCES

1. For a study of the attitudes and behavior of real estate brokers in the Chicago area, see Rose Helper, *The Racial Policies and Practices of Real Estate Brokers* (Minneapolis: University of Minnesota Press, 1969). For a summary of the real estate edu-

cational literature on the effects of housing segregation, see Luigi Laurenti, *Property Values and Race* (Los Angeles: University of California Press, 1960), pp. 8–16.

2. A detailed account of FHA policies and practices is contained in Leonard S. Rubinowitz and Elizabeth Trosman, "Affirmative Action and American Dream: Implementing Fair Housing Policies in Federal Homeownership Programs," *Northwestern University Law Review* 74 (November 1979): 496–621. A case study of the determination of public housing project location is contained in Cassandra W. Gottlieb, *The Effect of Site Selection Policies and Practices on the Success and Failure of the Federal Public Housing Program: The Case of Baltimore*, MA thesis (Baltimore: The Johns Hopkins University Press, 1978).

3. Rubinowitz and Trosman, "Affirmative Action and American Dream," p. 522.

4. Executive Statement by President Nixon on Federal Policies Relative to Equal Opportunity in Housing (11 June 1971), *Congressional Record* at 582.

5. William Lilley, III, "Housing Report/Administration and Congress Follow Courts in Promoting Residential Integration," *National Journal* 3 (1970): 2434.

6. Mary E. Books, *Lower Income Housing: The Planners' Response* (Chicago: Planning Advisory Service, American Society of Planning Officials, 1972), p. 11.

7. David Listokin, *Fair Share Housing Allocation* (New Brunswick, N.J.: The Center for Urban Policy Research, 1976), p. 2.

8. *Gautreaux et al. v. Chicago Housing Authority et al.*, 265 F. Supp. 582 (N.D. Ill. 1967); *Gautreaux et al. v. Chicago Housing Authority et al.*, 296 F. Supp. 907 (N.D. Ill. 1969); *Gautreaux et al. v. Chicago Housing Authority et al.*, 304 F. Supp. 736 (N.D. Ill. 1969); *Gautreaux et al. v. Romney*, 332 F. Supp. 266 (N.D. Ill. 1971); *Gautreaux et al. v. U.S. Department of Housing and Urban Development*, 448 F.2d 731 (7th Cir. 1971); *Gautreaux et al. v. Chicago Housing Authority et al.*, 436 F.2d 306 (7th Cir. 1970); *Gautreaux et al. v. Romney*, 457 F.2d 124 (7th Cir. 1972); *Hills v. Gautreaux*, 425 U.S. 284 (1976).

9. *Gautreaux et al. v. Chicago Housing Authority*, 296 F. Supp. 907.

10. *Gautreaux et al. v. U.S. Department of Housing and Urban Development*, 488 F.2d 731.

11. *Hills v. Gautreaux et al.*, 425 U.S. 284 (1976).

12. *Shannon et al. v. U.S. Department of Housing and Urban Development*, 436 F.2d 809 (3rd Cir. 1970).

13. *24 Code of Federal Regulations*, 1.4(b)(2)(i), quoted in the decision.

14. *Shannon et al. v. U.S. Department of Housing and Urban Development*, F.2d at 821.

15. Ibid. at 822.

16. *24 Code of Federal Regulations*, 880.206(b), (c), (d).

17. Title I, Section 101(c)(6), of the Housing and Community Development Act of 1974.

18. The 1974 HCD Act provides housing assistance that is tied to the construction and rehabilitation of dwelling units as well as subsidizes the rent for recipients in existing units. The Section 8 New Construction and Rehabilitation programs provide subsidies to developers so that rents to eligible families can be maintained at 30 percent of income. The Section 8 Existing Program is a housing voucher-like program. Income-eligible families seek housing in the existing market that meets minimum housing quality standards and rents for a moderate price. HUD provides a subsidy to the landlord for the difference between 30 percent of the recipients' income and the fair market rent.

19. The major reason was the extremely high cost of the program. Each assisted housing recipient received extensive counseling and financial assistance with relocation that were not normally available to assisted housing recipients. For example, in the Gautreaux Demonstration the average annual administrative cost per recipient household was $1,000, which is considerably higher than the average annual per recipient administrative cost in Section 8—$360.

20. Funding preferences included distributing an extra allocation of Section 8 Existing Certificates to complying PHAs.

21. The Discretionary Fund consists of funding, administered by the Office of Community Planning and Development, that the secretary can allocate for special projects within broad guidelines and without specific legislatively mandated appropriations.

22. *Federal Register*, vol. 42, no. 15, 24 January 1977, p. 4296.

23. Ibid., p. 4297.

24. Ibid.

25. Ibid., p. 4298.

26. The question of stabilizing tipping in private housing markets has been addressed in "Tipping the Scales of Justice: A Race-Conscious Remedy for Neighborhood Transition," *Yale Law Journal* 90 (December 1980): 377–99, and Michael J. Vernarelli, "Locational Distortion and Black Ghetto Expansion" (Ph.D. dissertation, Program in Economics, State University of New York-Binghamton, 1978), pp. 153–62.

27. *Evelyn M. King et al. v. Patricia Harris, Faymoor Development Co., et al.*, 464 F. Supp. 824 (E.D. N.Y. 1979).

28. Ibid.

29. *Dalzell et al. v. Harris et al.*, CA–1–78–28 (N.D. Tex. 1979).

30. Ibid.

31. *Stephen W. Langham et al. v. Landrieu et al.*, CA–1–78–28 (N.D. Tex. 1979).

32. *Roland N. Karlen et al. v. Harris et al.*, 590 F.2d 39 (2nd Cir. 1978).

33. *Secretary of U.S. Department of Housing and Urban Development v. Roland Karlen et al.*, 100 S.Ct. 497 (1980).

34. Ibid.

35. *Business Association of University City et al. v. Moon Landrieu et al.*, C.A. 80–3725 (E.D. Pa. 3rd Cir. 1980).

36. Ibid. at 14.

37. U.S. Department of Housing and Urban Development, Notice H–79–65 (HUD), 1979.

38. Title II Housing Assistance Programs, Section 216, Housing and Community Development Act of 1980.

39. U.S. Department of Housing and Urban Development, Notice H–81–2 (HUD), 1981.

40. "Desegregation Order Is Forcing Tenants to Switch," *Washington Post*, 8 December 1983, p. A20.

41. Seth Kantor, "HUD Push Centers on Integration," *Atlanta Journal*, 19 April 1984, p. 2A.

42. American Civil Liberties Union, "In Contempt of Congress and the Courts: The Reagan Civil Rights Record" (American Civil Liberties Union, Washington, D.C., 27 February 1984); Howard Kurtz, "White House Accused of Dismantling Laws," *Washington Post*, 12 June 1984, p. A6; Miriam Conrad, "Rights Leaders Claim U.S. Reversal on Desegregation," *Kansas City Times*, 31 May 1984, p. A1; U.S. Commission

on Civil Rights, *The Federal Civil Rights Enforcement Budget: Fiscal Year 1983* (Washington, D.C.: Clearinghouse Publications, June 1982), p. 71; Citizens' Commission on Civil Rights, *A Decent Home: A Report on the Continuing Failure of the Federal Government to Provide Equal Housing Opportunity* (Washington, D.C.: Center for National Policy Review, April 1983); Spencer Rich, "Tax Cuts Aid Minorities Least, Rights Unit Says," *Washington Post*, 5 May 1982, p. A8.

43. American Civil Liberties Union, "In Contempt of Congress and the Courts," p. 19.

44. George Lardner, "Compromise Apparently Reconstitutes Civil Rights Commission," *Washington Post*, 11 November 1983, p. A14; Margaret Shapiro, "Rights Leaders Charge 'Double Cross' by White House and GOP," *Washington Post*, 9 December 1983, p. A3.

Chapter Ten
Location and Racial/Ethnic Occupancy Patterns for HUD-Subsidized Family Housing in Ten Metropolitan Areas

ROBERT GRAY*

STEVEN TURSKY

This chapter describes location patterns and racial/ethnic occupancy patterns for HUD-subsidized rental housing for families in ten standard metropolitan statistical areas (SMSAs). The study was designed to answer three main questions:

1. Has HUD-subsidized rental housing for families been located in geographic areas occupied largely by minority households?

2. To what extent have families aided under HUD housing subsidy programs been members of minority groups?

3. Has the provision of assistance to families under the Section 8 program substantially affected overall location and occupancy patterns for HUD-subsidized housing?

The study addresses both the pattern and the extent of concentration of HUD-assisted housing.[1] The pattern of concentration is indicated by the percentage of HUD-subsidized housing units located in the central cities versus surrounding suburban areas, whereas the extent is indicated by the percentage of units located in minority-concentrated census tracts within each central city and suburban area. For the ten metropolitan areas under study, changes in the extent of concentration have in part been the result of a significant shift in the pattern of concentration between central cities and suburbs, a shift that began under early HUD programs and continued under Section 8.

The principal value of the study is that it provides, for a particular point in time, a comprehensive picture of location and occupancy patterns under all

*The data presented in this chapter were gathered by the Office of Policy Development and Research (PD&R) and the Office of Fair Housing and Equal Opportunity (FHEO), U.S. Department of Housing and Urban Development (HUD). The collection of location and occupancy data for the Section 8 Existing Housing Program and for housing built under prior programs was supervised by Mary Pinkard, former Director of the Office of Program Standards and Evaluation, FHEO; Eleanor Clagett and Beverly Butler assisted in the data analysis. The collection of location data for the Section 8 New Construction and Substantial Rehabilitation Program was supervised by Feather O'Connor, former Director of the Policy Development Division, PD&R; Jane Karadbil also had responsibility for analyzing these data. The authors wish to thank George Galster, James Zais, and John M. Goering for their comments on this work. The authors claim full responsibility for any errors, omissions, or misrepresentations. The opinions expressed do not represent the views of HUD or the U.S. government.

of the major HUD rental subsidy programs available for families in the ten metropolitan areas.

Data, Methodology, and Definitions

Information in this study resulted from two separate data collection efforts. From September 1977 to May 1978, HUD's Office of Fair Housing and Equal Opportunity collected location and occupancy data for HUD housing program activity in ten metropolitan areas. Subsequently, HUD's Office of Policy Development and Research collected location data for recently approved Section 8 multifamily housing projects for these same metropolitan areas.[2] The ten areas were originally selected for study because they provided a range of coverage regarding population size (of both SMSAs and central cities), minority percentage of the population, and geographic region. However, HUD program experience in the ten metropolitan areas is not necessarily representative of all metropolitan program activity.

Consistent with HUD's approach to site and neighborhood standards regarding concentrations of minority persons and of federally assisted persons, the data presented in this study exclude housing designed for or exclusively occupied by the elderly.[3] Thus, the data reflect location and occupancy patterns within family housing projects available for occupancy under selected HUD programs as of January 1978; families assisted under the Section 8 Existing Housing Program as of that date; and, for the Section 8 New Construction and Substantial Rehabilitation (New/Rehab) Program, approvals of projects for family occupancy, made by HUD under the Section 8 New/Rehab Program during FY 1977 to FY 1979 and used as a proxy to analyze locational patterns under the Section 8 New/Rehab Program.[4]

Terminology and Tract Classification

Three sets of terms, largely defined during the original FHEO data collection effort, are included in this study:

• *Projects* are identified as being either "minority," "racially mixed," or "nonminority," based on the racial/ethnic characteristics of the families receiving rental assistance. Projects in which 85 percent or more of the tenants were black or Hispanic have been described as "minority" projects. Projects with less than 15 percent blacks and Hispanics in residence are classified as "nonminority" projects. All others are considered to be "racially mixed" or "mixed" projects.

• *Minority persons* receiving HUD rental assistance are defined as blacks and Hispanics as reported on standard HUD forms.

• *Census tracts* are identified as either "minority" tracts, "racially mixed" tracts, or "nonminority" tracts, based on the percentage of households with a black or Hispanic head of household residing in the tract in 1970.[5] Tracts with 40 percent or more minority households are identified as "minority" tracts; those with 20 to 40 percent minority occupancy are "mixed" tracts; and those with less than 20 percent minority households are "nonminority" tracts.[6] The threshold of 40 percent used throughout the study to classify census tracts as "minority" tracts has been used extensively in determining site acceptability for HUD rental assistance programs.

Readers should be aware that the tract classifications reflect racial and ethnic occupancy patterns that existed in the ten SMSAs in 1970. The methodology may tend to overstate the true extent of location outside of minority census tracts, particularly for the Section 8 New/Rehab Program.[7]

The Location of HUD-Subsidized Units

Percentage Share in Central Cities

Before evaluating the extent of concentration of HUD-assisted housing in the ten metropolitan areas, it is useful to examine the central cities' share of HUD-subsidized housing (the pattern of concentration) in the respective SMSAs as it relates to the three indicators of need provided in the far-right columns of Table 1. The indicators are (1) the central city's share of income-eligible families, based on the number of families with incomes below 125 percent of the poverty level as of the 1970 census;[8] (2) the percentage of housing built before 1940; and (3) the percentage of estimated need for rental assistance, as indicated by the "Fair Share" formula, which was used in HUD rental subsidy programs to assure an equitable geographic distribution for new allocations of HUD rental subsidies.[9]

Compared with these three indicators, for most of the areas under study, the proportion of HUD-subsidized rental housing for families located in central cities exceeded the central cities' relative proportions of households in need. For the Public Housing Program, the percentage of units located in the central city was higher than each of the indicators of relative need provided in Table 1. These differences were substantial in many instances. For example, the central city's share of Public Housing units exceeded the central city's share of income-eligibles by 20 or more percentage points in seven of the ten SMSAs.

The locations of Section 236 units were much less concentrated in central cities than were those for Public Housing. The central city percentage of Section 236 units exceeded the percentage of income-eligibles in only three of the SMSAs (Newark, Denver, and Phoenix).

In comparing Section 8 activity to the three indicators of relative need, the central city share of Section 8 Existing Housing and of New/Rehab housing also exceeded the relative need percentages in many instances. For example, Hartford is shown in Table 1 as having 39 percent of current rental assistance need in the SMSA, but received 67 percent of Existing Housing units and 48

Table 1. Central City Share of Assisted Family Housing in Ten SMSAs, versus Selected Indicators of Need

SMSAs	Central City Share (%) of Units Under Programs Prior to Sec. 8				Central City Share (%) of Units Under Sec. 8			Central City Share(%) of Selected Needs Indicators:		
	Total	Public Housing	Sec. 236	"Other" (FHA)	Total	Sec. 8 Existing	Section 8 New/Rehab	Income-Eligibles	Pre-1940 Housing	"Current" Need
Hartford	71	99	52	50	56	67	48	54	46	39
Newark	78	78	96	67	61	55	63	50	28	33
Richmond	87	100	62	100	43	100	34	67	78	48
Atlanta	78	84	53	100	63	66	57	58	64	44
Dayton	59	87	21	23	71	75	58	46	48	35
San Antonio	97	97	95	100	77	76	82	83	84	81
Omaha	91	100	69	100	76	100	61	67	73	67
Denver	78	95	46	97	33	35	33	58	74	51
Phoenix	60	71	56	12	60	51	67	59	72	57
Portland	49	60	24	65	52	63	29	44	66	48

Notes:

1) Data describing the central city share of income-eligibles and of pre-1940 housing are from the 1970 census; data describing "current need" are derived from each SMSA's statistical "Fair Share" factors, adjusted to conform to 1970 SMSA boundaries.

Table 2. Percentage of HUD-Subsidized Housing Units Located in Minority Census Tracts, by Program

SMSAs	% Minority Tracts	Programs Prior to Section 8				Existing Housing	Section 8 New Construction/Rehabilitation		
		Total	Public Housing	Sec. 236	"Other" (FHA)		Total	New	Rehab
Hartford	8	63	90	48	37	27	16	–	26
Newark	22	89	88	100	91	48	62	67	57
Richmond	24	66	88	21	100	68	5	–	28
Atlanta	24	62	68	35	88	25	51	–	81
Dayton	12	36	55	9	23	33	–	–	N/A
San Antonio	43	77	97	22	51	49	38	38	N/A
Omaha	10	36	57	–	–	42	47	5	100
Denver	7	49	64	20	71	14	18	6	37
Phoenix	11	32	53	7	–	24	26	26	N/A
Portland	3	8	10	1	16	12	9	10	–

Notes:
1) N/A indicates absence of program activity.
2) Asterisk(*) indicates less than 0.5 percent.

Table 3. Percentage of HUD-Subsidized Housing Units Located in Minority Census Tracts, by Program (Central Cities versus Suburbs)

SMSAs	Central Cities						Suburbs					
	% Minority Tracts	% of Units in Minority Tracts					% Minority Tracts	% of Units in Minority Tracts				
		Prior Programs	Public Hsg.	Sec. 236	Sec. 8 Existing	Sec. 8 New/Rehab		Prior Programs	Public Hsg.	Sec. 236	Sec. 8 Existing	Sec. 8 New/Rehab
Hartford	27	89	90	92	41	33	–	–	–	–	–	–
Newark	61	91	89	100	66	91	10	82	84	100	25	13
Richmond	46	76	88	33	68	15	3	–	N/A	–	N/A	–
Atlanta	46	78	79	66	34	76	3	6	11	–	7	19
Dayton	33	53	57	16	43	–	2	11	38	7	6	–
San Antonio	59	79	100	23	57	36	15	–	–	–	24	48
Omaha	12	40	57	–	42	52	–	–	N/A	–	N/A	39
Denver	17	63	67	44	41	65	–	–	–	–	–	–
Phoenix	13	44	62	12	14	28	9	13	33	–	35	23
Portland	5	16	16	6	19	31	–	–	–	–	–	–

Notes:

1) N/A indicates absence of program activity.

2) Asterisk (*) indicates less than 0.5 percent

percent of New/Rehab units. In general, however, the central city share of Section 8 activity was much closer to both the Fair Share percentage and to the other need indicators than the central city share under prior programs (see the columns in Table 1 headed "Total"). The overall trend in these ten SMSAs has clearly been toward a more even distribution of Section 8 assistance between the central cities and suburbs—compared with the central city share of units provided under all programs instituted before Section 8. This is particularly true compared with the central city share of Public Housing units.

Location in Minority-Concentrated Areas

Considering the disproportionate share of program activity that has occurred in central cities, and utilizing the racial/ethnic categories of census tracts described previously, we now turn to the locations of HUD-subsidized housing for families in the ten SMSAs. Tables 2 and 3 indicate the percentage of units located in minority tracts (the extent of concentration) by program and central city/suburban location, versus the percentage of all tracts in each area that are minority tracts. The following discussion examines these relationships on an individual program basis, first for programs established prior to Section 8 and then for the New/Rehab and Existing Housing subprograms of Section 8.

Programs Instituted prior to Section 8. In nine of the ten SMSAs, Public Housing units represented at least half of all subsidized housing available for families under programs instituted before Section 8. This stock of Public Housing was heavily concentrated in minority census tracts. The percentage of Public Housing units located in minority census tracts exceeded the percentage of census tracts that were minority tracts in all ten of the central cities (Table 3). In five central cities, more than three-fourths of the Public Housing was located in minority tracts. In four of the suburban areas, none of the Public Housing was located in minority tracts; in three of the other four suburban areas that contained Public Housing, the majority of units were located outside of minority tracts.

There was a relatively high average project size among Public Housing projects located in the central cities, and this tended to limit the potential choices of locations for families still further. Except for scattered-sited housing, the average Public Housing project size exceeded 350 units in Hartford, Newark, and Atlanta and exceeded 200 units in four other central cities. Suburban average project sizes, as well as project sizes under programs other than Public Housing, tended to be much smaller.

For projects originally financed under FHA programs other than Section 236 (see the column headed "Other, FHA" in Table 4), the percentage of units located in minority tracts was relatively high. In the Newark, Richmond, Atlanta, Denver, and Portland SMSAs, the percentage of such units located in minority tracts actually exceeded the percentage located in minority tracts under the Public Housing Program. In most instances these represented a few very large

Table 4. Number and Percentage of Prior-Program Housing Units Located in the Most Active[a] Census Tracts in Each SMSA, by Program and Racial/Ethnic Category of Census Tract

SMSAs	HUD-Subsidized Units Located in the Most-Active Census Tracts			Number of Tracts by Racial/Ethnic Category			Number of Units by Category of Tract			% Minority Persons by Category of Tract[b]		
	Number of Tracts	Subsidized Units in Tracts	% of Such Units in the SMSA	Minority	Mixed	Non-Minority	Minority	Mixed	Non-Minority	Minority	Mixed	Non-Minority
Hartford	9	4,378	73	5	-	4	3,051	-	1,327	82	N/A	4
Newark	20	14,028	85	15	3	2	11,957	1,294	777	83	32	6
Richmond	7	4,454	69	5	-	2	3,309	-	1,145	92	N/A	6
Atlanta	12	11,243	50	11	-	1	10,009	-	1,234	88	N/A	3
Dayton	10	3,284	56	4	-	6	1,362	-	1,922	92	N/A	*
San Antonio	9	4,763	57	9	-	-	4,763	-	-	91	N/A	N/A
Omaha	7	2,614	76	2	1	4	1,222	480	912	83	30	1
Denver	16	5,458	68	7	2	7	3,308	483	1,667	62	27	11
Phoenix	12	3,547	63	5	3	4	1,502	989	1,056	59	28	9
Portland	13	1,934	57	1	-	12	119	-	1,815	57	N/A	2

Note: Asterisk (*) indicates less than 0.5 percent; N/A indicates absence of program activity in that category of tract.

a/ After listing all tracts in rank-order on the basis of the number of prior-program units located in each tract, the top five percent of tracts were identified as the "most active" tracts.

b/ These columns indicate the average minority percentage for persons residing in the most active census tracts. The percentages are based on 1970 Census data, weighted according to the number of prior-program units located in each tract.

projects located in central cities during the 1960s under the Section 221(d)(3) Below-Market-Interest-Rate (BMIR) Program.

Unlike housing built under the Public Housing and BMIR programs, Section 236 housing tended to be more evenly distributed among minority, racially mixed, and nonminority census tracts. In all of the central cities except Hartford and Newark, the percentage of Section 236 housing located in minority tracts was lower than the percentage of Public Housing units located in such tracts (Table 3). In the suburbs, Section 236 housing was for the most part located in nonminority tracts. As the data in Table 3 indicate, there were no minority census tracts in the suburbs of four of the SMSAs (Hartford, Omaha, Denver, and Portland); in the remaining areas, the percentage of census tracts classified as minority tracts was generally much lower in the suburbs than in the central city.

For programs instituted prior to Section 8, it was not unusual for one-half to three-fourths of the subsidized units for families to be located in only 5 percent of the census tracts in the SMSA (Table 4). These "most active" census tracts were primarily minority tracts in the Hartford, Newark, Richmond, Atlanta, and San Antonio SMSAs, but included many nonminority tracts in several other SMSAs. Within the most active minority census tracts, the average minority percentage among residents of the tract as of the 1970 census was approximately 60 percent in three SMSAs and exceeded 80 percent in the remaining SMSAs. Within the most active nonminority tracts, the average minority percentage among tract residents was generally 6 percent or less.

In summary, the overall locational patterns under the programs established prior to Section 8 indicate that:

• A disproportionate share of program activity has occurred in the central cities;

• Central city projects tend to be located in minority-concentrated areas;

• Units located in the suburbs are in less concentrated areas;

• The projects available in central cities are frequently very large Public Housing projects located in minority-concentrated areas; and

• More than half of subsidized units in the SMSA are located within a relatively small number of census tracts.

Section 8 New/Rehab Program. After construction of the subsidized multifamily projects whose locations are described above, additional projects for families were approved for nine of the ten central cities and for all of the suburban areas under the Section 8 New Construction Program. Also, Section 8 subsidies were approved for the substantial rehabilitation of multifamily projects located in eight of the central cities and six of the suburban areas. Almost 2,700 New/Rehab units for families were approved for the Newark SMSA, and between 1,500 and 2,000 units were approved for the Richmond, Atlanta, and Denver SMSAs. Very few New/Rehab units for families were approved for either the central city or the suburbs of the Dayton SMSA.

These numbers describe the amount of housing approved for development for families. But, significantly, the share of *all* Section 8 New/Rehab approvals allotted to family housing (i.e., not designated for the elderly) was frequently below 50 percent, which obviously limited the potential impact of Section 8 New/Rehab approvals on overall locational patterns for family housing.[10]

Most suburban Section 8 New/Rehab housing was approved for location outside of minority census tracts.[11] Within central cities, there usually was activity both inside and outside of minority tracts, although the percentage of units located in minority tracts varied widely among the ten cities (Table 3). For entire SMSAs, compared with the January 1978 profile of subsidized family housing, a lower percentage of Section 8 New/Rehab units was generally approved for location in minority census tracts (see the two columns headed "Total" in Table 4). However, housing approved for rehabilitation under the Section 8 program was much more likely to be located in minority areas than newly built Section 8 housing (Table 2). Virtually all of the substantial rehabilitation activity approved for Newark, Richmond, Atlanta, and Omaha involved buildings located in minority census tracts.[12]

In both the central cities and suburban areas, variations in the volume of activity and in the extent of location in minority areas provide some rather stark contrasts regarding the potential impact of Section 8 New/Rehab approvals on prior locational patterns. For example, in the suburbs of the Richmond and Denver SMSAs, a significant number of Section 8 New/Rehab units were approved for location outside of minority census tracts. Also, approximately 500 new construction units for families were approved for location outside of minority tracts in the central cities of both the San Antonio and Phoenix SMSAs. Conversely, over 1,500 units of Section 8 New/Rehab housing approved for location in the central city of the Newark SMSA were to be located in minority census tracts, representing a fairly substantial addition to the amount of subsidized housing located in the minority tracts of that city.

Section 8 Existing Housing. Because the Section 8 Existing Housing Program provides assistance on behalf of individual families rather than housing projects, it is fundamentally different from the other programs described above. Unlike the project-oriented programs such as Public Housing, assistance provided under the Section 8 Existing Housing Program has been dispersed over a relatively large number of census tracts.

Assistance under the Section 8 Existing Housing Program was not widely available in all of the ten areas as of January 1978. The central cities of Atlanta and San Antonio each had more than 2,000 families participating in the program, but assistance in each of the other central cities amounted to less than 1,000 families. The number of families assisted in the Newark suburbs was quite small in relation to the population of that area, and no Existing Housing assistance was available for families in either the Richmond or Omaha suburbs.

Within both central cities and suburbs, there was a wide variation in the percentage of families leasing Section 8 Existing Housing units in minority census tracts. In central cities, the percentage of families leasing units in minority census tracts ranged from 14 percent in Phoenix to 68 percent in Richmond (Table 3). For most of the central cities and suburban areas, however, the percentage of HUD-assisted families located in minority census tracts was generally much lower than the percentage of units located in minority tracts under the prior, project-oriented programs.

Racial/Ethnic Characteristics of Tenants

This section provides information on tenant characteristics of families occupying HUD-subsidized housing in the ten metropolitan areas in January 1978. The racial/ethnic characteristics of tenants are compared with the characteristics of income-eligible families, by program, for SMSAs (Table 5) and separately for central cities and suburbs (Table 6) in order to determine the extent to which families aided under HUD housing subsidy programs have been members of minority groups.[13]

Programs Instituted prior to Section 8

For all of the ten SMSAs, the percentage of families occupying HUD housing who were black or Hispanic was significantly higher than the corresponding percentage among income-eligibles. In seven of the ten SMSAs (all but San Antonio, Phoenix, and Portland), the minority percentage among tenants exceeded the minority percentage among income-eligibles by 30 or more percentage points. In all of the SMSAs except Portland, three-fourths or more of the families residing in Public Housing were black or Hispanic. The minority percentage among families residing in Section 236 projects was lower than the minority percentage among families residing in Public Housing, by at least 20 percentage points in nine of the ten areas (Table 5).

In each of the central cities, families residing in subsidized projects were primarily black or Hispanic. Except in Denver, the percentage of tenants who were Hispanic was roughly proportional to the Hispanic percentage among income-eligibles. However, the black percentage among tenants exceeded the black percentage among income-eligibles by 10 or more percentage points in each of the central cities (Table 6).

Generally, the percentage of tenants who were black or Hispanic was substantially lower in the suburbs than in the central cities. Yet, in all of the areas except Omaha, Phoenix, and Portland, the minority percentage among suburban tenants was significantly higher than the minority percentage among suburban income-eligibles.

In all ten of the central cities and in seven of the suburban areas, HUD-subsidized multifamily projects had racial/ethnic concentrations of 85 percent or more. These are classified as "minority projects." In six of the ten central cities, over half of the subsidized family projects were minority projects, and

Table 5. Percentage of Families with a Black or Hispanic Head of Household, by Program

| SMSAs | Income-Eligibles[a] | | Families Participating in HUD Programs | | | | | | | |
| | | | Prior Programs | | Public Housing | | Section 236 | | Section 8 Existing | |
	% Black	% Hispanic	% Black	% Hispanic	% Black	% Hispanic	% Black	% Hispanic	% Black	% Hispanic
Hartford	26	11	52	22	56	38	52	13	56	7
Newark	46	7	82	10	79	12	96	4	61	14
Richmond	57	*	89	–	99	–	65	–	96	1
Atlanta	52	1	90	*	94	–	72	*	88	*
Dayton	25	1	63	*	80	*	33	1	66	*
San Antonio	12	63	22	64	24	73	27	32	25	56
Omaha	20	2	53	1	79	*	28	2	79	–
Denver	10	24	26	41	27	54	28	17	17	20
Phoenix	9	28	22	31	32	51	14	11	32	24
Portland	6	2	30	2	43	1	8	2	24	1

a/ Racial/ethnic characteristics of income-eligibles have been estimated on the basis of the characteristics of families whose incomes were below 125 percent of the poverty level, as reported in the 1970 Census of Population.

Note:

1) N/A indicates absence of program activity. Asterisk (*) indicates less than 0.5 percent.

Table 6. Percentage of Families with a Black or Hispanic Head of Household, by Program (Central Cities versus Suburbs)

SMSAS	Central Cities						Suburbs					
	Income-Eligibles[a]		Program Participants				Income-Eligibles[a]		Program Participants			
			Prior Programs		Sec. 8 Existing				Prior Programs		Sec. 8 Existing	
	% Black	% Hispanic	% Black	% Hisp.	% Black	% Hisp.	% Black	% Hisp.	% Black	% Hisp.	% Black	% Hisp.
Hartford	45	20	66	29	72	9	3	1	17	4	21	2
Newark	66	11	84	12	67	24	27	2	78	4	58	2
Richmond	71	*	94	-	96	1	27	1	49	-	N/A	N/A
Atlanta	74	1	98	-	99	*	21	1	68	*	63	-
Dayton	47	1	86	*	82	-	6	*	20	1	18	1
San Antonio	13	68	22	65	27	62	9	40	39	34	21	39
Omaha	29	3	60	1	79	-	2	2	6	2	N/A	N/A
Denver	18	32	31	47	44	25	1	13	8	19	3	19
Phoenix	13	25	33	33	48	15	3	32	9	29	15	34
Portland	14	2	53	2	57	*	1	1	4	1	1	2

a/ Racial/ethnic characteristics of income-eligibles have been estimated on the basis of the characteristics of families whose incomes were below 125 percent of the poverty level, as reported in the 1970 Census of Population.

Note:

1) Asterisk (*) indicates less than 0.5 percent. N/A indicates absence of program activity.

numerous projects in the suburbs of the Newark, Atlanta, and Phoenix SMSAs met this definition of minority concentration. In each SMSA, minority projects comprised a much higher percentage of central city projects than of suburban projects, and they were more prevalent under the Public Housing Program than under Section 236.

The differences between the minority composition of central city versus suburban tenants, and between project occupancy categories of Public Housing projects versus those of Section 236, serve to highlight the relationship between the location of projects and the racial/ethnic characteristics of tenants who live there. This study noted earlier that the locations of projects built under programs instituted before Section 8 were limited to relatively few (and often minority-concentrated) census tracts. The racial/ethnic characteristics of tenants assisted under programs preceding Section 8 may be more representative of the characteristics of income-eligible families residing in the neighborhoods surrounding the projects than of income-eligibles located throughout the respective central cities and suburban areas.

Section 8 Existing Housing

In most of the SMSAs, the black/Hispanic percentage among families participating in the Existing Housing Program was significantly higher than the percentage among income-eligibles. The margin was 35 percentage points or more in the Richmond, Atlanta, Dayton, and Omaha SMSAs. Compared with minority percentage among tenants under programs instituted prior to Section 8, the minority percentage among Existing Housing participants was substantially lower in the Hartford, Newark, and Denver SMSAs, but it was much higher in the Richmond and Omaha SMSAs (Table 5). For six of the eight suburban areas that had Existing Housing activity, the minority percentage among participants was at least 10 percentage points higher than the minority percentage among income-eligibles.

Within the central cities, the individual racial/ethnic groups served by the Section 8 Existing Housing Program in some instances differed substantially from those served under programs instituted before Section 8. The Existing Housing Program was much more likely to serve black families in Omaha (79 percent vs. 61 percent under prior programs), in Denver (44 percent vs. 31 percent), and in Phoenix (48 percent vs. 33 percent). In Newark, families served by the Existing Housing Program were 67 percent black and 24 percent Hispanic, whereas those served by prior programs were 84 percent black and 12 percent Hispanic (Table 6).

For both central cities and suburbs, the minority percentage among Existing Housing participants was generally higher in minority census tracts than in racially mixed tracts, and was generally higher in racially mixed tracts than in nonminority tracts. Even in nonminority tracts, however, the minority percentage among Existing Housing participants was generally equal to or greater than the minority percentage among income-eligibles. Whether this means that the Existing Housing Program has significantly broadened housing opportunities for families cannot be determined, primarily because data were not collected regarding the origins of mover households, but also because the racial/ethnic categories of census tract classification used in the study are too broad to support such conclusions.

Conclusions

The first major conclusion of this study is that families receiving assistance under HUD's rental housing subsidy programs in the ten metropolitan areas studied were concentrated in a relatively small number of minority-occupied census tracts, and were headed primarily by minority persons. Second, these patterns of location and occupancy were markedly different for the pre–1968 housing programs (principally Public Housing) than for the housing built between 1968 and 1974 and post–1974 housing. However, the volume of assistance provided to families in these SMSAs between 1974 and 1978 was not sufficiently large to substantially change the overall locational and occupancy patterns established under earlier programs.

With regard to locational patterns in the ten central cities, most of the subsidized rental housing available through project-oriented programs instituted before Section 8 was located in minority census tracts. The suburban stock of such housing, however, was located primarily in nonminority tracts. Of the central cities, only Omaha, Portland, and Phoenix did not have a majority of housing in projects located in minority tracts. Among the ten suburban areas, only the suburbs of Newark had a majority of such family housing located in minority census tracts. In each SMSA, the locations of 50 to 85 percent of the housing in HUD rental projects for families could be traced to only 5 percent of the census tracts. Many of these were areas of minority concentration.

The locational patterns of projects built under the Public Housing Program were responsible for a large share of HUD family housing being located in minority-concentrated areas. Public Housing represented more than two-thirds of all HUD housing available for occupancy in four of the SMSAs, and comprised more than half of the HUD housing for families in four other SMSAs. This housing frequently consisted of extremely large, central city projects built during the 1950s to 1960s and located in minority-concentrated areas.

Housing built under the Section 236 program tends to be less concentrated in minority areas than housing provided under the Public Housing Program. Similarly, more recent program activity under Section 8 (including New Construction, Substantial Rehabilitation, and Existing Housing) has generally been less concentrated in minority areas. These changes in the extent of concentration in minority areas are in part the result of a significant shift in the pattern of concentration between central cities and suburbs, a shift that has occurred primarily since 1968. Data in the study show that, in the ten areas, Section 236 housing and particularly Section 8 housing have been more evenly distributed between central cities and the surrounding suburbs than earlier programs.

Because the Section 8 Existing housing subsidy is tied to families rather than to housing projects, the Existing Housing Program is fundamentally different from the others included in the study. Compared with locational patterns under the project-oriented programs that preceded Section 8, the Existing Housing locations were usually less concentrated in minority tracts. Also, in contrast with locational patterns under prior programs, for which the bulk of the subsidized housing was available within only a dozen or so census tracts, Section 8 Existing Housing activity was located in 100 or more census tracts in six of the SMSAs and in 50 to 100 census tracts in two other SMSAs.

Families served by all HUD rental programs were primarily black and Hispanic in the ten central cities, and were primarily nonminority in the suburban areas. Compared to the racial/ethnic characteristics of income-eligibles, minorities were generally overrepresented in both the central cities and the suburbs—for both the Section 8 Existing Housing Program and for programs instituted prior to Section 8.

Within the ten central cities, projects located in minority areas were frequently occupied to a large extent (i.e., occupied 85 percent or more) by minorities. It is important to recognize that the housing developed under programs preceding Section 8 was not subject to the requirements of site selection and affirmative marketing that govern current program approvals. Also, it is sometimes forgotten that many of the earlier HUD rental assistance projects, particularly under the Public Housing and Section 221(d)(3) BMIR programs, were built primarily to serve as relocation resources to support urban renewal efforts and, as such, were often intentionally located in or near minority-concentrated areas.

This study has found some variation regarding the degree to which the Section 8 program has begun to alleviate the scarcity of subsidized housing located outside of minority-concentrated census tracts. For example, in some of the metropolitan areas there was extensive Section 8 Existing Housing activity in many nonminority census tracts located in both the central cities and suburbs. In some suburban areas, such as Richmond and Denver, there was an extensive volume of Section 8 New Construction for families approved for location outside of minority census tracts. However, in five central cities the percentage of Section 8 New/Rehab approved for location in minority census tracts was at least as high as under prior programs, and in a number of suburban areas little or no Section 8 Existing Housing assistance was available.

A number of issues deserve more attention than this study could provide. In particular, it would be useful to analyze more recent location and occupancy data for a broader range of housing market areas. Although the data in this study cover only a limited number of metropolitan areas, they indicate considerable diversity in program outcomes across areas with regard to the pattern and extent of concentration, not only for the project-based programs but also for the Section 8 Existing Housing Program. This diversity suggests that a national strategy for providing additional housing assistance that relies on one particular program or approach may not be equally likely to expand housing opportunities for lower income and minority families. It also suggests that local housing assistance strategies (to the extent that the federal government allows for local flexibility in choosing among federal housing subsidy programs) should carefully consider the locational and occupancy characteristics of the subsidized housing provided in the area to date.

NOTES AND REFERENCES

1. Discussion of the pattern versus the extent of segregation can be found in John Yinger, George Galster, Barton Smith, and Fred Eggers, "The Status of Research into Racial Discrimination and Segregation in American Housing Markets," *HUD Occasional Papers* 6 (1979).

2. Data describing the more recent Section 8 project approvals are based on the metropolitan area boundaries that were in effect in 1980, whereas data for all other programs are based on the boundaries that were in effect in 1970. Section 8 project approvals that had been terminated through January 1980 were not included in the sample.

3. Although none of the projects included in the sample was designated for occupancy by elderly persons, the elderly percentage among household heads ranged from 10 percent in the Richmond SMSA to 30 percent in the Phoenix SMSA. The housing units occupied by elderly households are included in the location data because the units are available to nonelderly as well as elderly persons.

4. Throughout the study, the term "prior programs" is used to identify HUD-subsidized rental housing made available under the programs that existed before FY 1975 (i.e., before the Section 8 program was implemented). These prior programs include Public Housing, Section 236, and Section 221(d)(3) Rent Supplement and Below-Market-Interest-Rate (BMIR) housing.

5. See *HUD Socio-Economic Data from the 1970 Census Tracts of U.S. Metropolitan Areas* (Ithaca, N.Y.: National Planning Data Corporation, 1977), designed by the Grier Partnership.

6. For Section 8 New/Rehab projects, the same terminology has been used to identify "minority" tracts, but "mixed" tracts are not identified as a separate category. Throughout the study, census tracts are also classified as "central city" or "suburban." Split census tracts are classified as minority, mixed, or nonminority areas according to the demographic characteristics of the tract as a whole. Projects in split tracts are identified as central city or suburban, based on the street address of the project in question. For scattered-site assistance provided within all types of census tracts, the classification of central city or suburb is based on the identity of the PHA, and the classification of locations as minority, mixed, or nonminority is based on the characteristics of the individual tracts containing assisted families.

7. Relatively few HUD-assisted families were located in racially mixed census tracts in January 1978—the tracts tended to fall into either the minority or the nonminority

classification, which tends to limit the potential understatement of location in minority tracts. On the other hand, because the data for Section 8 New/Rehab projects are based on approvals, not completed projects, there is some potential for such understatement. Program experience indicates that family projects proposed for location in nonminority or racially mixed areas are more likely than other types of projects to be delayed or cancelled due to local government or neighborhood opposition. Also, data are not available to indicate the number of Section 8 New/Rehab units located in racially mixed tracts, which are considered more likely to have changed in minority status after 1970.

8. Actual income-eligibility limits vary by program and area. Also, significant changes in the income eligibility policy resulting from passage of the Housing and Community Development Act of 1974 were phased in from 1976 to 1979. These changes affected the admission of tenants to units in newly completed projects and to units with a change in tenancy, but did not affect the eligibility of tenants already receiving HUD subsidies. We have considered as income-eligible those families with incomes below 125 percent of the poverty level, as reported in the 1970 census, which on average is roughly equivalent to 50 percent of the median family income for the respective areas.

9. The Fair Share factor is an unweighted composite percentage representing an area's share of total population, population below the poverty level, housing units without plumbing, households living in crowded conditions, housing vacancy deficit, and renters with selected housing problems. See John Goodman, *Regional Housing Assistance Allocations and Regional Housing Needs* (Washington, D.C.: The Urban Institute, 1979).

10. In most of the SMSAs, the percentage of Section 8 New/Rehab units approved for family housing was significantly higher in FY 1979 than in the preceding two fiscal years.

11. Because data are not available to indicate the extent of location of Section 8 New/Rehab units in racially mixed census tracts, the distinctions made here are for locations that are either inside or outside of minority census tracts.

12. Beginning in June 1978, HUD procedures exempted Section 8 Substantial Rehabilitation proposals from the review for minority concentration that is included in the site and neighborhood standards applicable to all proposals for Section 8 New Construction.

13. Due to previously described difficulties involving the derivation of an appropriate income-eligibility limit, comparisons of the minority percentage among program participants with the minority percentage among income-eligibles should be approached with caution. Differences of less than 10 percentage points should not be considered significant.

Chapter Eleven
Race and Residential Mobility
The Effects of Housing Assistance
Programs on Household Behavior
JENNIFER L. STUCKER*

During the 1970s, the U.S. Department of Housing and Urban Development (HUD) developed a series of rental subsidy programs that made use of the existing, privately owned, rental housing stock in providing housing for low-income households. Unlike other HUD programs in which the subsidy is tied to a specific unit in a fixed location, these new programs were "tenant-based." The choice of unit was up to the assisted families (provided they met program requirements) and, if the families moved, they could take their subsidy with them. Because a primary objective of these programs was to increase freedom of housing choice, in the hope of promoting integration, HUD has undertaken a number of evaluation and demonstration projects to assess whether these tenant-based housing assistance programs result in some form of racial desegregation or integration. That is, do they "induce" low-income families to move and, if so, where do these families go?

To answer these questions, we will consider two aspects of household moving behavior. The first is household "mobility," the percentage of households that move during a given time period, and the extent to which the mobility of assisted households is influenced by housing subsidies. This will give us an idea of the potential impact such programs could have on the overall *extent* of desegregation. For example, if a tenant-based subsidy simply helps families to pay the rent in the unit where they lived before receiving the subsidy, the program cannot play much of an active role in integration. The second factor is locational choice, that is, to what degree do assisted households that move relocate to neighborhoods with larger or smaller proportions (or "concentrations") of minority households? This will define the *pattern* of integration associated with the program, indicating whether program recipients are increasing, decreasing, or making no change in the racial composition of their neighborhoods.[1]

The two major tenant-based subsidy programs that will be reviewed in this chapter are the Experimental Housing Allowance Program (EHAP) and the Section 8 Existing Housing Program. EHAP was a social experiment designed in the 1970s to test the concept of providing cash allowances to low-income households and to measure the impact on the households receiving the allow-

*The opinions expressed in this chapter are those of the author and do not necessarily reflect the views of the U.S. Department of Housing and Urban Development or the U.S. government.

ances, on housing markets, and on the agencies administering the program. Approximately 30,000 households were involved in the experiment in twelve sites across the country over a seven-year period.[2] Low-income households in EHAP were offered a direct cash allowance payment if they would occupy housing that passed the program's minimum housing standards. Generally, the allowance equaled the difference between the local cost of standard housing and 25 percent of the household's income. Because the subsidy was tied to the tenant rather than to the unit, selection and location of the unit were left entirely to the tenant, provided it passed the minimum housing standards. Before the final results of EHAP were available, Congress authorized the Section 8 Existing Housing Program—the operational version of the concept that was being tested in EHAP. Although EHAP ended in 1980, the Section 8 Existing Program currently assists over 800,000 families nationwide. Two major evaluations of the Section 8 program have been undertaken and these results, combined with those of EHAP, are the focus of this report.

EHAP consisted of three subexperiments—the Demand Experiment, the Administrative Agency Experiment (AAE), and the Supply Experiment (the only one for which homeowners were eligible)—each designed somewhat differently to answer a specific set of policy questions. For our purposes, we will only look at the first two.

The Demand Experiment is particularly useful in analyzing household moving behavior because it had a matched control group. Households in the control group were not offered a cash allowance nor were they required to live in standard housing. However, the same kinds of information were collected for the control households as were collected for the "recipient" households (i.e., the households receiving the allowance). Thus, comparisons can be made to determine whether the program incentives made any difference in household mobility or locational choice.

The Demand Experiment was conducted in two locations: Pittsburgh, Pennsylvania, and Phoenix, Arizona. During the first two years of Demand Experiment operations, 38 percent of the recipient households in Pittsburgh and 59 percent of the recipient households in Phoenix moved.[3] Among the control households, 35 percent and 54 percent moved in Pittsburgh and Phoenix, respectively. The differences between experimental and control households are not statistically significant, indicating that the allowance had little or no effect on the percentage of households that moved.[4]

Table 1 shows these proportions disaggregated by race.[5] None of the experimental/control differences are significant and the only significant difference between minority and nonminority households is among the control households in Phoenix. To explain these mobility rates, a model of household mobility was developed that included a variety of life-cycle, demographic, housing, and neighborhood factors, as well as measures of housing satisfaction and social bonds. When these characteristics are controlled for, the effect of the allowance across the two sites is an increase in a household's probability of

Table 1. Summary of Mobility Effects in EHAP and Section 8

	EHAP				AAE	Section 8 Urban Study
	Demand Experiment					
	Pittsburgh		Phoenix			
	Exp.	Control	Exp.	Control		
Proportion of Households that Moved:						
Total	38	35	59	54	45	49
Minority	40	33	73	74	60	61
Non-Minority	37	35	58	51	41	39
Proportion of Black Movers that Moved to Neighborhoods with Minority Concentrations that were: — Higher	12	24	32*	26*	27	15
— Same	71	67	11	47	20	52
— Lower	16	10	58	26	53	35
Mean Proportion Minority in Origin Neighborhood						
Minority Movers	52	42	40*	30	56	52
Non-Minority Movers	7	6	3	5	6	10
Mean Change in Proportion Minority from Origin to Destination Neighborhood						
Minority Movers	-4	+8	-4*	+4	-14	-13
Non-Minority Movers	-2	-1	-1	-3	-2	0

* Based on fewer than 20 observations

moving of about 7 percentage points above what it would have been if the household had not received the allowance. This effect is primarily concentrated among the households whose units did not meet the housing standards at enrollment (i.e., to receive the allowance, they would have had to move to a unit that met the standards or upgrade their current unit to meet the standards). For these households, the increased probability of moving was 10 percentage points above what it would have been without the allowance.[6] The implication of this finding is that the allowance caused households to move somewhat sooner than they would have otherwise.

Using census tract data, an analysis was conducted of changes in the characteristics from households' origin neighborhoods (i.e., the tract in which a household lived before becoming a recipient) to their destination neighborhoods (i.e., the tract in which a household lived after becoming a recipient). In general, the households that chose to move relocated to neighborhoods with slightly lower proportions of minority households than the neighborhoods from which they had moved. Control households that moved followed similar patterns, however, indicating that the allowance did not in itself induce a substantial change in household behavior. For example, 71 percent of the black movers in Pittsburgh moved to neighborhoods with minority concentrations similar to their origin neighborhoods, 16 percent moved to neighborhoods with a lower level of minority concentration, and 12 percent moved to more concentrated areas. Moves made by black control households were not significantly different (see Table 1). More specifically, black recipient households that moved in Pittsburgh reduced their level of minority concentration by an average of 4 percentage points. Black control households that moved increased their minority concentration by an average of 8 percentage points. However, these differences between experimental households and controls were not statistically significant. From Table 1, it appears that the patterns of locational choice of black movers in Phoenix are much different. But there were very few black experimental households in Phoenix and even fewer black movers. Hence the sample is too small to determine significance and may not even be representative.[7]

The important factor to keep in mind when analyzing locational choices made by minority households is that black households in both Pittsburgh and Phoenix tended to live in racially concentrated neighborhoods (i.e., neighborhoods with a substantial proportion of minority households). For example, in Pittsburgh the average minority concentration across all black recipients' origin neighborhoods was 54 percent. In Phoenix, it was 42 percent. Black control households, as well as black households that moved, lived in similar types of neighborhoods (see Table 1). Thus, even the households that moved to less concentrated areas, on average, were still living in relatively segregated neighborhoods.[8]

EHAP's Administrative Agency Experiment was conducted in eight sites. Overall, 45 percent of the recipient households moved to obtain program benefits. According to AAE analysts, movers tended to follow already established patterns of locational change, that is, white households tended to move to more segregated white neighborhoods, whereas black households tended to move to slightly less concentrated or transitional neighborhoods. Although they originated in neighborhoods similar to their Demand Experiment counterparts, minority movers in the AAE decreased their minority concentration on average by 14 percentage points. (See Table 1.) However, as was the case in the Demand Experiment, both black and white movers in the AAE remained in relatively segregated neighborhoods. That is, the average minority concentration in black recipient movers' neighborhoods was 40 percent, whereas the corresponding concentration for white movers was 4 percent.[9]

In the Section 8 Existing Housing Program, participants generally receive a subsidy equal to the difference between their rent and 25 percent of their income.[10] As in EHAP, Section 8 subsidies are tied to the tenant rather than to the specific unit, thereby leaving the selection of the unit to the tenant provided that it passes minimum housing standards. Two separate evaluations of the Section 8 Existing Program, the first conducted in 1976 and the second in 1979, provide information on the degree of change in neighborhood economic and racial concentration experienced by Section 8 program participants. The first study (herein referred to as the "national" study) was designed to provide a national overview of the Section 8 program's impact shortly after it was implemented. The second study (referred to as the "urban" study) took a further look at the program's effects in fifteen SMSAs where it had been operating for several years.[11]

According to the national study, almost half of the Section 8 subsidy recipients moved to obtain program benefits (44 percent of the nonminority households and 48 percent of the minority households). Approximately 70 percent of those households (or one-third of the Section 8 recipients) moved to new neighborhoods (again, the proportion of whites and blacks was about the same). Of those who moved to new neighborhoods, approximately 67 percent thought they had moved to a "better" neighborhood, 22 percent thought they had moved to a "similar" neighborhood, and about 16 percent thought they had moved to a "worse" neighborhood. With respect to racial mix, moves to neighborhoods that households thought were more racially mixed were offset by moves to neighborhoods that were perceived as less mixed. That is, approximately 32 percent of the households that moved said their new neighborhood was more racially mixed than their preprogram neighborhood, whereas about 28 percent said their new neighborhood was less mixed. The remaining 40 percent said the two neighborhoods were about the same. Offsetting moves occurred among black as well as white households. Among whites, however, moves to less racially mixed neighborhoods equaled moves to more racially mixed neighborhoods (30 percent for each), whereas among black households moves to more mixed neighborhoods exceded moves to less mixed neighborhoods by 15 percentage points (39 percent vs. 24 percent).[12]

Although these findings imply that Section 8 households are reducing their neighborhood level of racial concentration to some degree, we cannot specify to what extent in the absence of specific preprogram and program neighborhood characteristics. In the Section 8 urban study, however, census tract codes were recorded for neighborhoods lived in by each household both before (origin) and during the time they participated in the program (destination), thus providing census tract characteristics to analyze racial patterns of locational change.

The overall proportion of Section 8 recipients that moved to obtain program benefits was still about 50 percent when the urban study was conducted in 1979 (see Table 1). Disaggregating this proportion by race, 61 percent of the minority households and 39 percent of the nonminority households moved.[13] However, when other demographic factors such as age are controlled for, this difference is not statistically significant.[14]

Of the minority households that moved, 52 percent moved to neighborhoods with minority concentrations similar to their origin neighborhoods, 35 percent moved to neighborhoods with smaller proportions of minority households, and 15 percent moved to neighborhoods with a higher level of minority concentration (see Table 1). When averaged across all Section 8 recipients, the mean change in minority concentration from origin to destination tracts was a decrease of 4 percentage points. Although statistically this change is significantly different from zero, it nevertheless is not very large. For those who moved, however, the mean change in minority concentration was a decrease of 7 percentage points, and for black households that moved (26 percent of all recipients), the average was a decrease of 13 percentage points (see Table 1). This represents a 25 percent reduction from their average initial level of minority concentration. Thus, the mean change varies considerably, depending on which group of recipients is examined. Like many of their EHAP counterparts, Section 8 minority households that moved appear to be experiencing a sizable amount of neighborhood racial deconcentration. Yet their destination neighborhoods were still relatively segregated: the average level of minority concentration in destination tracts for black households that moved was 40 percent, whereas for white movers the average level was 9 percent.[15]

When comparing the results of the three programs, we see that mobility rates as well as the frequency of moves to less segregated neighborhoods seem to be higher in the AAE and Section 8 programs than in the Demand Experiment. This can be explained, at least in part, by the difference in the source of program applicants for the different programs. That is, in the Demand Experiment, a sample of the eligible population was invited to participate and those who accepted the offer applied for the program. The experiment's control group was also taken from this sample. In Section 8 and the AAE, families that needed assistance with their rent had to seek out the agency administering the program and apply for assistance. Because of this self-selection process, it seems reasonable to assume that Section 8 and AAE households as a group were more dissatisfied with their housing conditions (their unit, landlord, neighborhood, rent burden, etc.) than Demand Experiment households. Consequently, we would expect more of them to be "on the verge" of moving, which would explain their higher mobility rate and higher rate of moves to different types of neighborhoods (see Table 1).[16]

We know from comparing experimental households to controls in the Demand Experiment that the assistance payment per se does not induce many additional moves or moves to less concentrated neighborhoods than would have occurred in the absence of the program. Without a control group for AAE or Section 8 households, we cannot be sure whether the observed differences are attributable to the prevailing patterns of locational change among the population that participated in the different programs, the result of other program-specific differences, or some combination of both. Nevertheless, the reduction in minority concentration for some program participants appears to be significantly greater than that experienced by most of the low-income population. And even though households continue to live in relatively concentrated neighborhoods, the results of these evaluations suggest that the overall pattern of household moves seems to be in the direction of integration rather than segregation.

In view of these findings, what impact can we expect from these programs on the overall extent of racial integration? At a minimum, tenant-based subsidies do not inhibit desegregation, as is often the case with project-based assisted housing programs such as Public Housing. Households assisted under tenant-based subsidy programs generally follow existing patterns of integration set by unassisted households, implying that the program itself creates no additional constraints. As a result, the overall pattern of integration is not substantially altered by these programs—in either a positive or negative direction. However, by causing some program participants to move somewhat sooner than they would have otherwise, these tenant-based subsidies accelerate the current process, thereby increasing the overall extent of integration. Thus, the larger the number of families assisted, the faster the integration process takes place. Unfortunately, two important factors counteract this process, thereby limiting the program's actual impact on the overall extent of racial integration.

The first is program size. Unlike welfare programs such as AFDC and Food Stamps, for which all who are eligible for benefits are entitled to receive them, HUD's assisted housing programs are limited in scale by the program budget established each year by Congress. There are approximately 9.7 million households eligible for the Section 8 Existing Housing Program. However, because of budgetary limitations, it currently assists about 800,000 households. Thus, even if all 800,000 families moved to desegregated neighborhoods upon receiving Section 8 assistance, the overall impact on racial integration for the nation as a whole would be relatively small. This brings us to the second limiting factor. That is, only about half of the families that receive Section 8 assistance move from their preprogram units. This is due primarily to the fact that a large portion of the program's participants are elderly households, which for a variety of reasons choose not to move. Because we have little reason to expect the proportion of elderly participants to change substantially, the number of Section 8 households that move is equally likely to remain low.

Finally, the reader should bear in mind that the findings reported here are based on a static look at locational change and therefore are only partly accurate. The full impact of programs such as the Section 8 Existing Program can be assessed only if the racial composition of program participants' origin and destination neighborhoods are analyzed over time to see what integrative or segregative patterns follow. For the purpose of assessing the impact of a specific type of rental subsidy program on integration, we have limited our attention to moves made by the program participants. If assisted housing programs enable them to move to integrated neighborhoods, we conclude that the goal of increasing freedom of housing choice has been achieved.

NOTES AND REFERENCES

1. The reader should keep in mind, however, that analyzing the behavior of assisted households tells only part of the story. It tells us whether they are taking advantage of their increased freedom of housing choice and moving to less segregated neighbor-

hoods. But it does not necessarily indicate the program's final impact on housing deseg-regration. For example, if a minority household moves to a predominantly nonminority area, integration is enhanced. If, however, one or more nonminority households move away to another predominantly nonminority area as a result, the initial integrating effect may be canceled out. This leads us to the issue of racial "tipping," which is covered in depth in the racial integration literature and will not be analyzed here.

2. For a complete, concise description of the program and its principal findings, see *Experimental Housing Allowance Program: Conclusions, The 1980 Report* (Washington, D.C.: U.S. Department of Housing and Urban Development, February 1980).

3. The Demand Experiment tested a number of different subsidy designs. For comparability, only households that received the subsidy that was similar to that used for the AAE and Section 8 programs are included in this analysis.

4. Reilly Atkinson, William Hamilton, and Dowell Myers, *Economic and Racial/Ethnic Concentration in the Housing Allowance Demand Experiment* (Cambridge, Mass.: Abt Associates, June 1980), p. 47.

5. Ibid.

6. Jean MacMillan, *Mobility in the Housing Allowance Demand Experiment* (Cambridge, Mass.: Abt Associates, Inc., June 1980), pp. 3, 100.

7. Atkinson, Hamilton, and Myers, *Economic and Racial/Ethnic Concentration*, pp. 45–67. These findings are generally consistent with changes in patterns of racial segregation in standard metropolitan statistical areas (SMSAs) over time. See Ann B. Schnare, *Housing in Black and White: Patterns of Segregation in American Housing Markets* (Washington, D.C.: The Urban Institute, December 1977); Annemette Sorensen, Karl Taeuber, and Leslie Hollingsworth, *Indexes of Racial Residential Segregation for 109 Cities in the United States, 1940–1970* (Madison: Institute for Research on Poverty, University of Wisconsin, 1974); Karl E. Taeuber and Alma F. Taeuber, *Negroes in Cities: Residential Segregation and Neighborhood Change* (Chicago: Aldine, 1965).

8. Atkinson, Hamilton, and Meyers, *Economic and Racial/Ethnic Concentration*, p. 47.

9. Frederick T. Temple, William L. Holshouser, Jr., M. G. Trend, David Budding, and Mireille L. Ernst. *Third Annual Report of the Administrative Agency Experiment Evaluation* (Cambridge, Mass.: Abt Associates, Inc., August 1976), pp. 10, 48.

10. Although this was the case when the evaluations were conducted, the percentage has increased to 30 percent since that time.

11. See Margaret Drury, Olsen Lee, Michael Springer, and Lorene Yap, *Lower Income Housing Assistance Program (Section 8): Nationwide Evaluation of the Existing Housing Program* (Washington, D.C.: The Urban Institute, November 1978); James E. Wallace et al., *Participation and Benefits in the Urban Section 8 Program: New Construction and Existing Housing* (Cambridge, Mass.: Abt Associates, 1981). One caveat should be made when comparing the findings of the two evaluations, that is, the populations they represent, although similar, are not identical. The sample chosen for the national study represents a nationwide cross section of Section 8 participants (urban as well as rural) early in the program. The urban study reflects the behavior of a sample of households that became Section 8 recipients in late 1979, in fifteen SMSAs that represent a broad range of Section 8 program activity.

12. Household Survey from the Section 8 national study.

13. Wallace et al., *Participation and Benefits*, pp. 237–38.

14. Michael J. Vernarelli, "Mobility Behavior in a Housing Voucher Program" (Department of Economics, Rochester Institute of Technology, March 1982).

15. Wallace et al., *Participation and Benefits*, pp. 247, 253.

16. Dissatisfaction with present housing unit or neighborhood was one of the independent variables tested in the Demand Experiment logit analysis cited earlier. As we would expect, such dissatisfaction increases the likelihood that a household will search for a different unit. See MacMillan, *Mobility in the Housing Allowance Demand Experiment*, chap. 5.

Chapter Twelve
Public Housing Projects, Blacks, and Public Policy
The Historical Ecology of Public Housing
in Philadelphia
IRA GOLDSTEIN*

WILLIAM L. YANCEY

This chapter reports the results of research on the location and consequences of public housing in urban neighborhoods. Public housing and the neighborhoods in which it is located are paradigmatic of contemporary urban ghettos (see Salisbury 1954; Moore 1969; Rainwater 1970; Lewis 1966; Friedman 1966; Heumann 1979). Our interest focuses on the association between the location of public housing and black concentrations. The first counts of the 1980 census of Philadelphia effectively validated the continued rise in racial segregation forecast by the 1969 National Commission on Civil Disorders "toward two societies, one White, one Black, separate and unequal." Unlike the pattern experienced by other ethnic groups entering American cities, blacks have become increasingly more segregated, rather than less (Lieberson 1963; Hershberg et al. 1979). We seek to understand how, during decades marked by liberal domestic policies, a locally administered federal program such as Public Housing became increasingly associated with the conditions it was designed to eliminate—that is, the concentration of blacks in urban poverty.

Projects, Poverty, and Blacks: Alternative Hypotheses

There are three explanatory paradigms in the social science, legal, and planning literature for the association between public housing and concentrations of blacks. The first points to the "spillover" of race, poverty, and the culture of poverty of public housing into the surrounding residential areas. The second focuses on the site selection policies of housing authorities and urban political machines that tend to act largely as a function of the social characteristics of areas. The third posits that the position of neighborhoods in the historical ecology of the city is the determinant of both its housing and racial characteristics.

The first perspective argues that the causality flows from public housing to

*The authors would like to acknowledge the contributions and critiques of the members of the Urban Housing Seminar, Temple University: David Bartelt, David Elesh, George Leon, Jannet Shannon, and Ronald Turner. Our formulations have been aided by insightful critiques by Carolyn Adams, John M. Goering, Mark Haller, and Shirley Laska.

neighborhoods. The second perspective posits causality in the opposite direction—it is the racial, and concomitant social and political, character of neighborhoods, coupled with the racially based decisions of those in power, that determines whether an area will become the site of a public housing project. The third perspective says that the correlations observed between public housing and neighborhood characteristics, while strong, are spurious. These correlations can be understood in terms of the position of the neighborhood in the changing political, ecological, social, and economic structure of the city. As might be expected, there are arguments and evidence supporting each of these perspectives.

The Spillover of Poverty and Race

The primary explanation for the relationship between public housing, poverty, and black concentrations focuses on the impact of the project tenants on the surrounding neighborhood. Thus, according to a Chicago urban villager, project residents "have no sense of responsibility, they don't take care of their home or their children, and they have no initiative" (Meyerson and Banfield 1955:110). The presence of such people in neighborhoods apparently threatens important values and/or interests, such as safety, economic investment, and racial stability of the surrounding neighborhoods.

In Philadelphia, similar objections were raised against the siting of public housing in the 1930s (Bauman 1974). Recently, they have also been made by blue-collar residents of such Philadelphia communities as Whitman Park and by the wealthy newcomers to Society Hill. This sentiment was clearly expressed by the federal district court, which asserted that federally subsidized rental housing in a neighborhood "would seem to have the same potential for perpetuating racial segregation as low-rent public housing has" (*Shannon v. HUD* 1970:820). Concentrations of low-rent housing were believed, by the court, to contribute to urban blight. In this case, the court required the U.S. Department of Housing and Urban Development (HUD) to set up an institutionalized method to consider "whether the need for physical rehabilitation or additional minority housing at the site in question outweighed the disadvantage of increasing or perpetuating racial concentration" (p. 822).

Although a central component of the district court's decision, no evidence was cited supporting the hypothesis that public housing increases either urban blight or black concentrations. The research literature is somewhat contradictory on this point. Gold (1980:277) concludes her investigation of racial discrimination in New York housing with the suggestion that "many projects have been so distinctive in appearance that they have stigmatized the neighborhoods in which they are located and the tenants themselves." Laska et al. (1982:159–60) found that proximity to public housing was negatively related to levels of renovation activity. According to them, the strong negative correlation suggests that projects are "avoided as locations of dire poverty and the expected accompanying social problems." Yet, they add, "the strength of the statistics for other socio-economic measures does not suggest a complete avoidance of the poor."

Other investigators have reached different conclusions. Public housing is one of the least important predictors of violent crime in a community when social, economic, and housing characteristics of the neighborhood are taken into account (Roncek, Bell, and Francik 1981). Similarly, studies of real estate values indicate the insignificant effect of project proximity (Saunders and Woodford 1979; Schmidt 1980). Varady (1982:432) has observed: "This article's review of the social science literature provides little support for the widely accepted belief that government subsidized housing programs have neighborhood spill-over effects." He concludes: "In particular, the evidence on the relationship between housing programs and property values is contradictory and confusing."

Racism and Urban Political Structures

The National Advisory Commission on Civil Disorders (*Report* 1968:2) concluded its investigation of the conditions leading to the riots of the sixties with the following statement: "White society is deeply implicated in the ghetto. White institutions created it, White institutions maintain it and White society condones it." To the degree that public housing is implicated in the ghetto, it provides a means of examining some of the mechanisms by which a federally sponsored and controlled, or at least monitored, institution is involved in the formation and crystallization of the racial ghetto.

There are two explanations as to how public housing has been implicated in creating and maintaining racial segregation. First, blacks and whites have been (and continue to be) segregated within public housing projects. Second, public housing has become a black institution and white communities have successfully fought against it. Before the Supreme Court's rejection of "separate but equal," public housing projects were explicitly designated for blacks or whites. Since the 1960s, though no longer officially restricted to blacks or whites, projects have remained racially segregated. Rabin (n.d.) reports that, in 1970, 91 percent of blacks living in Philadelphia's public housing lived in projects that were over 75 percent black. Twenty years earlier, 87 percent lived in such predominantly black developments.

In general, the explanation of the association between public housing and black concentrations in surrounding neighborhoods refers explicitly to the policies of urban political machines and public housing authorities that base site selection on racial characteristics of the neighborhood. Meyerson and Banfield's (1955) investigation of the Chicago Housing Authority (CHA) during the early 1950s documents the impact of the political machines on the location of public housing in the city. Peel, Pickett, and Buehl (1970) mention Chicago's "Kean-

Murphy" deal, an informal arrangement whereby projects would not be proposed to the City Council until a particular alderman, Alderman Murphy, cleared the proposal with the potentially affected alderman. During the *Gautreaux v. Chicago Housing Authority* case, the CHA admitted that projects slated for white areas never reached the City Council for purely racial grounds. Another racially based strategy mentioned by Peel, Pickett, and Buehl was termed the "twice-as-many-as-needed" policy. This meant that many more sites than necessary were submitted to Chicago's City Council. In this way, the CHA could fill its HUD allotment and still veto sites on the basis of public pressure. Such an action was acceptable, given HUD's "prima facie" rule, because the CHA could show HUD that these were the only acceptable sites of all submitted. "The CHA site-selection procedures are a good example of what extreme local political authority over site approval can do and how the LHA (local housing authority) can acquiesce to and participate in discriminatory practices in site selection" (Peel, Pickett, and Buehl 1970:85).

Thus, neighborhoods with political organization, or strong aldermen, prevented public housing from being located within their areas. Welfeld (1976:125) reports that in Chicago "99.5 percent of the proposed units in White areas were rejected. Practically all projects were built in Black neighborhoods." In the mid-seventies the Supreme Court ordered the Chicago Housing Authority to construct new projects in predominantly white suburban residential areas. The primary impact of this decision was the sharp curtailment of new public housing (Heumann 1979:237; Welfeld 1976:118).[1]

There is a recognized need for public housing, yet the residents of black neighborhoods reject it on the grounds that it will perpetuate the ghetto, and the residents of white neighborhoods reject it on the grounds that it will create a ghetto. In essence, public housing has become the proverbial political football. Unfortunately, the fulfillment of a population's basic needs, through public housing, is often subjugated to the *desires* of neighborhood residents. It was refreshing to see that, in *Croskey Street Concerned Citizens v. Romney* (Croskey Street was the locus of a North Philadelphia citizens group), Judge Aldisert asserted: "Depriving the elderly of this facility, or even delaying access thereto, is to me important, if not the most important consideration of these entire proceedings" (*University of Pennsylvania Law Review* 1974:1355). In this case, the court allowed the construction of the project for the elderly.

On the whole, it appears that the resistance to public housing by Philadelphia's white communities was on a somewhat smaller scale than was the case in Chicago. In Philadelphia, before 1954 projects reserved for white tenants were in neighborhoods that were 99 percent white. Those reserved for blacks were constructed in neighborhoods with heavy concentrations of blacks (42 percent). Since 1954, projects have been constructed in 22 different neighborhoods or census tracts. While the black percentage of these tract populations was greater than the average for the city, projects were constructed in predominantly white neighborhoods. Thus, although there is a positive relationship between the percentage of a local population that is black and the subsequent location of a project, the weakness of the relationship suggests that other factors, besides political entities basing site selection on race, have determined the location of public housing in Philadelphia.

The Historical Ecology of the Ghetto

At the most general level, the perspective that we have labeled "historical ecology" is summarized by Taeuber and Taeuber (1965:125), who concluded their investigation of residential succession by writing that "the fortunes of residential neighborhoods in a city are to a large extent tied to broader changes occurring in the metropolitan areas and the economy as a whole." The involvement of the larger urban structure in the settlement pattern of race and ethnic groups has been documented by a series of social historians and sociologists (see Warner and Burke 1969; Ward 1971; Kusmer 1976; Lieberson 1963; Taeuber and Taeuber 1965). If we are to understand the formation of racial and ethnic communities and the locations of such institutions as public housing, it is necessary to specify how particular neighborhoods have been linked to the changing social and economic organization of the city as a whole, rather than merely examine their internal characteristics. The literature suggests that the economic character of neighborhoods, particularly the presence and stability of manufacturing employment, is central to understanding a neighborhood's ethnic and racial history. For example, European immigrants concentrated near centers of manufacturing employment (Pratt 1917; Greenberg 1981). Blacks, although initially concentrated in center city areas, and thus near centers of employment, were largely excluded from manufacturing jobs (Lieberson 1980).

Ericksen and Yancey (1979) have shown for Philadelphia that the pattern of racial transition is directly related to the ecological and economic position of the city's respective neighborhoods. In addition to the relative distance to large numbers of blacks in 1930, lower housing values and smaller concentrations of manufacturing jobs were present in those areas experiencing increases in the number of blacks. The manufacturing areas were residentially stable and thus did not provide easily accessible housing for the city's growing black population. The strong tie between work and residence for blue-collar workers and the lower proportions of homeowners who hold mortgages on their homes (Katona, Liniger, and Mueller 1965:39) enhance the residential stability of these communities.

In sharp contrast to the stable industrial blue-collar neighborhoods are the old streetcar suburbs. These communities were established around the turn of the century following the development of the electric streetcar, which made it possible for large numbers of urban workers to live farther away from their place of employment (Warner 1962; Ward 1971). The streetcar suburbs were inherently less stable in that they had no close ties to the workplace. They also contained a higher proportion of white-collar and professional workers, who with greater resources and earning power were more mobile. With the development of the more distant automobile suburbs in the 1950s, these areas were abandoned by families seeking greener spaces. Thus, these communities were more vulnerable to racial transition aided by the burgeoning intra-urban transportation systems. The ecological outcome of these historical processes has conformed with Schnore's (1964:333) observation that "the 'marginal work force' may be physically marginal to a given industrial community."

The characteristics of neighborhoods associated with increasing racial concentration are also associated with the location of public housing. Meyerson and Banfield's (1955) research on Chicago has been used to argue that it was the political efficacy of some local areas that determined the location of public housing. Logan and Schneider (1982) have suggested that the residential stability of local communities and their ethnic homogeneity are directly related to their political efficacy and, thus, to their ability to resist the invasion of blacks. Yancey and Ericksen (1979) have shown that the stability of white neighborhoods is the result of local manufacturing employment. Therefore, the presence of manufacturing jobs may be the antecedent condition to stability, community solidarity, and the ultimate successful resistance to public housing.

Public housing is likely to be located in areas that are being abandoned as a result of changes in major economic activities. The Chicago urban sociologists identified the "zone of transition" as those areas of the city being left fallow in anticipation of the continued growth of the central business district. We now realize that the zone of transition was being abandoned because of the decline of manufacturing and the decentralization of retail activity—not because the centrally located business district was expanding. Subsequent changes in the *relative* productive utility of neighborhoods leads to the creation of other zones of transition. For example, older industrial neighborhoods lose their stability with the loss of industrial employment.[2] Such areas are likely to have relatively unstable populations and thus are not likely to have the organization or connections necessary to use the political structure as a means of preventing public housing from locating there—given the will to do so. It is also reasonable to expect that the cost of land acquisition for public housing in these areas will be less—whether measured in political or economic terms.

In summary, we have found three rather different explanations for the relationship between the location of public housing and concentrations of blacks in urban neighborhoods. The "spillover hypothesis" suggests that the construction of public housing in a neighborhood will produce "white flight," the result being an increasing concentration of the black population. The racially motivated site selection argument suggests that the chief causes of the association between public housing and blacks are (1) the policy of racial segregation within public housing, (2) the growing proportion of public housing families that are black, and (3) the policy of locating public housing in predominantly black neighborhoods. In contrast to both of these explanations, historical ecologists have suggested that identifiable historical characteristics of neighborhoods (e.g., their proximity to the central business district, the level of manufacturing employment, their previous use as streetcar suburbs, and real estate values) have determined whether or not they have been abandoned by dominant institutions and middle-class populations, and thus become accessible to the growing black, poor population and public housing. Clearly, it is necessary to control for such factors before examining the direct relationship between race and public housing.

Data Sources

We have used census tracts for the city of Philadelphia between 1930 and 1980 as the units of analysis for this research. Because tract boundaries have changed several times over this period, we have grouped tracts to create a set of 248 areas whose boundaries were identical for the fifty-year period.

Information on the location of public housing developments in the city was taken from the public housing authority's annual reports, which provide the address, size, building types, and dates of construction of all housing developments owned and managed by the Philadelphia Housing Authority. In the analysis that follows, we have grouped the project developments into two categories to reflect the historical periods of their construction in the city. The first category includes the eight projects that were constructed before 1950—all of them low-rise buildings located in seven different census tracts. The second category includes the twenty-four housing projects constructed between 1950 and 1969; fourteen of these were dominated by high-rise buildings.

Data on the location of scattered-site housing was obtained through the Delaware Valley Regional Planning Commission, which reported the number of public housing units in each census tract in 1976.[3] Scattered-site housing units are units owned and managed by the Philadelphia Housing Authority that are not part of large developments. Although the development of scattered-site housing was approved by the Philadelphia City Council in 1958, most of it was constructed between 1967 and 1971. About 92 different tracts contain at least one scattered-site unit, yet 8 tracts contain more than 300 "scattered" units. Over 50 percent of the scattered-site public housing in the city is contained in these 8 tracts. The highly skewed distribution of scattered-site housing is mirrored in the distribution of all public housing in Philadelphia. Although 104 census tracts contain some public housing, five neighborhoods contain over 1,000 public housing units. Together, these five neighborhoods contain over 40 percent of the city's total public housing stock.

Given the highly skewed nature of the distribution of public housing in the city, we have created "dummy" variables to indicate the presence or absence of

Table 1. Racial Composition and Segregation in Philadelphia, 1930–1980

	1930	1940	1950	1960	1970	1980
White Population Size[1]	1,732	1,671	1,696	1,461	1,285	982
Black Population Size[1]	220	255	376	528	659	639
Percent Black	11.2	13.2	18.1	26.5	32.9	39.4
Index of Dissimilarity	59.9	67.0	70.7	78.7	76.6	84.0
Black Dominance[2]	34.3	45.8	56.9	71.6	74.3	79.8
Percent of Blacks in Tracts which are %80+ Black	0.0	12.5	22.7	52.5	59.2	74.6

1. In thousands
2. The average percent Black of tracts across the city, weighted by the number of blacks in each tract.

(1) pre-1950 projects, (2) 1950–70 projects, and (3) scattered-site housing in each tract.[4]

Data describing the social and economic characteristics of local populations and housing were taken from the published decennial census tabulations. Residential, housing, and journey-to-work data were obtained from the 1934 Works Progress Administration (WPA) Real Estate Survey. The survey, actually a census of the city, included many of the indicators currently found in the Census of Population and Housing. The variable "streetcar suburbs" has been operationalized as the percentage of the 1934 work force using public rail transit weighted by the average length, in time, of the journey to work for each tract.

The distance from the center of the city is measured in terms of the distance from City Hall, which is located (1) between the terminals of two commuter railroads serving the city and (2) above the intersection of two major subway lines. The City Hall tract is also the center of the census tracts with the greatest access to manufacturing jobs in 1928 and 1972 and with the largest number of nonmanufacturing jobs in 1970.

Information on the industrial structure of the city was taken from the *Industrial Directory of Pennsylvania*, published periodically since 1914. We have used the 1928 and 1972 editions of the directory and coded the locations of manufacturing in the city for those two years. These data show that industrial decline has been massive. In 1928 there were about 308,000 manufacturing jobs in the city. War industries provided a temporary renewal of manufacturing activity, but by 1972 the city lost 125,000 of the 328,000 manufacturing jobs present in 1947. Although the greatest loss of manufacturing employment has been in the areas of the city that contained the largest number of jobs in 1928, there remains a strong correlation (.70) between the number of industrial jobs in 1928 and in 1972. Between 1972 and 1978, manufacturing employment declined by an additional 25 percent.

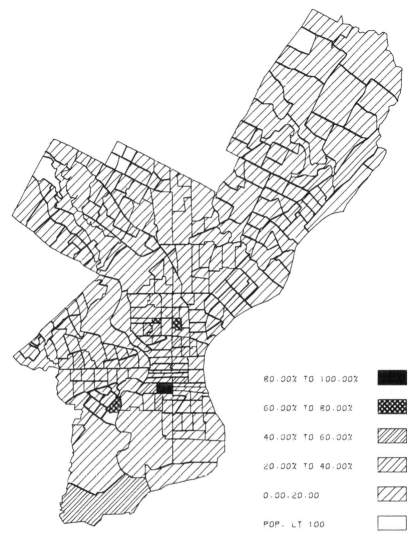

Figure 1. Percentage Black in Philadelphia, 1930

Results: Racial Change, Public Housing, and Black Concentrations, 1930–1980

The relative size of the black and white populations for each of the census years between 1930 and 1980 for the city of Philadelphia is presented in Table 1. The city's population grew until 1950, when, partially as a result of white suburbanization, there was a substantial decline in the number of whites. Since

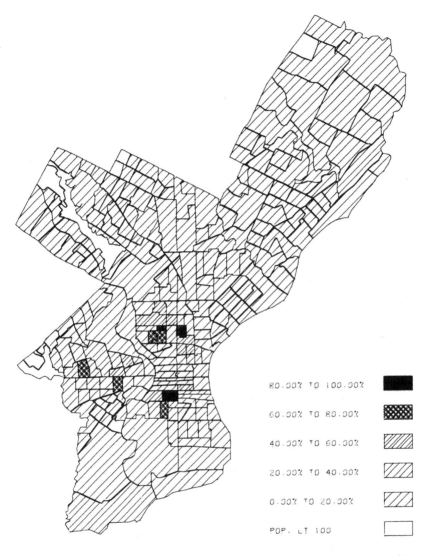

80.00% TO 100.00%	■
60.00% TO 80.00%	▓
40.00% TO 60.00%	▨
20.00% TO 40.00%	▨
0.00% TO 20.00%	▨
POP. LT 100	☐

SOC. SCI. DATA LIBRARY. TEMPLE UNIV.

Figure 2. Percentage Black in Philadelphia, 1940

1970 the number of blacks also has declined, although to a lesser extent than whites. As a consequence of these demographic patterns, the percentage of the population that was black increased from 11 in 1930 to 39 in 1980.

Also shown in Table 1 are three measures of racial segregation. First, the index of dissimilarity reflects the percentage of either the black or white population that would be required to move to a tract dominated by the other race in order to achieve racial balance. Second, the less frequently used measure of

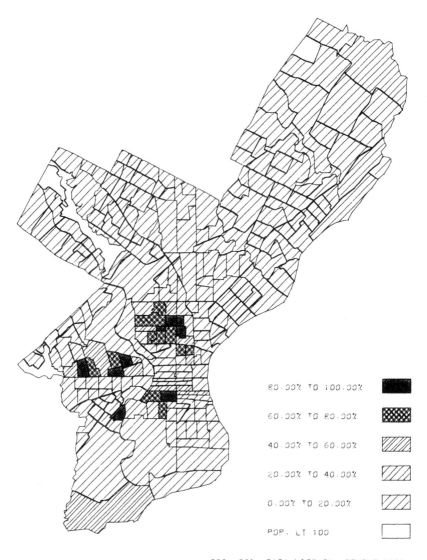

Figure 3. Percentage Black in Philadelphia, 1950

"black dominance" is the average percentage of the tracts' population that is black, weighted by the number of blacks in each tract. The third measure is the more straightforward percentage of the black population that lives in census tracts that are over 80 percent black. (See Figures 1–6.)

As can readily be seen, the level of racial segregation (measured by dissimilarity, dominance, and percentage of blacks in 80 percent black tracts) has increased steadily over the half-century covered by these data.[5] The exception

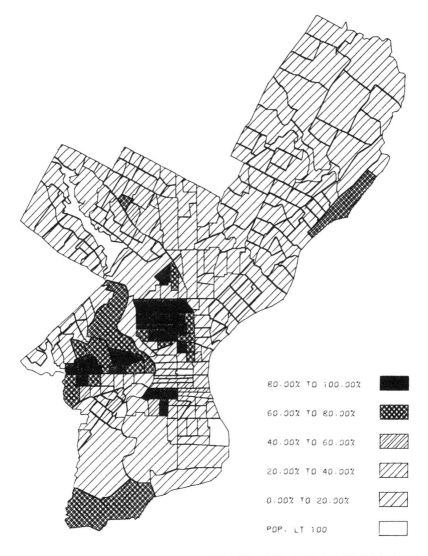

80.00% TO 100.00%

60.00% TO 80.00%

40.00% TO 60.00%

20.00% TO 40.00%

0.00% TO 20.00%

POP. LT 100

SOC. SCI. DATA LIBRARY. TEMPLE UNIV.

Figure 4. Percentage Black in Philadelphia, 1960

to the historical trend occurred in 1970, when there was a slight decline in the index of dissimilarity from the previous peak in 1960; by 1980 the pattern returned to its original form of increasing segregation. Apparently the 1970 census "caught" a relatively large number of neighborhoods undergoing racial transition. This "integration" was temporary.

The association between public housing and blacks is shown in Table 2, which presents the zero order correlations between the percentage of the tract's

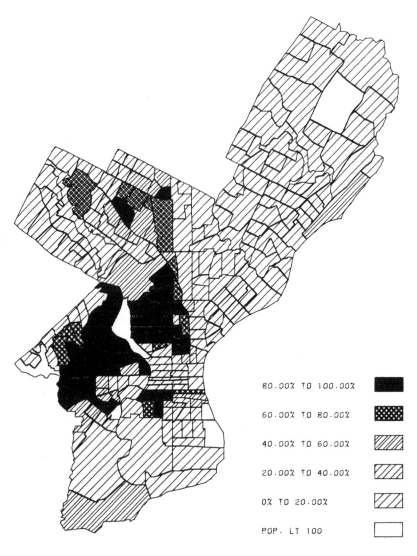

SOC. SCI. DATA LIBRARY. TEMPLE UNIV.

Figure 5. Percentage Black in Philadelphia, 1970

population that was black for each census year between 1930 and 1980 and the presence of pre-1950 public housing, projects constructed between 1950 and 1970, and scattered-site housing. (See Figures 7–9.)

We find there is no association between the pre-1950 projects and black concentrations. There are positive relationships between (1) the locations of post-1950 projects, (2) scattered-site developments, and (3) the percentage black. Yet these relationships are strongest for the census years preceding the

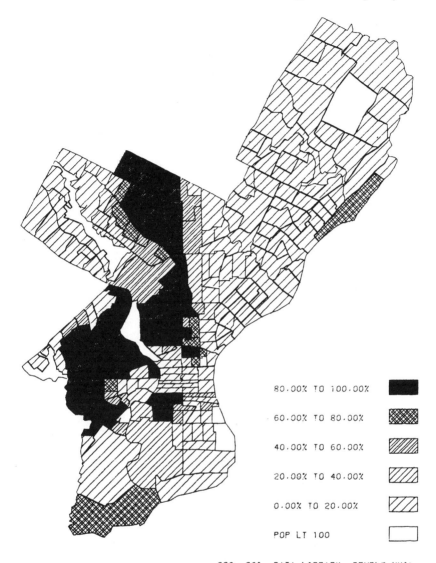

80.00% TO 100.00%

60.00% TO 80.00%

40.00% TO 60.00%

20.00% TO 40.00%

0.00% TO 20.00%

POP LT 100

SOC. SCI. DATA LIBRARY, TEMPLE UNIV.

Figure 6. Percentage Black in Philadelphia, 1980

development of public housing (e.g., 1950 and the large projects, and 1960 and scattered-site locations). These data do not support the hypothesis that public housing increased black concentrations in the neighborhoods in which it was placed.

The relationship between the location of public housing and the city's growing black population is also shown in Table 3, where we have grouped census tracts by the presence and nature of the public housing located within (i.e.,

Table 2. Correlations between Percentage Black in Tracts and Presence of Public Housing

	1930	1940	1950	1960	1970	1980
Pre-1950 Projects	.025	.008	.031	-.004	.002	.004
1950-1970 Projects	.325	.324	.352	.314	.302	.264
Scattered Site Housing	.355	.370	.433	.583	.672	.633

PRE-1954 PROJECTS

NO PROJECTS

SOC. SCI. DATA LIBRARY. TEMPLE UNIV.

Figure 7. Pre-1954 Public Housing Projects

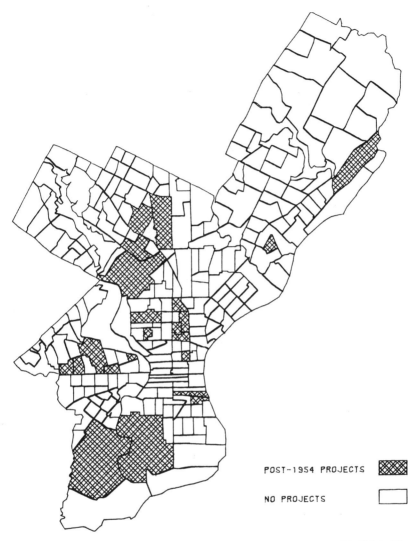

POST-1954 PROJECTS

NO PROJECTS

SOC. SCI. DATA LIBRARY. TEMPLE UNIV.

Figure 8. Post-1954 Public Housing Projects

no public housing, pre-1950 projects, post-1950 projects, and scattered-site housing). Three census tracts contain old and new projects. Seventeen of the 92 tracts containing scattered-site housing also have large projects. For each of these four categories, we have calculated the average percentage of the tracts' population that was black for each of the census years between 1930 and 1980. These data are presented graphically in Figure 10.

Areas containing public housing received disproportionate numbers of the

SOC. SCI. DATA LIBRARY. TEMPLE UNIV.

Figure 9. Scattered Site Housing in Philadelphia, 1976

city's growing black population. Although the black proportion of the population increased from 11 percent in 1930 to 39 percent in 1980, for those tracts that contained no public housing the proportion of black residents increased from 5 to 16 percent. The tracts that were selected to become the site of public housing after 1950 contained larger and growing proportions of blacks in the years before such siting decisions were made. As shown in Figure 1, the rate of increase in the black proportion of residents in public housing tracts either did not change or in fact began to level off after the introduction of public housing.

Table 3. Percentage Black of Census Tracts Containing Public Housing

	1930	1940	1950	1960	1970	1980
No Public Housing	4.6	4.7	5.3	7.1	11.4	15.8
Pre-1950 Projects	12.5	16.4	22.4	29.6	40.4	48.0
1950-1970 Projects	23.4	28.4	39.6	53.1	64.3	69.3
Scattered Site Housing	14.8	18.2	25.5	46.5	59.8	66.1

These data suggest three preliminary conclusions: (1) that some census tracts were more likely to experience racial transition—from black to white—before public housing was introduced, (2) that public housing was located in areas that were becoming increasingly black, and (3) that the introduction of public housing had little or no effect on the "trajectory" of racial transition.

Alternatively, we suggest that the character of neighborhoods—including their economic profiles, residential histories, distances from the central business district, and real estate values—is an important determinant of whether or not they experience racial transition and become the sites of public housing.

In order to more fully examine these hypotheses, we have relied on multiple regression analysis. This enables us to examine the impact of the racial character of neighborhoods on the location of public housing, while controlling for

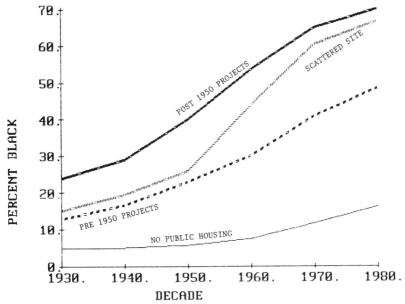

Figure 10. Average Percentage Black of Census Tracts Containing Public Housing

their historical and ecological character. Similarly, we may examine the impact of public housing on the subsequent movement of blacks, controlling for the neighborhood's ecological history.

The independent variables used to predict both housing project locations and black concentrations are (1) distance from the center of the city, (2) access to manufacturing employment in 1928 and 1972, (3) whether or not the neighborhood was a streetcar suburb in 1934, (4) the percentage black in 1930, and (5) the mean property value of a census tract in 1934.

These data permit tests of the impact of race on project location for projects constructed during the 1950s and 1960s, and on the development of scattered-site housing in the late 1960s and early 1970s. We have provided three tests of the impact of public housing on the movement of blacks in subsequent census years: (1) the impact of the old project locations on the concentrations of blacks in 1950, (2) the impact of both old and new projects on black location in 1970, and (3) the impact of scattered-site housing, constructed primarily in the late 1960s and early 1970s, on black location in 1980.

The results of these various analyses are summarized in Table 4. The regression coefficients for those variables found to be significantly related to the location of public housing, or to black concentrations, are also reported.[6]

Looking first at the results predicting the location of large projects, which ignore the location of blacks, we find that projects were likely to be located near the center of the city in neighborhoods with relatively low housing values and in neighborhoods that were previously streetcar suburbs. Industrial job access is not related to project location. When we include the percentage of the tract's population that was black in 1950, we find that the effects of distance to the center of the city and streetcar suburbs (both of which predict black location) are statistically insignificant. Previous housing values remain strong and significant. Race is the most important factor, indicating that projects built after 1950 were located in areas that were black in 1950. Finally, we find a small, negative, statistically insignificant effect of the older project locations on black concentrations. This means that there was not an overwhelming propensity to locate newer projects in tracts already containing public housing. In essence, then, our results indicate that projects were located in areas that were black or vulnerable to becoming black, but were not necessarily those with existing stocks of public housing.

The equations predicting the location of scattered-site housing are similar to those predicting the location of projects—in neighborhoods that are close to the center of the city, in the old streetcar suburbs, and in areas with relatively inexpensive housing. Including the percentage black in 1960 in the equation reduces the impact of each of these variables, although they remain statistically significant. The effects of project location on subsequent scattered-site locations are contradictory. We find that the effect of an older, pre–1950 project is negative, and that the impact of newer projects is positive (i.e., in general, there are

Table 4. Factors Affecting the Location of Public Housing and Racial Concentrations (Standardized Regression Coefficients)

Dependent Variables	Distance to City Center[1]	Industrial Job Access[2]	Street Car Suburb[3]	Housing Value 1934	PERCENT BLACK 1950	1960	1970	PUBLIC HOUSING LOCATION Pre-1950	1950-1970	Scattered Site	R²
Post-1954 Housing Project	-.157	n.s.	.114	- 259				n.s.			.117
	n.s.	n.s.	n.s.	- 222	.414						.232
Scattered Site Housing	- 339	n.s.	.135	- 171				- 124	.135		.225
	- 260	n.s.	.101	- 160		.191		-.118	.090		.248
Percent Black 1950	-.056	n.s.	.066	-.069	.878			n.s.			.851
Percent Black 1970	-.276	-.180	.162	n.s.	.572			n.s.	n.s.		.503
Percent Black 1980	n.s.	-.091	n.s.	n.s.			.966	n.s.	n.s.	.074	.878

[1] Miles to the center of the city, i.e., City Hall.

[2] The number of industrial jobs in 1927 (1972) within one mile of the census tract. Recoded to value of 1 if fewer than 1,000 jobs, 2 if 1,000 to 4,999 jobs, 3 if 5,000 to 9,999 jobs, and 4 if 10,000 or more jobs. 1972 data used in equation percent Black in 1980.

[3] Percent of workers using rail transport to commute to work weighted by the average length of time for commuting, 1934.

fewer scattered-site units in areas with pre–1950 projects, and more scattered-site units in neighborhoods containing the more recent developments).

The parallel nature of the results predicting both large public housing projects and scattered-site housing suggests that, although these are not the same neighborhoods, they are similar in historical-ecological terms. Both large projects and scattered-site housing are located in neighborhoods that are relatively close to the center of the city, in neighborhoods that have lower real estate values, and in old streetcar suburbs. These areas, because they were abandoned by whites moving to new suburban locations after World War II, provided greater opportunity for the development of public housing without the potential resistance of stable and politically connected communities. These historical-ecological characteristics are also associated with increasing black concentrations. Thus, it is expected that the inclusion of race in the prediction equation reduces their relative importance.

We now turn to the equations examining the impact of public housing on black concentrations. The first equation examines the location of blacks in 1950 and their relation to (1) the location of blacks in 1930, (2) the distance from the center of the city, (3) the value of real estate, and (4) streetcar suburbs. Of these, the most important factor determining the location of blacks in 1950 was their location in 1930. This is exactly what should be expected, given the little change in the spatial distribution of blacks over this twenty-year period. The change that did occur was largely one of increasing the percentage black in previously black areas. Areas that had lower housing values in 1934, were the old streetcar suburbs, or were close to the center of the city were also likely to experience growth in their black populations. We find no effect of the pre–1950 projects on the growth of black concentrations during this period.

The second equation predicting black location in 1970 tests the impact of the old (pre–1950) and more recent (post–1950) projects on surrounding neighborhoods. Between 1950 and 1970 numerous neighborhoods underwent racial transition. This was also the time when much of the city's public housing was constructed. Thus, this time period provides a good test of the "spillover hypothesis."

The results obtained indicate that, at least in terms of racial transition, public housing was not important. Rather, the 1970 location of blacks is best explained by economic and social forces reflecting the changing historical ecology of the city. Controlling for their previous locations, we find that in 1970 blacks were more likely to be concentrated in areas that historically had lower real estate values, in the old streetcar suburbs, and in neighborhoods nearer the center of the city. We also find a strong negative effect of industrial job access on black movement. Industrial neighborhoods, even though of generally lower housing value ($r = -.297$) and closer to the center of the city ($r = .733$), proved to be barriers to black movement. Unable to break these barriers, blacks became concentrated in neighborhoods without access to industrial employment.

When we control for structural characteristics of neighborhoods (such as historical housing values and employment base), we find that the relationship between projects and subsequent black concentrations is spurious. Blacks have moved into, and projects have been put into, the areas of the city no longer eagerly sought after by the higher income populations or by industry.

Looking finally at the equation predicting the location of blacks in 1980, we find that three factors appear to be important. Clearly the primary factor is black location in 1970. Beyond this, access to industrial employment, as measured by the location of jobs in 1972, continues to be a barrier to black movement. Scattered-site housing also has a significant, although small, effect on black movement.[7] Its effect, although significant, is infinitesimal, adding little to our understanding of black movement in the last decade. Previous real estate values and streetcar suburbs are no longer significantly related to black residential change. We suspect that such areas were largely "filled in" by 1970. In the last decade, we witnessed the first significant movement of blacks into areas that were previously of greater value and into the "first ring" of the automobile suburbs.

Summary and Conclusion

The results of this analysis lead us to a relatively straightforward general conclusion. The position of a neighborhood in the historical ecology of a city is the primary determinant of its internal, racial character. Except for the very small effect of scattered-site location on the concentrations of blacks in 1980, we find virtually no evidence—over the last fifty years of Philadelphia's history of black migration and movement—that the location of public housing in a neighborhood stigmatized the neighborhood so as to produce white flight or black invasion-succession. In short, the evidence presented adds little weight to the spillover hypothesis.

A very different conclusion must be drawn concerning the impact of race on the location of public housing. There is no relationship between the concentrations of blacks in 1930 and the locations of the housing projects constructed before 1950. After 1950, housing projects were most likely to be built in areas with lower real estate values, near the center of the city, and in the old streetcar suburbs. Yet, when tests control for these factors, it can be shown that public housing has been constructed since 1950 in neighborhoods with a disproportionate number of blacks.

Black concentrations, though not affected by the location of public housing, do appear to be generated in neighborhoods that are being systematically abandoned (i.e., areas with lower real estate values and areas being vacated by the suburbanizing middle class). Although there has been a significant decline in the level of industrial manufacturing in the city, blacks have not entered neighborhoods that are relatively close to industrial concentrations. These historical-ecological characteristics reflect a neighborhood's position in the emerging urban structure. They have been important determinants of the location of the black ghetto and, through it, the location of public housing.

At the most general level, it appears to us that the perspective suggested by historical ecology provides the most parsimonious explanation for public housing's role in the development of the racial ghetto. This understanding of the black community suggests that, rather than being a residual of past cultures or missed opportunities, it is indeed a product of modern times coupled with the investments and disinvestments of the past. It has emerged within the constraints imposed by the changing ecological relationships between the black ghetto and the economic activities that dominate the local political economy.

Limitations and Implications

There are several relatively obvious limitations to the present analysis. First, we have failed to directly test the hypotheses suggested by Meyerson and Banfield (1955) regarding the intervention of local political organization on the site selection process. By relying on the location and impact of public housing that was actually constructed, we have ignored the decisions leading to the selection and ultimate construction of housing in these particular neighborhoods.[8]

We have used relatively gross measures of "neighborhood" and of public housing. Census tracts are arbitrarily drawn boundaries that may, but often do not, approximate the social organization of a given community. Our measures of racial segregation and concentration are based on census tracts. Although this is appropriate for tests of the impact of public housing on the surrounding neighborhood, it assumes the even distribution of racial groups across the tracts and thus ignores the differential concentration of blacks and whites on different blocks within given tracts. It is reasonable to expect that public housing located on the edge of census tracts may have a significant impact on adjacent tracts, as well as on tracts in which it is located. Similarly, the impact of public housing may depend on the size and even architecture of the projects. More refined measures of public housing—including its size, architecture, and proximity— and of racial segregation may produce results different from those suggested by the present analysis.

One of the criticisms of our analysis is that we did not use information on the social characteristics of the project tenants to separate them from families living in the surrounding neighborhoods. The census reports summary data on the population of each tract without identifying families living in public housing. It has been suggested that the results of our analysis, showing no spillover effect, stem from the fact that the Philadelphia Housing Authority has successfully matched the racial characteristics of project tenants with the racial composition of the surrounding neighborhoods. If white tenants were placed in white neighborhoods, and conversely black tenants in black neighborhoods, the racial spillover effect would be minimized. We doubt this argument. Except for the residents of senior citizen projects, almost all new tenants of public housing since 1950 have been black. That the location of projects in neighborhoods did not have an effect on the neighborhoods' rate of racial transition, even though a black population was being added to a racially mixed population, adds even stronger support to our conclusion that public housing had no effect on the surrounding neighborhood. These somewhat anomalous results suggest that the contribution of public housing to racial segregation may have taken place at smaller geographic levels than census tracts, that is, through the creation of black enclaves within racially mixed neighborhoods.[9]

Albert Hunter (1979:269) has noted that "to try to understand the neighborhood solely by focusing on the internal structure and dynamics is to end up with carefully documented description, but a persistent failure to understand the causal explanations of the processes that create the variety of neighborhood forms and constrain the conduct of neighborhood life." The "failure of public housing" may be best understood, not in terms of the characteristics of the residents (Rainwater 1970), architecture (Yancey 1971; Newman 1973), or surrounding community, but rather in terms of the relationship of the community to the city's dominant institutions. This set of relationships and the resulting constraints on the poor are central to the emergence and maintenance of these communities in New York, St. Louis, Philadelphia, and elsewhere.[10]

NOTES

1. In an unsigned comment (*University of Pennsylvania Law Review* 1974) it was pointed out that courts, once involved in this sort of legal action, have three potential injunctive actions: (1) the negative injunctive—stop the construction, (2) the affirmative injunctive—begin building, and (3) the injunction that directs agencies to "carry out their ministerial duties." The weapon of courts to assure compliance with their rulings is the contempt citation. In very few cases has a court resorted to such action, and where it has it has still not seen great compliance. Thus, "courts appear to be ill-equipped to cope effectively with legal challenges to LHA site selection policies by ghetto residents. The intersection of complex housing statutes and political constraints with judicially ordered injunctive relief will very likely not lead to housing construction" (*University of Pennsylvania Law Review* 1974:1346).

2. Laska et al. (1982:198) have observed that in New Orleans old residential neighborhoods "were being abandoned by the wealthy and filtered to the lower classes. As a result of the disinvestment several public housing complexes were constructed during the 1950s in these same neighborhoods."

3. Temporary defense housing constructed in the 1940s and "senior citizen" projects have been excluded from this analysis.

4. Although this procedure leads us to ignore considerable variation in the data, there are good, substantive reasons for doing so—even if the data were not so highly skewed. It is reasonable to argue that there are in fact two decisions involved. The first

decision relates to where the project might be located; and the second, to its relative size. By creating "dummy variables," we are restricting our analysis to the outcome of the site selection process and ignoring the question of the number of publicly owned units constructed on each site.

5. Hershberg et al. (1979) have found that this trend goes back to 1850, when the black population in the city was, by today's standards, residentially integrated.

6. A special technique was used for the prediction equations of post-1950 public housing projects. Because only 22 census tracts contained projects (8.9 percent of all census tracts), something had to be done to make the dependent variable more nearly conform to the assumption in regression that the dependent variable, as well as the other variables, would be normally distributed. In each equation, all of the census tracts with public housing, and a random sample of census tracts without public housing, were used in an effort to produce a binomial distribution (i.e., tracts with public housing versus tracts without public housing) with the largest possible variance (i.e., .50). The same equation was derived 20 times, each time using a different random sample of tracts without public housing. The final results presented are the results of the 20 trials. A rough approximation of the "significance" of the coefficients can be made by building confidence intervals about the estimated means with the standard deviations provided below.

	Mean	Std. Dev.
R Squared	.195	.084
Housing Value, 1934	−.259	.091
Streetcar Suburb	.114	.123
R Squared	.318	.072
% Black, 1950	.414	.091
Housing Value, 1934	−.222	.094

For the analysis of public housing locations, we have run equations that include only the historical-ecological factors. The same equations were also solved including the racial composition variable.

7. Although not shown in Table 5, we have run this equation with scattered-site housing eliminated (even though it is found to be significant). With scattered-site locations included, the explained variance is .878; without it, the explained variance is .875.

8. Minimally, it is necessary to obtain information regarding the site selection process, including the specification of the neighborhoods that were originally proposed but did not receive public housing. Meyerson and Banfield suggest that there were significant differences in political organization and efficacy between neighborhoods that received public housing and those that did not.

9. The major weakness of the present analysis lies in the fact that it is limited to one city; thus, it is difficult to make clear generalizations from these results to other urban places. Although ours is a case study of a single city, Philadelphia shares basic characteristics with other northeastern cities currently undergoing the transformation from industrial to postindustrial metropolises. We have already noted the parallels between public housing in Philadelphia and in other cities. It is also similar to the conditions of the poor in Manchester in the nineteenth century. Engels (1935:77) quotes from the *Manchester Weekly Times* of 20 July 1872:

The smell there was so frightful that the healthiest man would have felt sick in a very short space of time. This disgusting hole was inhabited by a family of seven. ... She (a tenant) was of the opinion that the place was not fit for pigs to live in but on account of the low rent—one and sixpense a week—she had taken it, because her husband had been out of work a lot recently owing to sickness. The impression made upon the observer by this court and the inhabitants huddled in it, as though in a premature grave, was one of utter helplessness.

We find the similarity of the description of a Manchester "tenement" and observations of contemporary public housing projects striking. The disparity of time periods, cultures, political structures, and economic relations might suggest that there may be very different antecedents of poverty, and thus our analysis has specific limits in its generalizability. We disagree with this conclusion.

10. As a result of recent structural changes in the economy of Philadelphia (the decline of manufacturing and the growth of the centrally located professional-service economy), we are beginning to see neighborhoods that were previously abandoned, and thus selected for public housing, now being redeveloped. As a consequence, several housing projects are located in new, developing communities. Townhouses, complete with skylight, sundeck, and nineteenth-century facade, are renovated across the street from high-rise towers for the poor. Public housing appears to retard such development only to the degree that it removes real estate from the private market. Recent proposals to replace the nonelderly tenants with the elderly or to sell such projects to private developers—to turn them into condominiums or tear them down—are not surprising. We see no reason why the historical pattern of continued isolation of the poor from areas of value and growth will be broken now, and thus we object to such proposals. Indeed, these few communities represent the possibility of a change in the relationship between the poor and the city's dominant institutions. They provide a natural experiment, in which we may examine the impact of at least the physical integration of the poor with the not-so-poor and their institutions. We suspect that the outcome of these experiments will depend more on the social and economic integration, and less on the level geographic isolation, of the poor with the rest of us.

REFERENCES

Bauman, John F. 1974. "Black Slums/Black Projects: The New Deal and Negro Housing in Philadelphia." *Pennsylvania History* 41 (July): 311–38.

Engels, Frederick. 1935. *The Housing Question.* New York: International Publishers.

Ericksen, Eugene P., and William L. Yancey. 1979. "Work and Residence in Industrial Philadelphia." *Journal of Urban History* 5: 147–82.

Friedman, L. M. 1966. "Public Housing and the Poor: An Overview." *California Law Review* 54: 642–69.

Gold, Diana E. 1980. *Housing Market Discrimination: Causes and Effects of Slum Formation.* New York: Praeger.

Greenberg, Stephanie W. 1981. "Industrial Location and Ethnic Residential Patterns in an Industrializing City: Philadelphia, 1880." In *Philadelphia*, edited by T. Hershberg, pp. 204–29. New York: Oxford University Press.

Hershberg, T., Alan Burstein, Eugene P. Ericksen, Stephanie Greenberg, and William L. Yancey. 1979. "A Tale of Three Cities: Blacks, Immigrants and Opportunity in Philadelphia: 1850–1880, 1930, 1970." *Annals of the American Academy of Political and Social Science* 444: 55–81.

Heuman, Leonard F. 1979. "Housing Needs and Housing Solutions: Changes in Perspectives 1960 to 1978." In *The Changing Structure of the Metropolis*, edited by G. Tobin. California: Sage.

Hunter, Albert. 1979. "The Urban Neighborhood: Its Analytical and Social Context." *Urban Affairs Quarterly* 14: 267–88.

Katona, George, Charles Liniger, and Eva Mueller. 1965. *The 1964 Survey of Consumer Finances*. Ann Arbor: Institute for Social Research, University of Michigan.

Kusmer, Kenneth L. 1976. *A Ghetto Takes Shape: Black Cleveland, 1870–1930*. Urbana: University of Illinois Press.

Laska, Shirley, B. Jerrol, M. Seaman, and Dennis R. McSeveney. 1982. "Inner-City Reinvestment: Neighborhood Characteristics and Spatial Patterns over Time." *Urban Studies* 19: 155–65.

Lewis, Oscar. 1966. *La Vida: A Puerto Rican Family in the Culture of Poverty— San Juan and New York*. New York: Random House.

Lieberson, Stanley. 1963. *Ethnic Patterns in American Cities*. Glencoe: The Free Press.

———. 1980. *A Piece of the Pie*. Berkeley: University of California Press.

Logan, John R., and Mark Schneider. 1982. "Racial Segregation and Racial Change in American Suburbs." A paper presented to the American Sociological Association, San Francisco, August.

Meyerson, Martin, and Edward Banfield. 1955. *Politics, Planning and the Public Interest*. New York: The Free Press.

Moore, William. 1969. *The Vertical Ghetto: Every Day Life in an Urban Project*. New York: Random House.

Newman, Oscar. 1973. *Defensible Space*. New York: Macmillan Co.

Peel, Norman D., Garth E. Pickett, and Stephen T. Buehl. 1970. "Racial Discrimination in Public Housing Site Selection." *Stanford Law Review* 23: 63–147.

Pratt, E. E. 1917. *Industrial Causes of Congestion in New York*. New York: Columbia University Press.

Rabin, Yale. n.d. (ca. 1979). "The Whitman Park Townhouse Public Housing Project and Its Relationship to Black Population and Housing Policies of Government Agencies." Mimeographed.

Rainwater, Lee. 1970. *Behind Ghetto Walls: Black Family Life in a Federal Slum*. Chicago: Aldine.

Report of the National Advisory Commission on Civil Disorders. 1968. New York: Bantam Books.

Roncek, Dennis, Ralph Bell, and Jeffrey M. A. Francik. 1981. "Housing Projects and Crime: Testing a Proximity Hypothesis." *Social Problems* 29: 151–66.

Salisbury, Harrison. 1954. *The Shookup Generation*. New York: New York Times.

Saunders, L., and M. J. Woodford. 1979. "The Effect of Federally Assisted Housing Projects on Property Values." Colorado: Colorado State University Extension Service, Jefferson County.

Schmidt, J. H. 1980. "Kettering Square Property Valuation Survey." Montgomery County Fair Housing Center and Miami Valley Regional Planning Association. Mimeographed.

Schnore, Leo F. 1964. *The Urban Scene.* New York: The Free Press.

Shannon et al. v. U.S. Department of Housing and Urban Development (HUD). 1970. *Federal Reporter* 2, D series: 809–23.

Taeuber, Karl E., and Alma F. Taeuber. 1965. *Negroes in Cities.* Chicago: Aldine.

University of Pennsylvania Law Review. 1974. "The Limits of Litigation: Public Housing Site Selection and the Failure of Injunctive Relief." Vol. 122: 1330–65.

Varady, David P. 1982. "Indirect Benefits of Subsidized Housing Programs." *Journal of the American Planning Association* 48: 432–40.

Ward, David. 1971. *Cities and Immigrants: A Geography of Change in Nineteenth Century America.* New York: Oxford University Press.

Warner, Sam Bass, Jr. 1962. *Streetcar Suburbs: The Process of Growth in Boston.* Cambridge: Harvard University Press.

―――, and Colin B. Burke. 1969. "Cultural Change and the Ghetto." *Journal of Contemporary History* 4: 173–88.

Welfeld, Irving. 1976. "The Courts and Desegregated Housing: The Meaning (If Any) of the Gautreaux Case." *The Public Interest* 45: 123–35.

Yancey, William L. 1971. "Architecture, Interaction and Social Control: The Case of a Large Scale Public Housing Project." *Environment and Behavior* 3 (3–21 March).

―――, and Eugene P. Ericksen. 1979. "The Antecedents of Community: The Economic and Institutional Structure of Urban Neighborhoods." *American Sociological Review* 44: 253–62.

Chapter Thirteen
On the Possibility of Achieving
Racial Integration through Subsidized Housing

JOHN YINGER*

Achieving stable racial integration in residential areas is a pressing goal of many policymakers. Although not universally accepted, this goal has gained importance from several recent court decisions that require housing authorities in large cities, which depend heavily on federal housing programs, to provide housing in integrated environments.[1] Unfortunately, however, the operation of the private housing market and continuing high levels of racial prejudice among whites place severe constraints on the ability of government housing programs to promote racial integration. This chapter examines the social scientific evidence on these constraints. Policymakers must determine the importance of the goal of racial integration. This study is designed to assist policymakers by explaining the possibilities and the limitations of housing policy for achieving racial integration and by determining the provisions that would make a subsidized housing program, such as the Section 8 program, as effective as possible in fostering racial integration.

Stable racial integration can exist only if blacks and whites choose to live in the same neighborhoods. Any subsidized housing program that attempts to foster racial integration must therefore account for the way that black and white households choose their residential locations. Specifically, such a program must reflect the preferences of the low-income households it is intended to serve. For example, subsidized housing should not be located far from low-skill jobs. Second, a program must recognize that most whites are prejudiced against blacks and are likely to react to the placement of an integrated project in their neighborhood. Any program that ignores this prejudice will probably generate racial hostility and white flight and will fail to achieve stable racial integration.

Thus, in order to foster racial integration, a subsidized housing program must carefully balance the preferences of participants against the reactions of white suburbanites. This chapter begins with an examination of these two factors. The first section explains how an analysis of residential location decisions can be used as a guide to participants' preferences; the second section reviews the literature on racial transition; and the third section shows how our knowledge about racial transition can be used to predict white reactions to integrated housing projects. The implications of this analysis for the design of a subsi-

*This research was supported by a consulting grant from the U.S. Department of Housing and Urban Development and has benefited from conversations with William C. Apgar, Jr., John M. Goering, Mary E. Lovely, and J. Milton Yinger.

dized housing program are presented in the fourth section, and related programs that could increase the chances of successfully achieving racial integration through subsidized housing are explored in the fifth section.

Policymakers have been concerned with the integration of housing projects and with the integration of the neighborhoods into which housing projects are placed. To keep manageable the scope of my inquiry, I have assumed that subsidized housing projects themselves are integrated. Furthermore, I have assumed that a subsidized housing program is politically feasible. These are both strong assumptions. Individual projects have their own racial dynamic and strenuous efforts may be required to keep them integrated.[2] In addition, opposition to subsidized housing programs, particularly when they involve integration, is strong. Recent court decisions require existing programs to strive for integration, but they cannot force the federal government to appropriate money for such programs.[3] In effect, this study investigates whether stable racial integration of neighborhoods would be possible if these two obstacles were overcome. Finally, although the discussion focuses on the integration of blacks into white neighborhoods, it also applies to the integration of Hispanics and of several other minority groups.

To avoid confusion, several terms should be defined at the outset. Households' residential location decisions are guided by their *preferences*, that is, by their attitudes about the desirability of various locations. *Racial prejudice* is one type of preference; white prejudice, for example, is a strong aversion to living near blacks (or other racial minorities). *Racial discrimination* in housing is a type of behavior; in particular, it consists of actions by the sellers of housing that constrain the housing choices of blacks. *Racial segregation* and *racial integration* are descriptive terms. Segregation refers to a situation in which blacks and whites live in separate locations; integration refers to a situation in which blacks and whites live together. *Stable* integration, which is the focus of this chapter, exists when blacks and whites both live in the same location over an extended period of time. For some purposes, it is useful to measure the *degree* of integration (or of segregation), which is the extent to which blacks and whites live together (or apart).

The Preferences of Program Participants

Without zoning constraints or racial discrimination, the operation of the housing market would lead to the sorting of households by income and preference. High-income households would outbid low-income households for housing in desirable locations, and, in general, each class of household would cluster around its places of employment.[4] Zoning complicates this process by preserving old patterns of location. For example, it sometimes prevents low-income households from moving into a high-income jurisdiction despite the fact that jobs for low-income households have moved into or near that jurisdiction. In other words, zoning limits housing market adjustments to new circumstances. Racial discrimination constitutes an additional constraint on black households. Many blacks are prevented from moving to their desired locations because of racial discrimination against them.[5]

The household-sorting process is a reflection of household demand for the characteristics of various residential locations. People tend to live near their places of employment, for example, because they bid more for housing in locations where they can save on commuting costs. And high-income households live in the most desirable neighborhoods because the demand for such neighborhoods, like the demand for any "good," increases with income.

One important goal of a subsidized housing program is to provide low-income households with access to the high-quality public services in suburbs that they cannot now obtain because of restrictive zoning, racial discrimination, and their own low income. This goal can be achieved by locating subsidized housing in suburbs with good services. It may be difficult, however, for policymakers to decide where to place housing projects within a suburb. Program participants might prefer to live in the most desirable neighborhoods, but their presence would stir up the hostility of residents and of other suburbanites who are too poor to live in those neighborhoods but too rich to receive subsidized housing. In my view, policymakers should maximize the probability that the housing program will succeed by minimizing the potential conflict between residents and participants.

Conflict between participants and residents will be minimized when subsidized housing is located in neighborhoods where the residents' income and preferences are as similar as possible to the participants' income and preferences. The way to implement this conflict-minimizing rule is to simulate a market process without zoning or discrimination. In other words, the best site selection policy is one that places participants in those locations where they would live if they had somewhat more income and did not face restrictive zoning or racial discrimination.

Participants in a subsidized housing program also care about their social links with the neighborhood in which they live. It would be a mistake, however, to expect a subsidized housing program to generate significant social interaction along class and racial lines. Existing evidence implies that low-income households, especially low-income minority households, will not be assimilated into middle-class suburban communities. Even in an integrated community without much variation in income, blacks and whites may not interact to a significant degree.[6]

Furthermore, integration through subsidized housing is not likely to reduce the racial prejudice of white suburbanites. The many studies of the "contact hypothesis" conclude that equal socioeconomic status is a necessary condition for prejudice reduction through social contact. This condition is not met, virtually by definition, for subsidized housing in the suburbs.[7]

Nevertheless, project design can influence social relations in three important ways. First, no one wants to live in a hostile environment, so a project better serves its tenants if it avoids stirring up the hostility of white residents. The link between project design and white reactions is explored in the next section.

Second, people who live in large, conspicuous housing projects are likely to be labeled as project residents and to carry this social stigma into many of their social interactions. Suttles (1968) describes the negative impact of this labeling on blacks, especially teenagers, in one community. The project label is an obstacle for anyone, but its impact is particularly powerful for minority teenagers who already face more than their share of obstacles. In my view, therefore, projects should be kept small to minimize this severe social stigma.

Finally, projects must recognize participants' preferences concerning their neighbors. Because low-income households are not likely to interact with high-income households and because black households may not interact with white households, projects may require some critical mass to provide enough social interaction to make them attractive to participants.

The need for a neighborhood-based social network should not be exaggerated, however. Recent research shows that most people develop their important social interactions through their work, not through their residence.[8] Every project need not provide a complete social network. In my view, the best strategy is to acknowledge the range of participants' preferences by providing a variety of project sizes—from one unit up to a few small apartment buildings—and, to the extent possible, by letting each participant household choose the type of project it prefers. The mix of project sizes could be adjusted as one learns about the mix of participants' preferences.

Blacks' attitudes about integration in their neighborhoods are also relevant for deciding on project size. Many black households do not want to be the only blacks in a neighborhood, so they would not want to live in a one-unit project in a white suburb. The existing survey evidence suggests, however, that most blacks are quite open to living in integrated environments and that many blacks are willing to be pioneers in previously all-white neighborhoods. The survey by Farley, Bianchi, and Colasanto (1979), for example, found that 38 percent of the blacks interviewed would be willing to move into an all-white neighborhood and that 95 percent would be willing to move into a neighborhood that was 14 percent black. These types of neighborhoods are not the first choice of many blacks, but they are acceptable.

Suppose blacks are fairly evenly represented in all subsidized housing projects in all-white suburbs. Then the size of a project determines the racial composition of the neighborhood in which that project is located. The appropriate way to account for participant preferences is to provide projects of various sizes— and hence with a variety of implications for neighborhood racial composition—and, again to the extent possible, to let each black household choose the project it prefers.

Whites' Reactions to Market-Generated Racial Integration

Whites' reactions to the racial integration of their neighborhoods have been studied extensively. This section reviews what is known about racial integration generated by market forces; the next section expands this analysis to racial integration through subsidized housing. By way of preview, the outlook for widespread, stable racial integration through market forces is not encouraging at the present time. In most cases, the entry of a significant number of blacks into an all-white neighborhood discourages white movement into the area and eventually leads to complete racial turnover. However, integration through subsidized housing is different from market-generated integration in several important respects. An analysis of these differences indicates that, within certain limits, a carefully designed subsidized housing program probably could increase racial integration substantially.

In deciding where to live, households consider the price of housing, accessibility to jobs, housing characteristics, and neighborhood characteristics. From the standpoint of prejudiced white residents, the entry of blacks into a white neighborhood represents a decline in the desirability of that neighborhood. As soon as blacks move in, therefore, the most prejudiced whites move away to neighborhoods that remain all white. Other whites leave as the number of blacks grows. Thus, unless this decline in desirability due to black entry is offset by an increase in desirability from some other factor, such as improved local public services, all prejudiced whites are likely to move out of integrating neighborhoods.

Schelling's (1972) well-known analysis allows us to be more precise about the predominance of complete racial turnover in the private housing market. This analysis shows that racial integration cannot be stable unless the distributions of white and black preferences meet certain strong conditions. To be specific, the presence of many whites who do not mind a few black neighbors is not sufficient to sustain stable integration. Consider a previously all-white neighborhood into which some blacks move. This neighborhood cannot remain stable at, say, 10 percent black unless at least 90 percent of the original whites are willing to stay in a neighborhood that is 10 percent black. Otherwise, the neighborhood will not retain enough whites to stop racial transition at 10 percent black. Similarly, stable integration is not possible at a given racial composition, say 10 percent black, unless the number of blacks willing to move into a largely white neighborhood is at least 10 percent of the original white population. This analysis is summarized by the notion of a tipping point, which Schelling defines as the percentage black above which stable integration cannot be maintained.

The survey by Farley, Bianchi, and Colasanto (1979) asked white households if they would move out of neighborhoods with various proportions of black residents, assuming that the blacks and whites had equal incomes and educations. The results suggest a tipping point at 7 percent black. Ninety-three percent of the whites would stay in a neighborhood that was 7 percent black, but only 76 percent of the whites would stay in a neighborhood that was 13 percent black. In other words, not enough whites would stay to sustain a neighborhood at 13 percent black, but stable integration might be possible if blacks were a smaller percentage of the neighborhood population.

The survey by Farley et al. also asked black households whether they would move into neighborhoods with various racial compositions. The results suggest that black attitudes are not a barrier to stable integration; as noted earlier, 38 percent of the blacks interviewed were willing to move into an all-white neighborhood. Strictly speaking, however, this conclusion depends on the number of blacks who are potential migrants into the neighborhood. This pool of potential black immigrants must be large enough so that 38 percent of the pool, which is the number of blacks willing to move in, constitutes enough blacks to sustain stable integration. In most cities, racial discrimination limits the housing opportunities of black households. When a neighborhood does open to blacks, therefore, the pool of potential black immigrants is usually large and there are likely to be more than enough black households to sustain integration.

The logic of tipping is somewhat different in the long run. Because households move regularly for nonracial reasons, a neighborhood can remain integrated in the long run only if white households are willing to move into it. Farley et al. also asked whites whether they would be willing to move into a neighborhood with various racial compositions. They found that only 73 percent of the whites would be willing to move into a neighborhood that was 7 percent black. This result, like the result for black immigrants, must be interpreted with care. If the pool of potential white immigrants is much larger than the neighborhood in question, then 73 percent of the pool may constitute more than 93 percent of the neighborhood, so that the integration can be sustained at 7 percent black—or even at a higher black representation. Hence, the survey results do not provide a definitive answer to the likelihood of stable integration in the long run. My own guess, based on the assumption that the pool of potential immigrants into a neighborhood tends to be larger than the neighborhood population, is that widespread, stable integration may be possible in the long run as long as blacks remain a small percentage of the neighborhood population.

The survey by Farley et al. reflects the preferences of the entire white population. To keep these survey results in perspective, note that the whites in a particular neighborhood may be more amenable to racial integration than whites generally. In addition, some subsets of the white population may be more willing to move into an integrated neighborhood than are the whites in a representative sample. The survey indicates that integration is difficult to maintain with a representative sample of the white population; it does not rule out the possibility that integration would work with a low-prejudice sample. What we would like to know, but do not, are the racial preferences of the whites who could be attracted to a particular integrating neighborhood. Under the reasonable assumption that some subsamples of whites have less racial prejudice than do others, integration at a high percentage black may be possible in a few neighborhoods in many metropolitan areas. But to the extent that the Detroit survey by Farley et al. is representative of the nation as a whole, widespread, stable integration through market forces is unlikely at any racial composition above a few percent black.[9]

The Schelling model is a useful starting point, but a complete analysis of racial integration must consider several other factors. First, information flows play an important role in the process of racial transition. As many researchers have documented, racial transition often is accompanied by white fears of declining property values, of deteriorating schools, and of rising crime rates. Furthermore, these fears are sometimes magnified, or even created, by the behavior of unscrupulous lenders and real estate brokers.[10] If racial transition is not confounded by class transition, these fears are unfounded. But in many cases, these fears become a self-fulfilling prophecy. The first blacks to move into a middle-income neighborhood typically are middle-income blacks. But the pool of middle-income blacks often is not large enough to fill the neighborhood (even when it is large enough to sustain integration). Hence, if whites flee the neighborhood when the first blacks move in, then the middle-income blacks are followed by low-income blacks who, because of racial discrimination, have nowhere else to go.[11] In short, racial transition is often caused or accelerated by misinformation, and stable integration may not be possible without strenuous efforts by fair housing groups or local governments to provide good information and to combat rumors.

Second, Schelling's analysis leaves out housing prices. The importance of this omission is clearly shown in an excellent paper by Schnare and MacRae (1978).[12] In most cases, racial transition takes place at the edge of a largely black area and is triggered when blacks' bids for housing rise above whites' bids. Under these circumstances, racial compositions that appear stable in Schelling's analysis actually are not stable because blacks are outbidding whites for housing, and rational landlords and real estate brokers prefer to sell to blacks. Indeed, Schnare and MacRae show that stable integration is not possible unless blacks' bids for housing rise more rapidly than do whites' bids as the percentage of the neighborhood that is white increases. Given what we know about racial attitudes, this case is highly implausible. It follows that stable integration in a single neighborhood at the edge of the black area is unlikely at any racial composition without some kind of government intervention.

This analysis of information and of housing prices reinforces the conclusion that market forces are unlikely to generate widespread, stable integration with more than minimal black representation. This conclusion is supported by existing evidence. American metropolitan areas are highly segregated and few neighborhoods remain integrated for long. So far as I know, every case of a stably integrated community with a substantial black population, such as Oak Park, Illinois, or Shaker Heights, Ohio, involves intervention by a well-financed housing center and by local government.[13]

Given current levels of racial prejudice, the logic of the Schelling model indicates that stable integration may be possible without intervention as long as blacks remain a small percentage of a neighborhood's population. Because of white fears and the role of housing prices, this outcome is unlikely near a largely black area, but it may occur in scattered middle-income white areas, where massive black in-migration is unlikely. This conclusion is supported by recent evidence, which suggests that many previously all-white neighborhoods now have a few black residents.[14]

Finally, existing patterns of racial transition depend in part on the persistence of racial discrimination in housing. Without discrimination, stable integration would be much more likely. As explained elsewhere (Yinger et al. 1979:118):

> Most of the research on racial transition has focused on the notion of racial "tipping" . . . in a single neighborhood and has not asked the broader question of how racial transition is distributed throughout an urban area.
>
> Once racial transition begins in a neighborhood, the notion of tipping may be relevant. But by focusing almost exclusively on tipping, the literature has ignored the possibility that discrimination focuses racial transition into certain neighborhoods and thereby magnifies the pressures that lead to complete racial turnover.

In effect, racial discrimination preserves the option of white families to live in all-white neighborhoods. Some neighborhoods may open up to blacks, but whites know they can escape blacks by leaving those neighborhoods. Without discrimination blacks might live throughout an urban area so that whites, with no all-white communities to flee to, would not move at the first sign of integration. Abrams (1947:26) recognized this point over thirty-five years ago. As he put it: "The most effective method for stabilizing all neighborhoods is to ease the pressure for housing by all minorities, provide them with the living space they need. . . . If in fact there were no race covenants and no exclusions practiced, there might be a more even distribution of minorities in all neighborhoods and no fear of a shift in racial composition."

As I show elsewhere (1976), this argument is perfectly rigorous; integration in all neighborhoods is an equilibrium pattern of residential location, regardless of the distributions of black and white preferences. In an urban area without racial discrimination, therefore, the outlook for stable integration through market forces would be considerably brighter.

Whites' Reactions to Racial Integration through Subsidized Housing

Integrating neighborhoods through subsidized housing projects differs from market-generated integration in two important ways:

1. Placing subsidized housing in suburbs involves class integration as well as racial integration.

2. Integration through subsidized housing is generated by government policy, not by blacks outbidding whites for housing as the black residential area expands.

The first difference might make integration through subsidized housing even more difficult to achieve than integration through market forces. Suburban whites, largely middle class, do not want to live with low-income households or with blacks, let alone with low-income blacks. These preferences are reflected in the facts that housing projects involving class and racial integration are rare and neighborhoods involving both types of integration are even rarer.[15] However, as noted earlier, class and racial prejudice are already mixed as causes of racial transition; anticipated class integration appears to accelerate white flight. Thus, we cannot determine the extent to which the class dimension of subsidized housing will accentuate white reactions.

It is clear, however, that white reactions to racial integration through subsidized housing are potentially very strong. The evidence demonstrates that whites tend to react negatively to market-generated integration. The class dimension magnifies this reaction to some degree and therefore magnifies the need to design projects with white prejudice in mind. As discussed in more detail in the next section, projects should be located so as to minimize conflict between black participants and white suburbanites.

The second difference leads to a more optimistic outlook for the possibility of stable integration through subsidized housing. To begin with, a subsidized housing project does not represent an extension of the black residential area; that is, it is integration at a distance from the main black area, not integration as part of the expansion of that area. This fact will influence white attitudes toward the project. Real estate brokers and public officials cannot play on the fear of massive invasion by blacks, and homeowners will not feel the uncertainty about the future of their community that often drives them away in market-generated integration.

Second, the price dynamic in the Schnare-MacRae analysis will not take hold because integration is not caused by black demand for housing spilling over into a white neighborhood. Program participants will not bid for housing in the unsubsidized private housing market and landlords in that market will have no incentive to change their behavior. Thus, stable integration is possible if enough whites are willing to stay in the neighborhood (or, in the long run, to move in) and does not require blacks' bids for housing to increase more rapidly than whites' bids as the percentage of whites in the neighborhood increases.[16]

Third, a subsidized housing program, unlike ghetto expansion, is not guided by racial discrimination and need not be channeled into one neighborhood. Indeed, a widely dispersed subsidized housing program would affect not only the level of integration in a single neighborhood, it would also affect the desirability of the options for the white residents living there. In my opinion, the best insurance against white flight from subsidized housing projects is to scatter subsidized housing throughout a metropolitan area.[17] If whites found subsidized housing anywhere they went, they would have no incentive to move in order to escape racial integration.

Implications for the Design of a Subsidized Housing Program

The preceding analysis yields several principles to guide policymakers who are trying to achieve stably integrated neighborhoods. This section explains in detail how these principles can be applied to the design of a subsidized housing program. The discussion is organized around five topics: type of housing program, project design, site selection, geographic coverage, and tenant selection.

Type of Housing Program

Various types of housing programs have been used by or proposed for the federal government. The first question we must ask is which type of housing program is most likely to increase racial integration. Racial residential segregation has three primary causes: income differences between blacks and whites, racial prejudice, and racial discrimination. A subsidized housing program can reduce segregation (i.e., increase integration) only if it overcomes these obstacles.

Housing vouchers are one possible type of subsidized housing program. Let us consider a "pure" voucher program that provides a subsidy to low-income households and allows recipients to live anywhere they want, perhaps as long as the unit they select meets certain minimum requirements. These vouchers enable low-income households to move into neighborhoods, some largely white, in which they were unable to afford housing before the program.

Nevertheless, the impact of pure housing vouchers on racial integration is likely to be minimal. First, these vouchers cannot have a large impact on racial income differences because they provide assistance to low-income households of all races and because they only narrow, but do not close, the income gap between participants and nonparticipants. Further, housing vouchers cannot overcome the strong sorting process in the private housing market; even with their vouchers, recipients will be at the bottom of the bidding hierarchy and will be outbid for the housing in most middle- or high-income white areas. Finally, housing vouchers do nothing to account for racial prejudice and discrimination. Indeed, vouchers leave the process of integration up to the private housing market—which is the source of all the segregation we currently observe. It is no surprise, therefore, that the vouchers provided in the housing allowance experiments did not lead to any noticeable increase in racial residential integration. (See Rossi 1981.)

Another type of subsidized housing program, illustrated by the Section 8 New Construction Program, involves subsidies to promote the construction of low-income housing. This type of housing program has much greater potential for increasing racial integration than does a voucher program. First, it can provide participants with housing in locations where the private market supplies housing only for middle-income households. Most of these locations are all white. Second, by careful attention to project design, site selection, and geographic coverage of the new housing (following rules presented below), it can minimize the reactions of white residents and thereby maximize the chance for stable integration. Third, it can monitor the behavior of participating developers and landlords to ensure that black participants do not face discrimination.

These two types of housing programs define the extremes. My analysis of these extremes reveals two features that will enhance the ability of an intermediate program to promote integration. First, the program must apply to specific housing units. In order to maintain control over project design, site selection, and geographic coverage, all of which are crucial for maintaining integration, an intermediate housing program, unlike a pure housing voucher, must not allow tenants to select the units. The designation of specific housing units also enhances the ability of an intermediate program to monitor the behavior of landlords visited by participants.

A modified housing voucher program could apply to specific units. Indeed, the Section 8 Moderate Rehabilitation and Substantial Rehabilitation programs include modified voucher programs of this type; they give subsidies to tenants who live in specified rehabilitated housing. However, the "finders-keepers" policy of the Section 8 Existing Housing Program and of the recently enacted demonstration Voucher Program relinquishes control over unit selection to recipients. This policy may promote other goals, but it clearly weakens the ability of these housing programs to foster racial integration.

Second, if policymakers do not wish to limit racial integration to low-income areas, and thereby largely limit it to central cities, they must design a housing program that overrules the sorting process in the private housing market. Subsidies to households alone are unlikely to accomplish this objective; even a large subsidy would not allow a low-income household to pay for housing in most middle-income neighborhoods. Thus, a housing program probably cannot significantly expand the access of low-income households to middle-income neighborhoods without making it profitable for developers to build or rehabilitate low-income housing in such places. To ensure the necessary profitability, the program must guarantee subsidies to particular developers and provide direct construction or rehabilitation subsidies in addition to vouchers or other rent-related subsidies. These guarantees and subsidies are not possible with a pure housing voucher program because it does not apply to specific housing units.

The bottom line here is that it is expensive to promote integration in middle-income areas through subsidized housing. Policymakers must decide whether the goal of widespread integration is worth the large subsidies that it probably requires.

Project Design

Three rules for the design of individual housing projects emerge from my analysis. Projects should blend in with surrounding housing and should be relatively small but should vary in size within a single community.[18] The key point here is that projects need to be as inconspicuous as possible. A conspicuous project often imposes a social stigma on project residents, and it magnifies the negative reactions of white neighbors to the project. Given the pervasiveness and strength of white prejudice and the cycle of fear and hostility that can accompany racial transition, this point cannot be overemphasized.

Large projects are almost guaranteed to stand out and thereby stir up white residents and lead to hostility toward project tenants and/or to white exodus from neighborhoods near the project. One-unit projects, on the other hand, are very inconspicuous. For example, a housing authority could lease apartments scattered throughout a community and rent them to low-income households without attracting anyone's attention.

An entire program of one-unit projects would be undesirable, however. First, many suburbs do not have housing suitable for such a program, and single-unit projects are relatively expensive to build. Second, one-unit projects in white neighborhoods cannot provide a range of income and racial compositions to reflect the preferences of program participants. The exact mix of project sizes should be determined by the availability of suitable housing in the community, the availability of sites for new subsidized housing, and the distribution of participants' preferences.

The desirability of small projects is reinforced by the observation that stable integration is more likely if the percentage of blacks in the neighborhood is kept low. The existing evidence implies that under most, but not all, circumstances, stable integration of a neighborhood requires that blacks remain less than about 10 percent of the neighborhood's population. Thus, even holding visibility constant, large projects are more likely to generate racial transition than small projects scattered throughout several neighborhoods.

Small projects do not provide black participants with the opportunity to live in neighborhoods where the races are evenly divided, but such an outcome is probably beyond the capability of a subsidized housing program. The evidence indicates that under current conditions policymakers must either try to achieve integration at low percentages of black residents or limit integration to a few carefully selected neighborhoods.[19] As explained below, however, policy choices would not be so constrained if subsidized housing were placed in all suburbs or if racial discrimination were less pervasive.

Site Selection

The starting point for any site selection procedure is the principle that, all else equal, subsidized housing should be placed in neighborhoods where low-income households would be most likely to live without restrictive zoning or racial discrimination. This principle accounts for the preferences of program participants and minimizes the conflicts between participants and higher income residents.[20]

Several specific rules can be extracted from this principle. To the extent possible, for example, projects should be in neighborhoods that are accessible to jobs that participants are likely to have and to stores that low-income households are likely to use; do not have strong neighborhood organizations (unless they support racial integration); have a highly mobile population, such as young renters; and do not provide unusual amenities, such as good views.

In addition, certain neighborhood characteristics may help to make a project inconspicuous. New projects should be built in neighborhoods containing housing into which subsidized housing can blend. And, in some cases, neighborhoods that are somewhat isolated from the rest of the community may be more suitable for subsidized housing than other neighborhoods.

All the above rules for site selection apply to the choice of suburbs for subsidized housing as well as to the choice of a neighborhood within a suburb. All else equal, for example, suburbs near the relevant jobs and with highly mobile populations are preferable to other suburbs. In addition, it would be wise to avoid placing subsidized housing in suburbs near large concentrations of blacks.[21] As explained earlier, one of the key advantages of achieving integration through subsidized housing is that it need not take place in an environment in which whites feel threatened by the expansion of the black residential area. This rule is not costless, because it limits black access to the main black community, but it is probably a necessary condition for stable integration.

Geographic Coverage

My analysis yields two rules for the geographic coverage of a subsidized housing program. First, due to the pervasiveness and strength of white prejudice, a subsidized housing program that leads to a high black percentage in a single community will, under most circumstances, fail to achieve stable integration. This argument applies with added strength at the community level; even whites who accept a single integrated neighborhood within their community are likely to leave when all neighborhoods contain a significant proportion of black residents. Therefore, unless policymakers can identify a community that is receptive to racial integration, they should not concentrate subsidized housing in a single community.

The second rule is that the probability of successfully achieving integration in one community is greatly increased by the placement of subsidized housing in similar communities. This rule is crucial. The most effective insurance against white flight from a community with subsidized housing is the existence of subsidized housing in all the communities to which whites might flee. Downs (1973:141–2) makes a similar argument in discussing the integration of income classes through housing programs: "Quick attainment of broad geographic spread is more important than reaching any specific targets rapidly. It will convince middle- and upper-income households that they cannot escape less affluent neighbors by moving elsewhere in the metropolitan area."[22]

Note that these two rules reinforce each other. For any given number of subsidized units, the best way to satisfy each rule is to spread the units over a wide number of communities. Furthermore, if a significant degree of integration is desired, a large program is necessary. Unless one can find a receptive community, the best way to stabilize integration at, say, 20 percent black in a given community is to make sure that the communities to which whites can move have enough subsidized housing to generate similar racial compositions. Policymakers must recognize that it is probably impossible to achieve significant, widespread integration with a small subsidized housing program.

Tenant Selection

As explained earlier, racial integration is difficult to maintain with a high proportion of minorities. One possible response to this difficulty is to place an upper limit on minority representation in a particular location. Indeed, this type of policy, called a ceiling quota, has been used in some individual housing projects. In fact, however, ceiling quotas are a form of discrimination against minorities and they are entirely unnecessary in the context of a metropolitan-wide housing program.[23]

The temptation to use ceiling quotas arises when black demand far exceeds white demand for the housing in a given project so that it is difficult to prevent that project from becoming all black.[24] From a project manager's viewpoint, a ceiling quota is a costless way to divert black demand.

But ceiling quotas are not costless. A ceiling quota, just like old-fashioned exclusion, denies some blacks the same access to housing received by their white counterparts. It forces some black applicants to look elsewhere for housing and therefore imposes the cost of finding alternative housing, which may be substantial, directly on these black applicants. Further, a ceiling quota increases black demand for housing in other locations and may thereby both hasten racial transition and boost the price blacks must pay for housing in those other locations.[25]

In short, ceiling quotas differ from more familiar quotas, in which minority representation is brought up to some level, because their cost falls on members of the minority group—not on society as a whole. In my view, policymakers should have a strong presumption against a policy that promotes the integration of some members of a disadvantaged minority group into white neighborhoods at the expense of other members of that group.

Policymakers may believe that the only way to prevent racial turnover in a particular *neighborhood* is to use a ceiling quota to prevent racial turnover in the *project* or projects in that neighborhood. However, racial transition in a project poses a threat to stable integration in the neighborhood only when the project residents make up a large share of the neighborhood's population. Hence, this problem can be avoided entirely by following the rule, stated earlier, that projects should not exceed a small share of the neighborhood population.

Moreover, ceiling quotas do not make sense even for a project that provides a large share of the population in a single neighborhood. With a housing program that covers an entire metropolitan area, the costs of finding alternative housing for diverted black applicants can be spread out over many projects, and there is no excuse for imposing these costs on black applicants. A metropolitan-wide housing program provides housing in many different locations and therefore allows managers to direct black demand toward some projects and away from others. If sites are carefully selected so that they are all attractive to program participants, then good information and simple marketing should be sufficient to ensure that black residents will be fairly evenly spread among all projects. If some projects are more attractive to blacks than others, however, the program may have to offer special inducements, such as moving assistance, to promote the less attractive projects. In any case, the existence of projects in many locations provides program managers with ample opportunities to spread black demand throughout the urban area and thereby to avoid rapid turnover in a particular project—and to eliminate the temptation to use ceiling quotas.

Recent developments at Starrett City, a large housing project in New York City, dramatically illustrate the issues discussed here. Starrett City contains almost 5,900 apartments and is built on fill land near a poor, largely black section of the city. Despite extensive efforts by the management to make Starrett City attractive to whites, including the provision of large security and maintenance staffs, the project received far more applications from blacks than from whites. In an attempt to prevent racial transition, the management implemented a ceiling quota, which has kept minority representation at about 35 percent of the units.[26] Thus, the Starrett City management is maintaining integration by discriminating against blacks through a ceiling quota.

Several black applicants sued Starrett City and the state of New York, which provides subsidies for the project, on the grounds that they were denied equal access to the housing at Starrett City. After several years of litigation, the case was settled out of court in 1984. The state of New York agreed to take strong steps to increase minority representation in 86 state-subsidized housing projects around the city, many of which are currently all white. These projects contain almost 70,000 housing units. The settlement allows Starrett City to keep its ceiling quota, although the developer agreed to increase minority representation by about 8 percent.[27]

According to the principles developed here, this settlement is a large step in the right direction. The best way to take the burden of a ceiling quota off minorities is to provide them with housing opportunities elsewhere. And the best way to eliminate the temptation to use a ceiling quota is to divert black demand from a single project and to ensure that whites do not have all-white projects to which they can flee. Indeed, one strong sign that the settlement had been a success would be the voluntary elimination of the Starrett City ceiling quota in five or ten years.

Implications for Related Policies

Students of racial transition have discovered that the speed and extent of racial transition, if not its ultimate outcome, are influenced by many factors at both the neighborhood and metropolitan levels. For example, a high rate of migration of blacks into a metropolitan area leads to an increase in the number of neighborhoods that undergo transition. As Goering (1978) has pointed out, most of these factors are essentially beyond the control of policymakers. However, some factors, such as the responses of neighborhood institutions to racial transition, might be influenced by public policy. This section considers a few policies that would increase the probability of achieving stable racial integration through subsidized housing.

In both Oak Park, Illinois, and Shaker Heights, Ohio, the key ingredients for achieving stable racial integration were a well-financed, well-organized housing referral service and local government efforts to maintain the level of public services. These referral services attract whites into areas with black residents, calm the fears associated with integration, and correct the misinformation on which racial hostility grows. A federal program to finance such agencies in communities with subsidized housing therefore could make a significant contribution to stabilizing integration.

Similarly, many whites believe that integration will cause schools to deteriorate and crime to rise. These fears could be alleviated by local government efforts to provide special educational programs or extra police protection in neighborhoods with subsidized housing. Federal grants for such local efforts would therefore be a desirable complement to federal efforts to promote integration through subsidized housing.

As noted earlier, whites' fears about deteriorating schools and rising crime are often unjustified, but successful integration still depends on calming them.

Indeed, as Wilson (1979), Taeuber (1979), and others have explained, school integration magnifies the difficulty of achieving housing integration. To minimize the apprehensiveness of white parents about school integration, the federal government could finance programs to educate parents and teachers on racial issues. Moreover, special school programs and extra police protection would benefit program participants as well as the original residents of the neighborhood. Children who come from inner-city schools may be behind their peers and need special attention. And black residents may need extra police to protect them from the hostile actions of a few white residents.[28]

This logic can be carried one step further. Racial integration makes a community less attractive to prejudiced whites and therefore often induces them to move. This decrease in attractiveness could be offset by better local public services. It follows that the federal government could encourage whites to stay in integrated communities by providing those communities with general financial assistance.

Finally, policies to combat discrimination in housing would improve the prospects for integration. By channeling black demand for housing into certain neighborhoods, racial discrimination increases the pressures that lead to racial transition. Continuing racial discrimination may channel black demand into neighborhoods with subsidized housing and thereby encourage white flight. In addition, continuing discrimination preserves the all-white areas to which whites can flee. Effective federal policies to combat racial discrimination in housing, such as criminal penalties for landlords and real estate brokers who practice racial discrimination, would therefore be powerful allies in any struggle to achieve stable integration through subsidized housing.

Conclusion

The scarcity of stably integrated neighborhoods in this country testifies to the strength of the factors working against racial integration. Stable integration occasionally does occur in the private housing market, but only with vigorous support from citizen's groups and local governments. Similarly, stable integration could be promoted through a subsidized housing program, but only if that program were designed to account for the realities of racial prejudice. A program that sets unrealistic goals, such as a high percentage of blacks in a few suburbs, is bound to fail. But a program that acknowledges the existence of racial prejudice and attempts to minimize white reactions to integration would undoubtedly increase the number of stably integrated neighborhoods.

An analysis of racial transition is also valuable in deciding how many resources to devote to fostering integration. In particular, the amount of integration obtained is not a smooth function of the scale of a subsidized housing program. A small housing program could probably achieve a moderate degree of integration in a few receptive communities. And a large, costly, geographically dispersed program could probably produce extensive racial integration. But there does not appear to be a middle ground. A medium-sized housing program would have to spread black participants thinly throughout the suburbs, and thereby isolate them from other blacks, or concentrate black participants in a few communities. Unless all of these communities were receptive to integration, this type of program would encourage racial turnover.

To be more specific, assuming that racial integration is a high-priority goal, let us examine the options faced by policymakers. To begin with, the use of subsidized housing to foster integration in a few carefully selected communities could have a large payoff. Many urban areas probably have one or two communities that would be fairly receptive to integration. Placing subsidized housing in these communities would demonstrate that integration could work, with only modest spending on support programs such as housing referral centers or special school services.

Beyond this demonstration stage, however, the cost of integrating another community through a housing program would probably be large, at least until the program reached the critical mass necessary for it to cover an entire metropolitan area. Because of the strength of the factors working against racial integration, a subsidized housing program would not achieve racial integration in most suburbs unless it were accompanied by expensive efforts to correct misinformation and to boost local services. With medium-sized housing programs, therefore, efforts to extend integration beyond demonstration communities would have little payoff per dollar spent; it would be more cost-effective to direct federal resources toward other housing goals, such as the elimination of racial discrimination.

Finally, once the critical mass is reached, a subsidized housing program would probably be highly cost-effective in promoting racial integration, even without extensive support programs. These programs would not be necessary to prevent white flight because of the lack of all-white communities to which prejudiced whites could move.

NOTES

1. The cases mandating integrated housing are discussed in *Harvard Law Review* Staff 1980. Top officials of the Reagan administration, unlike many other policymakers, have explicitly rejected the goal of achieving racial residential integration (see Mariano 1984). Integration maintenance is also opposed by the National Association of Realtors (see DeMuth 1984).

2. For a discussion of maintaining integration in a housing project, see Milgram 1977, Ackerman 1974, or McFall 1974.

3. Hartman (1973:121) carries this argument one step further: "to insist upon racial integration as a sine qua non of housing improvement is to consign millions of American families, white and black, to their present slum conditions for years to come."

4. A basic discussion of sorting can be found in Mills 1980 and Downs 1981; an

analysis of sorting with racial composition as a neighborhood characteristic can be found in Yinger 1976; and an analysis of sorting with many income classes and racial prejudice can be found in Courant and Yinger 1977.

5. The existing evidence strongly supports the claim that racial discrimination is still widespread. See Feins and Bratt 1983; Wienk et al. 1979; Yinger 1979.

6. One study of an integrated community found little social interaction between blacks and whites (Molotch 1969). Another study found that new residents of a suburban community, black and white, had little interaction with their neighbors during their first year in the community (Hamilton and Bishop 1976).

7. Many studies support the contact hypothesis, namely that racial tolerance increases with equal-status interracial contact. See, for example, Ford 1973; Hamilton and Bishop 1976. The latter study finds that white suburbanites become more tolerant of a black neighbor over time even without significant interaction with that neighbor. The authors speculate that this response occurs because the whites' worst fears are not realized. Perhaps subsidized housing tenants also might be accepted over time.

8. In their review of the literature, Wellman and Leighton (1979) conclude that a person's social networks are more likely to revolve around his or her work than around his or her neighborhood. And one recent study (described in Collins 1984) found that middle-class black households in largely white communities "maintained close association with the black community" through various social organizations.

9. Wienk et al. (1979) discovered more racial discrimination in Detroit, where the survey by Farley et al. was carried out, than in 39 other large cities; this finding suggests that white prejudice in the Farley survey may be higher than the national average.

10. For studies of information flows during racial transition and of blockbusting by real estate firms and lenders, see Center for Community Change 1980; Goodwin 1979; Ginsberg 1975.

11. The correlation between racial transition and income transition has been studied extensively. Leven et al. (1976) conclude that the fear of income transition is the primary force behind racial transition, so that racial integration may be easier to achieve than class integration. Similarly, Downs (1973) argues that class prejudice is likely to be a more persistent problem than racial prejudice. In my view, however, racial prejudice is deep-seated and central to the dynamic of racial transition. Racial integration will continue to be difficult to achieve even without class integration.

12. A similar model, which describes racial transition in an apartment building, was developed by Yinger (1975).

13. The Oak Park case is described by Goodwin (1979); the Shaker Heights case is described by Milgram (1977). See also Berry 1979. A fair number of housing projects are stably integrated, but I suspect that these projects would not remain integrated for long without the active support and involvement of their management. See Milgram 1977; Ackerman 1974; McFall 1974.

14. The continuing high level of segregation in U.S. cities is documented by Taeuber (1983). Bradburn, Sudman, and Gockel (1970) found that 19 percent of the U.S. population lived in an integrated neighborhood, but two-thirds of these people lived in neighborhoods that were less than 5 percent black. The evidence provided by Sorenson, Taeuber, and Hollingsworth (1975) and by Schnare (1977) indicates that, between 1960 and 1970, blacks became more concentrated in largely black neighborhoods and became more likely to live in a largely white neighborhood. For an explanation, see Yinger 1979. Segregation indexes calculated by Taeuber (1983), which show somewhat

more integration in 1980 than in 1970, suggest that these trends continued in the 1970s. Some less formal evidence is available for several cities. For example, one study found 24 suburbs of Cleveland with at least 50 black households in 1980, compared with 11 suburbs in 1970. See Cuyahoga Plan of Ohio 1982.

15. To my knowledge, the only community with stable racial and class integration is Mt. Airy, Pennsylvania. See Schermer and Levin 1968.

16. This conclusion may be too optimistic. With continuing racial discrimination in housing, black demand for housing is channeled into certain areas. Brokers and landlords may decide to sell or rent to blacks in neighborhoods with subsidized housing, so that unsubsidized, middle-class black demand is channeled into these neighborhoods. This channeling will increase the pressure for racial turnover.

17. Downs (1973) makes a similar argument. Note that this argument provides strong support for "fair share" housing allocation plans, such as those described in Rubinowitz 1974.

18. Downs (1973) offers a similar set of rules to guide income integration through subsidized housing.

19. Some individual housing projects have remained stably integrated with an equal number of blacks and whites. Such a high degree of integration might be achieved in a neighborhood with unusually receptive whites or in a community that was willing to spend money to entice whites to stay. In Oak Park, for example, the housing center has placed blacks in all parts of the community and encouraged whites to move into neighborhoods where some blacks lived, and the local government has maintained or even improved local services in neighborhoods into which blacks have moved. See Goodwin 1979.

20. This principle could be applied in a rigorous manner. The first step would be to estimate hedonic regressions for housing. These regressions could then be used to estimate demand or bid functions for neighborhood characteristics and then to determine the locations where participants are most likely to outbid higher income people. For example, all else equal, low-income households are more likely to outbid other households in a location close to the jobs held by low-income workers. For a detailed discussion of neighborhood demand functions, see Freeman 1979.

21. This rule has been proposed by others. See McFall 1974.

22. In addition, Downs points out that subsidized housing should be placed in distant suburbs as well as in inner suburbs because the traditional escape route for the middle class is to move farther from the city.

23. For a legal analysis of ceiling quotas, see *Harvard Law Review* Staff 1980. That article uses the term "benign quota," which I regard as highly misleading. My argument is similar to one made by Ackerman (1974), who says that ceiling quotas are justified only if alternative housing is made available to minorities.

24. It is tempting, but incorrect, to say that the ceiling quota keeps the black population below the tipping point. In fact, the tipping point is endogenous; policymakers can move it to a higher percentage black by alleviating white fears in that project or by fostering integration in other projects.

25. For a review of the literature on the effects of racial exclusion, see Yinger 1979.

26. For a description of the steps taken by the Starrett City management, see Rosenberg 1982. The severe impact of the Starrett City ceiling quota can be seen by comparing the waiting list, which is 75 percent minority, with the project itself, which is 35 percent minority.

27. For a description of the settlement in the Starrett City case, see Blair 1984. The reader should know that I was involved in this case—as a consultant to the plaintiffs.

28. Violence against black "pioneers" is still disturbingly common. See, for example, Wycliff 1979.

REFERENCES

Abrams, Charles. 1947. "Race Bias in Housing." American Civil Liberties Union, New York.

Ackerman, Bruce L. 1974. "Integration for Subsidized Housing and the Question of Racial Occupancy Controls." *Stanford Law Review* 26 (January): 245-309.

Berry, Brian J. L. 1979. *The Open Housing Question.* Cambridge, Mass.: Ballinger.

Blair, William G. 1984. "Accord in Minority Suit Provides for More Subsidized Apartments." *New York Times,* 3 May, p. B4.

Bradburn, N. M., S. Sudman, and G. L. Gockel. 1970. *Side by Side: Integrated Neighborhoods in America.* Chicago: Quadrangle Books.

Center for Community Change. 1980. "Response to Crisis: A Study of Public Policy toward Neighborhoods and Fair Housing." Washington, D.C.

Collins, Glenn. 1984. "A Study of Blacks in White Suburbia." *New York Times,* 30 July, p. 26.

Courant, Paul N., and John Yinger. 1977. "On Models of Racial Prejudice and Urban Residential Structure." *Journal of Urban Economics* 4 (July): 272-91.

Cuyahoga Plan of Ohio. 1982. "Black Homeownership in the Cleveland Area: Patterns of Residence in 1970 and 1980." Mimeographed report.

DeMuth, Jerry. 1984. "Integration Maintenance Opposed by Realtor Group." *Washington Post,* 21 July, p. E1.

Downs, Anthony. 1973. *Opening Up the Suburbs.* New Haven: Yale University Press.

————. 1981. *Neighborhoods and Urban Development.* Washington, D.C.: The Brookings Institution.

Farley, Reynolds, Suzanne Bianchi, and Diane Colasanto. 1979. "Barriers to the Racial Integration of Neighborhoods: The Detroit Case." *Annals of the American Academy of Political and Social Science* 411 (January): 97-113.

Feins, Judith D., and Rachael G. Bratt. 1983. "Barred in Boston: Racial Discrimination in Housing." *American Planning Association Journal* (Summer): 344-55.

Ford, W. Scott. 1973. "Interracial Public Housing in a Border City: Another Look at the Contact Hypothesis." *American Journal of Sociology* 78: 1426-47.

Freeman, A. Myrick. 1979. "The Hedonic Price Approach to Measuring Demand for Neighborhood Characteristics." In *The Economics of Neighborhood,* edited by D. Segal. New York: Academic Press.

Ginsberg, Yona. 1975. *Jews in a Changing Neighborhood: The Study of Mattapan.* New York: The Free Press.

Goering, John M. 1978. "Neighborhood Tipping and Racial Transition: A Review of Social Science Evidence." *American Institute of Planners Journal* (January): 68-78.

Goodwin, Carole. 1979. *The Oak Park Strategy*. Chicago: University of Chicago Press.

Hamilton, David L., and George D. Bishop. 1976. "Attitudinal and Behavioral Effects of Initial Integration of White Suburban Neighborhoods." *Journal of Social Issues* 32: 47–68.

Hartman, Chester W. 1973. "The Politics of Housing." In *Housing Urban America*, edited by J. Pynoos, R. Schafer, and C. Hartman. Chicago: Aldine.

Harvard Law Review Staff. 1980. "Benign Steering and Benign Quotas: The Validity of Race-Conscious Government Policies to Promote Residential Integration." *Harvard Law Review* 93: 938–65.

Leven, Charles L., James T. Little, Hugh O. Nourse, and R. B. Read. 1976. *Neighborhood Change: Lessons in the Dynamics of Urban Decay*. New York: Praeger.

McFall, Trudy Parisa. 1974. "Racially and Economically Integrated Housing: Can It Work? Under What Conditions?" Paper submitted for presentation at Confer-In 1974.

Mariano, Ann. 1984. "Fair Housing Law Questioned." *Washington Post*, 11 July, p. A1.

Milgram, Morris. 1977. *Good Neighborhood: The Challenge of Open Housing*. New York: W. W. Norton.

Mills, Edwin S. 1980. *Urban Economics*. 2nd ed. Glenview, Ill.: Scott, Foresman.

Molotch, Harvey. 1969. "Racial Integration in a Transition Community." *American Journal of Sociology* (December): 878–93.

Rosenberg, Robert C. 1982. "Starrett City Created a Model Integrated Community." *Real Estate Review* 12: 63–68.

Rossi, Peter H. 1981. "Residential Mobility." In *Do Housing Allowances Work?* edited by K. L. Bradbury and A. Downs. Washington, D.C.: The Brookings Institution.

Rubinowitz, Leonard S. 1974. *Low-Income Housing: Suburban Strategies*. Cambridge, Mass.: Ballinger.

Schelling, Thomas. 1972. "A Process of Residential Segregation: Neighborhood Tipping." In *Racial Discrimination in Economic Life*, edited by A. Pascal. Lexington, Mass.: Lexington Books.

Schermer, George, and Arthur J. Levin. 1968. "Housing Guide to Equal Opportunity." The Potomac Institute, Washington, D.C.

Schnare, Ann B. 1977. "Residential Segregation by Race in U.S. Metropolitan Areas: An Analysis across Cities and over Time." Contract Report 246–2. The Urban Institute, Washington, D.C.

———, and C. Duncan MacRae. 1978. "The Dynamics of Neighborhood Change." *Urban Studies* 15 (October): 327–31.

Sorenson, Annemette, Karl E. Taeuber, and Leslie J. Hollingsworth, Jr. 1975. "Indexes of Residential Segregation for 109 Cities in the United States, 1940 to 1970." *Sociological Focus* 8: 125–42.

Suttles, Gerald D. 1968. *The Social Order of the Slum*. Chicago: University of Chicago Press.

Taeuber, Karl E. 1979. "Housing, Schools, and Incremental Segregative Effects." *Annals of the American Academy of Political and Social Science* 411 (January): 157–67.

———. 1983. "Racial Residential Segregation, 28 Cities, 1970–1980." Center for Demography and Ecology Working Paper 83-12. University of Wisconsin, Madison.

Wellman, Barry, and Barry Leighton. 1979. "Networks, Neighborhoods, and Communities." *Urban Affairs Quarterly* 14 (March): 363–90.

Wienk, Ronald E., Clifford E. Reid, John C. Simonson, and Frederick J. Eggers. 1979. *Measuring Racial Discrimination in American Housing Markets: The Housing Market Practices Survey*. Washington, D.C.: U.S. Department of Housing and Urban Development.

Wilson, Franklin D. 1979. "Patterns of White Avoidance." *Annals of the American Academy of Political and Social Science* 411 (January): 132–41.

Wycliff, Don. 1979. "Rosedale Is Black, White, and Seething." *New York Times*, 9 September, p. E5.

Yinger, John. 1975. "A Model of Discrimination by Landlords." Institute for Research on Poverty Discussion Paper 251-75. University of Wisconsin, Madison.

———. 1976. "Racial Prejudice and Racial Residential Segregation in an Urban Model." *Journal of Urban Economics* 3 (October): 383–96.

———. 1979. "Prejudice and Discrimination in the Urban Housing Market." In *Current Issues in Urban Economics*, edited by P. Mieszkowski and M. Straszheim. Baltimore: Johns Hopkins.

———, George C. Galster, Barton A. Smith, and Frederick Eggers. 1979. "The Status of Research into Racial Discrimination and Segregation in American Housing Markets: A Research Agenda for the Department of Housing and Urban Development." *Occasional Papers in Housing and Community Affairs*. Vol. 6. Washington, D.C.: U.S. Department of Housing and Urban Development.

Chapter Fourteen
Postscript
Unresolved Themes in the
Evolution of Fair Housing
ROBERT W. LAKE

The 1980s have emerged as a critical period for fair housing. The extended recession of 1977–82 relegated civil rights issues to a low priority in the national consciousness. The hard-won national mandate that made the gains of the 1960s politically possible has largely evaporated. The administration in Washington has eviscerated the federal civil rights effort and sent out strong signals of a pullback in federal commitment. Recent efforts to strengthen federal fair housing laws have suffered defeat in the Senate, while strong pressure exists to make enforcement even more difficult by requiring proof of intent to discriminate. Reflecting these trends, the civil rights movement today seems troubled by uncertainty over objectives, dissent over methods, and difficulty in placing its concerns on the national agenda.

The papers collected in this volume aptly mirror the times. Within a common emphasis on desegregation and housing policy, the papers address a broad range of issues; adopt a variety of assumptions, definitions, and perspectives; and arrive at multiple and sometimes conflicting policy conclusions. Several authors, focusing on the original and continuing challenge of eliminating segregation, call for stronger enforcement of antidiscrimination statutes. In this view, the problem is defined in terms of existing racial concentrations, perpetuated by discriminatory barriers to equal housing access. Others address the parallel issues of preventing resegregation, an effort that may require, in Gary Orfield's words, "special efforts" reaching beyond the present fair housing laws in support of stable integration (Chapter 1).

In addressing these various concerns, the authors raise questions for which there are as yet few firm conclusions. Can the competing goals of equal access and stable integration be reconciled? What is the appropriate role of public policy in the prevention of resegregation? Should the level of white tolerance for integration establish the pace of desegregation? Can housing subsidy programs contribute to integration? Is integration *per se* a demonstrable benefit for black homeseekers?

The preceding chapters reach varying conclusions on these and other questions. A synthesis of disparate and conflicting viewpoints into a unified analytic and policy perspective presents an awesome and perhaps, at present, unattainable goal. However, the reasons for, and sources of, these differences can be identified, leading to the promise of eventual resolution.

Where differences are rooted in ideology, their reconciliation is a political rather than an analytical problem and lies beyond the scope of this essay. At a more fundamental level, the disparity in approaches and conclusions is directly linked to the evolution of residential segregation as an analytical and policy problem. Change over time in both the nature and the context of housing segregation has introduced new and sometimes conflicting challenges for those seeking guideposts for fair housing policy and research. As the question evolves and becomes fragmented, with ongoing problems coexisting with new ones, analysis and policy become fragmented in turn as they address discrete segments of an increasingly complex issue.

The diversity of approaches and directions encompassed in fair housing in general, and in the present volume in particular, to a large extent reflects this multifaceted and changing nature of the problem. In the following discussion, I trace out some principal dimensions of recent evolution in the fair housing arena reflecting the varying perspectives presented in these essays, both to summarize the current debate and to sketch an agenda for continuing research and policy development.

That advocates of fair housing may fail to speak with one voice is less a symptom of dissension or disharmony than an indication of the problem's complexity and changing nature. Seventeen years have passed since the Fair Housing Act of 1968 was signed. While segregation and discrimination remain, over time the problems have evolved, are redefined, and reemerge in new forms and guises. New complexities are introduced even as old wounds continue to fester. Cycles of initiative followed by retrenchment mark the historical ebb and flow of progress in civil rights. Further progress is limited not only by the persistence of discrimination and segregation but also by new conditions that have emerged (e.g., suburban integration succumbing to resegregation) even as *some* barriers have been overcome. The endurance of discrimination prompts calls for strengthening existing enforcement programs, while the price of success is the introduction of unanticipated consequences, such as selective integration and resegregation, requiring new policy responses. A further level of complexity is introduced by the danger that solutions and policy directions prompted by new and emerging issues may conflict with those adopted earlier to contend with longstanding and continuing problems. The case of suburban communities exempting neighborhoods within their boundaries from enforcement of local fair housing ordinances in order to stabilize integration provides a troubling example of such potential conflict.[1]

In the following discussion, I consider four basic elements of change in the fair housing arena that underlie the diversity of perspectives represented in this volume. The first is a *historical reorientation* of assumptions that has come about as a result of changes since passage of the Fair Housing Act in 1968 as well as changes introduced by the act. After seventeen years, fair housing is in large measure hostage to its own history. Both its successes and its failures have contributed to a new context that will influence future analysis and policy.

Analysts tend to differ in their problem statements, definitions, and assumptions depending on how they interpret this new context and its implications for policy development.

The second dimension of change is the growing *geographic displacement* of the fair housing issue from the central cities to the suburbs. This geographic refocusing complements the time element discussed above, with the particular historical period of the 1970s encompassing major demographic and metropolitan shifts in black and white population distributions. These shifts have introduced changes in the ecological and political units confronting the fair housing issue (e.g., many small autonomous suburbs instead of a few large cities and subordinate urban neighborhoods), introducing new issues, problem definitions, and policy needs. Once again, analysts may differ depending on the specific geographic focus they have selected.

The third dimension, and perhaps the most central to the disparity of views in the current fair housing debate, is the *emerging goal conflict* between the objective of initiating integration by eliminating discrimination and the goal of promoting and maintaining stable integration. This conflict is partly a function of the temporal and spatial changes discussed above: temporally, the issue of maintaining stable integration arises only *after* some integration has been achieved; geographically, the political autonomy of suburban jurisdictions permits a breadth of policy responses not available to urban neighborhoods. Central issues in this debate focus on the separability of access and integration as avenues to good quality housing, the municipal versus regional scale of targeted effort, and the appropriateness of race-based methods for achieving stable integration. Analysts are likely to differ, with reason, on each of these issues.

A fourth element to consider is the potential impact on fair housing goals (whether defined as integration or equal access) imposed by *changes in other minority objectives* such as political power and social cohesiveness. Implicit here is the problem of fluctuating priorities as well as the need to distinguish between integration perceived as a means to attain other objectives or as an end in its own right.

These elements of evolution within the fair housing picture raise difficult problems for those attempting to chart a course for the future direction of policy and analysis. The above list is clearly only a partial selection of the possible sources of differences in perspective, definition, and direction. It encompasses, however, many of the principal items of contention within the current fair housing debate. Identification of the dimensions of diversity and their possible sources is the first step toward eventual agreement on goals and methods.

Historical Reorientation

In describing the expected results of passing the Fair Housing Act, the sponsors of Title VIII offered a bright scenario in 1968. The end result, in Senator

Mondale's often quoted phrase, would be "truly integrated living patterns," to be brought about through the elimination of discrimination in the housing market. Alexander Polikoff, in Chapter 3, notes the implicit causal connection within the "twofold" purpose of Title VIII, as clarified by the U.S. Department of Housing and Urban Development (HUD), whereby "the abolition of racially discriminatory housing practices would ultimately result in residential integration." Significantly, the sponsors of Title VIII envisioned a world in which the elimination of discriminatory barriers was an implicit guarantee against resegregation. An all-white neighborhood once opened to blacks would not quickly become all black because, free from discriminatory constraints, blacks who could afford to would select housing in stable integrated neighborhoods elsewhere and thus relieve the pressure of resegregation.[2]

The passage of time has uncovered serious weaknesses in the numerous assumptions inherent in this scenario. The clean line evidently foreseen by the act's sponsors leading from nondiscrimination to stable integration is instead fraught with unanticipated pitfalls and confounded expectations. Foremost among these is the reality of partial, or spatially discontinuous, integration. Rather than barriers falling everywhere at once, the path to nondiscrimination has been pursued slowly on a case-by-case basis. The problem, as a result, has been redefined. Whereas the original motivation for Title VIII was *universal discrimination* preventing access to housing, now some access has been attained and the problem is one of *partial discrimination* funneling integration into limited areas.

The emerging reality of piecemeal, checkerboard integration presents a new and difficult set of issues evidently not anticipated in the effort to eliminate discrimination at once with the stroke of a pen in 1968. What are the consequences for the integrated community in a discriminatory setting? What policy responses are appropriate and available, both at local and higher levels of government? How is this emergent issue to be reconciled with the ongoing and undiminished importance of Title VIII's original objectives? The controversial issue of public intervention designed to slow the pace of resegregation is addressed below in "The Emerging Goal Conflict." For the present, there is virtually no systematic information available on the dynamics of checkerboard integration. There is a fundamental research need for monitoring a wide array of community settings in which integration is proceeding within a discriminatory regional context. What social, economic, and demographic changes occur both within the community and in the ties between community and region? How do institutional actors—realtors, lenders, planners, and others—external to the community influence the community's internal composition, and what is the community's ability to reach these external influences? Development of effective policy awaits answers to these research issues.

Closely related to the spatial discontinuity of integration is the length of time evidently required to generate change. A hard look at the evidence from the vantage point of more than seventeen years since passage of Title VIII might suggest the need for a reevaluation of earlier expectations and an examination of assumptions. Do we continue on the same path or look for new initiatives? A major difficulty arises from the lack of adequate measuring devices to accurately evaluate the extent of change attributable to the Fair Housing Act. At the least this implies the need for more detailed and repeated measures of the extent of discrimination, along the lines of HUD's Housing Market Practices Survey.[3] Beyond this, we need more comprehensive measures not only of the *amount of change* in the incidence of discrimination, but also, though far more difficult, of *change in the pace of change.* Has progress slowed after an initial burst of reform, or is momentum just beginning to build? Evidence of widespread albeit subtle discrimination compels a sobering recognition that Title VIII is weak and easily flaunted. Continued discrimination despite the Fair Housing Act has become the new status quo, introducing the danger that further reform will succumb to lost momentum and a dissipated national commitment. Has the potential for change introduced by Title VIII run its course, or is its full capacity yet to be tapped?

In a related vein, the important question may no longer be how much progress has been made toward fulfilling the promise of 1968, but rather what new directions are needed in the 1980s? This is surely not to abandon Title VIII but rather to ask what it means in today's context and how this has changed from the way the world was seventeen years ago. What are the consequences of change in the economic, social, and political setting for the continued effectiveness of the Fair Housing Act in promoting integration? To what extent has the progress foreseen by the act's sponsors in an expanding economy and liberal sociopolitical climate been subverted, in both pace and direction, in a recessionary economy and conservative political atmosphere?

Of final concern in this discussion of historical shifts in the fair housing arena is the marked expansion in recent years of the black middle class. That income alone does not account for residential segregation was demonstrated by John Kain more than ten years ago. He, as well as George Galster, marshals new evidence here to restate and update that conclusion (in Chapters 5 and 6, respectively). Evidence from housing audits in a wide range of locales (with testers matched by income) confirms that discrimination does not cease upon black attainment of income parity with white homeseekers.[4] Despite this consistent evidence, racial segregation is all too commonly equated with low income, and researchers are constantly required to reinvent the wheel in documenting the strong independent effects of discrimination. Black access to good quality housing and neighborhoods is clearly separate from and broader than the question of the supply and distribution of low-income housing.[5] Monitoring the middle-class black experience in the housing market through an expansion of audits and related research would provide an important barometer for evaluating progress toward eliminating discrimination in housing markets.

Despite the separability of economic and race effects on housing patterns, both public discourse and public policy appear to emphasize the issue of housing subsidies as a means to residential integration. Continuing problems confronting middle-class black homeseekers provide a reminder that housing subsidy programs, though undeniably important, should not overshadow the need for a strong fair housing enforcement effort. Thus, there is a need to maintain a clear conceptual distinction between compensatory antipoverty programs, including various forms of housing subsidies, and prohibitory anti-discrimination programs providing for equal housing access *ceteris paribus*. A real question therefore arises—in light of Title VIII's requirement that HUD administer its programs so as to affirmatively further the purposes of the act—concerning the efficacy of evaluating antipoverty programs against integration objectives.

The evidence reported herein on the effect of housing subsidy programs on integration makes for sobering reading. HUD data analyzed by Robert Gray and Steven Tursky (Chapter 10) substantiate the widespread perception that subsidized public housing for families is highly concentrated in minority neighborhoods and disproportionately occupied by minority households. Housing units under Section 8 are somewhat more geographically dispersed but nonetheless still racially segregated. It has also been found that affirmative marketing designed to facilitate integration has had little impact on the racial composition of subsidized housing. Ira Goldstein and William Yancey (Chapter 12) find the explanation for these patterns in the "ecological history" of neighborhoods selected for subsidized housing developments. Court-mandated site selection criteria designed to avoid increasing minority concentrations have been largely ineffectual and, as Michael Vernarelli reports (in Chapter 9), have generally succumbed to pressures to redirect housing assistance efforts back into minority neighborhoods. Jennifer Stucker (Chapter 11) concludes that neither Section 8 nor the housing allowance experiment contributed significantly to the spatial deconcentration or residential integration of program participants.

Numerous conclusions can be derived from these rather dismal findings, among them perhaps that the wrong yardstick is being applied. The primary objective of housing subsidy programs is to improve housing affordability; the primary route to residential integration continues to be via strengthened enforcement and elimination of discrimination.

Geographic Displacement

The historical evolution of the fair housing debate is paralleled by a geographic evolution that has shifted attention from the central cities to the suburbs. Better than half of the papers collected here have a suburban focus. If written ten years ago, this book would implicitly have assumed a central city locus; as it is, the word "ghetto" rarely appears in the preceding pages. The expanding metropolitan scale, continued high residential mobility, and accelerating suburbanization of blacks in the last two decades have made residential segregation a regional rather than simply a central city issue.

Several factors can be identified to help explain this geographic displacement of attention. First, of course, is the "urbanization of the suburbs": suburbia itself has evolved, taking on many of the characteristics of the central cities. Substantial evidence suggests that much of the recent suburban black population growth represents a replication of central city segregation in the suburbs rather than a lessening of segregation.[6] In the state of New Jersey, to cite just one example, fully two-thirds (66.5 percent) of the 1970–80 black population increase in the state's 551 suburban municipalities was concentrated in just 12 communities, which on average increased from 23 percent black in 1970 to 43 percent black in 1980.[7] To some extent, then, the suburban reorientation in the fair housing issue simply reflects a replication of long-standing patterns in a new setting.

In several other respects, however, the new suburban focus represents real change in the nature of the debate. A case can be made that in the current political and economic climate, the problems of many cities, especially those with black majorities, have simply been relegated to a low priority by both policymakers and the general public. Relative income characteristics of rural-to-urban versus city-to-suburb black migration streams are depleting the cities even further.[8] As middle-class blacks depart the cities for the suburbs and are replaced by lower income black in-migrants, the growing central city concentration of low-income blacks at best translates the city's racial problem into an economic problem and at worst compounds the problems of race and class. The result is an intractable dilemma, leaving the cities with a voiceless constituency and no ready solution other than to await a redirection of the political climate and a refocusing of national priorities.

The suburban capture of the fair housing issue reflects not only the diminishing voice of the central city, but also the newfound significance of the suburbs. As cities fall heir to either the extremely wealthy or the very poor, the suburbs represent the greatest potential source of good quality housing and neighborhoods available to black homeseekers. It therefore seems inevitable that the pressure for equal access currently should be greatest in suburban locations.

Perhaps the most significant explanation for the attention devoted to suburban fair housing, however, is that, with the suburbanization of blacks, growing numbers of suburban middle-class *whites* are feeling themselves actually or potentially affected. To be blunt, the issue of maintaining stable integration and preventing black resegregation is a problem perceived far more readily by whites than by blacks. Wilhelmina Leigh and James McGhee (Chapter 2) report a substantial ambivalence concerning the value for blacks of integration per se, an issue discussed more fully below. The newfound concern for suburban integration may rest largely in the fact that it is there, far more than in the cities, that the white majority is being forced to confront the issue—and it is these white concerns that are reaching the public forum.

The Emerging Goal Conflict

The attempt to maintain stable integration following initial black entry in a community raises a fundamental conflict over both goals and methods of the fair housing movement. Methods used to achieve the goal of promoting and maintaining racially integrated residential patterns, described by Rose Helper in Chapter 8, include the dispersal of black concentrations, slowing of black in-migration, encouragement of continued white in-movement, and possible use of quotas—all steps necessary to counteract steering and self-selection, which contribute to black resegregation. In contrast, promoting freedom of choice in housing is aimed at ensuring that minority homeseekers have a realistic choice of housing throughout a metropolitan area, without mandating a particular racial residential pattern. Relevant methods to achieve this objective involve eliminating racial steering, improving the dissemination of housing market information, and removing restrictions on black housing search.

The conflict is clear-cut. Under the integrationist approach, intervention in the housing search process (i.e., integration counseling—cf. Alexander Polikoff) aims at maintaining stable integration. Information about housing vacancies may be selectively disseminated to achieve this goal. Under the choice approach, intervention in housing search is aimed at providing equal information and equal choice to all homeseekers, regardless of the resulting spatial pattern. The test for success in each of these approaches is quite different: for the choice approach, equality of the housing search *process* is the key criterion, whereas the integrationist approach looks to the resulting residential *pattern* to validate its methods.

Paradoxically, the severity of the debate over these objectives is testament to the partial success of improved housing access and increasing black incomes, for it is only as *some* access has been attained, and with it the prospect for continued access, that the issue of racial transition is reached. The need to develop an appropriate response to racial transition (or resegregation) provides, in Gary Orfield's words, "an agenda for the next generation of efforts to achieve racially integrated urban neighborhoods." The debate on the nature of those efforts is intensifying, as reflected in a growing and complex set of legal proceedings.[9] Numerous questions, both implicit and explicit, still await resolution.

First, is this a new problem or simply a renewed manifestation of the old tipping point controversy? It is interesting to note the resurgence of this debate after its relative quiescence during most of the 1970s. It was first raised as an issue with the breaching of urban neighborhood (and school) barriers in the early 1960s; its reemergence today marks the initial integration of suburban neighborhoods. Are there any lessons from the earlier inner-city cycle and its literature that can be applied in the current suburban context? The classic works from the 1950s and 1960s described racial transition as inevitably culminating in resegregation.[10] To what extent do similarities and differences between the current and earlier periods suggest the continued validity of that conclusion today? A potentially significant difference arises from the ecological and political characteristics of urban neighborhoods versus suburban communities, in which the manageable size, definable boundaries, and ordinance-passing capability of the latter allow for a greater degree of control.[11] These very characteristics, however, simultaneously limit the suburb's ability to effectively reach institutions and actors centered beyond its borders. Additional differences might arise from variations in behavioral expectations of urban and suburban residents. Considerably more research is needed, however, on the process of racial transition in a wide variety of neighborhood and community types to be able to discern the relative uniqueness of current trends.

A second, as yet unresolved, issue concerning the integration objective centers on the nature of regional efforts in integration management or integration counseling. The effort to maintain stable integration in a community is often coupled with the attempt to deflect black homeseekers to other, presently all-white, communities. On the surface, this strategy appears congruent with the equal access objective: it expands the range of housing choices for blacks. In practice, however, a program designed to integrate all-white suburbs is likely to take a significantly different form than one intended to curb black access to already integrated suburbs. In the latter case, housing information is disseminated selectively to achieve an integrated residential pattern.

Closely related to this issue is the question of whether integration management efforts divert attention from the broader goal of nondiscrimination. The integration objective of Title VIII, as summarized above, is to be achieved by eliminating discriminatory housing practices. It might be argued that the undeviating policy objective is to push on with this unfinished task at the broadest possible scale. Management of stable integration within specific neighborhoods or communities might divert resources and attention from this larger task, especially in an era when financial and political capital for fair housing is extremely limited.

An alternative argument raised in support of intervention for stable integration, however, is the value of successful examples of integration in influencing other communities to lower exclusionary barriers. Do limits on resegregation in one community encourage other nearby communities to be more receptive to initial integration? Alternatively, is a more likely scenario one of limited integration in the first instance and continued exclusion in the second? The latter alternative may be a more likely outcome if the effort required to prevent resegregation is perceived as excessively difficult, legally problematic, or unduly costly. Research is needed on how integrated communities are perceived within their surrounding metropolitan regions, and how these perceptions in turn influence the behavior of other communities, realtors, and homeseekers.

Ultimately, however, controversy over the integration objective reduces to the appropriateness of race-based methods for achieving stable integration. The issue is tackled directly here by Alexander Polikoff in summarizing the two-tiered test required to justify racial distinctions under the Equal Protection Clause of the Constitution. To be justifiable, such distinctions must serve a compelling interest, and must be a necessary and not burdensome means to serving that interest.

The latter test is the most difficult because, as Polikoff concedes, "any race-conscious counseling program presents a risk of appearing to stigmatize blacks." The solution for Polikoff is in the distinction between persuasion and coercion. The final decision is left to the black homeseeker, "who may choose to ignore the views and information provided through counseling" (i.e., entreaties to seek housing elsewhere, in a predominantly white community, to prevent black concentrations and resegregation). It would appear, however, that the imputation of stigma has been reached once such entreaties are made, and not only if they are acted upon. The effect is the same, even given a certain lack of intent.

Finally, proponents of intervention for stable integration proffer the hope that such intervention is justified by contributing to the goal of increasing the number of stably integrated communities. Here, perhaps, the conflict is most clearly joined. Is the goal one of increasing the *number of integrated communities*, each capable of supporting a highly constrained number of black households? Or, alternatively, is it rather one of maximizing the *number of black households* with equal access to housing opportunity, even if this leads to limited integration? Adding to the complexity of this debate, is equal housing opportunity possible without integration, that is, can separate be equal? Can these issues be reconciled based on clear priorities, and do they conflict with yet other objectives on the agenda of black Americans?

Establishing Priorities

What is the principal objective of the fair housing effort? Is agreement on priorities likely, or even possible? The setting of priorities is an inherently ideological and political process in which policy analysis and research can contribute interpretations and empirical evidence to help place priorities on a realistic footing. The preceding chapters provide sometimes contradictory signals, yet a coherent message can be discerned.

Is integration a means to the attainment of broader objectives or an end in and of itself? From the perspective of several authors, integration is preponderantly a means. As Wilhelmina Leigh and James McGhee interpret the minority perspective, if residential integration contributes to providing good quality housing, then blacks "are willing to accept integration as a useful although not essential outcome." Gary Orfield takes an unequivocal position: separate is inherently unequal and integration is a mandatory condition for ensuring a good quality residential environment. Indeed, for Orfield, integration is the only real alternative to ghettoization, with all the negative consequences implicit in the latter term.

Yet several conflicting objectives intervene. Despite strong evidence that the alternative is, in Orfield's words, "undesired segregation and permanent inequality," Leigh and McGhee are able to cite several arguments in opposition to integration. Suburban integration may dilute central city black voting strength and rob central city black communities of potential leadership. Integration of black central city neighborhoods may be nothing more than gentrification preparatory to displacement to even less desirable neighborhoods. Integration that depends on relatively low black proportions for stability preempts the potential for social cohesiveness and maintenance of a black identity. If separate is indeed unequal, then blacks may be left with a difficult choice: on the one hand, a good quality integrated residential environment but relative social isolation and dispersed political power, or, as the other alternative, black concentration and political representation but greater socioeconomic heterogeneity and, consequently, lower housing and neighborhood quality. It seems unlikely that achievement of all of these goals will be possible simultaneously.

An equally sobering policy constraint is suggested (in Chapter 13) by John Yinger's pessimistic assessment of the potential for achieving residential integration. "The prospects are not encouraging," Yinger concludes, "for achieving stable integration through market forces." Intervention for integration through housing subsidies is even more problematic as racial issues are compounded by class issues. Nonetheless, Yinger identifies several mitigating factors that improve the potential for integration through a subsidy program: subsidized housing need not raise fears of ghetto expansion, and it need not be concentrated in particular neighborhoods. Stringent siting and design criteria must also be adhered to: projects should be small and blend in with surrounding housing, and should be placed in neighborhoods where low-income households would be most likely to live in the absence of discrimination.

The implications of this prescription—as of Rose Helper's prerequisites for stable integration—are sobering indeed. The basic assumption of the integration objective (cf. Leigh and McGhee; Orfield) is that integration provides access to better quality housing, neighborhood environment, and municipal services. Paradoxically, the very requirements for successful stable integration directly obviate such access for more than an extremely limited number of black households. In the case of subsidized housing, as Yinger argues, projects must be small ("as inconspicuous as possible"), limited to very small numbers of black households, and located in low-income neighborhoods and in isolated areas to contribute to their invisibility. This is not the description of a good quality neighborhood environment with good municipal services.

Yinger's prescription for subsidized housing appears to apply equally in the unassisted market. In either case, stable integration rests on maintaining an extremely small black population. A 1970 national survey found that integrated neighborhoods that were attracting both black and white in-movers had a median black population of just 3 percent.[12] Yinger interprets more recent data compiled by Farley et al. in Detroit to suggest a "tipping point" at 7 percent black.[13] Whatever the actual black proportion conducive to stable integration in a given situation, the white tolerance threshold continues to be extremely low.

The paradox is evident. Blacks express a willingness to accept integration if it leads to a better quality housing and neighborhood environment, but the basic requirement for stable integration is to limit access to a very small number of blacks. An integration program might well increase the number of stably integrated neighborhoods, but it would thereby have very little effect on the vast majority of black households; indeed, it would leave the vast majority of black households in all-black ghetto areas. If attainment of stable integration is contingent on the constraints imposed by white fears and prejudice, a reconsideration of goals is inescapable. Is the amount and type of integration that could be achieved under these constraints—that is, comprising very low black concentrations and consequently available to relatively small numbers of black households—a worthwhile policy objective?

The underlying objective of Title VIII is to achieve integration through the elimination of discrimination. If integration has not yet been achieved, then either the premise of Title VIII is incorrect—nondiscrimination does not lead to integration—or the premise still holds but discrimination has not yet been subdued. All indications point to the latter conclusion.

The unyielding implication is the need for a reinvigorated, broad-based attack against lingering discrimination and in support of equal access to housing. This goal should constitute a powerful force forging a coalition between integrated communities and advocates of equal access, groups that all too frequently are adversaries in integration management cases but who share a common interest in eliminating discrimination in the housing market. The renewed assault on discrimination must be aggressively and affirmatively pursued by all levels of government. It is insufficient to challenge quotas aimed at stabilizing integration, as the Reagan administration has done, without simultaneously attacking discrimination in a determined and comprehensive manner.[14] Quotas and other integration maintenance devices are symptomatic of pervasive discrimination. The means to eliminating the need for stabilizing quotas is the elimination of discrimination—the continuing, undiminished objective of the Fair Housing Act. A strengthened and expanded enforcement effort remains the highest priority.

Conclusions

The essays in this volume are a document of the times. Appropriately, the essays raise far more questions than they answer, but these questions signal the current status of progress toward desegregation. It is unlikely that all the issues raised herein will ever be resolved. Some issues will resolve themselves. New issues will arise as fair housing continues to evolve. This volume stands as a marker of racial residential patterns in the 1980s, the progress that has been achieved, and the substantial distance still to be traversed.

In addition, these essays in aggregate contain an implicit agenda for continued research. The focus of needed research spans the interacting poles of discrimination, transition, and integration. First is the need for extensive and comprehensive monitoring of both the frequency and the form of housing market discrimination. This effort is the responsibility of all levels of government, which must affirmatively seek to document the full magnitude of the problem. To require the victims of discrimination to cry foul before a problem is acknowledged, is akin to expecting the victims of environmental pollution to be solely responsible for monitoring air and water quality.

Closely related to the issue of measurement is the need for a fuller understanding of the rationale and incentives to discriminate. It is not sufficient to measure symptoms without seeking to understand and counteract the causes. Third, research is needed on both the direct and indirect effects of discrimination on black housing search and residential mobility. This includes analysis of how the search for housing is influenced directly by discrimination, and indirectly by black adaptation to the expectation of discrimination.

In addition to analysis of discrimination and its manifestations at the individual level, research is also needed on the linkages between discrimination and both segregation and transition at the macro or collective level. This research would focus on institutional effects on racial patterns, and on relationships both within and between communities, including the ability of communities to respond to institutional influences centered beyond their borders.

A logical extension of this question focuses on the progression of transition itself, in particular analyzing the course of transition in a broad variety of ecological and institutional settings.

Finally, analysis is needed to monitor the progress of intervention in racial transition in the form of integration management efforts. The issue for policymakers is to ensure that integration management is coupled with strong anti-discrimination efforts, bringing analysis full circle to the unfinished objective: achieving desegregation by eliminating discrimination in the housing market.

NOTES AND REFERENCES

1. Brian J. L. Berry, *The Open Housing Question: Race and Housing in Chicago, 1966–1976* (Cambridge, Mass.: Ballinger, 1979); Carole Goodwin, *The Oak Park Strategy: Community Control of Racial Change* (Chicago: University of Chicago Press, 1979); Robert W. Lake and Jessica Winslow, "Integration Management: Municipal Constraints on Residential Mobility," *Urban Geography* 2 (December 1981): 311–26.

2. 114 *Congressional Record* 2539–40 (remarks of Senator Mondale), cited in Leonard S. Rubinowitz and Elizabeth Trosman, "Affirmative Action and the American

Dream: Implementing Fair Housing Policies in Federal Homeownership Programs," *Northwestern University Law Review* 74 (November 1979): 563.

3. Ronald E. Wienk, Clifford Reid, John C. Simonson, and Frederick J. Eggers, *Measuring Racial Discrimination in American Housing Markets: The Housing Market Practices Survey* (Washington, D.C.: Office of Policy Development and Research, U.S. Department of Housing and Urban Development, 1979).

4. For a summary of recent audit studies of the extent of housing discrimination, see Harriet Newburger, *Recent Evidence on Discrimination in Housing* (Washington, D.C.: Office of Policy Development and Research, U.S. Department of Housing and Urban Development, 1984).

5. Robert W. Lake, *The New Suburbanites: Race and Housing in the Suburbs* (New Brunswick, N.J.: Rutgers University Center for Urban Policy Research, 1981).

6. John R. Logan and Mark Schneider, "Racial Segregation and Racial Change in American Suburbs, 1970-1980," *American Journal of Sociology* 89 (January 1984): 874–88.

7. U.S. Bureau of the Census, *1980 Census of Population and Housing*, PHC80-V-32, Final Population and Housing Unit Counts, New Jersey.

8. Thomas A. Clark, *Blacks in Suburbs: A National Perspective* (New Brunswick, N.J.: Rutgers University Center for Urban Policy Research, 1979).

9. Walter Goodman, "Dispute over Quotas at Starrett City: Complex Mix of Principle and Politics," *New York Times*, 13 July 1984.

10. Otis D. Duncan and Beverly Duncan, *The Negro Population of Chicago: A Study of Residential Succession* (Chicago: University of Chicago Press, 1957); Karl E. Taeuber and Alma F. Taeuber, *Negroes in Cities: Residential Segregation and Neighborhood Change* (Chicago: Aldine Publishing Co., 1965).

11. This point is central to Carole Goodwin's comparison of racial change in urban and suburban neighborhoods of Chicago: see her *Oak Park Strategy*.

12. Norman M. Bradburn, Seymour Sudman, and Galen L. Gockel, *Racial Integration in American Neighborhoods: A Comparative Study* (Chicago: National Opinion Research Center, 1970), p. 30.

13. Reynolds Farley, Howard Schuman, Suzanne Bianchi, Diane Colosanto, and Shirley Hatchett, "'Chocolate City, Vanilla Suburbs': Will the Trend toward Racially Separate Communities Continue?" *Social Science Research* 7 (December 1978): 319–44.

14. Goodman, "Dispute over Quotas at Starrett City."

Concluding Remarks

JOHN M. GOERING

One of the great luxuries of social science is that it does not have to take responsibility for its failed promises. Policies and programs based on applied research are the responsibility of policymakers and elected officials, because it is they who must live with the consequences. Indeed, social scientists should hesitate before making recommendations about issues as contentious and complex as racial segregation when it is all too clear, from a reading of the preceding essays, that there are dozens, if not hundreds, of research issues left unexplored. Without clearer research evidence, social scientists' hunches are no better than anyone else's.

At the same time, virtually all of the contributors, as well as myself, have strong feelings about the immorality or inequity of racial prejudice, discrimination, and segregation. Each of us, like the majority of Americans, prefers a racially open, free society. Few of us are fully certain how to best reach this goal.[1]

The difficulties of reaching reasonable recommendations are complicated by the fact that most Americans seem unwilling to be reminded that prejudice and racism are commonplace. Concerns about economic growth, budget deficits, and the entitlements of the poor are foremost in the minds of Congress and citizens. What, then, is the best means to prick the conscience of those distracted by other concerns?

It now appears that the triumphant passage of civil rights laws in the 1960s was a highwater mark in this country's efforts to eliminate racism. The passage of these laws may have signaled to Americans that they had paid their debts, done enough. The accompanying efforts to eliminate poverty, along with discrimination, wound up confounding efforts to do either well. Minority benefits soon appeared to be disproportionate to the economic and social gains insured to the white majority. Affirmative action became a symbol of doing too much in the name of racial equity. The relatively clear moral choice of ending discrimination became compromised by the inevitable partisan politics of program funding levels and concerns about program inefficiency.

It is therefore difficult as well as frustrating to draw policy conclusions when there may be no one willing to listen or to act. What is fair becomes compromised by what is possible. Conclusions may be all too clear but there may be no means to address the findings. There is, then, no easy means of balancing social science evidence and the availability of new policies and programs.

Most conclusions that can be drawn from the foregoing are also a mixture of certainty and doubts. These concluding observations are prescriptions for new research questions, focused on these unanswered issues rather than a restatement of what others in this volume have offered as recommendations for action.

The first conclusion is that it is a serious mistake to underestimate the power of racial prejudice—of racism—in the operation of housing markets throughout the United States. Public opinion polls have lulled many people into believing that racial tolerance has increased and discrimination has concomitantly decreased. The hollowness of such expressed beliefs is, however, revealed virtually each time and in each place that a concrete program aimed at desegregation is proposed. Certainly there are fewer people who sound prejudiced but, as Bobo, Schuman, and Steeh's careful assessment points out, their real values are tested only when principles turn into programs. The academic face of their analysis turns uglier when racial antipathy has been revealed to journalists from the *Dallas Morning News*, the *New York Times*, the *Miami Herald*, and the *Chicago Reporter*.

Second, recent declines in the level of racial segregation in cities have been caused by factors we know little about. The fact that we know so little about the reasons for this decline means that it is presumptuous to discount the possibility that either declines in prejudice and discrimination or increases in fair housing enforcement have been responsible. We just do not know enough to say who or what should get the credit.

The most reasonable conclusion is, however, that a host of national, regional, and local institutional and personal factors has been responsible. Some of these same factors are also likely to be responsible for the perseverance of modest numbers of racially diverse neighborhoods and communities scattered throughout the country.

Is it possible, then, that the dynamics of urban growth—the historical ecology of cities—are changing; that they permit more racial diversity in housing? Is the decline in the growth rate of minority populations and the increasing number of middle-income black, Hispanic, and Asian households a reason to expect further "natural" increases in stably integrated communities? If such areas can survive even in the midst of Chicago's racial violence, can they perhaps blossom in other locations?

If more were known about the number, characteristics, and effectiveness of the integration programs used by such communities, it would be easier to be encouraged. Until there is comparative research on stably integrated communities, with and without maintenance programs, it would be cavalier to conclude that more are likely to emerge. Until more is known about the legality of the means used to "maintain" integration it would also be unwise to predict federal enthusiasm or funding.

Also, if more were known about the expectations and experiences of middle-class minority households as they locate in nonghetto areas, it would be easier to point to reasonable trajectories for the future. How many experience the bombings and racial insults found in Chicago? How many silently and passively move next door to neighbors who remain indifferent or unconcerned? How many, in fact, prefer racial diversity for its own sake?

In brief, we do not know enough about how integration or residential diversity works in the private market to understand how public policies can help or hurt the process. There has been a long history of recommendations to promote diversity on a metropolitan or regional scale, but most of the evidence from policy research indicates that no tools are available to promote such interconnections. All the evidence shows, in fact, quite the opposite. Interjurisdictional or regional sharing of any scarce good—or tax—is anathema to those wealthier areas receiving the "fair" share of the poor or minorities. The heterogeneity of most suburbs means that they will have enough of their own poor or ill-housed to accommodate before accepting the needy from other jurisdictions. A few efforts at cross-jurisdictional exchanges of housing assistance have, nevertheless, survived after the termination of federal support. It goes without saying that research assessments of such programs are needed.

A third conclusion is that for most Americans, and for local officials, there is no clear-cut way to separate economic and racial integration fears. For over one hundred years, blacks have been associated in the minds of white Americans with their worst fears—crime and the devaluation of their property. Virtually nothing has been done, or perhaps can be done, to address the illegitimate bases of these fears. Social scientists continue to document their deadly interconnection, but no one seems able to separate the malleable from the inevitable.

A fourth conclusion is another admission of ignorance. Little is known about the effectiveness and limitations of either voluntary or mandatory efforts to desegregate. There has been surprisingly little documentation of the impact of school desegregation decisions on housing patterns, and no information about the effect of court orders and consent decrees on communities required to desegregate their public housing. There is a curious disinterest by researchers and policymakers in knowing how well or poorly courts have done in using public programs to reduce housing segregation. In many cases, decisions have been too recent to be able to detect clear changes, and the circumstances of each trial may be too variable. However, no other institution currently has the power or inclination to require broad-scale housing desegregation. It seems essential to spend more time assessing what has worked and with what consequences in jurisdictions subject to court decisions.

Fifth, there is little leadership by civil rights organizations to promote a stronger constituency for desegregation. The doubts of the National Urban League, expressed in the essay by Leigh and McGhee, are apparently shared by other advocacy groups. There appear to be other priorities and tradeoffs to be focused on before worrying about housing integration. The absence of a cohesive civil rights agenda for the decade ahead, in which housing desegregation is a part, makes it difficult to establish how low or high integration ranks as a priority. If established civil rights leaders are reluctant to press for desegregation and integration, Congress and federal agencies are unlikely to fill the void. Lake, in his postscript, poses the insightful questions, central to the formulation of this agenda: "Is equal housing opportunity possible without integration, that is, can separate be equal? Can these issues be reconciled based on clear priorities, and do they conflict with yet other objectives on the agenda of black Americans?"

Another conclusion is that federal housing programs succeed and fail for many reasons unrelated to race and desegregation. The cross-pressures on housing and community development programs mean that scarce resources often attempt to accomplish too much, producing inconsistencies and confusion at the local level. Also, HUD's small share of the rental housing market is unlikely to grow in the short run. State and locally financed housing programs are already being designed and implemented in ways that sometimes will complement and at other times conflict with HUD's efforts to promote housing desegregation. More attention, then, should be paid to nonfederal housing assistance programs as they affect federal civil rights mandates.

A clear, although at times implicit, conclusion is that federal fair housing laws have failed to achieve their objectives. Over twenty years have elapsed since Title VI of the Civil Rights Act of 1964 was passed, and the bulk of public housing tenants and projects is still segregated. The failure to eliminate segregation and discrimination in public and private sector housing is partly due to the inadequacy of the laws themselves. Inadequate enforcement procedures, cumbersome and time-consuming hearing procedures, and congressional ambiguity have led to frustrations and ineffectiveness. Inadequate staffing, the failure to develop regulations, and a host of other reasons have been given for the failures of federal fair housing laws. For each of the past five years, Congress or the Executive Branch has proposed new fair housing amendments designed to strengthen Title VIII. Discussions are even now being held to determine what form the Fair Housing Amendments Act of 1986 will take. There is bipartisan agreement that stronger laws are needed, but it remains uncertain whether this session of Congress will have the time and inclination to pass the amendments. With new legislation, there will be added incentives to determine how well they work in reducing discrimination and private sector segregation.

A related conclusion is that federal agencies, especially HUD, almost perfectly mirror the confusion, apathy, and shortsightedness of Congress, civil rights leaders, and the public. Ambiguity about the requirement or need to promote housing desegregation is echoed, and amplified, within the corridors of HUD, the Department of Justice, and the Office of Management and Budget. No federal agency is likely to develop a coherent, comprehensive desegregation strategy when it is whipsawed by congressional and budgetary pressures and when its "natural" allies remain silent, confused, or antagonistic. Also, how does an agency begin systematic desegregation efforts when there is judicial uncertainty about the legality of the race-conscious tools needed to desegregate? As funding for housing construction, rehabilitation, and public housing modernization programs is further reduced, how does the federal government become a major actor, with minor resources, in creating new nonsegregated housing opportunities?

The federal government is unquestionably liable for either tacitly or overtly supporting the segregation of conventional and assisted housing over the last fifty years. HUD and its predecessor agencies often became hostage to local practices of segregation and discrimination. This liability may be more or less clear when specific cities and specific practices are examined for causal influences. Local elected and congressional leaders, in conjunction with local administrators of public housing authorities, had most of the practical operating authority and most of the incentives to maintain segregation—and not to rock the boat of racial customs. How hard did federal officials try to change such local practices, were their incentives and disincentives clear and powerful enough, and were political pressures able to circumvent the limited control of civil rights field staff over resources and decisions? How, in brief, does a single program, housing a fraction of the residents in a local community, work to disestablish deeply entrenched, fear-driven practices of segregation?

The temptation to look for solutions is one most appropriately assigned to plaintiffs, courts, Congress, and elected officials. Social scientists should resist offering advice without having done all the homework needed to establish proof of causality for the specific circumstances and cases in which federal or local legal liability has been raised. It is, however, a far cry from such case-specific fashioning of remedies and the assessments required to create a national agenda for housing desegregation. Yinger's assessment comes as close as possible to recognizing all of the forces impinging on federal desegregation policy. He, like the National Academy of Sciences over a decade ago (Social Science Panel 1972), looks to small-scale demonstrations and programs to illustrate the feasibility of integration efforts. Such programs could provide federal, state, and local officials with a clearer view of the potential utility of the incentives, punishments, disincentives, and costs of promoting desegregation in all or portions of a local housing market. Such incentives should aim at linking public housing agencies, local officials, and private real estate interests in supporting both the social and programmatic changes needed to establish and then maintain racial diversity.

The maintenance of stable racial integration remains a thorny legal, programmatic, and research question. How long do incentives and laws need to be in place in order to eliminate or counterbalance pressures for resegregation? What nonrace-conscious techniques exist that can sustain racial balance without the use of exclusionary practices? In what types of markets and neighborhoods do different blends of incentives and law enforcement work best?

Whatever strategies or demonstrations are created, they must be sufficiently varied and maintained over a long enough period of time to be certain that the outcomes are stable. Such efforts will help to answer the question of when to let go of the integration or desegregation program and allow market choices to take over. Recent actions by HUD to end public housing segregation in Texas and other parts of the South may provide the first evidence of how far federal pressures can go to create long-term change. Within several years it will be clear whether recent initiatives have been effective, challenged and dismissed in federal court, or once again circumvented by local officials. In the short run, more information about the success of various scattered-site housing programs in promoting racial diversity would be extremely useful.

In light of the evidence, it is clear that there are no quick or painless fixes— no simple solutions. If there were, they would have been tried because such simplicity would surely be less costly. Racial segregation and discrimination persist for the obvious reasons that they are in someone's best interest and their elimination will cost more than decision makers can easily risk. A serious effort to generate federal or state actions would require the potential massive redistribution of housing, people, resources, and fears—fear of the unknown matched by fears of unwanted neighbors and unwanted government action. Such a resolution will not come about easily or soon.

Proponents of desegregation must establish a framework for long-term actions at the local, state, and federal levels. There must be the pressure of real experiences of real people wanting to fight through each obstacle to gradually construct the programs that will work best for specific cities and specific groups in need. Such an action program should include an assessment of all of the benefits and costs likely to be experienced by minority and white households— including those of schooling, job opportunities, social networks, and interracial tolerance. This assessment must try to strip away the economic liabilities of ghetto life and at the same time evaluate the housing options for those who wish to live with varying proportions of their own race or nationality. The freedom to choose one's neighbors will remain a necessary ingredient in any voluntary plan to achieve broad-scale desegregation. How big this loophole is is anyone's guess. It is, however, certain to be smaller than the current number of segregated neighborhoods.

The compartmentalization, and virtual isolation, of the various disciplines that focus on race and housing in America must be part of the changes needed to create better concepts and programs. The analysis of racial segregation, for example, has become highly technical and narrow in its focus on measurement at the expense of theory. Studies of discrimination have seldom been connected to real-life measures of antidiscrimination programs, limiting the practical character of their findings. Program evaluations, in their inevitably myopic fashion, lead to recommendations that often lack the breadth that social science desperately needs. Case studies are endlessly fruitful as well as frustrating in their mastery of local failures and successes at the expense of understanding interconnections to broader markets and national policy influences.[2]

Looking back at all these recommendations and questions can be a chilling experience. It is appalling how little is known, how little has been effective, and how mountainous are the obstacles to change. The costs of segregation are so severe, and the pace of change so dreadfully slow, that one can despair of any progress within the next decades. Perhaps that is how the first civil rights sit-ins in restaurants began. Perhaps frustration can build and lead to the necessary laws and programs. There may again be another critical period for civil rights reform where major breakthroughs are achieved. For the foreseeable future, however, I suspect that progress will occur only in small steps and that watershed victories are unlikely. The movement for housing desegregation will be lucky to hold its own for the next decade. All too many forces exist at the national and local levels to subvert efforts for major changes, new programs, or a dramatic reconfiguration of interests and resources.

The next decade of housing research has plenty to accomplish and a great deal to offer to the policy process. If the interests of social scientists do not stray elsewhere, for hotter topics or more ample funding, the next volume on housing desegregation should be more systematic, conclusive, and relevant to the actual desegregation of all housing in America.

NOTES

1. Fifty years ago it was relatively easy to offer policy recommendations for the issue of "Negro housing." The President's Conference on Home Building and Home Ownership, in 1932, recommended that states improve the quality of low-income housing for blacks. The conference went on to observe: "In so far as the Negro is the victim of special handicaps, such as those arising from segregation, low wages, rent profiteering, and unusual difficulties of adjustment, special measures must be taken for him. Education—training the Negro to seek and maintain higher standards of housing—is perhaps of primary importance" (Gries and Ford 1932:VIII, 114). For the very poor, the conference recommended that "civic-minded people be induced to establish adequate financing agencies at reasonable interest for people with low incomes" (p. 115). Addressing the issue of racially restrictive covenants, the conference proposed "the removal of legislation restrictive of Negro residence in desirable sections of the city where they are able to rent or purchase." The conference did not, however, support any new fair housing legislation. "What is needed," it stated, "is not new legislation but protection against discriminating interpretations and applications of the basic laws now existing" (p. 51).

2. Theoretically, many of these academic limitations could be remedied in court cases in which there is a synthesis of social science evidence, program performance, and personal experiences—all with a view to establishing causality or liability. All too often, however, such trials are contests between the resources and articulateness of experts that leave significant gaps in the conceptual and methodological rigor of trial testimony. Moreover, it is not unknown for social scientists to become partisans of legal conclusions. Back 1971; Wolf 1981.

REFERENCES

Back, Kurt. 1971. "Sociology in the Desegregation Process: Its Use and Disuse." In *Racially Separate or Together?* edited by Thomas Pettigrew, pp. 89–127. New York: McGraw-Hill.

Gries, John, and James Ford. 1932. *Negro Housing.* Washington, D.C.: The President's Conference on Home Building and Home Ownership.

Social Science Panel. 1972. *Freedom of Choice in Housing: Opportunities and Constraints.* Washington, D.C.: National Academy of Sciences.

Wolf, Eleanor. 1981. *Trial and Error: The Detroit School Desegregation Case.* Detroit: Wayne State University Press.

Contributors

Lawrence Bobo, Assistant Professor in the Department of Sociology at the University of Wisconsin at Madison, received a Ph.D. in sociology from the University of Michigan. He has published in the journal of *Personality and Social Psychology* and is coauthor, with Howard Schuman, of *Racial Attitudes in America: Trends and Interpretations.* His research interests include social psychology and racial and intergroup attitudes.

George C. Galster, Associate Professor of Economics and Chairperson of Urban Studies at the College of Wooster, received a Ph.D. in economics from MIT. He has served as consultant to the MIT-Harvard Joint Center for Urban Studies, the National Committee Against Housing Discrimination, and HUD. His papers have appeared in the *American Economic Review*, *Land Economics*, *Urban Affairs Quarterly*, *Environment and Behavior*, *Regional Science Perspectives*, and *American Real Estate and Urban Economic Association Journal.* His current research interests include racial segregation and discrimination, ghetto economic development, and neighborhood change.

John M. Goering directs and conducts civil rights research and evaluation studies for the Office of Policy Development and Research in HUD. He received a Ph.D. in sociology from Brown University and has taught at the University of Leicester, Washington University in St. Louis, the Graduate Center of the City University of New York, and the University of North Carolina at Chapel Hill. He has published extensively on the subject of housing and neighborhood racial change and public policies and is author of *The Best Eight Blocks in Harlem.*

Ira Goldstein is Assistant Director of the Social Science Data Library at Temple University, where he received a Ph.D. in sociology. His research interests include the impact of mortgage redlining on neighborhoods and the antecedents and effects of residential segregation. A comment on color stratification and Hispanics has recently appeared in the *American Journal of Sociology.*

Robert Gray, an economist with the Office of Policy Development and Research in HUD, received a B.A. in economics from the University of Maryland and an M.A. in economics from the University of New Mexico. His interests include urban housing market analysis, federal housing subsidy programs, and, more recently, housing block grants.

Rose Helper, Professor of Sociology Emerita at the University of Toledo, obtained a doctorate in sociology from the University of Chicago. She was Research Fellow in Race Relations at Fisk University; Research Assistant for the Committee on Education, Training, and Research in Race Relations at the University of Chicago; Research Associate for the Research Center for Human Relations at New York University; and Research Associate for the Commission on Race and Housing of the Fund for the Republic. She is author of *Racial Policies and Practices of Real Estate Brokers*; "Neighborhood Association 'Diary' Records History of Citizen Effort to Adapt to Racial Change" (*Journal of Housing*); "White People's Reactions to Having Black People as Neighbors: Current Patterns" (*Research and Edu-*

cation); and "Social Interaction in Racially Mixed Neighborhoods" (*Housing and Society*).

Franklin J. James, Associate Professor in the Graduate School of Public Affairs of the University of Colorado at Denver, received a Ph.D. in economics from Columbia University. He directed HUD's Urban Policy Staff during the Carter administration and has done research on urban policy and housing issues at The Urban Institute, the Center for Urban Policy Research, and the National Bureau of Economic Research. His current research focuses on issues relating to Hispanics, including their economic and jobs status, access to health care, and participation in federal social programs.

John F. Kain is Professor of Economics and of City and Regional Planning at Harvard University, where he is a member of the faculties of Arts and Sciences and the John F. Kennedy School of Government; he formerly served as Chairman of the Department of City and Regional Planning. He has been a consultant to the U.S. Commission on Civil Rights, Environmental Protection Agency, HUD, Department of Health and Human Services, and several foreign governments, and has initiated a three-year study in Dallas of the growth and development of the Dallas-Fort Worth region over recent decades. He is coauthor, with John R. Meyer and Martin Wohl, of *The Urban Transportation Problem*; with Gregory K. Ingram and J. Royce Ginn, of *The Detroit Prototype of the NBER Urban Simulation Model*; with John M. Quigley, *Housing Markets and Racial Discrimination*; and, with William C. Apgar, Jr., *Housing and Neighborhood Dynamics*, a book on the development and use of a large-scale microanalytic computer simulation model of urban housing markets.

Robert W. Lake, Associate Professor in the Center for Urban Policy Research at Rutgers University, received a Ph.D. in urban geography from the University of Chicago. He is author of *The New Suburbanites: Race and Housing in the Suburbs* and of numerous articles on race and housing policy in the United States, and is editor of *Readings in Urban Analysis*. His current research focuses on the role of minority real estate brokers in urban restructuring in the United States and Great Britain.

Wilhelmina A. Leigh, a housing policy analyst with the Congressional Budget Office, received a Ph.D. in economics from Johns Hopkins University. She previously taught at Harvard University and was employed by the U.S. Bureau of Labor Statistics, HUD, and The Urban Institute. She coauthored Chapter 2 of this volume while a Senior Research Associate/Economist at the Research Department of the National Urban League. Her research interests cover many issues relating to the housing market, including estimating depreciation/replacement rates, housing affordability, and housing finance.

James D. McGhee, former Director of Research for the National Urban League, received a Ph.D. in social psychology from Washington University in St. Louis. Previously he was a former staff member of the U.S. Commission on Civil Rights and a lecturer at Howard and George Mason universities; he has also held a variety of teaching and administrative positions. He is author of numerous publications and reports, including *A Dream Denied: The Black Family in the Eighties*.

Gary Orfield is Professor of Political Science at the University of Chicago, where he received a Ph.D. He has served as a court-appointed expert in school desegregation cases in St. Louis and Los Angeles and has published extensively on the subject of school and housing desegregation, including *Toward a Strategy for Urban Integration.*

Alexander Polikoff has been Executive Director of Business and Professional People for the Public Interest (BPI), a Chicago public interest law center, for fourteen years; previously, he was a member of a large Chicago law firm. He is also director, and has long been a cooperating attorney, for the Illinois Division of the American Civil Liberties Union (ACLU). For both BPI and ACLU he has carried on important litigation in the civil rights and environmental fields. He is author of articles on civil liberties and urban affairs issues and of *Housing the Poor: The Case for Heroism.*

Howard Schuman, Professor of Sociology and Director of the Survey Research Center of the University of Michigan, received a Ph.D. in sociology from Harvard University. He is also President of the American Association for Public Opinion Research. His primary research interests are in public opinion research, race and ethnic relations, and survey research methods. He is author or coauthor of seven books and numerous articles, including research on racial attitudes in the Detroit Area Study.

Charlotte Steeh is a Research Associate for the Office of Affirmative Action at the University of Michigan, where she received a Ph.D. in history. She previously was employed by the university's Institute for Social Research.

Jennifer L. Stucker, Social Science Analyst for the Office of Policy Development and Research in HUD,

received a master's degree from the Institute of Public Policy Studies at the University of Michigan. She is author of a number of published and unpublished papers on a variety of public issues related to HUD's rental assistance programs, including household mobility, housing standards, and program administration and costs.

Steven Tursky, an analyst for the Office of Information Resources Management in the General Services Administration, received a master's degree in public administration from the University of Southern California. Previously he was a Program Analyst in the Office of Fair Housing and Equal Opportunity at HUD. His research interests center on the impacts of assisted housing programs on the poor and minorities.

Eileen A. Tynan, Assistant Professor in the Graduate School of Public Affairs of the University of Colorado at Denver, received a Ph.D. from the University of Colorado at Boulder. She previously was a research associate in the university's Center for Health Services Research. She currently is working on a study of Hispanic utilization of health care services.

Michael J. Vernarelli, Assistant Professor of Economics and Chairman of the Economics Committee of the College of Liberal Arts at the Rochester Institute of Technology, received an M.A. and a Ph.D. in economics from the State University of New York at Binghamton. His research interests include fair housing, mobility behavior of low-income households, and urban revitalization. The research for Chapter 9 of this volume was conducted while he was participating in the Visiting Scholar Program, Office of Policy Development and Research, HUD.

William L. Yancey, Professor of Sociology and Director of the Institute for Public Policy Studies at Temple University, received a Ph.D. in sociology from Washington University in St. Louis. He is coauthor of *The Moynihan Report: The Politics of Controversy*, with Lee Rainwater, and of numerous articles on urban sociology, neighborhood structure, and industrial change. His current research interest is in the changing industrial character of cities and its impact on neighborhoods.

John Yinger, Associate Professor of City and Regional Planning at the John F. Kennedy School of Government, Har-vard University, has served as a senior staff economist for the Council of Economic Advisors and as a consultant to HUD, the city of Boston, and several private fair housing centers. His research has concentrated on urban housing markets, particularly their financial dimension, and on state and local public finance. His published papers on racial aspects of housing markets include theoretical work on the effects of prejudice and discrimination on urban structure, an analysis of the incentives that lead real estate brokers to practice racial discrimination, and an empirical study of black/white price differentials in housing.

Index

DATE DUE

Aug 20, 03 lu	
OCT 2 3 2003	